Forty Years Master

MARINE, MARITIME, AND COASTAL BOOKS

Sponsored by Texas A&M University at Galveston

William Merrell and Stephen Curley, General Editors

FORTY YEARS MASTER

A LIFE IN SAIL & STEAM

DANIEL O. KILLMAN

Edited and Annotated by

JOHN LYMAN *and* HAROLD D. HUYCKE JR.

Compiled by REBECCA HUYCKE ELLISON

With an Introduction by BRIAN J. ROULEAU

And an Afterword by DAVID HULL

TEXAS A&M UNIVERSITY PRESS College Station

First edition

This paper meets the requirements of
ANSI/NISO Z39.48-1992 (Permanence of Paper).
Binding materials have been chosen for durability.
Manufactured in the United States of America

Library of Congress Cataloging-in-Publication Data
Names: Killman, Daniel O., 1860–1936, author. | Lyman, John, 1915–1977, editor. | Huycke, Harold D. Jr., 1922–2007, editor. | Ellison, Rebecca Huycke, 1957– compiler.
Title: Forty years master : a life in sail and steam / Daniel O. Killman ; edited and annotated by John Lyman and Harold D. Huycke Jr. ; compiled by Rebecca Huycke Ellison ; with an introduction by Brian J. Rouleau and an afterword by David Hull.
Other titles: Marine, maritime, and coastal books.
Description: First edition. | College Station : Texas A&M University Press, [2016] | Series: Marine, maritime, and coastal books | Includes bibliographical references and index.
Identifiers: LCCN 2015038788 | ISBN 9781623493806 (cloth : alk. paper) | ISBN 9781623493813 (ebk.)
Subjects: LCSH: Killman, Daniel O., 1860–1936. | Killman, Daniel O., 1860–1936—Travel. | Ship captains—United States—Biography. | Pacific Coast (North America)—Description and travel. | Pacific Area—Description and travel. | Peru—Description and travel. | Steamboats—United States—History—19th century. | Sailing ships—United States—History—19th century.
Classification: LCC HE569.K55 K55 2016 | DDC 387.5092—dc23 LC record available at http://lccn.loc.gov/2015038788

Frontispiece : Daniel O. Killman. Courtesy San Francisco Maritime National Historical Park, Harold Huycke Collection

To our brothers departed

Contents

Illustrations

Maps

Series Editors' Foreword

Emily Dickinson famously wrote, "There is no Frigate like a Book / To take us Lands away." In some sense a book about ships doubles the payoff. For generations, land-bound readers have feasted on first-person sea memoirs. In the tradition of Richard Henry Dana's *Two Years Before the Mast* (1840) and Frederick Pease Harlow's *The Making of a Sailor or Sea Life Aboard a Yankee Square-Rigger* (1929) comes Captain Daniel O. Killman's *Forty Years Master*.

We are fortunate that this manuscript exists at all. In the 1970s—forty years after it had been written—Killman's daughter gave it to Capt. Harold D. Huycke Jr., who collaborated with historian John Lyman to turn the collection of typed and handwritten pages into a coherent narrative. Then, in 1977, Lyman died unexpectedly, and once more the manuscript lay forgotten, until 2007, when Rebecca Huycke Ellison rediscovered it among her late father's papers. She completed the editing and the annotation, and the resultant work won the 2013 Karl Kortum Award for Maritime History, presented by the Friends of the San Francisco Maritime Museum Library.

What a tale Killman has to tell! Listen to his bare-knuckled anecdote of what he had to do in the 1870s to survive as a greenhorn third mate aboard a 539-ton bark hauling ten thousand barrels of oil out of New York harbor. After he gave his first order, a crewmember contemptuously "told me he would not do it, and if I did not like it I could fight." As Killman saw it, his career was on the line: "it was up to me to lick Jack or stop going to sea." The crew formed a ring around the two men to watch as they "went at it":

> He was surely a hard man. At first he had the better of me, but in some twenty minutes he began to weaken, and I put him to sleep. I was badly smashed up, but he was much worse. He came to and said he had had enough, and he went and did what he had been told to do.

Afterward a delegation of sailors told Killman he didn't need to fight anymore. He had passed the test. The young officer summed it up succinctly: "After this I was obeyed without any talk, and there was a lot of work done." No moralizing, no overelaboration, no extraneous details—Killman leaves us with the unadorned statement of fact. This is prose with hair on its chest, a masculine eloquence that is at once direct and understated. Killman's classic memoir of real men on a workaday sea does indeed take us lands away.

Now, for the first time, a fully annotated version of Killman's narrative is widely available to readers interested in the transformative era when wooden sailing vessels made way for iron steamships. We proudly offer it as the second in our new series of books.

—Stephen Curley and William Merrell
General Editors

Preface

In the more than eighty years since the words in this book were originally written, the world has changed in dramatic ways. Lives have been lived and lives lost, generations have come and gone. Few things have remained untouched by the passage of time. The events of the past, however, although long receded from sight and memory, still live in yellowed handwritten pages, old newspaper clippings, government archives, letters between friends and acquaintances, and photographs. So it is with the life of Captain Daniel O. Killman.

Forty Years Master is the title given by Captain Killman to the memoir he wrote before his death in 1936. His memory of more than fifty years at sea, forty as master, was clear, and he recalled events and people, vessels and places, weather and seas, in detail.

Exactly when and why he wrote his memoirs is not certain, but his daughter, Sydney Killman Pierce, believed that they were written after her father's retirement in 1929 at the suggestion of Jim Bashford, a newspaperman in Tacoma and a good friend. Sydney recalled that the manuscript was written in collaboration with Norman Reilly Raine, who wrote "Tugboat Annie" stories for the *Saturday Evening Post*. Probably Captain Killman wrote the original in longhand and then someone else, perhaps Sydney or her sister, Catherine, typed it. The majority of the existing manuscript is typed, with handwritten penciled notes in the margins and the final several dozen pages in Captain Killman's own hand.

When finished, the manuscript was laid aside. Forty years passed. In the mid-1970s Mrs. Pierce was put in touch with my father, Capt. Harold D. Huycke Jr., a well-known maritime historian. In September 1975 she gave him the manuscript, saying, "You may have it. Yes. So, if there's any way that you can preserve it, and think he deserves it . . ." He did think it deserved to be preserved. He judged it "exceptionally good"; "very extraordinary"; "a rare autobiography, definitely worth preserving"; "great reading." He enlisted the help of Dr. John Lyman, a friend and fellow maritime historian. Lyman also realized its value, writing that he was "very enthusiastic—it is a real sociological document," "a real contribution to maritime history." They agreed that publication of the manuscript was important, with minimal but necessary editorial work done in regard to punctuation, paragraphing, and chapter breaks. Captain Killman's style, opinions, and words would be preserved throughout. Supplemental notes would provide exact dates, vessel particulars, names, cargoes, and corroborating accounts of events. As my father told Mrs. Pierce when he first received the manuscript, "What I'm trying to do is get as honest a picture, warts and all, as they say. . . . We have no ulterior motives. All we're trying to do is preserve an accurate history of [this kind of] life as it used to be and the people that took part in it. So, if there was something good about him, we get that. If there was something bad about him, we get that, and we are not judges, we are recorders."

When working for a living (and putting three children through college) limited my father's ability to conduct unpaid research, the recently retired John Lyman and Mitchell, his wife, typed and retyped the manuscript. Dr. Lyman spent innumerable hours over many months researching vessel particulars, court documents, and consular papers in the National Archives and the Library of Congress. From the West Coast my father sought supplemental information from his many friends, acquaintances, and correspondents, tracked down photographs of people and vessels, and verified dates and names. His two-part piece about Captain Killman and the resurrection of his manuscript, which ran in the *Marine Digest* in April 1976, concluded with these words: "It is the hope of Dr. Lyman and myself, coeditors of this extraordinary manuscript, that anyone who remembers this shipmaster and may have passed through his sphere of influence, may provide some authentic and personal recollections to revive the otherwise undocumented details which must surely exist, somewhere. The trail is almost too cold to follow, but for this one last chance, and a full backward glance at seafaring as it used to be, we solicit and welcome the assistance of anyone who may have trod the old wooden decks of those long vanished ships—with Captain Daniel O. Killman undisputedly in command."

"Undisputedly in command." Those few still living who might have known "Crazy Killman" (as he was known for years on the Pacific Coast) would most certainly remember him as undisputedly in command, either through personal hard experience or by reputation. When and how he earned the nickname is unknown, but *why* he was known by such a handle becomes clear as one reads his own account of his experiences through the years. This insight was an unpleasant surprise to Mrs. Pierce. She knew her father had gotten into fights, and she knew he had had to be tough to survive a long, hard life at sea. But she had not heard the old waterfront nickname until my father asked her about it. Sometime during the ensuing months she must have begun to doubt that the father she remembered fondly—a family man, a perfect gentleman, a man who never threw his clothes down, who always put his coat on for meals, who was a friend to his daughters' friends, and who advised his neighbors about the weather—would receive fair treatment in the appended notes. My father and Dr. Lyman made every effort to assure Mrs. Pierce of their desire to preserve his history as accurately and objectively as possible, but they found her purposely and consistently unavailable. Without her full agreement, they would not proceed with publication. They put the project aside, but with the hope that eventually Mrs. Pierce would see the project more objectively and grant permission. Weeks stretched into months. Then, in the fall of 1977, a few short weeks after a diagnosis of cancer, Dr. Lyman died. My father retrieved the Killman manuscript and the notes and once again laid it aside. As he continued with his own research projects, the months stretched into years. In a letter dated 4 May 2000 he wrote, regarding the autobiography, "A high sense of urgency sweeps over me again." But in early 2007 my father died with the unfinished work still filed away.

After his death, our family donated the majority of his collection of books, research files, and artifacts to the San Francisco Maritime Museum Library, where Dr. Lyman's collection also resides. The Killman manuscript and notes, however, we did not donate.

In the summer of 2012, I contacted Sydney Killman Pierce's family in an effort to reopen the discussion about the edited but unpublished manuscript. Mrs. Pierce had died some years before, as had her sister Catherine, but I learned that Mrs. Pierce's son-in-law, Frederick Hokanson, lived a couple of hours south of me. We met for lunch on a hot day in July, and he enthusiastically approved my proposal to publish *Forty Years Master*.

After another forty years the document has been re-edited. I have preserved Captain Killman's words, style, and opinions as much as possible. Comparing his original manuscript with Dr. Lyman's typed copy,

I made minor grammatical adjustments that seemed warranted. I knew I could not improve upon my father's and Dr. Lyman's knowledge and research. What I could do, however, was take advantage of resources available through the Internet, and by doing so (often with the generous help of librarians, archivists, and genealogists) I found documentation to supplement the existing notes.

Dr. Lyman wrote in a letter, "I've grown mighty fond of old Killman." After all the time I have spent with Capt. Daniel O. Killman, I too have grown mighty fond of him. I can even say that I have come to admire him "warts and all."

—*Rebecca Huycke Ellison*

Acknowledgments

I would like to express my sincere thanks to the many people who helped and encouraged me along the way. The list is extensive! Very special thanks go to my husband, Drew, for his unending patience and his technical support. Thanks also to my children, David, Gregory, and Rosalie, and to my brothers, David and Artie, and their families. I am grateful to Frederick Hokanson and Mitchell Lyman for encouraging me to continue when the others had to leave off. David Hull, John Kortum, Steve Hyman, E. Kay Gibson, Bill and Jennifer Bunting, Bob Browning, Gary White, Chuck Fowler, Norman Brouwer, and Donna Stock offered help, encouragement, and advice. Special thanks to Mike Mjelde for his assistance and advice. Librarians at the following public libraries responded to my requests: Seattle, Tacoma, Aberdeen, Everett, Multnomah County, Contra Costa County, Oakland, San Francisco, San Francisco Maritime National Historical Park Research Center (special thanks to Gina Bardi!), Denver, Howard at Ramsey County Library (Minnesota), Washington State, Hawaii State, and the State Library of Victoria (Australia). Further thanks to the Australian National Maritime Museum; Joy and Ed at the Washington State History Research Center; Brita, Chris, Ken, John, and Mark at the National Archives at Seattle; San Bruno, and Washington, DC; Kris at the Clark County Historical Museum; Nathan at the Maine Maritime Museum; Anne at Phillips Library; Peabody Essex Museum, Salem, Massachusetts; Bill at Piper-Morley Funeral Home, Tacoma; and volunteers at the Family History Center, Everett, Washington. Finally, I would like to acknowledge my reliance for definitions of nautical terms on these sources: René de Kerchove, *International Maritime Dictionary*, 2d ed. (New York: Van Nostrand Reinhold, 1961), keyshistory.org/ASS-Amer-Sail-Ships.html, Eugene Edward O'Donnell, *The Merchant Marine Manual* (Boston, MA: The Yachtsman's Guide, 1918), Merriam-Webster.com, National Marine Institute website: www

.marineinstitute.org, *The Sailor's Word-Book: An Alphabetical Digest of Nautical Terms*, by William Henry Smyth and Edward Belcher (London: Blackie and Son, 1867), Thefreedictionary.com, Wikipedia.org, and Working-the-Sails.com

Introduction

From the end of the 1960s onward, there has been a consistent trend in maritime history toward accounts of the past told "up from the lower deck." That is, the lion's share of scholarly focus has been on the lives of ordinary seamen—poor, physically abused, disenfranchised, and often exploited. These histories have provided remarkably detailed descriptions of what it meant to occupy the cold, wet, cramped confines of a ship's forecastle, eating lousy food, drinking fetid water, and suffering violent reprisal for anything an officer might term "mutinous conduct." Long gone is the intellectually stale stereotype of "Jolly Jack Tar," tattooed, intoxicated, and womanizing as he staggers through his dockside haunts. Instead we have a richer understanding of a global maritime culture, more or less shared by working-class sailors who constituted a nineteenth- and early twentieth-century deep-sea proletariat. It was a culture defined, in many ways, in opposition to, or defiance of, their officers and employers. It provided the tools required to resist often-oppressive conditions aboard oceangoing vessels. Indeed, many historians go so far as to champion ordinary seafarers as the progenitors of the organized labor movement: when maritime collectives agreed to "strike" their sails and refuse work, they birthed a term and a tactic that became increasingly popular among industrial workers. Sailing ships thus could be considered some of the first factory-like industrialized operations. Ordinary sailors, then, had much to teach us about not only the history of the sea, but also the origins of capitalism and working-class activism.[1]

But perhaps the pendulum has swung too far in one direction. The vogue for a "people's history" of the maritime world has led to the publication of countless seafaring narratives written by ordinary sailors, but this worked to the detriment of equally fascinating chronicles penned by officers and other officials. If earlier maritime histories overlooked commoners before the mast and redounded to the credit of "great men" or "heroic navigators," more recent accounts often caricature elite figures as uniformly monomaniacal and vicious Ahab-like figures. Rather than treat sea captains uniformly as villains who wielded absolute power in service of floating despotism, we might read their accounts with an eye to recapturing some of the attitudes and pressures that shaped their distinct perspective on the maritime world. None of this is meant to endorse a return to the "wooden ships, iron men" genre of maritime history, but it is to suggest that we have as much to learn about the waterborne world from those above as from those below.[2]

Enter, then, the memoir of Captain Daniel Killman, who spent more than fifty years of his life afloat, and most of that time as a commander of some sort. Born in Maine in 1860, Killman left home after the death of his mother and went to sea aboard a ship operated by his brother. He rapidly ascended the ranks, and he found particular success in the Pacific, running short-haul coasting voyages within the Pacific Northwest and longer trips to Hawaii, Australia, and the Far East. Only in 1929 did Killman finally retire from seagoing service, and by then, he had seen and done extraordinary things: socialized with the king of Hawaii, found himself immersed in the Klondike gold rush, witnessed the outbreak of World War I in German South West Africa, and become involved in contentious legal proceedings in Australia and elsewhere. His memoirs contain the sort of amusing yarns, perilous storms, hairbreadth escapes, and courageous flirtations with death that have long made nautical nonfiction such an exciting read. But this is also a historically significant document that provides interesting insight into a number of issues.

Two themes stand out in particular. The first is violence. Even a cursory reading of these pages finds Killman constantly—one is tempted to say habitually—involved in some kind of rough altercation with either the sailors under his command or some port official. Most, consisting of a few black eyes and broken noses, read like relatively minor affairs. A few appear to have been more severe, with at least one young seafarer under Killman's command dead on arrival. Indeed, while Killman gives some of the more-serious episodes short shrift in his story (autobiographers tend to censor material reflecting negatively on themselves), the historical record seems to show that Killman was on multiple occasions successfully sued by subordinates for assault and battery. And yet, for Killman, those lawsuits and the monetary damages levied against him were treated almost as the casual cost of doing business. They represented an inconvenience at most, a tax on what it meant to be a good commander. He never did reform his ways; he never stopped resorting to sometimes-brutal methods meant to extract labor from his men. In fact, as Killman tells it, these episodes seemed actually to burnish his reputation as a man who could be trusted to whip a crew into shape and get results. Indeed, it is fascinating to hear him describe (and justify) such abusiveness as a managerial style. Without irony (but with much understatement), Killman at one point muses, "I don't think I was liked by the sailors." "But," he continued, "it did not bother me in the least, for the better you use Jack the less results you receive." Spare the rod, in other words, and you spoil the child.

One gets the impression that it was an unlucky seaman who had to serve under Killman. He makes it clear throughout the memoir that he was aboard a ship to serve the owners' interests and not those of the men beneath him. In several places, Killman remarks quite explicitly that whatever success he enjoyed in his career derived from neither luck nor a charitable spirit while afloat. As he had it, "One must take advantage of everything," and, "The only way to do that is to stay on deck, trust no one, and drive, drive, all the time." By his own admission, Killman rarely respected the customary privileges and free time ordinarily allotted to sailors below: "if I thought the ship could stand more, [the crew] were called out at any time, as I always said that that was what they were there for." Time was money, after all, and so this captain had little patience for what he considered the common seafarer's inveterate laziness. Complaints were dealt with summarily and harshly. At one point, Killman even boasts that a crew that deemed one of his vessels unseaworthy—and so refused to work—had their rations stopped and were starved into submission. (Nor does he express contrition when reporting that the ship, once underway, did begin to sink.)

But threats, violence, and intimidation used to cow ordinary sailors seem particularly fascinating because of their larger context. Killman commanded ships along the West Coast at a moment in American maritime history when laws governing conduct afloat were starting to shift, and maritime laborers themselves were experimenting with unionization meant to combat the sort of imperiousness embodied by Daniel Killman.

He himself observed that the start of his career afloat coincided with "the beginning of the sailors' union." He was referring to the Sailors'

Union of the Pacific. First formed in 1885, it was overshadowed later by the much larger International Seamen's Union (ISU). Led for much of its early life by waterfront organizer Andrew Furuseth, the union worked to improve conditions for working men at sea, increase wages, and eliminate draconian punishments for desertion. Unlike other workers at the time, seamen were not freely contracted employees with the right to "quit" an objectionable job. They still could be coerced into laboring against their will. As union leaders saw it, the Thirteenth Amendment to the Constitution, which abolished slavery and involuntary servitude, had yet to be applied to seamen. Indeed, an infamous 1890s Supreme Court case upholding punitive incarceration for striking sailors became known among mariners as the "second Dred Scott decision." Passage of the Seamen's Act in 1915 did afford the ISU limited success, decriminalizing desertion and promoting fair treatment for sailors at sea, but the earliest years of the unionization effort were met by judicial setbacks and by fierce resistance among officers and shipping firms. As one might expect, Furuseth and his fellow activists received little sympathy from the likes of Killman. Indeed, the captain's memoir provides both a fascinating insight into the mindset of those opposed to expanded rights and protections for seafarers and an unblushing record of tactics they used to defeat the organizational efforts of workers. In that sense, *Forty Years Master* is a highly significant text.[3]

Because Killman's time was one of technological flux as well as labor transformation, the second overarching theme of his life history is the shift from sail to steam and from wood-hulled to iron- or steel-hulled ships. Of course the transition to greater mechanization at sea was not unique to the United States. The change was global. In fact, even though many early steam trials took place in American waters, the transition to steam and steel was not one in which the country could be said to have led. For a variety of reasons, such as disadvantageous materials and labor costs, tariff laws, and a relative lack of government subsidization, the United States lagged behind Britain in adopting new propulsion technology and shipbuilding techniques. But this is not to say that American shipping did not adapt at all. Killman's narrative clearly registers those growing pains. Indeed, Killman proved remarkably prescient when, early in his career, he elected to become educated as a steamship engineer—"passed for steam," in his words—thus learning the ins and outs of a still-developing but soon-to-be-dominant machinery.[4]

By the time of his retirement, in 1929, Killman was waxing nostalgic for a "simpler," "quainter" time, when sailing ships glided atop the world's waves. Drifting into Washington through the Strait of Juan de Fuca on his final voyage, he wrote of "the great changes that had taken place" since his first voyage. Whereas before America had boasted "some of the finest sailing ships in the world," "now you see a cloud of smoke coming down the Sound, you know it is a steamer, and you pay no attention to her." They are "operated by machinery and [have] no charms for anyone." And at the last he sighs, "Sailoring is a lost art, or nearly so." Embedded in this eulogy, however, was an appreciation of broader historical trends in the maritime world. Not only was propeller-driven steam (and diesel) navigation the dominant force in transoceanic commerce, but, in addition, America's merchant marine had been almost wholly displaced in international shipping lanes. What national maritime traffic remained consisted largely of coastal and riverine craft. The "American" carrying trade still afloat now flew "flags of convenience," registering their ships in foreign countries and hiring foreign crews to skirt regulations and reduce overhead. Congressional committees inquired into the causes of this decline and sought to reverse it. Fingers pointed in all directions as to the root cause. People such as Killman, caught up in the transition, could only marvel about a lost world, in which "at [one] time, the American ship was the pride of the ocean." But no longer. A nation that in 1860 had carried 90 percent of its foreign trade in its own ships had by the first decades of the twentieth century seen that number fall below 10 percent. Thus, America's post-1870 industrial takeoff required the exporting of domestic manufactures aboard foreign bottoms. Historians, armed with reams of data, sought to explain America's waning international maritime presence, but no single explanation sufficed. More important (and revealing) are the ways in which those living at the time described that shift. The melancholic conclusion of Killman's memoir speaks powerfully of defeat and disempowerment within the higher ranks of the maritime community. It is tempting to see this one captain's retirement from the sea as representing America's broader retreat from its once-expansive saltwater frontier.[5]

Above all else, however, Daniel Killman's memoir reminds us of the individual personalities—the mass of contradictory virtues and vices—that constitute the sweep of history. To generalize when discussing the past is too easy. In doing so, we paper over the fascinating particularities that seem to defy the process of simplification inherent in the historian's craft. Scholars often are more interested in saying something about the forest than about the trees. Captain Killman's memoir reminds us that there is much to be gained by occasionally narrowing our focus, fixing it on individuals telling us tales of extraordinary value. *Forty Years Master* is one of those unique perspectives on the past, and, now preserved, should be enjoyed by both casual readers and serious scholars for years to come.

—Brian J. Rouleau

Forty Years Master

I Early Life

I was born the 22nd day of June, 1860, in the State of Maine on the banks of the Penobscot River. I went to sea with my parents, as my father had been master of many fine ships from when he was a very young man.[1] I was with them when my youngest sister was born on the way from Bourgeois to Queenstown[2] for orders in a new bark named the *George Treat*.[3] My father had been many years with Treat & Company, and took command of every new ship.[4] He had some stock in the company. They failed and paid practically nothing. He stayed in the bark for some time, but my mother's health started to fail and he stopped going to sea.

My father had a farm and thought he could make a living on it; however, I think he knew but very little about farming. I was next to the last of a large family of ten.[5] My mother's health failed slowly, and when I was seven she passed away.[6] I stood at her bedside, and I can see her today as plainly as I could then. I was very fond of my mother, and I have cherished her memory. She always said she would like to live to see me raised right, and if she had lived it might have made a big change in my life. In a few years my father married again. I had grown to be a large boy and was not afraid of work, and when my father told me of my new mother I left home and never returned.[7]

I went to work for my board and went to school. This farm had a lot of stock, and I was kept very busy. On Saturdays I went into the woods hauling wood to the main road so that it could be hauled to the wharf after the snow had gone. After school had finished in the spring I went to work for a man by the name of Emery Martin. His farm was small but was kept in very fine shape. I was to have seven dollars a month for eight months. Martin was home only a small part of the time as he was a house carpenter and had lots of work during the summer. I worked hard—up every morning at four o'clock and rarely finished before seven-thirty in the evening.

The people were very good to me, but after I had finished my eight months I took my money, bought some clothes, and went to work for my uncle, James Killman, for ten dollars a month. I had not been there long when one night about midnight the house caught on fire, and by the time I had given the alarm the fire had reached my room and all of my new clothes were burned.

After that I went to work for a man named Thomas P. Shute on an excellent farm. When school started I got only my board and had to get up at four in the morning and work late at night. The schoolhouse was only a short distance, so it was very handy. Some days I couldn't get through feeding the stock in time to get any breakfast, so I would grab something in my hand and run for school and at recess would run back home for lunch. I worked there all winter and when school closed went on wages of eleven dollars a month.

My brother, Thomas Killman, came home that winter after being dismasted off Cape Horn in the bark *Courser*[8] loaded with a cargo from New Zealand. He put back to Valparaiso and the bark was condemned. He took command of the bark *Masonic*[9] in New York, and I wrote him and asked him for an ordinary seaman's position. He sent for me at once. I was very happy when I got his letter for I wanted to go to sea and see the world, and I was sure I would get to be master.[10]

I went at once to New York and went on board the *Masonic* as an ordinary seaman. I got a sailor's mattress and pillow stuffed with straw, two cotton blankets, a pint dipper, tin plate, fork, knife, and spoon and a sheath knife and belt, all of which were a sailor's stock in trade at that time.

We went to the Standard Oil Company wharf and loaded case oil for Nagasaki, Japan. After loading, we went to anchor in the bay and bent sail. After the crew came on board and the ship was ready for sea, a tug came and towed us a short distance outside. We made all sail, dipped the flag three times, received the three long whistles from the tug, and started on our long voyage toward Nagasaki.[11]

At once I was ordered to the wheel. The captain asked me if I could steer, and I told him I could. The course was given to me, and I took the wheel. In a short time the sea got larger, the bark dipped to the swell, and I became deathly seasick. I had to stand there for two hours but it seemed weeks to me. If I could have gotten back to dry land then, I don't think I would ever have gone to sea again, but it was too late. No one has ever been seasick more than I have during my life at sea.[12] But it made no difference in the *Masonic:* I must work as the other men did.

The captain, my brother, would sometimes ask me how I was getting along and told me that as long as I had started the hard life of seagoing I must make good. Learn to make every knot there was to be made; learn all the different splices; do everything that a sailor can; and work one hour every watch below in fine weather. He gave the first mate these orders and said he would expect good reports from him. I soon learned to do any sailoring there was to do.

Shortly after leaving New York they started overhauling the sails. I was given a palm and needle, and it was but a very short time before I could sew as fast and as well as anyone on board. I took great interest in everything. There was one sailor in the forecastle who belonged to London and who had English master's papers, but drink got the best of him, and he shipped as a sailor. He taught me more than anyone else did and would always stay part of his watch below showing me all kinds of knots and teaching me how to make them. I was soon master of them all. We had the usual weather through the Northeast and Southeast trades, and it was not long before we were getting down to strong westerly winds. We shifted sails and bent the best ones, and everything was in order to meet the strong winds of the South Atlantic and the Cape of Good Hope.

In a few days we were running hard with the wind on the quarter. One morning after my watch one of the sailors went on the forecastle head, looked over the bow, and made a dive as we all stood watching. We hollered, "Man overboard!" but the ship was running before a gale of wind and it was impossible to bring her to the wind without shortening sail. He came up once, went down, and was never seen again. That afternoon we were all called aft and signed the official log. His clothes were sold at auction, but as he had but little the sale was soon over.

One afternoon, a few days later, the two topgallant backstays carried away, and the mast went over the side. We soon had the rigging fixed and the spare mast aloft, but had a lot of trouble with the rigging from then on, and had to go easy on carrying sail and had many stoppers on before reaching Anjer Point. I will never forget the night we went through the Straits of Sunda. The wind was from the island of Sumatra, and the fragrance coming from the Island of Spices, as the sailors call it, was wonderful.

We anchored at Anjer Point at one thirty in the morning and in a few moments the ship's side was lined with bumboats. After the sails were furled and all the ropes coiled, the mate let them aboard. They had fruit and birds of all kinds and monkeys, which they exchanged for old clothes. There was liquor on some of them, and I remember that one of the sailors got a good licking the next morning for giving the mate some back talk. The captain went ashore in the morning and in a short time a water lighter came alongside and filled the water tanks. The stores also came along, yams, chickens, ducks, fresh meat, fruit, and vegetables. At two p.m., we heaved up anchor and bade Anjer good-bye. A fine new Swedish ship had left a short time before we did and was soon out of sight. He was the only ship under sail that I ever saw with royal studdingsails set. Before we left Bangka Strait we passed him at anchor.

We kept on, and that night we went into the straits and anchored. Soon this same ship came up close and anchored. This is the only place that I have ever been in where we had to plug the hawse pipes to keep out the sea snakes. There were many large ones in sight alongside.

At four in the morning we weighed anchor and were away on our voyage. After passing through the straits, we headed for the Palawan Passage. There we had very squally weather, and the rigging began to go again, so the captain decided to put into Manila for new rigging. Going through the passage we were in company with the English bark *Matilda.*[13] He sailed a little faster than we did and passed us. We talked with the flags for some time. He too was bound for Manila.

At one in the morning we saw rockets going up and light flashes. The captain said the *Matilda* was too far to leeward and must be on shore. We hove to until morning and at eight we saw the bark coming. We waited until he came up with us. He had been on shore. The water was as smooth as glass, and he went aground at low tide. He ran a kedge anchor out, and at high water he hove the bark off. The captain was very excited, but the bark was not hurt. We arrived at Manila the same day he did.

After a survey was held we started to send the topgallant masts down and fitted new backstays to topmasts and topgallants. We had a customs officer on board the whole time, who walked the deck with a long rifle with a bayonet on the end of it. We had been there but a few days when the steward stabbed my brother.[14] I was asleep at the time the crime was committed, but the alarm was soon given, and in a short time the captains of all the fine ships in the bay were on board. They talked strongly of lynching the criminal until one of the captains made a long talk telling them that it would be a disgrace to all of them if ship masters took a hand in anything like that. My brother lived only three hours. The steward was handcuffed and taken on shore by the water police, who were around the bay all the time.

My brother was buried the next afternoon under the Masonic honors, and a fine headstone put at his grave. The steward was taken to San Francisco and as near as I know was let go for lack of evidence. The first officer was put in command,[15] but as I did not care to stay after the death of my brother the Consul paid me off, and I went on board the bark *Elmiranda*,[16] a fine ship, almost new, built where I was born and commanded by Isaac Lanpher of Stockton, Maine. She was discharging coal from Newcastle, Australia.

After discharging we loaded sugar for New York. The sugar was in small vats weighing about seventy-five pounds, and it was as black as coal. The *Masonic* finished her repairs and went to sea before we did but in a few days put back with the loss of sails and some of her light spars. She repaired again and went to sea but was put ashore a total loss.

After loading, we went to sea and had fine weather until we got close to Sunda Strait. There we struck very bad weather, the wind coming in dead ahead. We saw a large fleet of ships anchored close to the island of Sumatra and went there to anchor. It was a fine anchorage, well protected from the wind and sea. There were a lot of very fine ships laying there with expensive cargoes; some with tea, sugar, rice, and general cargoes bound to all ports of the world. There was a lot of visiting among the captains and first mates. Most every day some of them would get under way early in the morning when the weather would look fine, but as soon as the sun turned it would thunder and lighten and blow very hard, and they would come back to anchor again. The *Thermopylae*,[17] one of England's fastest clippers, was there with another clipper, both loaded with tea. One night the two captains were on board one of the ships with other captains. During the evening one clipper captain said to the other, "Let's you and I try it in the morning."

"Very well," said the other, "and you will turn back first and shorten sail first."

"You are very much mistaken," said the other. They shook hands on it, and in the morning there was a large crowd of men on board each ship to help get them under way. It took only a few moments before the anchor was at the cathead and all sail set, and they were on their way. All the ships dipped their flags three times, and each gave three cheers for a good sendoff. The breeze was very light, and they did not get very far before a heavy squall came up from ahead. Everyone was looking to see what was going to happen, as they all knew that both ships had very clever captains and smart officers.

The squall struck them with all sail set, and neither ship took any sail in. The last we saw of them, their fore and main topgallant masts were hanging over the side, and lots of sails had blown away. But neither came back, and we later heard that both ships arrived at their ports of destination.

The next day, five of us got under way: the *Elmiranda* and four others. The American ship *India*, one of those bound in ballast to the guano[18] islands of Peru, came in stays about three a.m. At the same time a small Spanish bark started to tack under her lee, and the *India* missed stays and came down across the bark's bow, carrying away the jibboom, fore topmast, and fore and main topgallant masts.[19] The ship did very little damage to herself. We all lowered boats and sent an officer with what men we could spare, and all turned back. By dark, all were back to anchor.

Next morning a big crowd of men and some officers were sent to look out for the bark, and by dark that night she was jury-rigged. The next morning she got under way and went to Batavia for repairs. She was loaded with rice from China and bound for the West Indies. After a day or two we got under way again. I was sure we would not put back as I had heard the captain tell the first mate that he would not come back again if his spars stood.

We had a very bad night. In the morning the wind hauled, and we got out clear and were all glad to be on our way home. Once again we had strong winds beating around the Cape of Good Hope and were in company with many fine ships. After passing Good Hope, we had fine weather and fine southeast trade winds. One morning the island of Barbados hove into sight, and at four p.m. we anchored there. The captain went ashore and got some vegetables and what stores we needed, and the next day we left for New York, arriving there in March.[20]

After passing the doctor we went to Hunters Point to discharge. The ship was made fast, and after she was pumped out, decks washed, and everything in order, we were told that they were through with us. Supper was ready, but I don't think anyone stopped for it. Salt beef had lost its flavor, and fresh meat sounded good. I know I had a fine big steak at the Fulton Market.

I had been master for years before I saw the bark *Elmiranda* again. She came to San Francisco and loaded a general cargo for Australia. I went down to the wharf and had a good look at her. Her rigging had all been changed from hemp to wire, and although she was well along in years she looked very well. She was lost years afterward in a hurricane in the West Indies.

After staying in New York for two weeks, I shipped in a three-masted schooner, going to Wilmington, North Carolina, and loading southern pine for Martinique, one of the Windward Islands, owned by France. From there we went back and loaded southern pine for New York. I stayed in New York only a few days and then shipped again, going to the West Indies with general cargo and back with sugar.

After another trip to Cuba and back to New York, I returned to Maine, where I found my father had passed away.[21] I did not see his wife, as I only stayed a short time. I had one sister there and other relatives. My grandmother Killman was living. She was past ninety at the time and very smart.[22] I danced with her, and she was as light on her feet as a young girl. She lived to be over a hundred years old.

My grandmother was born on an island off the coast of Maine and raised a family of eleven children. She and her husband took up wild land on the Penobscot River and cleared a large farm, where they raised their family. On her hundredth birthday her relatives came from all over the United States to see her.[23] She gave a very good speech, and it was printed in the *Belfast Journal.* She remembered George Washington well, and the last time I saw her I asked her many questions about him, as she loved to talk about him and loved him as a brother. She saw the British Redcoats come up the Penobscot River and was armed with a flintlock rifle of her own that I have seen. She told me of the time that the tea was poured into Boston Bay. She was a grand old lady when I saw her last and had done enough hard work to kill many of the present generation.

I went back to New York and shipped second mate of the brig *David Owen.*[24] I was sure I was capable of filling the position. She lay at Hoboken, on the Jersey side of the Hudson River, and was to start loading railroad iron for Galveston, Texas. I found one sailor on board, and a cook, besides the captain's wife and son. The captain told me in the morning that I was to tally in the cargo and get the headsails and staysails bent. It was not much trouble to tally the cargo as it came in cars.

The next day, after we started to load, the sailor and I were repairing one of the jibs on the forecastle head, when we heard them shouting, "Man overboard!" We looked over the bow, and I saw the captain's son come up. I jumped overboard from the forecastle head, and as he was going down for the last time I dove and got him. We took him on board, and in a short time we brought him to. His mother was very frightened, and when the captain came on board I was in the cabin with them. She told him that I had saved their son's life, and the only word from him was that that was what he was paying me for.

I at once left the cabin and went to my work. When the boy's mother left, after the ship was loaded, she came to me, and the tears came to her eyes as she kissed me and said that was all she had to give me for saving her boy.[25]

The mate and the crew came on board when we were nearly loaded. We bent the rest of the sails and got everything ready for sea. I finished tallying the cargo and gave the receipts to the captain. They turned out to be correct. When we went to sea I was sure that the brig had too much cargo in the lower hold, but the captain was there and I said nothing. We had not been out long when we got a strong northwest wind, and then they knew that the cargo was not put in right. The wind let go with a heavy sea running—and such rolling!

In a short time the fore topgallant backstays carried away, and overboard went the topgallant mast and half of the jibboom. We saved the topgallant and royal yard, and as we had no spare spars we had to get along without those sails, which made progress slow. We arrived at Galveston in due time and had two lighters outside the bar. We had a great time getting out the cargo on account of the brig rolling so much, but we finally finished lightering and went inside and completed discharging.

Galveston at that time was a great city for gambling. I used to go to the gambling houses in the evening and watch the games. They were playing poker, each player with a revolver alongside of him. They served free drinks, but if anyone made any noise he was put out at once.

After discharging, we sailed to Pensacola to load for Santos.[26] We arrived all safe and started to load, but when we were almost finished loading I was paid off as I refused to go to Santos. It was one of the most deadly ports in the world. The yellow fever took thousands of lives then, although today, due to modern sanitation, it is safe. I never heard whether the brig got away without a lot of trouble or not.

After I was paid off, I went to a boarding house run by Tommie Glennon. He was a noted character, but I had no trouble whatever with him. He asked me one day to go and look at a Norwegian bark which was loading for Europe. I went and was allowed to go on board and talk with the mate. The bark had two big cables around her, set up with four-fold blocks. I think she was the hardest ship I ever have seen. The mate told me that she was not as bad as she looked, and I told him that I hoped not. All the crew had left, and they were offering a big run across the Atlantic.

When I got back to the boarding house, Glennon asked me what I thought of the bark. I told him that it would be almost impossible for any ship to look worse and keep above water, and he asked me if I wanted to go in her, that they were offering sixty pounds for the run across. I told him I would let him know in the morning. He said, "You needn't mind. I will not let you go in her if I can help it."

So I let it drop, as you could not get a ship out of Pensacola unless he said so. The Norwegian bark got across all right, even though it was the dead of winter.

In a few days a fine three-masted schooner[27] came in from New Orleans to load for Portland, Maine. One man was sick and had to be paid off. Glennon told me that the job was for me, and in a day or two I went on board. She was one of the largest schooners at that time and in fine shape. Wages then on the coast were twenty dollars per month for sailors.

We left the last of January and had a lot of bad weather. The mate was a square-rig man. We were reefing the fore staysail one afternoon, the mate bossing the job, and I knew the sail would blow away when it was set. I told him that he had done it the wrong way, and that the sail would burst when it was set. I was told to mind my own damn business or I would get into trouble. I said no more. When the sail was hoisted it went to pieces. I went to the wheel soon after that, and the captain came on deck and asked me why the staysail went. I told him I didn't know, but he said he knew I did, so I told him why. The only thing he said was that the mate should have listened to me, and the sail would be all right now, as it was almost new.

We got nearly to Portland and had to go to sea again. It was bitter cold, and we got so much ice on the vessel that we went into the Gulf Stream to get it off. After we got in and made fast, the captain went ashore and got money, and paid all hands off. I was the last one to be paid. The captain's wife was with him, a very nice looking lady, who paid out the money. The captain asked me what I was going to do, and I told him that I would go to Boston on the first boat and go to sea again at once. He told me to bring my clothes aft and go second mate, as he was taking the second mate as mate. I told him that I did not care to go second mate as I had been before the mast. His wife talked to me very kindly and said that she and her husband had talked it all over some days before and that they were sure that I could do second mate's work. But I would not stay and said goodbye to them, thanking them for their kindness, as I was looking forward to big ships and Cape Horn.

The next day the boat left for Boston, and I was on board. I had very little money. On arrival in Boston, one of the sailors took me to a boarding house on North Street, as I was a stranger there and he was acquainted. It was a hard looking shop. The boss weighed at least two hundred and forty pounds and was a hard case, one of the old type of sailors' boarding house keepers. We had supper, such as it was, and my chum and I went out and looked around until ten o'clock, and then went back and were shown where we were to sleep. There was a large room with at least forty bunks in it. They were three high, with some loose straw in them, a straw pillow, and one small quilt. I told my partner that I was going to get out in the morning. About one o'clock in the morning the crowd came rolling in, some of them very drunk, others fighting mad. In a few minutes a free fight started.

By this time I had my shoes on and was waiting for what might occur. They were talking every language but English. We tried to keep out of trouble, but it was practically impossible. Two of them made a run for us with knives, but we side-stepped them, knocked them down, and took their knives away from them. About this time the boss and two of his runners appeared, armed with black jacks, and in a very short time these tough boys hauled down their flag and a peace treaty was signed.

The boss came to us and said that we didn't look as though we had been frightened very much. We had some blood on us, and two knives that we had taken away from the two fellows who had tackled us. He told us to come up and have a wash. He fixed my right hand, which I had hurt a little, and we were soon in bed; however, I can truly say that I did not sleep.

Next morning we were up early, and as soon as the bell rang for breakfast we were there. After breakfast we went out, as my chum knew where the shipping offices were. As soon as they were opened we went in and found out that they wanted two men for a big two-masted schooner going to Long Island to load for Charleston, South Carolina, but that we would have to wait and see the captain. He came in and asked us if we knew anything about a schooner, and we showed him that we had just left the *Grace Bradley* in Portland.

We were at once signed on the articles and went back to the boarding house to get our clothes. We asked our landlord what our bill was for the night's lodging and two meals, as we had shipped and were going to sea that night. He told us that he would look after our bill and that he had a fine three-skysail-yarder loaded for San Francisco for us.

We said no more but went immediately to the shipping office and explained our trouble. They sent a man to the police station, and very shortly two policemen came back and after asking us a lot of questions told us to come with them and we would get our clothes. They asked if we had money to pay for the meals and lodging, and we told them we did, and of the fun we had when the mad crowd came in.

We went to the boarding house, where they both seemed well acquainted. They asked the boarding house master if we had stayed there one night and had two meals, and told him he had better give us our clothes. We paid him, and he seemed to be in good spirits and said, "Come again, boys," but I said to myself, "Never, if I know it." The policemen showed us the way to go to find our schooner, and we thanked them for their trouble and parted.

In a short time we reported to the mate of the schooner and were soon ready for work. We got everything ready for sea, and at seven that night the tug came. It was bitter cold, everything ice and snow, but as I was young and hard I did not mind it. As soon as we got the hawser on board and the lines in, I was sent to the wheel. They started to make sail, and in setting the jib the mate was knocked overboard. They saw it from the tug, and I at once ran forward and told them to let go the hawser, which they did, and the tug picked him up.

I felt very badly, for he was an old man, but it did not seem to hurt him, for as soon as he got his clothes changed he was at work again and had no bad effects from it.

In the morning it started to snow hard, and at one p.m. we went to anchor in Provincetown, Cape Cod. We were very glad to get there as we had a very heavy snow storm, which lasted for thirty six hours before it cleared off. We got underway then and went to Dennis, Cape Cod, as the captain and mate lived there. The next day the captain, his wife, two daughters, and the mate came aboard, and we once more started for Greenport, Long Island Sound, arriving there in due time.

We anchored and sent the captain on shore, and as soon as he came back we had to go some eight miles to the place where we were to load. It took us only a short time to get there. We went alongside a wharf, and the next day started to load pogy[28] scraps. They took the oil out of the fish, and we took the rest. I have never encountered anything that smelled as bad as they did. They came down in carts hauled by a span of horses and were put on board in tubs.

After we had been there four days, a very heavy storm occurred, and the tide came in so high with a heavy sea that it looked as if the schooner would surely go ashore. The wharf was going to pieces, and the local authorities came down and advised the captain to abandon the vessel. He and his wife and little daughters went on shore with the crew, bag and baggage.

But my chum and I would not go. We thought we would stick by the ship. I could not see any great danger if the ship should go on shore; the only thing was to keep away from the spars if they carried away. We watched our chance after a squall. The ship ran out some distance. We let go the other anchor and had lots of slack chain, so when the next squall came we had both anchors down.

The tide came in so high that several families had to leave their homes, as there was so much water in them. It lasted but a few hours; then the wind went down and the sea with it. The wharf was in bad shape, and it took three days to fix it before we could start to load again.

After we finished loading we went to sea and had very bad weather for several days. We had a lot of ice on the vessel and had to go into the Gulf Stream to get it off, but arrived safely in Charleston, South Carolina. We were all very glad to get discharged, as the odor was anything but pleasant. One could not stay in the hold over one hour before the blood would come from the eyes and nose. Some of the crew could not stand it at all. Even the Negroes could stay in the hold only one hour at a time before they would have to go on deck for a while to get some fresh air in their lungs.

We loaded guano there for Wilmington, North Carolina, and from there went to Georgetown, South Carolina, and loaded southern pine ship planking for New York. The planking was long, and the stevedores stowed the lumber in the hold as the crew put it in through the bow ports. The pile was much higher than the bow ports. When the piece dropped from the pile, we would sing out, "Look out below!" Two of the Negroes thought they could hold the end down and lay across it, but when the piece of lumber fell from the pile it threw them against the 'tween-deck beams and killed both of them. One of them was dead before we could get him on deck, and the other man died in a few hours. They were buried the next day.

The captain asked us to go to the funeral, and we did, of course. It was conducted very well. Several other white men were there, including the manager of the mill and the captain of the schooner.

After finishing loading, we sailed for New York, arriving in due time. After docking, we were all paid off, and the captain asked me to stay and go mate, but I thought I had had enough of schooner sailing. I had learned how to handle one, or thought I had, and wanted to get back into square-rigged ships again.

2 From Third Mate to First Mate

In a few days I shipped third mate in the *Louis Walsh*,[1] a large ship, to load barrel oil for Bristol, England. In order to go above Brooklyn Bridge we had to send down the fore and main topgallant masts. We loaded at Hunters Point, at the Standard Oil Company dock. They were very careful about fire at that time. No fire was allowed on board, but we got good meals at the company's eating-house there. We took over ten thousand barrels of oil. It had the same blue shade that it has today.[2]

When we finished loading, we towed below the bridge and sixteen Western Ocean sailors came aboard. They were all sailors and hard cases, some of them, and it didn't take me long to find it out. After sending the topgallant masts aloft with their yards, we bent the sails, and the tug came and towed us to sea.[3] It was summer, and we had very fine weather. The first mate went to his room sick shortly after we left, and I had the port watch to handle myself. I gave one of the men an order, and he told me he would not do it, and if I did not like it I could fight. So it was up to me to lick Jack or stop going to sea.

A ring was formed, and we went at it. He was surely a hard man. At first he had the better of me, but in some twenty minutes he began to weaken, and I put him to sleep. I was badly smashed up, but he was much worse. He came to and said he had had enough, and he went and did what he had been told to do. Two of the men came up to me and told me that I need not fight any more; they would do it for me. After this I was obeyed without any talk, and there was a lot of work done.

We anchored off the port of Bristol after a good passage across the Western Ocean, as the sailors call it. Two tugs came to take us in, bringing a pilot and two men to steer. After we passed under the Clifton Bridge,[4] we had to wait for some time for the tide to come up so we could get up to our berth, as we were the largest ship and drew more water than any other ship that had been to Bristol up to that time.

By the time we were ready to start we had only six men left. Ten had run away. We went to our berth, and the next morning I had only two men left. The mate was paid off, and by noon the second mate was drunk, so he likewise was paid off. Two men on a hand winch took out all the cargo, one barrel at a time. I tallied the cargo out, and it came out right with the bill of lading.

The captain went to Liverpool, where he stayed most of the time we were there. I was made second mate as soon as the other one was paid off, and the ship was left under my care. I wrote to the captain every night, telling him how everything was, how much oil we put out each day, and how much we still had on board. When we were almost discharged, he came back, bringing a first mate and third mate. The first mate's name was Fitch, and he was surely a hard case among the sailors.

We shipped fourteen seamen, very poor men for those days, and sailed for Saint John to load deals for Liverpool, England.[5] The first mate made a slaughter shop of the crew all the time across. He had no use for me, as I could see, but I said very little and carried out his orders to the letter to give him no chance to complain, for I was sure he wanted me out of the ship.

We made a fair passage to Saint John, and after docking the crew were all paid off if they had anything coming to them, for they had gotten a month's pay in advance in Bristol. The mate got money from the captain, and then came the whiskey. He was giving the carpenter and me more work than six men could do. Twenty casks of salt beef and salt pork came to the ship one morning. We waited until the ship fell even with the dock and rolled them onto the after deck. They were to go down aft, so the carpenter and I put a bight of rope over one of the after bitts and were slacking them below, the easiest and safest way, when the mate came aft and asked me what in the hell I was doing.

"Well," I said, "you should be able to see."

His reply was, "You put this beef below seaman fashion or there will be trouble."

I asked him why he didn't take off his coat and help and told him not to give so many orders. "All the sailors have gone that you could lick," I said.

"Well, I am going to give you the damnedest licking you have ever had," he said, "and drive you out of this ship."

"Well," I said, "come out on the main deck, and the best man will win."

The carpenter told me he was sorry for me, but we went up to the main deck, and at the start it was as hard a fight as I have ever had. He took a lot of beating before he gave in. He was in awful shape and I felt sorry for him, but it could not be helped. I was not hurt with the exception of my hand, and it was in bad shape. The carpenter put my knuckles back and bandaged my hand, and we went back to our work.

"Well, carpenter," I said, "I expect this ends me here, but there are more ships than churches." I did not want to be fired, as I might get a bad discharge, which could have stopped me from getting into some ship that I wanted to go in.

In a short time the captain and the boss stevedore drove down to the ship. As they came over the gangway the captain called me, and I went to him at once. He gave me a good looking over and then asked me where the mate was. I replied that he was in his room, and I was told to tell him that the captain wanted him at once. I did and then started back to my work. The captain told me to stay there. Then he called the carpenter, and he came and stood by me. The mate came on deck, a hard-looking sight.

"Well, what is the matter with you?" was the greeting from the captain.

"I have had trouble with the second mate," he said.

"But," said the captain, "the second mate doesn't look any different than he did when I went ashore. You have had it in for the second mate ever since you came on board, and you want him out of the ship. When you got half full of whiskey, you thought you could lick him and that he would leave, but you should not try to lick one of the State of Maine boys."

Then he turned to me and said, "Mr. Killman, you lick the mate every day or I will give *you* a damned licking."

"Very well," I said.

In a short time the mate went ashore. He came back with an express man, took his things on shore, and did not come back. He did not even say goodbye. I saw him once later in Astoria, Oregon, where he was mate of a small steamer, discharging cargo there. I was master at the time, getting a crew to go to sea. I went down with the steamer's captain for lunch, as he was a friend of mine. On the wharf I walked up to the mate, took him by the shoulder, turned him around, and asked him if he wanted to have one more chance at me. He asked me to please leave him alone, and I walked away. I had to tell the captain the story, and as the mate did not come to the table for dinner we both laughed and thought it was a good joke.

We finished loading the *Louis Walsh*, and a new mate had come. We got a third mate and sixteen sailors, who came the last moment before leaving the wharf, all drunk as usual. The tug and eight riggers came, and we took the ship out in the stream near Partridge Island, rigged out the jibboom, bent the headsails, and got the deckload secured, so that we could get underway from our anchors the next day.

Next morning the captain and pilot came on board, up came the anchor, sail was made, and we were off for Liverpool.[6] Winter had come, and one gets plenty of wind in the North Atlantic. We had average weather until we were some six hundred miles from the St. George Channel.[7] The barometer went very low, the wind came from the northeast, and at twelve-thirty noon I left the deck. The ship had three lower topsails, a reefed foresail, and fore and main spencers. Everything was in the best of shape, and the ship was going very easy.

At three p.m. I awakened. The ship was laboring very hard, and I went on deck at once. It was blowing a most horrid gale. I asked if the captain was on deck, and the mate said that he had not been on deck since one-thirty. I got my watch out, and we took the foresail in and got it furled. The wind was increasing very fast. As soon as we got on deck the fore lower topsail went. We hauled the sail up and got men on the weather braces to square the yard in to try and save some of the sail, as it was new and had been bent only a few days. I was down to leeward, slacking the braces, when the carpenter hollered, "Look out!" and ran up the main rigging. I looked to windward and saw this mountain of sea coming. I hung on to the fore brace, and then I was struck by this wall of water. When I came up I was twenty feet from the ship, with the lumber from the deckload all around me. I saw three men hanging to lumber, but I could look out only for myself. One of the braces came near enough for me to get hold of, and I hung on to it, going hand over hand for the ship.

I got near, and the ship righted some, and I got on deck. The five seamen that were washed overboard at the time were not seen again. We could do nothing, even if we wanted to, for our boats were all gone. No boat could live in such a sea, anyway. The main and mizzen topsails soon went, then the fore and main topgallant masts and the jibboom went over the side.

By this time it was very dark. The lee bulwarks had all gone, and the main rail was gone from the fore rigging well aft to the stern. I had lines on the man at the wheel, also relieving tackles on the tiller. The wind was still blowing a horrid gale. The carpenter was aft with me and we didn't know whether any of the crew was left or not. We had no idea if the mate and third mate were still alive. The carpenter and I hung on to the weather mizzen rigging. It was bitter cold, and we had very little clothing. During the first part of the night the carpenter got close to me and said, "Mr. Killman, I think this is the last storm we will ever see."

I made no reply. I was wondering if anyone was left on board. I was sure the captain was in the cabin, but I did not know if he was all right or not. After midnight the wind started to moderate fast, and when we got into the cabin we found the captain there and all right. There was two feet of water in the cabin, and the steward was working hard to clear things up. I found the mate and third mate both below, but both of them had been hurt by the deckload. I got them bandaged.

We started forward and found the cook with a broken left arm. I told him that we would fix him as soon as daylight came. I found eleven of the men under the forecastle head, but they came out quickly on my order, and I sent three of them aft to get the water out of the cabin. Then, with the carpenter, I got to the pumps and found seven feet of water in the hold of the ship. We got steam on the engine, and in two hours and a half we had the main pump going.

The yards were swinging from one side to the other, and the fore yard had fallen on deck and broken, one half going overboard. The first thing after getting the pumps going, I went to the cabin and asked the captain if I should not throw the rest of the lumber overboard. He said to get clear of it as soon as possible. There was not much left, and that was badly broken, so we soon threw it over the side. By that time they had the water out of the cabin, and we had breakfast. It had been nearly twenty-four hours since we had eaten.

After breakfast I set the cook's arm. The ship was in a horrid mess. I got the yards secured, and as the braces were nearly all gone new ones had to be rove. The weather had gotten fine, almost calm, and I was sure the next wind would be fair. We got a main lower topsail bent before dark that night and about eight o'clock a breeze sprang up from the west. I set the main lower and upper topsails, also the fore upper topsail and what headsails we had left. The ship paid off and soon got steerage way.

I went aft to ask the captain about setting the mizzen topsails and found the rudder head sprung above the deck. We put a hemp seizing around it, and it was a long job as it had to be put on so tight, but we got it finished by midnight. We had pumped all the water out of the ship and found that she was not leaking any to speak of. I sent half the men below to get a few hours' sleep, for they had worked very hard and willingly.

At four o'clock in the morning the captain was on the warpath. I can assure you that the mate and third mate came on deck very quickly. The captain gave the mate orders not to call me, but I slept only my four hours and was on deck when my watch came. The captain gave the mate an awful dressing down and told him and the third mate to get out as soon as the ship was fast.

We had fine weather and a fair wind the balance of the way to Liverpool and went into the Canada Dock to discharge.[8] As soon as the ship was made fast, the mate, third mate, and what was left of the crew left. The captain returned on board and made me first mate.[9] I asked him if he thought I was capable of filling the position, and he told me that he thought he knew what he was doing. I said that I would do my best and that in his absence he need have no fear about me not being at my post.

After our repairs were finished and the cargo discharged, we loaded a thousand tons of salt in the hold and four hundred tons in the 'tweendecks for a return voyage to Saint John. After finishing loading we got the usual crowd of sailors, all drunk, but as soon as they were on deck we had to go to sea. The jibboom had to be rigged out and the headsails bent before we got to Point Lynas, where the pilot and tug would leave us. It was one job to get finished and be ready to make sail, but it had to be done, and the mate was the man held responsible. Some of the crew would want to fight and had to be handled roughly, but no matter what came the ship must be ready for making sail.

We had an easterly wind, something one does not expect, that carried us nearly the whole way across the North Atlantic. We had a wonderful passage, nineteen days, and very few ships have ever beaten it.[10] The captain was a very strange man, but I soon learned his ways and got along fine. I worked and made everyone else do the same. I was surely mate all the time, and I knew I was getting much better with experience.

At Saint John we went to the dock, and as soon as we passed the doctor we started to unload. The crew all ran away the first night, as they had drawn a month's wages in advance and were only twenty days on board. I was always glad to see them gone. I had good second and third mates whom I had hired in Liverpool, and a good carpenter. We could do everything there was to do. The ship had improved in looks and was in fine order. I felt very proud of myself, as I was very young to be mate of a ship of that size.

We went back to Liverpool, and there was the same thing over again—sailors put on board by the boarding house master, and there was a hard crowd of them in Saint John. A sailor had little to say, and if he said much he was knocked down until he was willing to keep still. They had very few clothes, but they were most always sailors after the poor liquor was worked out of them.

We had a very fair passage back to Liverpool in the early spring. We towed from Point Lynas to an anchor in the river. I rigged the jibboom in and got everything ready for docking. The pilot stayed on board, as there was such a very strong current in the river. Before noon I sent the pilot and the second and third officers to dinner, and I went aft to see that the ship was kept dead to the current, as it was running very fast. Everything was fine when the pilot relieved me. I was at dinner when he ran to the cabin and told me that the chain had parted.[11]

I ran forward and let go the port anchor, but the chain fouled under the windlass. The ship was very crank and had swung across the current and lay over with a big list. One of the big tugs was close by. He came to our assistance and heaved a heavy line on board. I asked the tug captain what he was going to charge, and he said the same as for docking. The pilot and the rest of the officers said they were witness to this.

We hauled in the hawser and made it fast, and he went ahead full. But a long scope had to run out before it got to where it was fast. When he brought up, we were moving in the other direction, and the hawser parted, hitting one of the men and breaking his arm.

I thought we surely would land on the beach, but I cut the gaskets adrift on the topsails forward. Then I set them and the foresail. The wind was strong, and the ship was hard aback. I got the mainsail down, and by this time the ship's bow ran into slack water. She turned, the sails filled, and we started to go ahead. The pilot said that we hit bottom forward, but I am not sure of that. We had all sail on the main and were going ahead.

By this time, the tug got his hawser in and came back, but I refused to take his hawser again, for I knew we were quite safe. I got the anchor chain clear ready for letting go the anchor. We sailed up the river some distance and anchored. Shortly after the cable broke, we were going straight for a big English ship, and I hailed him and told him to put his wheel hard to starboard. We didn't clear him more than five feet.

After we were safe at anchor again, a boat came with a letter from the captain telling me to have nothing to do with the tug and that if the windlass was harmed to buoy the anchor and slip it when the tugs came in the morning to put the ship in the Canada Dock.

The tugs came early the next morning, and as soon as they were fast I slipped the chain and we went to the dock. By the time we were fast, we didn't have a sailor left. That afternoon a lighter came with both anchors and chains.

The tug sued for salvage, but as soon as the pilot and I had finished with our evidence the judge stopped the case, ruling that it was the fault of the captain of the tugboat by going ahead too fast with a large ship going the opposite way, and that the tugboat company should pay the cost of court and the repairing of the ship. I got a big write-up in the papers for the way I had handled the ship and sailed back to anchor without getting into the hands of the tugboat company.

We took part cargo of salt and some general cargo, went back to Saint John again, and loaded for Liverpool, arriving back in good time.[12] It was a fine sight to go around the docks and see the American and English ships, all kept in such fine order. At that time the American ship was the pride of the ocean.

A few days after arriving, the captain told me that we were going back in ballast to Belfast, Maine, for repairs, because the main and mizzen lower masts were getting bad and the main deck was to be put in new. I asked him if he would pay me off when we were discharged, as I did not care to go back to Maine. When we were nearly discharged he told me to come to the American Consul's office and he would pay me off. I met him at John Dernot's office, and he made me acquainted with the captain of the American ship *Thomas M. Reed*,[13] which was loading for San Francisco, California. I shipped in the *Reed* and went on board that day with my clothes, going to work the next morning.

The *Reed* was almost new and a beautiful ship, painted white. Captain Work was her master, Work by name and work by nature, as I often called him. We loaded a cargo of coal, and when we were finished loading, twenty sailors and two boatswains came on board. I had bent the sails with riggers, and we started on our long voyage around Cape Horn for San Francisco, with a channel pilot on board. Shortly after we released the Liverpool pilot, we started off with a fine northeast wind, the wind increasing as we went, and by the time we got down the Irish coast to Waterford it was blowing a moderate gale. There were no fishermen out to take the pilot off, so we kept on with him on board. Our only hope was that we would see a ship bound to some port in Europe.

Days passed by and we sighted nothing. We were getting down close to the Azores when, one morning, a ship was in sight far ahead and on the lee bow. We kept off some, and it did not take long before we were close to him. It was an English ship, bound for London. We hove to, put a boat overboard, and bade the pilot goodbye. The pilot was a very happy man when he got into the boat, for he had a wife and three children in Waterford. The boat was soon back and hoisted aboard, and once more we were off on our voyage.

We had a fair run to the Line. We had some men that I did not like, but there was nothing that would give one any clue against them; they worked hard and said nothing. Getting down close to Buenos Aires, we spoke a bark two days out of that port. We exchanged signals for a short time, asking him to report us on his arrival in New York.

About four-thirty the next morning, the alarm was given that the ship was on fire. The cook had gone forward to go down in the 'tween-decks to get some kindling, as his fire was not burning well. Seeing a big light below and smoke starting to come up the hatch, he knew that something was wrong. He started to run aft but was grabbed by one of the men. Being a very able man, he laid the sailor out and got aft, reporting the ship on fire.

I had not been below but a short time. Hearing the alarm, I was soon on deck, armed with two good revolvers. I ran forward, fired one shot in the air, and it was not but a moment before I had the men lugging water below, and the fire was soon out. I then called the captain, and he gave me orders to put the irons on the watch that went below. I did this and locked the forecastle up.

After we had talked the affair over and called the men aft one by one and asked them if they knew who was guilty, with no results, we put the ringleaders in irons and locked them up. The others whom we thought guilty we put in a room in the after part of the forward house. They had planned this for some time, as they had saved small pieces of oakum that they had picked up from the deck where the carpenter had been caulking on the forecastle. They also used rags wet with coal oil from the forecastle lamps and two barrels of pitch. If the fire they had started had ever gotten along, and the pitch had burned, no one could have gotten below on account of the smoke.

We had very bad weather off the Horn, twenty-six days from latitude 50° South in the Atlantic to latitude 50° South in the Pacific. One night we sighted a ship on fire. It was blowing hard. We stood by until morning but found no signs of life. She was loaded with coal, and the foremast was the only spar standing. It was a great sight. As the ship rolled the iron plates would become red hot, and when she rolled back they would send a cloud of steam in the air. The crew had all been saved, as we learned on our arrival in San Francisco. Many ships loaded with coal caught on fire in those times. We spoke an English ship bound for San Francisco, loaded with coal from Cardiff, Wales, three times during the voyage. The last time, we were just across the Line in the Pacific, and four days afterward she was abandoned on fire. The crew were all picked up by an English ship and brought to San Francisco, arriving a few days after we did.[14]

On our arrival the captain entered charges against the two men whom we had had in close confinement for so many days. They were taken out of the ship and put in jail. One of these men was English and the other French. The French sailor lived only a few days, but the English sailor got a five-year sentence on McNeil Island.[15]

Shortly after we had docked, I left the ship. The *Thomas M. Reed* was a fine ship, and I don't think I ever have seen a ship that was so clean. She was painted white outside and inside. There was nothing that we did not do to make her look fine. It is possible that the crew was worked harder than they would have been if the ship had not been set on fire, but I could not forgive them. It might have cost our lives, and although we got the two ringleaders the rest were just as bad in my estimation. The *Reed* a few years later burned in port at Liverpool, loaded with coal.[16]

3 Twice around Cape Horn

I shipped then in the ship *Carrollton*,[1] loaded with wheat for Havre, France. We had to pay three months' advance wages and sixty dollars blood money. The sailors were most all handled by a boarding house manager by the name of Shanghai Brown. I knew him very well, and his word was as good as a government bond, but he had a gang of runners who did all the dirty work for him. He got all of the American ships. Men were very scarce, and we were three days getting a crew, but as soon as the last one was on board we went to sea.

We sailed into the Black Sea Dock at Havre after a most wonderful passage for a slow ship—one hundred and one days.[2] We were quarantined twenty-four hours for not having a French bill of health. We had sailed on a French holiday, and the French Consul was to send the bill of health. It came a few days after we arrived. The crew ran away as soon as we were fast—to my pleasure, for a crew on board in port is no good, as they are drunk all the time and apt to cause trouble.

After discharging, we took ballast and sailed for Philadelphia. The crew came on board in the morning, and we took the tug's hawser on board, let go the lines, and away to sea! The captain and pilot were on top of the after house. After passing through the dock gates, the orders were given to square the yards and set the topsails. I gave the orders to man the braces. One of the sailors made no attempt to move, so I took him by the shoulders and told him to go to the braces.

As quick as a flash, out came his sheath knife, and he made a dive for me. I jumped to one side, the knife just clearing my breast, and knocked him down. Some of the other sailors started in to help him, but it did not take long for the second mate and two boatswains to take all the fight out of them.

The captain called me aft. The pilot had gone to haul the American flag to a position that would call a police boat and stop the tug, but I got aft very quickly and grabbed the pilot by the throat, telling him that if he knew when he was well off he would let the flag alone and mind his own business, or he might have to swim back to Havre. I am sure he understood what I meant, because he was very fine after that. In a few moments the pilot left, and when the tug gave three long whistles, we dipped the flag three times and were away under full sail.

We had a lot of trouble with the crew going across as they were hard cases, most of them, but it did not do any good to be hard as they got the worst of it at all times. We had the usual weather going across the Atlantic, as we left Havre the last of February and made a northern passage. Lots of wind and lots of reefing of sails and putting them on again.

We arrived off the Delaware, and the captain made a bargain with the tugboat captain to anchor the ship below Philadelphia. It was in the evening when we passed the breakwater, and about midnight we anchored. I was all packed, and the tug landed me in Philadelphia. The captain gave me some money that he had, and I was off as soon as a train left for New York.[3]

I got a room in Brooklyn and wrote the captain my address, and in nine days he sent me a telegram to come back by a certain train. He met me at the train with the captain of the ship *Norris*, which was to load railroad iron for San Francisco. I had my things sent to the *Norris*.[4]

Her captain's home was in Maine. He had been away many years without seeing his family, and Captain Lewis of the *Carrollton* gave me a fine name to him. He told him that the ship was safer in my hands than it was in his, for I had the knowledge and youth and strength to back up anything I said and would pay strict attention to my business.

He took me to the ship chandler and introduced me, telling them to give me anything I needed for the ship and what money I should want, as I had a steward and night watchman and one boy on board. That night he left for Maine. He gave me a letter to give to the stevedore, telling him that I was in charge of the ship while he was away.

The next morning we started to load. The rails came on flat cars, and I tallied each car. It was very simple to count the rails as they had a man count against me and give me a receipt every night for the amount we took in each day. I wrote the captain a letter every night telling him how everything was going, and a few days before we finished loading I sent him a telegram saying that we would finish on such a date. The day the ship finished, he arrived with his wife and daughter, a young lady, and two sons, one of them to be second mate, as well as the managing owner's son, who was to go third mate.

I was in a tight place with these two young men, neither of them ever having been officers, not even sailors. I would have asked for my money if it had not been for my old captain. I was afraid he might be hurt, so I said nothing and decided that I would see it through. I had a ship chandler list made out of what there was on board and what I thought we needed, also a list of all the stores on board. The captain looked the chandler list over carefully and came to me and asked me if I had enough. I told him that I had been all over the ship aloft and could judge pretty near what was needed, but that the only thing I could not tell was how much canvas would be wanted, as I did not know the condition of his sails or how many new ones were coming. That night I helped him with the store list, and early in the morning he went ashore. By noon the stores were coming. The next day everything was on board, and the ship cleared.[5]

The crew came in fairly good shape, the cook being the only one that was really drunk. About ten a.m. we took the tug's hawser and the pilot came. We started for sea with a lot of work to be done, jibboom to be rigged out, and all the sails to be bent. I had a fine crew and, you might say, sober. The cook, however, had had more than his share of spirits and bothered me so much, telling me that he was no cook, had never been to sea before in his life, and did not know what to do with ladies on board, that finally I had to put him in irons.

We came to an anchor at six that afternoon. The captain told me at supper time that I would have lots of time in the morning, but there was a fine full moon, and I kept on until the ship was ready for sea with all sails bent. I went to the cook's room, and he had become quite sober by that time and begged that the irons be taken off so he could go to the galley. I told him that I wanted coffee for all hands in forty-five minutes, and he promised to have it ready. He turned out to be one of the best cooks that I have ever had.

Morning came, and we heaved the anchor up and were on our way down the Delaware. The tug towed us but a short distance, as there was a fair wind blowing. The pilot left, and the tug's hawser was let go. Blowing three long whistles, and dipping the flag three times, the topsails and foresail were set, the captain gave me the course, and in a few minutes every sail was set to the lovely breeze. I sent the studdingsail booms aloft and set topmast and lower studdingsails, stowed the anchors on the forecastle head, and put everything away. I picked the watch, as the men had worked hard and very willingly since coming on board and needed rest.

We had fine weather, and there was a lot to be done, as the ship was not in very good condition. The third mate was no good whatever. It was not long before I told the captain that he was useless to me, and from then on he was rated as boy, and a poor one at that. We had very good weather off the Horn; only one heavy gale. The cargo was stowed well, and the ship was very easy. After reaching fifty degrees south in the Pacific we had fine weather again. We had a lot to do, so I stayed on deck all day and saw that everything was done right.

The second mate, the captain's son, was a good young man but had no idea how to set men to work. I had one very good sailor in my watch, and after getting into fine weather, if I got too tired I would let him come aft and keep my watch for an hour or so, and I would lie down on the grating in the coach house. I got the ship in fine order before reaching San Francisco, and we had a good passage, one hundred and twenty six days, which was good for the *Norris*, a slow ship but very well built.[6]

We docked at Oakland Long Wharf, and everyone was paid off. The second mate and the owner's son who came to go third mate finished their careers as officers, and neither went to sea again. We lay some three months before chartering. Wheat freights had taken a decline, but at last we chartered railroad ties, timber, and some general cargo for Salina Cruz, Mexico. They were building a railroad across Mexico, but very little had been done to the road on the Pacific side when we arrived there.[7]

We anchored just before dark, at least a mile from the shore, and in the morning the doctor came on board but did not stay long. The captain's boat was then lowered for the captain to go on shore. The boat was in fine shape, because I had cleaned it, and it had an awning the whole length of it. Four men and the second mate manned it. We did not watch them go, but shortly I saw the boat coming back with no awning up. It soon came alongside, and I saw that they had had trouble, because they were all soaking wet.

I got the captain on deck and learned that there was a heavy surf on the beach, and that the boat had turned over and had landed with the captain underneath. He was hurt, and they had quite a time getting him out. Some natives helped them turn the boat over and swam it out through the surf. The captain went to his cabins, and it was some two hours before I was sent for. He told me that he would not go ashore again if he could help it and that I would have to go to Tehuantepec in the morning to enter the ship.

We got all ready for discharging, and after the captain had told me what to do I started for shore and had no trouble getting there safely. I found that I could enter the ship there but that the American Consul was in Tehuantepec City. They would start discharging at one p.m., so I held the boat on shore until I got finished. Then I went back to the ship and told the captain that I would go the next day after things got going all right.

The discharging went very slowly. It was winter when we got there, and the wind comes from the land at times in great force. We would have both anchors out, and all our chain. One bark loading there dragged both anchors and went to sea. It was eleven days before he was able to get his anchors, because his windlass was poor; he was lucky to get them at all. The first chance I had, I took the papers to the Consul and was glad to get back to the ship. The northers would come up at short notice, and the second anchor needed to be placed correctly. The captain, who was getting along in years, looked to me to attend to everything that I could, and I can truthfully say that I did to the best of my ability. As soon as the gales let go, I at once heaved up one anchor, no matter what time it was, to keep from getting turns in the chains.

This was a hard place to get water, and very poor water at that. I used to take four men and a cask that held one hundred and fifty gallons, go close to the breakers, and anchor the boat. Then bend a line onto the cask, let it go on shore, and then swim through the surf to the shore, leaving one man in the boat. We had to roll the cask about a hundred and fifty yards, fill it with water, and then get it afloat. Then the men would swim to the boat and haul the cask out to it. I would stay with the cask until it was through the breakers. It was not a pleasant job, but there was no other way to get water, and we did not want to use up our good water and have nothing left but that Mexican water. By doing as I did, we had ample water to get home with by the time we were through discharging.

One morning, one of the coast steamers came in and discharged four lighters of railroad iron. The first three lighters got ashore all right, but the last one could not, as the wind began to blow. Although they were all pulling hard in the lighter, they were being carried out to sea the whole time. I watched them for a short time. Then I told the captain that I would go and take the men off, taking a coil of rope with me to anchor the lighter, as it might be saved. The ship *Ida Lilly*[8] was there, and I asked her mate to go with his boat also, as I would not be able to take all the lightermen and still have room to pull. We lowered his boat, and he too took a coil of rope.

It did not take long to get to the lighter, as we had a strong wind after us. We got the rope on board and soon had the lighter anchored. Then came the job of getting back. There were ten men on the lighter, so we each took five and started. It was blowing strong by this time, so we could make very little headway. We were eight hours pulling back. We had no water and suffered with thirst, but at eight p.m. we made the *Ida Lilly*. Our tongues were so swollen that we could hardly talk. The next morning the lightermen got ashore and were very thankful to us, for they would all have been drowned, and the lighter and railroad iron would have gone to the bottom.

In a few days a steamer landed some more iron, the last lighter being a big one. As it left the steamer, I saw that it had a big list and kept listing more and more. All at once, over she went! I lowered my boat and picked up both of the men, who were cut badly. I took them on board and gave them first aid, and a boat from shore came after them in a few days. For saving the men, I got a letter of thanks, and two hundred and fifty Mexican dollars for saving the lighter and iron.

After finishing discharging our cargo, we had to take one hundred tons of ballast at five dollars a ton. The last thing, I went to Tehuantepec, got the ship's papers, and did everything else there was to do. I was glad when we were cleared of that port. The water was alive with shark, and you could go as high as the main top and count one hundred at any time. It became a well-known port after the railroad was finished. They built a breakwater, drydock, and wharves, and a lot of freight went across from west to east, but as soon as the Panama Canal was built it took all the business away.[9]

We made a good passage to San Francisco, going to the dock to lay up for a while.[10] All hands were paid off, but the steward and I stayed a few days.

4 Master in Steam and Sail

I thought it would be a good time to pass for steam, so I told the captain what I was going to do. He told me that I was doing the correct thing. I went to school for a few weeks and passed for steam. I got master's papers for six hundred tons, and very shortly I got the job to take the steamer *Planter*[1] to Honolulu. She was new, built by the Hall Brothers at Port Blakely, to run between the islands carrying passengers and freight, returning with sugar to Honolulu. She was a fine boat and made eleven knots.

We left San Francisco with holds full and a big deckload, and had a strong north wind. The second day out the *Planter* commenced shipping water. The president of the company and the superintending engineer were on board. I saw that Mr. Foster[2] was a little frightened, so I put the steam to half speed, and they seemed very well pleased. Mr. Foster came to me and said that he was glad I did it, since we went so much easier. After a few hours, however, the wind fell light, and I went full speed again. We made very good time and only had to stop three times to tighten up some of the bearings.

The last twenty-four hours, I noticed that the superintending engineer came to my room a lot and asked me to show him where the ship was, but I did not think anything about it, as I was sure of my position if the chronometers were right. After dinner the evening before we arrived, Mr. Lash, the engineer, came to me and asked me what time I would make the light on Molokai. I had just placed the ship on the chart and told him that if the ship made the same speed we would see the light a few moments after midnight. I paid no attention to the question and went to the cabin.

A little before midnight I asked the president of the company if he was getting anxious, and he said he was very anxious. I told him that he would be home early in the forenoon. At midnight, eight bells having just been struck, Mr. Lash came along and said that we should soon see the light on Molokai. I went up a few steps in the main rigging and told him that it was one and a half points on the port bow. By the time I came down, you could see it from the bridge. Mr. Lash looked at it and said that that was wonderful navigation. He went aft and sent Mr. Foster up. He came and looked at the light, saying that it was very fine, and shook hands with me.

Still I thought nothing of it, thinking he surely would be glad to get home with his new steamer. They went aft to the cabin, and in a few minutes Mr. Lash came and asked me for the key to the purser's room. It was locked, as there was a lot of liquor left from the trial trip. Mr. Foster had had the key once before and had gotten whatever he wanted out of the room. In a short time Mr. Lash came to me and said that Mr. Foster wanted me in the cabin. I went with him, and we had a bottle of champagne and some sandwiches.

Mr. Foster told me that they had something to tell me, but that I must promise not to get mad. I told them that they should know whether or not I would be justified in getting mad. Mr. Foster said that I would be very mad, but to be governed by his decision. They told me that the mate had been telling them that I had no idea where the ship was and that I never would find the Hawaiian Islands, that I was hundreds of miles from my course. I listened until they finished. I didn't speak for some time, for I could hardly believe my ears. Then I assured them that the mate would tell them no more lies and got up to go, but they were both beside me and asked me to pay no more attention to what he had said. The mate was a man of forty years of age, I should say, but what he expected to make out of it I have never been able to learn. He came on deck at four o'clock in the morning. Mr. Lash, who was on the bridge with me, stopped him, and told him that he had better go back to his room if he knew what was best for him, and to get ashore as soon as we got to the dock, that there was no more room for him in the company.

The commodore captain was to take her on arrival, which I knew, and I was to go mate. I went mate, but from the start I saw that the captain did not likc mc. Hc was no navigator, for if hc had bccn hc would havc gone to San Francisco and brought the boat to Honolulu, as she was under the Hawaiian flag. After some work was done on her at Honolulu, the *Planter* was ready for the trade, and we started on our first trip. We made eight ports each way, and had a load each way. It was a hard run, and for a stranger that did not know any of the ports it was worse. The freight was all handled in boats. Each way we had five big surf boats, one being the boat that carried the mail and most of the passengers. The captain of the mail boat was a big, strong Kanaka[3] who had been in the Arctic whaling and had the rest of the natives afraid of him.

I noticed the second voyage that the mail boat was behind, so I went to the boat captain and asked him what was wrong. When he said nothing was the matter, I told him to wake up. But I could see no difference—always last, and should be first, as he got five dollars more a month than the captains of the other boats.

I saw that something had to be done. Captain Bates, the captain of the *Planter*, came to me and asked me if the captain of the mail boat was mate. I told him not yet, and then I knew that they had framed on me and that I had to lick the captain of the mail boat or leave the steamer. I knew that Captain Bates was at the head of it. So the only thing to be done was to give the big Kanaka a good licking or take one myself.

After the freight was all ashore, I told the captain of the mail boat to do some job with his crew. He told me to do it myself. I told him that he was going to get the damnedest licking he ever would get, so we went at it. He was very strong, and I saw that he was trying to get a hold on me so that he could throw me overboard, but I kept clear of him. In a short time he began to get tired, and I soon put him out. He was in bad shape, and I was very mad, as my hands were bad. I went to Captain Bates and told him if he could think of any of his Kanaka friends who could do any better than his boat-steerer to send them along. From now on, I told him, I would see that there were no pets on board, for if there were I would soon make them pets of mine, and if he did not like it he might try his own luck. We never had any conversation with the exception of business, and I stayed in the steamer for one year.[4]

I must say that I had a very fine time in Honolulu. It was during King Kalakaua's reign.[5] I became well acquainted with the King and had several pleasant evenings at the palace. At that time there was no place where one could enjoy himself more for a few months than Honolulu, but after a year I saw that it was no place for me. The barkentine *Discovery*[6] wanted a mate, and I was acquainted with the captain, so I went to him and told him that I would go mate. He told me to get my things on board, which I did. In a few days we left, loaded with sugar and all the passengers that we had quarters for. We made San Francisco in good time,[7] but as soon as we docked I got my few dollars and went ashore, as I did not like that kind of seagoing. We were under water[8] all the way to San Francisco. I might relate that the captain's name was Lee, a big, good-hearted man, who had reverses and in a few years committed suicide.

I had been in San Francisco but a few days when my brother[9] arrived in port and wanted me to go mate with him. After some delay I agreed to go, telling him that I might not suit, as I would not allow the sailors on the California coast to run me the way that I had heard they ran other mates. I went on board the day before the *Arkwright*[10] was discharged.

It was the beginning of the sailors' union, and the bark belonged to Pope & Talbot,[11] who would have no union men at that time. After getting discharged, we went into the stream for a crew. We got a few the first day, finished the following day, and went to sea. We had been out but a day or two when I went aft and found the man at the wheel steering very poorly. Consequently I went into the wheelhouse and told him that I wanted him to steer the ship straight when he came to the wheel.

I did not use any bad language, but he looked at me and laughed, telling me that I had better go away, as they didn't pay any attention to what a mate said on the California coast. I stood and looked at him for a short time and asked him again what he had said. His reply was that I had better get out or be put out. I lost all control of myself. The man at the wheel went over the top of the wheel, and the next time went head-first out through the lee door. He got up and started to run forward, singing out for the rest of the crew.

The captain ran aft and took the wheel, and the rest of the crew soon became like lambs. I brought the same man back to the wheel who had told me that they did not pay any attention to the mate on the California coast. He and the balance of the crew had changed their minds. The captain, my brother, sent for me as soon as it was my watch below and told me that it would not do. I told him that I would leave as soon as we got in because, naturally, I did not want to do anything that he did not want done, but that I would be mate until we did get in and that the crew would fly once in a California coaster and they surely did. I kept the afternoon watch up, and in fact they got very little rest the remainder of the way to Port Ludlow.[12]

As soon as we got fast the captain told me that we were going to load for Australia and that there was a lot of work to be done on the ship, and he did not want me to think about leaving. So I stayed. As soon as the whistle blew at six p.m. (we worked from six to six those days) I called the crew aft and asked them if they paid any attention to what the mate said, and the next morning at five-thirty when I went to breakfast the steward told me that the crew had all gone. When my brother got up I told him about it, and I knew he did not like it; not that he cared himself, but he thought the company would not like it. Things like that didn't bother me because I was young and could pick most any ship I wanted to go mate of in San Francisco in the foreign trade.

I was on the wharf doing something a few days following. Mr. Cyrus Walker[13] came along and asked me if I was not Mr. Killman, the mate of the *Arkwright*. I replied that I was. He then told me that he understood that the sailors had found one mate that they could not handle, but that it had always been his impression that the young State of Maine men were very hard to handle if they got mad. He has always been a very good friend of mine.

We loaded after the repairs were finished and cleared for Melbourne, Australia.[14] We had a long passage because the ship was very foul, and it had been years since her bottom had been seen. We discharged at the old pier in Melbourne, and were some time, as we had most all big timber. What an amount of cargo was going over that dock! Nothing but fine sailing ships with all kinds of cargoes, and loading tallow, wool, and hides for Europe.

After our cargo was discharged, it was taken to some vacant lots and sold at auction, bringing a good price. While we were there the barkentine *Kitsap*[15] went up the river to Melbourne with some two hundred thousand feet of lumber, this being the first ship to go up the Yarra River to Melbourne. After we finished discharging, we went back to Port Gamble in ballast and had a fine passage home.

We stopped at Port Townsend, passed the doctor and entered the customs house, and went direct to Port Gamble, taking the US Shipping Commissioner with us. As soon as the ship was moored, we paid all hands off and took a cargo of piling in the lower hold, with lumber and laths in the 'tween-decks. It was my first experience at stowing piles, but I did very well. I had a short talk with the expert pile stevedore there, who told me in ten minutes all I wanted to know. He told me that I could do better than he because I could handle men so much better.

After loading we sailed for San Francisco. We had the usual weather, it being early spring, and on our arrival[16] I told the captain that he must get a new mate, that I would stay only until the ship was discharged.

The port captain came to the ship in the morning and asked me what time we would be discharged. I told him about eleven, and he told me to change my clothes and he would take me to Mr. William Talbot's[17] office. I did so at once, leaving a new second mate to look out for things while I was gone.

I was taken to Mr. Talbot's room, and after passing the usual greetings he told me that my brother wanted to stay ashore that voyage and that he wanted me to take command of the *Arkwright* for the trip. I had promised one of the Eastern captains that I would go mate with him, taking wheat to Liverpool. When I told Mr. Talbot this and that if I was going master only for the voyage, I had better go in that fine, big ship to Liverpool, he told me that he would see that I would have one of their ships. So I told him that I would. The port captain and I went to the customs house and changed the papers.[18]

It was not long before I had a full crew on board and articles signed. I took the second mate as mate and shipped a new second mate, and the ship was all ready for sea before six p.m. The next morning the tug came and towed us to sea. He let go his hawser at the Four Fathom Bank,[19] as we had as thick a fog as one could have, but everything went well. The wind hauled to the south, and before night we had a fair wind and were going along with all sail set.

The fourth day, I got a shift of wind to the southwest, and the fore topgallant-mast carried away. I saved the topgallant yard, but the sail and the fore royal and its yard went overboard. I sailed to the mill at Port Gamble and made the passage in six days, the best the *Arkwright* had ever made. Mr. Walker came to me and shook hands, saying that I had made a good passage and that I was not afraid to carry sail. I told him that I was not, but that it showed poor judgment to lose spars and sails. He assured me that I should not let it bother me.

I had spars made there, and it did not take me long to get them aloft again. We went back to San Francisco, and on our arrival my brother took charge of his ship again and went back to Port Gamble.[20] I took charge of the bark *Atalanta*,[21] which had been laid up there a year or more. I found her fore lower rigging and part of her backstays gone. I put on her what rigging she required to be able to go to sea, and loaded for San Francisco. We had a fair wind all the way down and made a good passage, considering that the ship was very slow and in awful condition.[22]

After discharging, we went back to Port Ludlow to load for Honolulu.[23] The office sent a letter saying that they had always had to anchor outside and lighter the deckload. Mr. Walker came to see me about not taking any deckload. After I told him that I was well acquainted with going into Honolulu, he told me to take all the cargo I wanted to, so I put on her usual deckload. Before leaving, I got a round spar to rig out across the forecastle head, with a place on it for the hawser.

Off Honolulu, I hove to, and the pilot came aboard the first thing. He told me that we would have to come to anchor, as this ship always lightered outside; but I assured him that I was going in. I suggested that he go ashore if he wanted to, but that if he stayed he would have nothing to say because I knew the way in. The tug was but a short distance off. I went on deck and asked her captain if he could tow me in. I took his hawser on the starboard bow and gave him my hawser on the port bow and insisted that he keep close to the ship and go slow in the narrow place.

In a few moments the sails were all furled and we started in through the reef. The pilot said something, and when I told him to keep his mouth shut he said that he expected trouble when he saw that I was captain of the *Atalanta*. I assured him that he had not been disappointed. We went in as fine as any ship ever did. Captain Fuller, the harbormaster, came on board and suggested that we anchor for the night and moor in the morning, but I said that I was going to moor then and be ready to discharge in the morning. It wasn't long before we were moored and well ready for our next day's work.

The cargo was for Wilder & Company. I was well acquainted with the boss of their lumber department, and it was not long before we were putting off the deckload and the 'tween-decks at the same time. Everything went fine, and I had a very quick dispatch. I went around and saw the pilots, as I was acquainted with them all, but when I was ready to go out I didn't bother them, as the pilotage was paid in the customs house.

We made sail at the dock with a line out aft, and when sufficient sail was made we let go aft, and then, as all bills were paid, we were at sea in a short time. We had fine northeast trades leaving, the wind going to the east southeast. Before I got to the Sound, the old bark began to leak a lot, I think because I had carried sail too hard. But I had wanted to make time and had fitted the ship out so one would hardly know her. I sailed to Port Townsend, where I had to enter the customs house. I was gone fifty-three days on the voyage, which is very good time and has been equaled but a very few times, if ever.[24]

From Port Townsend I went with the *Atalanta* to Port Gamble. When I went ashore there I was told to take my things off and wait for the bark *Emerald*[25] and that there was a captain there to take the *Atalanta*. I told them that the bark was leaking badly and that something should be done to her before she went to sea again. The next day a telegram came saying that the *Atalanta* would load for Honolulu and asking me to make one more trip in her before taking the *Emerald*. So I went back on board the *Atalanta* and went to Utsalady to load.

The bark leaked worse as we put the lumber in, so I sent a telegram to Port Gamble stating the condition of the vessel and received a reply to stop loading. A tug came with a carpenter and caulkers, and we hauled the bark onto the beach, bow on. They thought that it was the wood ends under water forward, but I didn't think so. We had a big hawser around a grain warehouse, and when the tide went out the hawser parted. We tried again the next day but could not hold her up, the beach was so steep. So I hauled back and finished loading, putting only a very small deckload on, then towed to Port Ludlow and put a donkey engine on the main hatch.

After getting finished, and with a lot of good firewood for the engine and a good carpenter to attend to the engine and pumps, we went to Port Townsend to get a crew. I did not expect any trouble with the ship as the pumps were in most excellent order, and we had oceans of fresh water for the boiler.

I shipped a crew in the morning, and at two p.m. the flag went up, union down. I went on board at once. The crew and mate had stopped work. The carpenter, second mate, cook, and boy were at their posts. The Commissioner came on board, and the crew had a lot to say that didn't amount to much. There was a revenue cutter at anchor in the bay, so I set the flags,[26] and they came on board. After talking with the crew, one of the revenue men came to me and asked if I was willing to go in the ship. I told him I was, and he said if that was the case then the crew must go too, so he put them all in irons, mate and all. I told the captain of the cutter that I would look out for them and that they would be good men in a short time.

I finished my business on shore, and at eleven that night the tug came. I had ten men from shore to heave the anchor and had the second mate at the wheel. Less than three hours out of Port Townsend the steward came and said that the men wanted to see me. I went forward and unlocked the forecastle and was assured that they were all willing to go to work. I told them that if they started any more trouble they would get the worst of it, and that they well knew. I took the irons off them and had the cook give them their supper, as they had had nothing to eat. While the rest got a bite to eat, I drove half on deck. I then went aft and took the irons off the mate and threw him out on deck head first. He was never more willing to work in his life. I told him to watch his step, and he did, I can assure you.

The barometer was low and falling, but with the wind at southeast the ship must go to sea. The tug *Tyee*,[27] the biggest tug on the Sound, had me in tow. Captain Gove was her captain, a very dear friend of mine who told me many times after that he had never before hauled in a hawser from a ship that he hated as badly to see go to sea as mine that day in the face of a heavy storm, knowing the condition of the ship and the way the crew had acted.

After we had let go the hawser, he came and asked me if everything was all right. I told him that I would never put back, but that I would make some port. He blew three long whistles and in a few moments was out of sight. I made what sail the bark could stand and drove her off shore as fast as possible, for I knew I would soon be under small canvas. The barometer was falling fast, and there were all the signs of a gale of wind, but I was able to get a good distance from the land before it began to blow.

The pumps were able to keep the ship free the first twenty-four hours out, until it began to blow very hard. It did blow when it started, so I took in all sails but a goose-winged main lower topsail, fore topmast staysail, and reefed main topmast staysail. For twenty-four hours it blew with hurricane force. I took in the staysails, leaving nothing on but a main lower topsail, goose-winged. The water was gaining on me in the ship's hold, but there was nothing to do as the pumps were working fine all the time.

The wind finally jumped to the southwest in a horrid squall. I saw the shift coming and had gotten the bark off before the wind before it struck.

She took a sea over the port quarter, which landed me under the forecastle head. I thought for a moment that I was overboard until I brought up under the windlass. I soon got out and aft and got the yards around. It blew very hard for a while, then it backed into the southeast again.

We were able to get the water down to eight feet in the hold when it moderated and the sea went down. The cabin had been part full of water and everything wet, which made it anything but pleasant, but I was young, strong, and determined and did not know what it was to be beaten. I did all I could to ease the bark in heavy weather. We had one gale after another and made slow progress.

I saw that it would be almost impossible to make Honolulu, so I made up my mind that I would make San Francisco. I said nothing to anyone of what I intended to do. I was getting worn out, as I had been on deck most of the time since leaving Port Townsend. At last I got a fair wind, but I found that I could not get the water in the ship's hold below eight feet. If anything should happen to the pumps making it necessary to stop them for any length of time, I knew that the bark would fill.

On the night of the twenty-second day out, at two in the morning, I was close to Point Reyes. I knew that there would be a tug out there, because there was strong competition among the tugboat companies. I saw a tug coming, so I had the carpenter haul the fire out of the boiler. In a few moments the tug came up on my weather quarter and hailed me, asking what bark it was. When I told him, he asked me what I was doing there.

"You are bound for Honolulu," he said, and I replied, "If you are so damned smart and know more than I do, you had better come on board and take command, if you think you can get away with it."

He then said that I was listed in the *Guide*[28] for Honolulu, and I told him that he was too smart to be captain of a small tug. Then he asked me if I wanted to tow. I told him that I would tow, but that I did not want to buy his tug. He said that he would tow me for a hundred and twenty-five dollars. I offered him one hundred dollars and no more. In a few minutes he said to stand by the hawser, and we were all ready.

As soon as the hawser was well fast, I hailed the tug and told the captain to tow us in mid-channel, as we had water up to the 'tween-decks and drew at least thirty feet, and to run the bark up in the mud at the foot of Third Street. The carpenter was making steam again, and in a very short time both pumps were going as hard as we dared to drive them. We had no trouble and put the ship as hard up in the mud as the tug was able to.

Mr. William Talbot was on the wharf when I got ashore and was glad to see me. I was in bad shape, my legs swollen three times their usual size.[29] He told me to give all my accounts to the port captain,[30] who would take me to the Baldwin Hotel. I stayed there until I felt that I could get around, then went back to the ship.

After the lumber was taken out, the ship went on drydock and was caulked and coppered, but the cargo was never sent on to Honolulu.[31] As soon as the bark was finished with her repairs, I was sent for to come to the office. Mr. Talbot told me to take command of the bark *Emerald* at Oakland, which would be finished discharging that day and would go to sea at ten a.m. the next day. I went to the customs house with the port captain and had the ship's papers changed, shipped a crew, and went to sea in the morning.[32]

The *Emerald* was a much larger ship and much better than the *Atalanta*, so of course I was glad of the change. She had very fine cabins with four fine staterooms for passengers, having been built for the Western Ocean trade. I went back to Port Gamble, loaded for San Francisco, and made a fine passage. Luck seemed to follow me, but I can assure you that it is not all luck, for one must take advantage of everything. The only way to do that is to stay on deck, trust no one, and drive, drive, all the time, if you want to make time.

I needed very little sleep, and by watching the weather night and day I was able to get all there was to be gotten out of the wind. I never waited for a watch to come on deck to make sail. Instead, if I thought the ship could stand more, they were called out at any time, as I always said that that was what they were there for. I don't think I was liked by the sailors, but it did not bother me in the least, for the better you use Jack the less results you receive. This I found out by a very long, hard life at sea.

In 1887 I loaded twelve hundred tons of English railroad iron at San Francisco for Port Ludlow, to build a logging road on Hood Canal. The stevedore who was discharging the lumber was putting in the iron all wrong, so I went to the office and told Mr. Talbot. I knew, because I had had two cargoes, one around Cape Horn. He called the port captain, who said that it was stowed right, so that was all of that. I finished the iron and took some general cargo in the 'tween-decks for the store in

Port Gamble, also some marble for Mr. Walker's new house that was being built at Port Ludlow.[33]

After finishing, we went to sea. The wind was from the southeast, it being February, but before long it shifted to the northwest with a strong breeze. In a short time it made a nasty sea, and the ship gave a heavy lurch as the iron in the 'tween-decks shifted to leeward, breaking some of Mr. Walker's marble and fixtures and giving the ship a very heavy list. I wore around and shifted everything I could to take the list out, but it did very little good, if any, as the cargo in the lower hold had shifted.

The bark did not leak, so I kept on, but it was very disagreeable. The ship was over on her side so much that she would not sail and handled badly. You had to use all precaution as it took a long time for her to wear and tack, and I found that there was no use trying to tack her, so I gave it up. I found my compass out some three points on a north course after the cargo had shifted, and it was impossible to find out the correct deviation as the sun was out so little that time of year. But I made Cape Flattery without any trouble and had a fair wind up the Sound.[34] I was reported from the Cape as being on my beam and full of water.

When I was abreast of New Dungeness, I saw a Whitehall sailboat coming toward me, and I wondered what he was doing so far down the Sound. As he came alongside, I threw him a line and saw Henry Rothschild, who was agent for the company and whom I knew very well. He was soon over the rail and aft, shook hands with me, and told me that I was lucky to get there.

"Oh, I don't know," I said. "If she had sprung a leak I might have been up against it."

When he asked me if I was not full of water I told him no, that I was full of railroad iron and general cargo, which had shifted, and that was what the trouble was. We went on into Port Townsend, as the cargo had to be entered in the customs house,[35] and from there towed to Port Gamble to discharge the freight for the store.

When I was nearly finished I went to the office and told them that I would be through at a certain time. Mr. Walker was there and said that they had nothing to tow me to Ludlow with, and that they didn't know when they would be able to get a tug, because they were all at anchor with booms of logs. The weather was so bad the tugs couldn't start with them. Consequently I would have to sail to Ludlow. I looked at him and told him that I didn't think the *Emerald* could be sailed to Ludlow. He assured me that he knew I could do it, and I promised to do my best. I went back to the ship, and as soon as the cargo was ashore I got ready to make sail.

The mill had a small tug that towed logs around the bay, and he came and hauled the ship's head around. I made lower and upper topsails and fore topmast staysail and jib and let go from the wharf. In a few moments I had plenty of wind and set the foresail and main topgallant sail. As I passed Whiskey Spit, the main topgallant sail went into a thousand pieces, and it looked to me as though I were up against a very hard job. I was sure that I would not be able to get into Ludlow, but there was no turning back.

I got both anchors ready to let go at a moment's notice. As I hauled into Ludlow, I was hanging to windward as much as I could, to avoid the rocks. All at once the wind started to haul out of the bay. As I was where I could not wear around and run out, I hauled up the foresail, let go the topsail halyards, and let go the starboard anchor. When I could see which way the chain was bearing, I let go the other anchor and gave the ship one hundred fathoms of chain, and when she brought up to her anchors I was but a very short distance from the rocks.

I got the sails furled as quickly as possible, for I had a very good crew who saw the danger, and they worked with a will. At midnight it fell calm, and I heaved up the port anchor and some chain on the starboard anchor. At nine in the morning the breeze came from the west. I at once made sail and heaved up the anchor, for I had only a mile to go. It was but a few moments before I let go the anchor a short distance from the wharf and ran a line ashore. I was soon alongside the wharf where I was to discharge the railroad iron.

I was getting the gear up to discharge when Mr. Walker came down to the ship. He came up to me and said, "You surely are some sailor, and you did well. I thought the bark was going, and the cargo too. But it would have been all my fault."

I told him that it looked very close to me, but after I had stopped the ship with all that chain out I felt safe. The only thing I was frightened of was that I might break one of the cables before I could stop the ship, as she was going astern very fast with the sails only half hauled up.

5 Commanding the *Kitsap*

After the railroad iron was unloaded, I loaded lumber for San Francisco and continued in the coast trade. In October 1887 I was called to the office and told that Mr. William Talbot wanted to see me. I went to his office, shook hands, and was told to sit down.

"Killman," he said, "there is a man on the way from Searsport, Maine, to take your ship."

"That is all right with me," I replied. "There are lots of good ships, and if I cannot get a master's job I can go mate again, but not on this coast. I will go back to the Cape Horn trade. I should never have left it for a master's job on the California coast."

"But," he explained, "you are not going to leave this employ. I want you to go to Port Ludlow and take command of the new schooner that is on the stocks."

This was a surprise. I told him that I did not want the new schooner they were building, that he had some good men in his employ much older than I, and very able shipmasters with lots of experience.

"Yes," he said, "that is true, but I don't think they are as able to take command of that big schooner as you are."

I repeated that I thought they were more able and that it would make hard feelings, but if he thought I was deserving of a better ship to give me the *Bonanza* or the *Palmyra*.[1]

"I can get lots of men to take those ships," he said, "but I want a man for the schooner *Kitsap*.[2] You should care if the rest of the captains like it or not; in fact, you don't care for any man—that is very well known."

"Well, sir," I said, "I suppose it is either take the new ship or get out."

Mr. Talbot assured me that this was not what he meant but that it was his wish that I would take the new schooner and rig her. I thought for a moment, knowing that I was taking some job, and then told Mr. Talbot that I would take the schooner, rig her, too, and sail her after she was rigged.

"That is all settled," he said. 'The new captain will be here day after tomorrow. You give him any advice he needs and tell him everything about the ship that he wants to know. You go to a hotel, and when the steamer goes north, go to Port Ludlow. I will give you a letter to give to Mr. Walker. You will have command, and anything you think should be changed for the benefit of the ship, have it changed. Go to the riggers where the rigging is being made and get what data you want. Before you go, come to the office, and your hotel bill will be paid and a ticket will be here for you for your passage to Port Townsend."

The port captain was outside when I had finished my business with Mr. Talbot and asked me if I was going down to the ship. When I told him that I was he said that he would drive me down. We had not gone far before he asked me if I was going to take the new ship they were building at Ludlow, and I told him that I was. He asked me if I was able to rig her. I told him that if I wasn't, it was a sure thing that I would not come to him for any information. I told him that he needn't worry about my taking the ship, as I didn't think it would make any difference in his wealth, no matter what I did. He had no use for me, and I was anything but civil to him. He was aware that I was on to his game and knew that he was dishonest, so, consequently, he wanted me out of the employ.

I went to Ludlow on the first steamer, the *George W. Elder*, and took command of the *Kitsap* on the stocks. She was launched a few days after my arrival.[3] Mr. Wright, the master mechanic, was a very fine man and a good friend of mine. If I saw anything that I thought should be changed, I talked it over with him and then went to Mr. Walker and got him to look at the change that I thought would be a benefit to the ship. He was always in favor of anything that I wanted done.[4]

I got the shears up to step the lower masts and put garlands on them. One afternoon Mr. Wright came to me saying that he had something to talk to me about and asked me to come to his room at eight o'clock that night. I told him that I would with pleasure. That evening at the appointed time, I went to his room. He received me and asked me to sit down.

"Captain," he said, "I don't want you to get mad with me, as I take a great interest in you and your abilities. But as I hear the men talking and laughing, I think it is my duty as a friend to relate this to you. I do not know who started it, but I do know that they are very careful not to say anything while you are around, as they have a lot of respect for your right hand and your temper.

"This is what they say: you have the garland lashings so far down on the lower masts that they will go up with the wrong end up. I am no rigger and have not even looked to see how you have the masts slung. The only thing is that I don't want anyone to be able to laugh behind your back—something they would not dare to do to your face."

I had not spoken while he was telling me what he had heard, but when he was finished I said, "I know I have some enemies, and there are captains in this employ that should have this new ship. I told Mr. Talbot so when he asked me to take her, and that I would much rather he chose one of them, as I well knew it would cause hard feelings among some of them. But he said he did not care if they liked it or not, as he was sure that I could fight my own battles. And in regard to the masts being slung wrong, you need not worry about that. I can assure you that I have the garlands on correctly and in the right place."

And Mr. Wright said that if I said they were right then he knew it was so. I then told him that if I could find out who started that report I would make him eat one of the masts, but I never found out, and in fact did not try, as I had plenty to do without bothering about something of that kind.

When the ship was ready for her masts, I hauled her under the shears. The first mast was the jigger, the after mast, and everything went fine. I put only the trestletrees and a gantline on before sending the masts aloft. By four p.m. that day I had the three lower masts in, and at midnight I put the foremast in. I had to wait for the big run-out of the tide, as this mast went through the forward house.[5] It was a cold night, and there was a very heavy frost, but I used a lot of fine sand on the barrel of the engine of the company's pile driver which I was using, and everything went fine.

It did not take long after I started to land the mast in its step on the keelson. Mr. Walker was on the dock watching how everything was going, as it was the biggest spar that had been put in a ship on Puget Sound at that time.[6] After it was in her, Mr. Walker and Mr. Wright came and told me that I had done a very clever piece of work, and that I surely knew what I was doing. Mr. Wright told me afterwards that he never heard the men say one word about how the masts went in.

I then hauled the *Kitsap* to her loading berth and started to load below decks. By the time the hold was full, I was finished with the rigging. I did not bend the sails until I got the ship loaded. I was shipping men all the time, but they would stay one day and disappear that night, as they had never been on a schooner of this size[7] and they thought that it would be impossible to handle her. When I got ready for sea, I went to Seattle and shipped a crew for the bark *Sycamore*[8] and landed them on board the *Kitsap*, bound for San Francisco. They were all very drunk and did not know when they were taken on board.

I had the ship out at anchor and men from shore to heave the anchor up and take the tug *Tyee's* hawser. At two a.m. I started on the first voyage of the *Kitsap*. I had two officers and a cook that I had shipped by the run. I had the second mate at the wheel, I sent the mate below, and took the lookout myself.

The ship steered fine, as I found out as soon as we got started and out clear of Ludlow Rocks and the tug had gone ahead full speed. At six in the morning I went forward and called the crew out, telling them to get some coffee and get on deck. It was a fine morning with a fresh east wind. In a few moments I saw all the men on deck, and I went to the deckload where the men were all standing looking at their new home and talking to each other. I told one to go aft and take the wheel from the mate and the rest to wash the ship off fore and aft and to do it as quickly as possible, for the lower masts and topmasts must be greased down before we got to the Cape. The sails were very heavy, and we had no engine to hoist them up. The mate had come along by this time, the men started for the buckets and brooms, and I went aft where I belonged.

After the foremast was finished, I set the foresail and jibs. The men all worked with a will and said nothing. It was not long before we were out past Cape Flattery, and the tug blew his whistle to make sail. It did not take long for them to get them up, as they were all good men. After the lower sails were set, the tug blew to let go the hawser, which we did, and after the tug got his hawser in he came close and asked me if everything was all right. I told him everything was fine. He bade me goodbye, blew the usual three whistles, and in a few moments he was out of sight astern.

The *Kitsap* was very fast but very crank for a single-deck vessel, although I was sure she would go over only so far. The barometer was down, and I knew that I was going to have a gale of wind. At midnight I took in the gaff topsails, and the ship straightened up some. She was going fast through the water and behaving fine. By this time I had made a lot of distance and was in a good position for everything that came along.

The wind stayed in the southeast for forty-eight hours before it shifted to the southwest. I carried three lower sails and three headsails through it, but everything had to be new and the ship had to be good to stand the amount of sail I was carrying. As soon as the wind shifted to the southwest, I wore around on the starboard tack. There was a heavy head sea running, and the *Kitsap* made some very heavy dives, putting the whole bow with bowsprit and jibboom under water, but she must go, as I knew that she could stand it.

The head sea soon went down, and the good ship was going fine and fast through the water. Before long we had all sails set and were making eleven knots. As we went south the wind fell light, but I arrived in San Francisco in six days, to the great surprise of the waterfront critics.

We went to the dock at once and began discharging. Mr. Walker had told me before sailing that lumber was going to fall in price two dollars a thousand New Year's Day, and if I could get to San Francisco and get discharged before New Year's it would mean a lot of money for the company, but not to take any chances, as there was no insurance on the ship. I told him that I surely would do my best, and I would bring the ship safely into port. We had over a million feet of lumber on board, the exact amount I cannot remember, and were discharged several days before December was gone.

After the deckload was off, a fine hoisting engine was installed, connecting with the windlass, a winch was put on the forward house to heave the sails up by steam, and steel tanks also were put in the forward house for fresh water. The cabins were finished and painted, and by the first of the year the ship was completed.

I took in some two hundred tons of cargo and sailed for Port Gamble, arriving there after four days and some hours, one of the quickest passages ever made to the Sound by a sailing ship. At Dungeness the tug *Goliah*[9] picked me up and towed me to Port Gamble. She was a big powerful side-wheel tug that had sailed out from the East Coast around Cape Horn and was used mostly in log towing.

I loaded back for San Francisco and had the usual good luck making a quick passage. I arrived off the whistle buoy in the night, off the bar. We were not allowed to sail in at night, for to try it was considered to be taking too many chances. There was no lightship off the Golden Gate then to help the sailor, as there is now, with two fine lights and a steam whistle that can be heard several miles.

When morning came I started in, having a fine fair wind at the time, with tide that had just turned flood. As we neared the heads, the wind fell light, and when we were abreast Point Bonita[10] it was calm, not a breath. We were as near the center of the channel as one could judge. The pilot boat *Lady Mine*[11] was also going in, a little ahead of me and nearer Point Bonita, when he started to cross my bow to get across under the south shore. Not being able to judge my speed, and losing steerage way, he came down across my bow, my jibboom going between his fore and main masts.

We had some trouble getting him clear, but I got a big block out on the end of the jibboom and, having steam on the engine, heaved him clear. By this time my ship had gotten across the tide, and there was nothing you could do as it was flat calm. We were drifting in fast toward Lime Point,[12] and it looked as if the *Kitsap* would surely hit. The man attending to the fog whistle on the point was talking to me and telling me that the spanker boom would not go much clear, if any. I looked out and saw a little tug coming out of Sausalito, and he was soon down to me.

I knew the tug captain, Dan Thompson, and he told me that he had a line all ready for me and that it would cost twenty-five dollars. However, when I told him his tug wasn't worth that much money we agreed on twenty dollars for the job. The line was aboard in a second. I told him to pull her head off, for she would go herself, and I would anchor off Meigg's Wharf.[13]

He went ahead, and it was not long before we were leaving the danger, but we were awfully near. In another twenty minutes she would have landed if the current did not shift and set off from the shore, although one can never tell how it will act in a place like that. I was very glad when I saw our fine ship leaving those rugged rocks.

In a short time we had steerage way and were moving up San Francisco Bay. I looked ahead and saw a tug coming down, the smoke belching from her stack. He rounded to, came alongside, and told me to let go my hawser as he was sent after me. But I firmly told him that I was all O.K. and that the little tug was going to do my towing.

After I got up the Bay I came to an anchor and went ashore at once to go to the office, where I was told that Mr. Talbot wanted to see me. I went to his office and we shook hands. He asked me if the *Kitsap* had struck the rocks off Lime Point, for the government lookout thought she did. I assured him that she didn't, but we were very close. Mr. Talbot then asked me how much I had to pay the little tug, and wondered if I had been able to get him to tow me for ten thousand dollars. When I told him that I was to pay him twenty dollars, he put his hand in his pocket and passed me a twenty dollar gold piece, asking me to pay it at once and bring the bill back to him. He told me that I would dock at Third Street at slack water.

I left and went to the office at Steuart Street from where the tug was operated and paid the bill. They asked me if I would speak a good word for them to Mr. Talbot, and I assured them that I would. The captain of the tug was there, so I asked him and the owner to go and have a drink with me. When I got a chance, I gave the captain of the tug a five dollar gold piece and told him that it was a new hat for him. When I took the bill in duplicate back to Mr. Talbot and related what I had done, he told me I had done right and gave me another twenty dollar gold piece. I told him what I had spent.

"Well then," he said, "there is a new hat for you, too, and you surely deserve one."

The pilot who had been in charge of the *Lady Mine* when she got across my bow was at Third Street when I docked. We looked over the damage that had been done to the *Kitsap* by the pilot boat, and he had everything repaired in fine shape but asked me not to give the reporters any more data than I could help. Of course I didn't, because all the pilots were friends of mine, and it was no fault of theirs. However, it is risky, crossing a ship's bow—even in a pilot boat—when she is not handling all right.

I stayed in the *Kitsap* some fifteen months[14] and had wonderful luck. The longest that I was at sea on any passage during that time was eight days. Mr. Walker would say, "The *Kitsap* is out so long; have a tug sent to Cape Flattery," and by the time he got there I would be coming in.

I surely worked hard to make time in the *Kitsap*. Never once when I was in her did I take off my clothes at sea when I went to bed. I must admit that I had very favorable winds and no calms. The ship sailed very well, but to make time on the California coast you must take advantage of every possible chance to make a mile. Don't wait until the change of watch to make sail. Call them out at any time, if you think the ship can stand more sail. That is the only way to make time.[15]

Capt. Daniel O. Killman at the wheel of (probably) the schooner *Ella A.*, sometime between 1920 and 1928. Courtesy San Francisco Maritime National Historical Park, Harold Huycke Collection.

The bark *George Treat*, built in 1866 at Frankfort, Maine. Killman's sister was born on board this vessel. Courtesy Peabody Essex Museum, Salem, Massachusetts.

The bark *Masonic*, on which Killman first served as a seaman, in his brother's command. Courtesy Peabody Essex Museum, Salem, Massachusetts.

The *Elmiranda*, Killman's second vessel.
Courtesy Peabody Essex Museum, Salem, Massachusetts.

The *Louis Walsh*. Courtesy San Francisco Maritime National Historical Park, Morrison Collection.

The *Thomas M. Reed*. While serving as the *Reed*'s mate, Killman arrested several crewmen for starting a fire on board. Courtesy Maine Maritime Museum, Bath, Maine.

The *Carrollton*. Courtesy Maine Maritime Museum, Bath, Maine.

The *Norris*, at anchor off Le Havre.
Courtesy Peabody Essex Museum, Salem, Massachusetts.

The shipyard of Pope & Talbot, owners of the *Arkwright*. The four-masted schooner *Okanogan* appears along the quay to the right. Courtesy San Francisco Maritime National Historical Park.

Schooner *Kitsap*, Puget Sound, ca. 1910–15. Courtesy San Francisco Maritime National Historical Park, Plummer/Beaton Collection.

Steamer *West Coast* loading at Fort Bragg wharf, about 1885. Courtesy San Francisco Maritime National Historical Park.

Steam ferry *Benicia*. Courtesy San Francisco Maritime National Historical Park.

6 The Wreck of the *Julia H. Ray*

I left the *Kitsap* to take command of the *West Coast*,[1] one of the early steam schooners, trading between San Francisco, Mendocino ports, and San Pedro. We would coal at San Francisco, go to one of the ports on the Mendocino coast and load for San Pedro, go back to one of the ports, and then to San Francisco with lumber as we would have to fill our coal bunkers by that time.

The *West Coast* was small, with not much power, so we had to depend on our sails in strong head winds and beat in ballast. Loaded, we could do very well and rarely had to make sail in head winds.[2] There were a lot of small sailing schooners on the coast at that time, and I used to keep close in, going north. As soon as these small ships were loaded, they would want to get away. It was hard to get out of the outside ports, as it was calm inshore, and what wind there was generally came ahead and was dangerous. I soon got to know all the captains and got a lot of towing. They would have their flag up, and I would go in and put them two miles offshore, so they could get on their way. I charged them twenty-five dollars, and the owners were very well pleased. In one day, going north, I towed as many as eight out into the breeze. We lost some time, of course, but it paid us to tow them out, and it gave others a chance to load.

One morning, as I was leaving the dock, the managing owner came to the end of the pier and called me back. I went alongside the dock again, and he and another gentleman came to my room. They wanted my opinion on towing the ferry steamer *Benicia*[3] from San Francisco to San Pedro. After we had talked it over, we made a bargain to tow her to San Pedro for a certain sum. They were to furnish the hawser, and I would not be responsible for the breaking of the line, but if his line was not good and did break, I had fulfilled my contract.

Notes were made of the agreement, and a copy was to be on the steamer when I came in after her. I then went to the Albion River and loaded ties for San Pedro, sending a telegram when I left to tell them when I would arrive in San Francisco for the tow.

I got there at five in the morning, went to the sea wall alongside the steamer, and got a copy of the contract. I asked him to let me see the hawser. Knowing the man I was dealing with, I was almost sure that he would buy some old hawser, and when I looked at it I asked him if he thought that that old piece of rope would tow his steamer to San Pedro. He said he was sure of it, so we made the hawser fast and went ahead, everything being in good shape. The side wheels of the steamer were uncoupled so they would revolve as we went ahead.

The wind was strong down the coast from the northwest, and I made sail before reaching Point Bonita, keeping off to the south through the South Channel. It was not long before the tow signaled to me to go slow. But he was all right, so I kept on. The wind was soon well aft, and we went much easier. The wind increased, and it was a wonder to see that old line stand the strain, for we were towing fast through the water.

At three in the morning, the hawser went in the middle. Before I could get sail on and the hawser in, I must have been a mile from him. I turned around and went back. There was a heavy sea running, and the side-wheeler was rolling beyond description in the trough. I went near enough to hail him through the megaphone and asked him if he wanted to be taken off his unpleasant home. He said they would all drown and begged me to save them and the steamer. When I told him he had no hawser he said that I had a lot of good ones, but I assured him that they cost money.

The steamer was going sideways so fast that I found I had some job to get one of the heavy hawsers aboard him, as it was wet and heavy, and he had but a few men to haul it in. After a while, we succeeded in getting it in and fast, and I again went ahead and made sail. In a few moments we were going fast through the water with nothing to fear, because I knew my hawser was strong, and had no chance to carry away.

Everything went fine from then on, and we anchored outside San Pedro at three a.m. In a short time the *Benicia* went inside, but I had to wait until high water, as in those days there was very little water going in to Pedro. At six a.m. I went ashore to settle with the captain, as he had a check signed by one of the Southern Pacific Railroad managers, which only needed filling out.

I met the captain in Captain Banning's[4] office, and was greeted with a warm handshake. He praised me for what I had done for him, saying the steamer would soon have been on shore if I had not picked her up. I told him that a man of his abilities ought to be ashamed for buying an old second-hand hawser to tow a steamer that was owned by the Southern Pacific Railroad, for I was sure that they had not ordered him to do anything of the kind. He had nothing to say. I then told him that he had better settle with me, as I wanted to get a few hours' sleep, and I asked him how much he was going to make out the check for. He answered that it would be what we had agreed on in San Francisco.

I immediately assured him that that wouldn't do, since I had had to pick him up in a gale of wind and use my hawser.

"Well," he said, "I will go on to San Diego."

"Not if I know it, you won't," I replied. "You might go to the hospital, and I will libel your ship. Don't get funny with me, because I am not in a good humor this morning."

I then told him that I would read the contract to Captain Banning and explain what I had done for him and then hear what he had to say. He read the contract over very carefully and then turned to me and asked, "What more have you done than tow the steamer to San Pedro?"

I explained that the captain had bought an old second-hand hawser from a junk dealer, and that I had told him before leaving that it was no good and could not tow him to San Pedro, but that he had assured me that he knew what he was doing. He then turned to Captain Polhamus and said, "I am surprised at you for buying an old condemned hawser. You know that the railroad company does not want you to endanger their property by trying to save a few dollars. You have not got a foot to stand on, and Captain Killman will not stand many of your bluffs, I can assure you. I know this young man, I think, much better than you do, and I would advise you to make an amicable settlement with him."

I then told him that I wanted seven hundred and fifty dollars beside the figure we had agreed on. Captain Banning said that he thought it was very fair and advised him to pay it at once, as delays were dangerous. He gave me a check for the amount I asked for and walked out of the office. I have never seen him since. We did not hear from the railroad company, so they must have been satisfied with the settlement.

When I got back to San Francisco, the managing owner still had the check, as he had heard from me only by telegram that I was sending the check. As soon as I got there he wanted to know how I got so much money. I told him, and he, being a very good man, wanted to know if I didn't think I had charged them too much and if he shouldn't send some of it back. I responded that they would laugh at him if he did anything of that kind.

When I went into the office that afternoon, he passed me five twenty-dollar gold pieces, saying that I deserved it as I had done most of the work. I thanked him for his kindness and shortly afterward went into the ship chandlery that I dealt with to leave an order. Mr. York came to me and said that Captain Nelson[5] of the Oregon Coal & Navigation Company wanted to see me at once. I told him that there must be some mistake, as I did not know Captain Nelson, but he said he would take me to his office and assisted me into a buggy.

I went into the main office, and one of the clerks asked me who I wanted to see. I told him that I didn't want to see anyone but that a Captain Nelson wanted to see me. I was shown into his office, and he got up, shook hands with me, and asked me to take a seat. He said that the captain of the steamship *Arago*[6] had resigned and he wanted me to take command of the ship on her return the day after tomorrow.

I told him that there must be some mistake. In the first place, my master's papers were not large enough,[7] if the *Arago* was the ship I thought it was. And in the next place, I had never been to Coos Bay in my life.

"I am aware of that," he said. "I know it is a very bad bar, and the navigation in the bay is not too good for a ship of that size. But you are young, with a lot of stamina, and learn quickly. I want you to take the ship. I have seen Captain Freeman, and he says he will make your papers as large as you want them."

But I told him that I didn't think I cared for the job, for I was getting along fine where I was. The *West Coast* was making good money, and I would not do one thing wrong to Mr. Garthwaite, as he had been very kind to me in every way.

"I am sure of that, Captain Killman," he said, "but if you intend to go in steam, the *Arago* is a big step up from that little steam schooner. You think it over tonight and let me know in the morning. Your wages will be seventy-five dollars more than you are getting now, and that is a big item."

"Yes," I said, "that is a big item. We are all working for that almighty dollar, but I think one would earn the extra in the *Arago*."

He agreed, saying it was a hard job but that he would not have asked me to take it if he had not thought that I could do it. I told him that I would let him know in the morning, and left. I went directly to the manager of the *West Coast* and told him of the offer from Captain Nelson. He listened carefully and said, "Captain Killman, if I was a young man with your abilities, seamanship, and strength, I surely would accept Captain Nelson's offer and take the *Arago*, as much as I hate to lose you. In regard to the wages, you can have as much as he will give you if you will stay. I have put myself in your place and have told you what I would do."

I told him that if he felt that I should change ships then I would, but that I would not go if it was going to put him to any inconvenience. He asked me to find a master for the *West Coast*, if I knew one. I told him I knew one that was not doing anything, but that I could not recommend him as I knew nothing about his abilities. I went out and found the man, bringing him to Mr. Garthwaite. He told him to stand by, and if I left he could have the steamer, but that I would fit her out for the next voyage and see her to sea.

The next morning I went to the Oregon Coal and Navigation office and told Captain Nelson that I would take the *Arago* but must have someone to give me information on the bar and the channel to the coal bunkers, as I would not be able to take the ship in over the bar and up the bay by myself. He told me that he would have the present captain stay for a voyage and tell me all about everything, so I would have nothing to worry about. He would also introduce me to the agents at Empire City and Marshfield and to the manager of the coal mine.

"You come down at nine in the morning, Captain Killman," he said, "and I will go on board with you and fix everything. Then we will go and change the ship's papers, and you can get your papers changed at the same time. The *Arago* will go to sea the next afternoon at two p.m."

I took my departure and got the *West Coast* away at four that afternoon with her new captain.[8] Going to the office, I reported to Mr. Garthwaite that she had gone and everything was O.K. He settled with me, shook hands, and wished me all the good luck in the world with my new command.

The next morning I reported to Captain Nelson, and we went at once to the *Arago*, which had arrived an hour and a half before. We went to the captain's room, where Captain Nelson introduced us and told him I was to take command of the *Arago*, as he wished to be relieved. Captain

Nelson asked him to stay for one voyage to show me all about the bar and the bay inside. His pay would go on until the ship got back, and he could take any stateroom he wished. He was also to make me acquainted with the agents and give me all the information he could in regard to the ship.

After Captain Nelson had finished, he responded that he would not go in the ship with any new master. They could get their knowledge from some other source than from him, as he did not wish to impart to anyone what he knew about Coos Bay and the steamer *Arago*. This made Captain Nelson mad, and he told him to vacate the ship as soon as he could, and that his presence was not wanted in the office again. We went away, after getting the ship's papers. We then went to the office of the Inspector of Hulls and Boilers and had my papers changed and then went to the customs house where he had the ship's papers changed to my name as master.

I also had the combination of the safe changed, as at times we carried treasure for Wells Fargo up to sixty thousand dollars. The safe was built-in in my room. A new chief engineer and chief steward came aboard. We were lying at the coal bunkers at the top of Vallejo Street wharf, with tugs on the other side of the wharf. The captains of the tugs came to me and said, "Killman, you will have some time getting that steamer out, as she handles very badly. She draws only a few inches forward and some twelve feet aft. The wind catches her bow, and she will swing down on those big sailing ships at the other dock, so, whatever you do, be very careful. You will find the *Arago* much different from the little *West Coast*."

"Well," I told them, "I think I can get out all right, but I surely will be careful, as I don't want to have any trouble the first time I leave the wharf."

The captains of the ships at the other dock came over to see me. I knew them all, as they were ships from New York. They all joshed me and said that they would be on board their ships to see me take some of my yards down. About an hour before we were to sail, I was at the office and Captain George Holt came in. He was over-looker of the new ship[9] that they were building and would command her when she was finished. Captain Nelson introduced me to him and told him that the other captain would not go one trip with me. He asked him if he would go, and he said he would and that he would do all he could for me.

He was a peculiar man but very smart. He was on board when the Wells Fargo treasure came, and as soon as the packages were over the rail the gangway was hauled in. I counted their number and signed for them, put them in the safe and locked it, and then went on the bridge, but no Captain Holt. He was as far aft as he could get.

I was sure that he would be on the bridge to tell me the best way to take the ship out, as he had had the *Arago* built and was master of her until they started to build the new steamer.

At once, I ordered the lines taken in aft, put a spring out forward, went ahead slowly to throw her stern out from the dock, then reversed the engine to half astern. To the surprise of all the onlookers standing on the dock to see me get into trouble, I went out the finest that I ever did in all the times I took that ship out from Vallejo Street wharf. My friends in the big sailing ships all dipped their flags to me. I went down the bay, watching how much the compass was out, if any,[10] and went out through the north channel.

As I got through the channel, it shut down with thick fog. I passed Point Reyes, and it was very thick. I then hauled her to the north, but gave the land the benefit of the doubt. I had my dinner in my room, and as soon as I was finished I took the bridge. The fog was bad, and the mate came to me and told me the course from Point Reyes to Cape Mendocino. I told him that when I wanted any information from him I would surely ask for it.

I never did see the light on Cape Mendocino, as the fog did not lift. It was as thick as could be. I had not seen Captain Holt since we backed out from the dock, and I did not look for him as I felt it was his place, under the existing circumstances and from what I had heard Captain Nelson tell him, to come to the bridge and render his knowledge. But he did not and it was sure that I would not go and ask him anything.

The fog kept the same, and when I got up abreast of Cape Blanco I had to find out where the ship was, as it was not far from there to Coos Bay. I called the chief engineer and told him that I was going to haul the ship direct for the land and see if I could pick up Blanco Reef. I told him to have a full head of steam, and when I sent in full astern to give her all there was to give. I also told this to the first assistant who was on watch.

The chief engineer came back on the bridge with me. I slowed the ship to half speed, and it was not long before we made Blanco Reef dead ahead. The fog was getting thinner, and I changed the course for Arago

Head. In a few moments, Captain Holt came on the bridge and asked how I was, saying that I surely had some fog and he didn't think he had ever seen it thicker.

He put his hand on my shoulder and said, "Killman, you are some man. I can give you one good recommendation. You have not left the bridge since sailing, have you? I wanted to find out if you knew anything, and I surely have. You do not want any advice from anyone.

"Now, Killman, I will take charge and give you all I know. This is the course to Coos Bay whistle buoy. I will tell you all I know about the bar and the bay, and you and I will be friends. I had a good chance to try you out, as I will be expected to give a report about you to Captain Nelson and Mr. Lewis, the owner of the coal mine and the ships, and it surely will be a good one, as you don't sail your ship by any man's compass but your own."

We became good friends, and after the new steamer was completed he tried very hard to beat me. He did not know what fear meant and took great chances, but made good. He did not last long, for he fell dead on the ferry boat one morning coming to his ship to go to sea,[11] and I lost a great friend. I made many voyages to Coos Bay in the *Arago*, had good luck, and made good time.

W. S. Ray had built a new steam schooner that had been in commission for a few months, and he kept after me to take a piece of her and go captain. At last I made up my mind that I would, as I thought I could make more money for myself. So I resigned from the *Arago* to take the *Julia H. Ray*.[12] The captain of the steamer *Arcata* took the *Arago*.[13] He had been a long time in the *Arcata*, which was owned by the Oregon Coal & Navigation Company. I told him everything about the *Arago* that I could, showed him the combination to the safe, and opened it several times. I gave him the combination in writing and told him to put it in his pocket.

He went to sea, and the next day I went away, bound for Coos Bay to load lumber for San Francisco. I arrived at Coos Bay and went directly to the mill where I was to load, without stopping at Empire City. Before I got to North Bend, I saw the *Arago* coming out, loaded. In a few moments he stopped and blew a call signal. I went slow ahead until I could speak to him. He said he wanted me to come on board and unlock the safe, as he had forgotten the combination. He sent his boat for me, and I went on board and unlocked the safe. It had some fifty thousand dollars in it. I asked him what he had done with the written combination, and he explained that in his excitement he had put it in the safe and locked it up. They were going to blow it open if I did not arrive before sailing time for the *Arago*. I took my departure, and the captain of the *Arago* was feeling much better. He was a very nervous man when I went aboard.

I loaded and went to San Francisco and back to Coos Bay. When I got to the bar it was very rough, but no rougher than when I had crossed many times before. I got the bearing and started in. The second big sea that struck the steamer carried away the rudder, and the ship landed on the North Spit. I at once talked to the chief engineer, who was in the engine room at the time, and told him to be very careful and not break anything, and I would get the ship out all safe. In a few moments I went full astern, and she came off and was going out fine.

All at once the engine stopped. The engineer told me that he had broken some part of the engine, and it could not be used again. At once I saw the fate of the *Julia H. Ray*. It was not long before we struck the South Spit, and there was no hope of saving the steamer. Soon it was dark, and it was a long, hard fight. The seas broke over the ship something awful, and the only place we could stay was on the forecastle head.

We rigged life lines to hang onto, and it was not long before the ship was full of water, but she kept heaving in. The after mast went over the side, then the smokestack and wheelhouse, and by morning she was a total wreck. When daylight came, the lifesaving boat came and took the crew off, as there was nothing one could do. She was breaking up fast but had heaved in so far that at low water one could almost walk to shore.

I stayed until that afternoon; then I abandoned. I went to Empire City to notify the owners, and the underwriters told me to sell the wreck at auction on such a date. I got money, paid the crew, and sold the wreck at auction, but did not get very much. Nor did the buyers get anything that amounted to much, as the hull soon broke in two pieces, and the boiler sank deep into the sand.[14]

7 Whalers in the Arctic

I went to San Francisco very much discouraged, not caring which way the tide ran. The Pacific Steam Whaling Company sent for me and told me that they had a bark they were going to send to the Arctic Ocean as a tender for the whalers and would like me to take command of her. I accepted the position and took command of the bark *John & Winthrop*,[1] a little bark that was built at Bath, Maine by Goss and Sawyer. She was but a few years old and fine-looking. I fitted her out, and after putting in a lot of ballast with some stores between decks sailed for Nanaimo, British Columbia, to load coal for the steam whalers in the north.

I got to sea and made all sail, the wind being very light. That afternoon it breezed up, and I never have seen such a crank vessel. She lay over something awful. I sent down the fore royal yard, but when it was on deck I took a good look at it and told the mate that we would not send down the main, as I could almost take it on my back and carry it aloft. But I kept on, and it was not long before I had a light fair wind and carried it.

I passed in by Cape Flattery and had a fine fair wind up the strait. One of the big tugs came within hailing distance and asked me where I was bound. I told him I was bound to the Arctic Ocean. He thought I was going whaling, as I had five whaleboats hoisted in the davits and two on the boat skids.

"What are you doing in here?" he asked. I told him I was going up through the Inside Passage.

"I don't think you can make it," he replied. I told him I was sure I could.

"Then you don't want a tow, do you?" He wished me the best of luck, and away he went. I knew that captain well, but he never thought of me as being in a whaler, and in a few days I saw him in Nanaimo where we had a good laugh over it.

I went into Royal Roads and put up my flags for a pilot. In a short time a Victoria pilot came off. I told him I wanted a Gulf of Georgia pilot, and one very soon came off, a man I knew very well.

"What do you want a pilot for?" he said. "You aren't going to try to sail to Nanaimo, are you?"

I told him I was going to sail to Nanaimo, but he said that he didn't know anything about handling a square-rigged ship. I assured him that I only wanted him to be there, and that was all. By this time we were on our way with a fresh west wind, and I was quite sure that it would let me through, as the wind had been from the south for several days. I was also sure that it would draw from the land.

It was very strong at times, and we had to settle the topgallant sails, as she would lie over so far. The pilot was very uneasy, but I assured him she would not turn over. The wind kept fair with the yards on the backstays, and at two in the morning we were some five miles off Nanaimo. The wind fell calm, and we lay there until eight a.m., when a light breeze came fair, and we squared the yards for the harbor.

In a short time I saw two ships' boats coming, and their captains were soon on board. One was Captain Staples of the *Robert L. Belknap* and the other, Captain Gibson of the ship *America*.[2] Captain Staples came from the same town in Maine as I did, and Captain Gibson was a friend of mine. They gave me a warm handshake, as it had been many years since a ship had sailed to Nanaimo. Captain Staples said that I must sail alongside the wharf without anchoring, so I told him to take charge, and I would see that every order was carried out very quickly. He refused, and I told him then that I would do it in order to show him that it could be done.

I could see where I was going to discharge my ballast and had fenders put over. The men from the other two ships took hold with a will, and we could handle all the sails at one time if I wanted to with the number of men we had. I took in the royals, topgallant sails, and the fore and main lower topsails, and furled them. When I was near the wharf, I lowered the upper topsails down and had them hauled up snug, and when I had headway enough, I hauled the foresail up, threw heaving lines on the dock, and put her alongside as easily as it could be done by an expert tugboat captain. We were seven days and twenty-two hours from wharf to wharf.

We discharged ballast and loaded coal for the steam whalers. A few days before I was ready to leave Nanaimo, I received a letter from Captain Knowles[3] of the whaling company, directing me to take four fat cattle to the Arctic for the whalers. I had to go to Victoria with the ship, as I could not get them in Nanaimo. I towed to Victoria, bought the cattle, and had a well-padded house made for them on deck. I took grain and hay for them, and they grew fatter on the voyage north. I took a lot of pleasure keeping them curried clean. They got so when they saw me they would moo for me, and I would go and pat them.

Off Unimak Pass I got a gale of wind down from the north and was under lower topsails standing to the west, when all at once we were surrounded with thousands of fur seals. They were trying to get up over the ship's side and by some force were washed over the rail on deck. I had them put overboard, as I did not have the heart to kill the curious little things.

I got up off St. Lawrence Island, where one of the whalers was to meet me and tow me into Port Clarence, but no one was there, so I kept on. I went down to King Island, did some trading with the Indians, and bought boots for the men. It was all ice as far as I could see, packed solid. It shut down thick fog, so I held the ship there. In three days it cleared off, and I went down to King Island again. I was getting down close to the island when I saw two barks standing toward me.

They soon hove to, lowered boats, and started toward me, and when I got in the right position I hove to also. They were soon up to me and on board. They were the captains from the *Mars* and *Cape Horn Pigeon*.[4] They came to my cabin, as I had a big supply of liquor put on board by the whaling company for open house for all the captains. They told me that it was impossible to get into Port Clarence, as they had been trying for ten days. However, they believed the steam whalers were all in there but would not come out through the ice, as it was very dangerous. When they left they were surely lit up to a high degree. I gave them each a bottle of good scotch to take with them, and we parted.

It shut down thick fog, and the wind fell to nearly calm, with flat calm at times. I knew the current to be running to the north, and I was trying my best to keep the ship to the south. It was as thick as it could possibly be for three days. When it lifted for a short time, I saw I was close to the ice pack in the Arctic Ocean. I had drifted up through Diomede Strait past Diomede Island[5] and Cape Prince of Wales, never seeing anything.

I made fast to the ice, as it was smooth as a lake, and lay there some twenty-four hours.

Then the wind came from the north, it cleared off, and I started back toward Port Clarence. As I was through Diomede Strait and approaching King Island, I saw the same two barks standing back and forth. As I got near them the *Mars* hove to and lowered a boat, and the captain came on board. I asked him what he thought of the ice, and he said it was impossible to get through it. It would be sure to punch a hole in my bark if I tried it, as she was deep loaded, and one could not stop her headway as quickly as he would want to.

I listened to him until he finished, and said, "Well, Captain, I cannot lay around here, as the feed for my cattle is getting short. I am going to Port Clarence, and I think I will make it."

But he still advised me not to try it, because he was sure I would sink my bark. About three p.m. I gave orders to square the main yard. We shook hands, and he told me I had some nerve to try it.

It was not long before I was down to the ice, and now came the trouble! In a short time the ship hit a cake of ice very hard, and I saw that it would never do. I at once went up to the fore topgallant yard, where I could look down on the ice, and it made a big difference. I could see the ice under the water and could swing the main yard aback, letting the ship strike easy, and then fill away again.

By so doing, I was getting along fine and making a lot of distance. In a few hours I could see the ships at anchor in Port Clarence. But no one made a move; in fact, they were all asleep, as it was in the night. Yet it was daylight all the time—the sun went down, and in five minutes it was coming up again. When I was about a mile from Port Clarence, I ran out of the ice.

I was coming in under easy sail, and as I was nearing the end of the spit, heaving two leads, a whaleboat came alongside from one of the steam whalers. The captain came aft and made himself known, and the next thing he said was that I need not throw the lead any more. I don't think I was in a very good frame of mind, as I had not had any sleep for forty-eight hours, and had been twelve hours on the fore topgallant yard, piloting the ship through that ice pack, this being my first experience of that kind.

I looked at him for a second and said, "You damn fool, I am captain of this ship, and if you don't think I am, take off that big fur coat, and I will soon show you!" My coat was thrown on deck. He made no reply, and I looked at him for a second, saying "Get to hell out of my way and sight."

I stooped down and picked up my coat, putting it on, and he went to the gangway. In a few moments, Captain Weeks of the steam whaler *Thrasher*[6] came on board. He ran aft and gave me a warm handshake, for we were old friends. He then moved away, knowing I was busy, and I shortly let go the anchors. As soon as I was finished, I went to Captain Weeks and asked him if he thought I needed a nurse to assist me in bringing a ship into Port Clarence.

"If you do," he said, "I don't want the job, Killman, knowing you as I do."

He knew that the other captain had said something to me that I did not like. By this time all the captains were on board except the captain of the steam bark *Grampus*,[7] which was anchored about six miles south in clear water. But the ice was so bad a short distance from him that he could not break through and had to wait until it moved north.

"Now, gentlemen, if you will come to my cabin I will give you all a drink and all your mail."

We all went below, and I served liquor to them all and gave them their mail, telling them to make themselves at home. Leaving plenty of liquor on the table, I told them that I was going to lie down for a short time and have a little sleep, which I was badly in need of. I gave orders to the first officer when to call me and asked Captain Weeks to come back later.

After a short sleep, I was on deck at seven a.m. to make the arrangements about the cattle and getting the coal out. I had a letter to Captain Baker[8] of the steam bark *Jesse H. Freeman*, owned by Captain Knowles and Captain Griffith,[9] not the Pacific Steam Whaling Company. Captain Weeks and Captain Baker came on board, and we went to the cabin, where I read them the letter that Captain Knowles had written me at Nanaimo, saying that I should go to Captain Baker for any advice that I might need, and that he would take charge of the cattle and divide them up among the ships as he saw fit.

Captain Baker then said, "Now, Captain Killman, I have met you and seen what you have done. I will carry out Captain Knowles' letter if you wish, but I am aware that you need no help from anyone here in regard to your business. As for the cattle, you will do me a great favor if you will take them off my hands. We will send men to kill and dress them and clean your ship up again, but I wish you would divide the meat to suit yourself. If anyone is not satisfied with what you do, and how you divide the meat, it is just too bad for him, but we are sure that they won't say one word to you."

"Well, Captain Baker," I replied, "If you feel that way I will do as you have suggested."

Captain Weeks said he also thought it was the correct thing to do, and that no matter how the meat was divided there would be talk among some of the captains. It was all settled, and in a short time there was a gang of butchers and two of the mates of the steamers to look out for them. It did not take long before they had the cattle all dressed and hung up, and very finely done, too. Every part of them that could be eaten was saved. The next morning I gave each ship an equal share, not saving an ounce for my ship. They seemed to be satisfied, and if they were not, it was all right with me. Captain Weeks and Captain Baker each brought me a fine piece of meat and said that I was foolish not to keep my share, as I surely deserved it.

One of the steamers came alongside me next morning for some coal. They had a pair of scales. It was all weighed, and the mate checked every bit of it to see that they got just what they asked for. I had orders that if the man-of-war *Thetis*[10] came in there I was to sell him two hundred tons and to arrange the price with her commander. It would be all right in San Francisco.

One morning the *Thetis* arrived, being the first man-of-war ever in the Bering Sea. The commander came on board and wanted two hundred tons of coal, which I told him I could let him have. We agreed on the price, twenty dollars a ton. I had bought the coal in Nanaimo at three dollars a ton, making a profit of seventeen dollars a ton. The *Thetis* came alongside and started taking the coal, weighing every basket. When it was finished, I protested the weight, as the ship had come up out of the water more than I thought she should.

Lieutenant Stockton was in command, and he felt badly about my protesting against the weight. He was up there showing the Indians what they could do with their machine guns, if it was necessary. I was on board once when there were a number of chiefs watching the demonstration. I watched these Indians, and it did not make the slightest impression on them, as they were not the least bit interested.

After I had gotten the coal out and the ballast, whale oil, and furs in, I made out all the bills of lading, signed them, and gave them to the captains who had shipped anything. Everything was insured, as the whaling company had made very careful arrangements. Everything went fine with all the captains except one who was captain of a small two-masted schooner for some company in San Francisco. The captain, who was a great trader, carried a good stock of trade and had caught one big whale. He shipped his bone, furs, and ivory, of which he had a lot, and after it was on board I made out the bills of lading, signed them, and gave them to him.

He looked them over and went away. The next day he came back and said that they were not made out correctly. He had been drinking a lot. I said I was sorry and asked him to give them to me. I went into the cabin, got three bills of lading, and gave them to him. I asked him to make them out, and if they were correct I would sign them.

I then said, "I have no right to make out bills of lading. I am not the shipper. The only reason I am doing it is that I know you don't know how. You have had no experience of that kind."

He was very ugly and gave me the bills that I had made out and signed. I took them, tore them up, and tossed them over the side. He went away, and that afternoon he came back in a bad frame of mind. He passed me the bills that he had made out, and asked me to sign them. I looked at them very carefully and told him that I would not sign them, as they were not right.

"Then give me my goods back," he said.

"No, that I won't do, either," I replied. That was enough. He was knocked down so quickly that he didn't know what it was all about. He came back for more, and I felt sorry for him; his face was in a horrid shape. After he said that he had had enough, I took him by the arm, led him to the rail, and told his boat's crew to take him on board and not fetch him back if he was under the influence of liquor. I also told him that when he came to me like a man and apologized I would make out a set of bills of lading for him and sign them.

He left, and the next afternoon he came on board. He apologized very humbly, and I told him that I was sorry that I had to tame him down to normal. I wrote out another set of bills, signed them, and gave them to him. He was surely glad to get matters straightened out, as I had all his bone, furs, and ivory. Captains Baker and Weeks came on board and told me that I had done right, that he needed what he got, and that I needn't worry about any more trouble, that that had given them a good sample of the goods that I could deliver if called on. He was called a hard case, but I could see nothing but a silly man.[11]

After I got finished at Port Clarence, the *Thetis* put two crazy men on board for me to take to San Francisco. The whaling bark *Little Ohio*[12] had been wrecked in the early spring, and the crew got ashore on an uninhabited island in the Bering Sea. Several died, and some of them went crazy, for they went through very severe hardships.[13] The law was, at that time (and I think it still remains the same), that the government could compel any merchant ship to take one distressed seaman to every one hundred tons net register of the ship.[14]

We went into the Arctic and took what whalebone there was from the ships of other companies and then sailed for San Francisco. We had a lot of fog working down through the Bering Sea. One of the crazy men was giving us some trouble. He was getting very violent and had to be watched closely. I had him scraping the hardwood on the skylight aft. It was just before noon, the sun was trying to burn out through the fog, and I was standing aft of the man at the wheel with my sextant in my hand, when the man at the wheel sang out, "Look out, Captain!"

I turned quickly to see this crazy man with a big knife over his head, diving for me. He would have stabbed me if it had not been for the man at the wheel. He jumped and shoved him enough so I stepped clear. Then I hit him, very hard, and by that time the mate had arrived on the scene. I at once put him in a strait jacket, and he became very vicious, so I kept him locked up the rest of the passage home and had to keep a very close watch over him.

Ten days before arriving at San Francisco, one of the sailors stabbed another. I did not think he would live to reach port, but he did. When I got up to the Bay, I got a tug and towed in, docking at the Arctic Oil Works.[15] I put the man that had done the stabbing in irons, and when the tug got hold of us I set the police flag. The police and doctor came off and took the sick man and the prisoner. The doctor said I arrived just in time, as an operation had to be performed, and one more day would have been too late. As it was, he recovered.[16]

They would not take the two crazy men that had been sent by the government. We went to the dock, but as it was Labor Day there was no one there but a watchman. I sent for a hack, taking the two crazy men with me, and went to the police station with them, but the police would not take them. They told me to take them to the Home for Inebriates.

So I went there, and they would have nothing to do with them. By this time, I was not in a very good frame of mind.

I went back to the police station and asked them if they were going to take the two men. They said no. I told them that I was through with them, so I went to the hack and told them to get out. As I started to take off the strait jackets, telling them that they could go wherever they wished as far as I was concerned, you should have seen the police grab them! In less than a minute they were locked up.

The sergeant on duty laughed and said, "Killman, you should have done this the first time. It would have saved you a lot of trouble."

I was in court several times before they were finally sent to the Insane Asylum. After the papers were made out and sent to Washington, their passage was paid by the government. The sailor that did the stabbing came to court, and the one that had been stabbed had recovered so he could come to court. He testified that it was his fault, and he did not care to have anything done with the man, so he was let go free.

The bark *John & Winthrop* was laid up, that being her first and last voyage as a merchant vessel.[17] She was sent whaling to the Arctic the next year. Captain Knowles wanted me to go in one of the steam whalers the next year, just to look on and learn the whaling business, but I knew it would cause a lot of friction among the whaling officers. I talked it over with him. He told me that after I had gone one season to the Arctic I could take command of one of the steam whalers. I declined, for I did not seem to take to whaling; yet I might have done very well. There is one thing sure, if I had gone in a whaling steamer, I would have worked hard to catch whales, and I might have been the lucky one. There is a lot of luck in being at the right place at the right time.

8 Alaska and the Salmon Trade

I then took command of the small steamer *Hattie Gage*[1] for a canning company that had a salmon cannery at Karluk, on Kodiak Island, Alaska. I went away very early in the year—the last of February—as we had a big wharf to build at Uyak Bay. We cut the piles for the wharf in the woods on Rosebury Strait,[2] anchored the steamer with two anchors, and hauled over one hundred piles into the water by steam with a very long wire rope. We boomed them, watched our chance for fine weather, and towed them to Uyak Bay.

I had two carpenters with me, and we built a pile-driver, using timbers we took from the San Francisco Bridge Company. As soon as the pile-driver was finished, we started driving piles. The wharf had to be long enough for the bark *Hope*[3] to lie alongside afloat at low water, drawing twenty-one feet. It was a long wharf, and some days we had a lot of trouble, as the wind would be too fresh to hold the steamer. We had four anchors out, and even then some days we did not do too much. But when it was fine we got along well, and fast, too, as we went to work at four in the morning and worked until six and sometimes seven in the evening.

It was fine and cool there, although the snow had been some trouble to us getting the piles out. They would start from a side hill after we got a wire on them and the engine started, but often they would get going so fast that they would get out of our control and jam themselves in some unknown way, causing a lot of hard work to get them out. But we got the wharf built, and a big warehouse too, where we stored case salmon and the surplus supplies that the bark *Hope* had brought up with her. It did not take long to unload her, as she had some fifty fishermen besides the cannery workers.

Everything was all ready by the time the fishing started. The *Hope* went away but was back late at the end of the season to get what salmon we had packed. I had brought all the salmon back to Uyak Bay and stored them in the warehouse when the *Hope* arrived. It did not take long to load her and get all the fishermen and cannery workers on board.

I towed her to sea on a very bad morning, and she had a narrow escape from going ashore in a blinding snowstorm.

After the bark had sailed, I had anchors and buoys to take up, and some two hundred and fifty barrels of salt salmon to take on board. Then I took up the fresh water pipes that I had laid at Uyak Bay so I could get fresh water for the steamer. After finishing, I started for San Francisco but got as far as Kodiak, putting in there, as I was getting a lot of ice on the ship. I stayed there for three days before the cold wave passed away, and then I was off for old San Francisco.

We had very fine weather, easterly winds and smooth sea, until we were down below the Columbia River, where we got a heavy gale from the southeast, shifting into the southwest. But by that time we had used a lot of our coal and were all ready to meet any kind of weather that might come along. We arrived in San Francisco some ten days before Christmas; the bark *Hope* arrived just before Christmas. I stayed by the steamer at the dock for some time. Then I took her and another of the company steamers, the *Gertie Storey*,[4] up the Sacramento River to Black Diamond[5] and put them both in fresh water.

I was changed to the *Gertie Storey*, and when it was time to get ready for the cannery business, I took caulkers and caulked both vessels' topsides and decks, as they were built the year before [in 1889] and needed caulking. I also painted them outside and in, and the two chief engineers and two machinists did what work was to be done below. By the time I was finished the engines were in good shape, and I took them to San Francisco with steam on the *Gertie Storey*, towing the *Hattie Gage*.

Then I put them on the drydock, did what work there was to be done on them, painted them with copper paint, and they were both ready for sea. The company told me that I had saved hundreds of dollars for them by doing this work at Black Diamond. I was sure that it was done well, as I had but a small gang of men and was able to see how everything was done. I fitted the *Gertie Storey* out at once, as we wanted to get away long before the other boats did, for they were opening a new cannery that had been built the summer before. The Alaska Commercial Company also had built a new cannery at the same place the summer before, but neither cannery had been run. I had the two superintendents and head engineers of each cannery with what men I could take, as well as freight, with some lumber on deck.

We had some very bad weather going north. I was driving the little ship as hard as could be under sail and steam. We shipped a sea and smashed in the end of the pilot-house, breaking the wheel and losing the compass overboard. After getting the wheel fixed so we could steer, I was in what I thought was some fine fix with no compass. I started looking through the spare gear, as there might be one, but since I had not seen any I was in doubt. But, as you might say, luck was with me, and I found a card compass.

At once I got that to the pilot-house, but as soon as I got there I saw it was five and six points off, flying around like a jack-in-the-box. I had reefed the foresail and mainsail and set the jib and knew that the wind had not changed while I was fixing the wheel, so it gave me a good idea of how much the compass was out on the course I was steering. I had no trouble in making the land off Unimak Pass, and I could follow the land then to Thin Point,[6] where the canneries were built.

We arrived in good time and found everything in good shape. There was eleven feet of snow on one side of the cannery when we got ashore. I stayed only until the next morning, as I had the mail for Unalaska, and they wanted it delivered there as soon as I could. When I got over to Unimak Pass, it was blowing a gale of wind with blinding snow. I had to lie to for some eight hours, as I would not attempt to go in thick weather with a compass of that kind. When it stopped snowing I started on my journey and had no trouble reaching my port.

They were all very glad to see me and get their mail, as it had been months since they had heard from the outside world. I went to the dock and could get fresh water, so I blew the boiler down and then washed it out, and as soon as the engineer was ready I left for Thin Point.

When we got there I went on shore to look at the cannery. I also wanted to see the river and lake that I had heard the two superintendents talking about all the way from San Francisco. The two canneries were fitted out to pack eight thousand cases each, and the superintendents were talking about salting five hundred barrels each. They showed me the two canneries and the other buildings, and I can assure you that they were all very fine and in perfect shape.

"Now," I said, "I have seen this. You surely have two fine modern canneries. Now show me the river and lake. If the lake is not too far away, I would like to go to it."

"Surely," they said. "It will not take long to go to the lake."

The river was just back of the cannery. It had a small entrance, but the water was quite deep. We walked along the edge of the river. It became very small, and at last we came to the lake. There we were in full view of the lake, still covered with ice and snow, and very small.

"Well," I said, "I don't think I know much about lakes or salmon but it does not look good to me. I don't think you will get many salmon if this is all you have to depend on."

Of course they laughed at me and said, "You wait and see, Captain."

I replied, "I only hope I am wrong, as there has been a lot of money spent here."

They said that they had another river some fifteen miles from there which was as good as this one. They would keep a gang of fishermen there and would keep me busy night and day hauling the fish from there. I told them that I hoped so, because that was what I was there for. We went to the other river to look at it, and I must say that it looked much better than the river at Thin Point. I could get quite close to shore with the steamer.

In due time the steamer *Jeanie*[7] came with the fishermen, cannery men, and supplies. It did not take but a few days to discharge her, and everything was soon ready for the big run of salmon. We built a house for the fishermen at the other river and made everything in the best of order. Then we waited for the salmon to come. They said they knew the time that the fish would start running.

The time came, and a few salmon came, but very few. I had hunted the country over for miles for rivers that might have salmon come to them to spawn, and they all did have a few, but it takes a lot of fish to run two canneries.

Well, we put up seven thousand cases, and the Alaska Commercial Company put up five thousand. It was a complete failure.[8] When I saw that there were no more salmon, I went to the superintendent and told him that we would make some dories, and I would see if I could not catch some codfish. I immediately started the carpenter on the dories, went to Belkofski[9] for lines and hooks, and started a codfish station, hiring outside men as there were a lot of beach-combers there at the time. I gave them so much per fish. We had a lot of salt, and in a few days I had three stations running full blast. They were surely catching codfish as long as they ran.

The best place was off Cape Pankof.[10] They were catching them very fast there one day, but the next day they were all gone. Yet we did fine, and I salted between two and three hundred tons.

When the steamer *Jeanie* came the second time, to take the salmon, fishermen, and Chinese cannery men away, all the cannery men went on board. I went back and got the fishermen, taking them alongside. I had told Captain Porter of the *Jeanie* that I thought that there was going to be trouble with them, as one of my men had told me that one of the fishermen was a ringleader,[11] and the rest would all do as he said. I had had trouble with him early in the season, and he was very civil when I was around.

We took the men alongside the steamer, with all their effects. They at once started talking about what they were going to do. I went out of the pilot-house and told them that they would do no talking on board my steamer, as I did not want to know anything about their troubles. Captain Porter would deal with them. So they all went on board, and Captain Porter asked them what their troubles were.

They said that he had not boats enough. He responded that he had sufficient boats to go to Prince William Sound, and there they would get more men and more boats. He would give them ten minutes to make up their minds if they were going or not. At the end of the ten minutes, he gave orders to heave away the anchor. The men all came back to my steamer, and I set them back on shore again. The *Jeanie* blew three long whistles, I replied, we dipped our flags, and she was soon out of sight.

I started then to take in coal, water, and stores for the return trip to San Francisco. The next day the superintendent sent on board for me to come on shore and have dinner with him. I knew that there was something besides dinner on his mind, and I could not help him. Going on shore, I went to his office, and he asked me what they were going to do with the men.

I replied, "That is not my business, and I am going to have nothing to do with it, either."

He said that they were talking about suing the Pacific Steam Whaling Company, which owned the *Jeanie*.

"They have no case," I said. "It is possible that they might have had if they had gone in the steamer, but as they did not they have no case against her.

"Furthermore, it is all your own fault. You well remember the first of the season when I told you that you were not handling the men right. I had to have trouble with the ringleader myself, and I was able to give him a good licking. That settled the affair as far as I was concerned. You did not like it, and you even told the men that you wished some of them could lick me, but there were none of them that cared to take on the job. They saw that they had you where they could handle you, and they have. It was lucky for you that there were no more salmon than there were.

"Your father, Mayor Pond,[12] as you well know, asked me in your presence to help you in any way I could in regard to handling the men and making a success. I told him I would. I have done all I could to find salmon, but they are not here. If there had been a lot of fish and the men had started any trouble, I would have come on shore and straightened them up. Now you know the truth of the whole affair.

"What do you want of me? I know it is not dinner that you have sent for me to have with you, and I will tell you what you have in your mind. If I am not mistaken, the fishermen see that there is no more steamer to get away in. They have come to you and told you that there is room in the *Gertie Storey*'s hold and that they can get along all right.

"This is what you have sent for me for, am I not right?"

"Yes," he replied, "I want you to get the men away. What can you do about it?"

"Mr. Pond," I answered, "you see your mistake now when it is too late. In the first place the *Gertie Storey* has a passenger license for just so many, and if I should take all these men to San Francisco the inspectors would take my papers away from me. If you had put your foot down and told them that they would have to go, I would have helped you out, but you knew what was coming and stayed away.

"I expected this, as one of my men had told me that he had heard that they were going to have trouble. As soon as they started to talk on my steamer, I told them to keep their mouths closed, as I did not care to hear any of their troubles. Now, as far as I am concerned, they can stay here forever. I will not take one of them, and you can tell them that, or I will, as you wish."

He was feeling rather badly, but that was all there was to it. There were lots of stores left there, and there was no danger of them starving.

The next day I went ashore to check over the stores that I wanted to come on board to take me to San Francisco, telling the passengers that were coming with me to get on board. As soon as that boatload of stores was on board, I was off. As I went to the beach to go on board, the men all met me and begged me to take them away. I gave them a good talking to and told them that I hoped that they would have a pleasant winter, also a fine summer.

I went on board, and in a short time everything was on board, so I blew three long whistles and left them all standing on the beach, the saddest looking crowd of men I have ever seen.[13] We arrived at San Francisco in good time.[14] I took the steamer to Black Diamond, laid her up, and resigned, as I could see nothing in that business that I wanted.[15]

9 A Married Man

In a few days, I took command of the ship *Mercury*,[1] belonging to Renton, Holmes & Company of the Port Blakely Mill Company. She had been a very fine ship in her day, but she was very old. We went on Hunters Point Dry-dock the first thing after I took command of her and caulked and coppered her. She was very fast and handled the best of any ship that I have ever commanded, could sail the fastest, and, I might add, leaked the worst.

As soon as she was loaded and got to sea she started to leak, and I doubt if it would have been possible to stop it, as the topsides worked so badly. After the Civil War, the government bought her and rigged her into a training ship. She still had the plates on the 'tween-decks where the guns had trained and the portholes where they went through. The gunports, of course, were planked over on the outside. After that, she became a merchant ship again.

One morning on sailing day I was at the office and learned that the ship *Dashing Wave*[2] was also sailing that afternoon. She was very fast and made wonderful passages, always having smart men in command of her, and was the favorite ship on the coast. I was continually being stopped and asked if I wanted to bet on a race between my ship and the *Dashing Wave*, they always taking the *Dashing Wave*. I told them all that I expected to get beaten, but I would get there as quickly as I could.

I went into G. M. Josselyn's, the largest ship chandlery store in San Francisco, to sign my bills, as we dealt there. There were a lot of ship owners and masters in the store. As soon as I got inside, they all said this would be the time I got a good beating, and I told them that I expected to. They all did a lot of talking and offered to bet, but I declined. The captain of the *Dashing Wave*, George Morehouse, a San Francisco man who had made wonderful time in her, came in. They all asked him by how much he was going to beat the *Mercury*.

He said, "Well, gentlemen, I don't think I am going to beat her. She is a very fast ship, and as to my friend, Captain Killman, there is no man on this coast or any other coast who can teach him anything about his business of sailing a ship. As for myself, I would not bet one cent if I was a betting man. But we will both get to the Sound, I trust."

We bade them all goodbye and went away together. As we were at different wharves, we went in and had a drink, then parted for our ships. We both towed out at the same time, the *Dashing Wave* a little ahead of me; both made sail at the nine-fathom buoy, and let go the tugs' hawsers and started out on our own. The wind was from the northwest and very fresh. The *Dashing Wave* was going to windward more than the *Mercury*, but we were sailing faster.

For a while the next day, the wind backed to the west. I tacked ship, and in a short time the *Dashing Wave* was in sight standing on the port tack, as was I in a short time. I crossed his bow some three miles to windward. We were both going very fast and both carrying a lot of canvas, only the three royals being fast. We did not see each other again. The wind soon backed to north and west, and I went around on the starboard tack again.

We had strong winds all the passage and sailed a lot of distance. I lost some sails trying to keep up with my friend, but as soon as one went, night or day, another one was bent and set. After we got a long distance offshore, the wind came from the west with thick fog, the one thing that a shipmaster dreads. I steered for Cape Flattery, but the fog kept on, no sun and thicker than ever at night. I was some six hundred miles off when it shut down thick, and it did not lift once until I was nearly to Port Townsend.

At midnight I got a cast of the lead and got bottom as I expected, but I was not sure whether I was too far north or too far south. It was very dark, with thick fog, and at one in the morning I hove to, as I did not have the nerve to go any farther. It was June, and daylight started to break at three in the morning. The wind was falling light at four a.m., and I was squaring in the main and crossjack yards when the tug *Sea Lion* came in sight a short distance off.

He came alongside, bade me good morning, and sent on board some papers and a big beefsteak for breakfast. He told me that the tug *Tyee* was putting a hawser on board a ship two miles to the north but said that we would be by the Cape first as the *Sea Lion* could tow faster in smooth water with the wind fair. I asked the captain if he wouldn't go in between Duncan Rock and the Cape,[3] as I wanted to set my numbers so they could be reported in San Francisco. He said he would, and I was sure that Captain Gove of the *Tyee* would not go between those rocks unless it was fine and clear, as he was very careful.

The hawser was soon on board, and we were on our way. I was in a fine position, and if I had kept on would soon have gone up the straits and heard the whistle on Cape Flattery. We set the ship's numbers or signal letters as we passed the signal station. He replied, and I knew that in a few moments it would be on the blackboard in the Merchants' Exchange.

It cleared up that afternoon when we were nearly up to Port Townsend, and the *Dashing Wave* was some five miles astern. On my arrival at Port Blakely that afternoon, I got several telegrams from friends of mine, congratulating me for beating the *Dashing Wave*. But it was very close. When I got back to San Francisco, I went on board the *Dashing Wave*, and we compared notes. He did not have to heave to, as his distance was not up. We figured that the *Mercury* was fifteen miles ahead of the *Dashing Wave* at the time that I hove the *Mercury* to.

There were very few ships, if any, that could beat either the *Dashing Wave* or the *Mercury* at that time. While I was in the *Mercury* I never saw any ship pass me. The *Dashing Wave*, I should say, was a very close rival, and it would be a chance bet on either ship. The *Mercury* was more desirable to go in, as she had very fine cabins.

After nearly two years in the *Mercury*, I resigned to go in the barkentine *Catherine Sudden*.[4] I bought a large piece in her, as I thought I could do better by owning an interest in the ship. She was built by Hall Brothers at Port Ludlow and sailed very well; in fact, she was very fast. I made some very good passages in her, including, I think, one of the best round voyages that was ever made. I went from San Francisco to Aberdeen, Grays Harbor, loaded a full cargo of lumber, and was back in seventeen days; the same voyage took eighteen days from Aberdeen to San Francisco and back to Aberdeen. I am very sure no vessel has ever beaten that.

At the time I bought into the *Catherine Sudden*, freights were very low. I chartered to go to Portland to load at Inman & Poulsen's mill.[5] They had a clause in their charter party that I should use their tug in and out over the bar, and they would furnish the tug for river towing. I had a quick run to the Columbia River, but the wind was from the east when I got to the bar, so I had to wait until I could get the tug that was to tow me in. I was spoken every day by other tugs, but I would not take them.

After five days, their tug came and towed me to Astoria. Then one of the Oregon Railroad & Navigation tugs came and towed me to Inman and Poulsen's mill. It was January, and when I was loaded I went to the office and gave them notice in writing that I would be ready to tow to Astoria at a certain time. The tug came, and there was a heavy freshet in the river at the time, so I went to the office and told Mr. Inman that the tug was alongside my vessel and that I would like him and Mr. Poulsen to go and ask the captain of the tug if he could take the ship through the bridges. I would hold them responsible for any damages that might occur.

They came to the ship and asked the tug captain if he could take my ship through the bridges safely. He said he could. I then asked them if they were satisfied, and they both firmly declared that they were. So we let go the lines. I told the captain of the tug that he would be all right if he did not get too much headway on the vessel, but he must keep backing all the time so that the ship would not go too fast. If she did take a sheer, he would be able to stop her very quickly by going full astern.

I was on top of the deckload, obtaining any orders that the captain of the tug gave me, and we went through the first bridge fine. Then he went ahead slow with his tug in that strong freshet. The ship started very fast, and a short distance from the next bridge we took a wild sheer. He went full astern, but it was too late. We struck the stonework at the bottom of the bridge and smashed all the woodwork on the port side of the forecastle head. The cathead went, and the anchor went to the bottom; the fore topgallant mast, jibboom, and several yards broke, and the deckload was covered with iron from the bridge.

The mate of the tug quickly let go the head line on the tug, and she fell astern. We gave him a line when he was astern, so he kept us from going broadside onto the stone abutment. If that had not been done, the ship would have swung broadside, the driftwood would have piled on her, and in a few moments she would have been full of water. The only thing that could have been done then would be to dynamite her, as they had to dynamite the driftwood at times to save the bridges.

In a short time, we heaved our anchor up, got the tug fast again, and had no trouble getting through the other bridges. The captain of the tug asked me what I wanted him to do with my vessel now. I told him that it was a sure thing that I was not going to sea, and inasmuch as he had done the damage I would leave it to him. So he put me to the company dock.

As soon as we were fast, the captain came on board my ship, feeling very badly about the affair, but I said nothing of it. He asked me if I would go to the office of the owners of the tug, as he could not tell the manager the names of the things that were broken. I told him I would, but that I had nothing to do with them myself, as I would hold Inman & Poulsen responsible.

We went to the office of the Oregon Railroad & Navigation Company, the owners of the stern-wheel steamer that ran us into the bridge. The first thing the manager asked the captain of the tug was why in hell he smashed the barkentine into the bridge. The captain told him that he could not avoid it, as the current caught the vessel and he was unable to stop her before she struck the bridge. I was then introduced, and the manager turned to me and asked what the hell I wanted up there.

That was enough for me. I said, "I want nothing from you, you big damn fool, only a civil tongue. You bluff your own captains all you like, but if you say one word more to me I will smash your face so badly that you will land in the hospital."

I stepped up close to him, but he did not speak, so I turned and walked out. As I was leaving, the captain of the tug thanked me for coming up with him.

"Don't mention it," I said. "I will be more than pleased to come here any time and meet that damn fool sitting over there. I would make a man out of him if he had enough brains."

I then went to the office of Inman & Poulsen and gave them a letter stating that the barkentine *Catherine Sudden* was lying at Ainsworth Dock after receiving serious damages by striking the bridge in tow of the tug that they had furnished by the terms of the charter party. Also that the said ship's lay-days had expired at noon that day, and I should hold them for demurrage and all the repairs to the ship's hull, spars, rigging, and sails until she was ready for sea. Demurrage to be due day by day.

They asked me a few questions as to how it happened, and I told them that they would be able to find out from the captain of the tug or at the office of the Oregon Railroad & Navigation Company. I did not wish to express my opinion, as the captain of the tug was supposed to be a most competent master. The next day, I gave them the same written notice. They took it and seemed to be in the best of humor.

This kept on for five days. Then they wanted to know what it all meant. I told them if they did not know that they should get legal advice, as delays were costing them a lot of money. They asked me if I knew anyone to go to that would give them the correct information. I told them that I thought the firm of Sutton & Beebe[6] could furnish them with what they wanted, as Colonel Beebe was very well posted on ships' business.

So I went with the secretary, telling him to bring the charter party with him, as I was sure Colonel Beebe would want to read it. He met Colonel Beebe, and I at once walked out of the office, because I wanted him to have his talk without my being present. In a few moments I was sent for, and Mr. Wylie said, "Captain Killman, you go ahead and get your ship fixed up again to your own satisfaction. Bring the bills to us, and we will give you the money and the demurrage."

I told him that was no way to do, as I was afraid the bills would be larger than they thought, and that they should call for bids on the job. He replied that they knew nothing about ships and that Inman and Poulsen were willing to leave the whole affair to me, because they were sure I would do the right thing. I asked them to kindly give me this in writing, which they did, and I got Mr. Inman and Mr. Wylie to go to the ship and have a look at the wreck, as I had not touched anything.

Going to work at once, I rushed things through as fast as I could, but it took some time before it was completed as we had a lot of snow and rain and cold weather that winter in Portland. After everything was finished and the sails bent, I took the bills over to the office. They immediately asked if I had gotten everything fixed up to my satisfaction. I told them that I had and that I had tried to keep the bill as low as I could. They did not even read over the bill but gave me a check for the full amount. I paid all the bills and that night left for Astoria, had a fine run to San Francisco, and did very well on the voyage.

I then chartered to take peeled piles from St. Helens, on the Columbia River, to Redondo,[7] southern California, for the Santa Fe Railroad. I made several voyages for them and did very well, considering that it was an outside port. I had to have several hawsers but bought second-hand ones, and as luck was with me I had no trouble. I found the railroad company were very fine people to do business with. As soon as the cargo was out, I went to Los Angeles, and the freight was paid. Mr. Wade, the manager of the office with whom I did my business, gave me a pass over the road.

On August the fifteenth, 1894, I was married at the assistant auditor's house in Los Angeles to Miss Minnie Campbell, born in North Carolina.[8] After we were married, Mr. Wade also gave her a pass over the Santa Fe. After the ship was discharged, my bride went to sea with me. We made several trips for the railroad, and Mr. Wade always came on board the *Catherine Sudden* and had lunch with us, saying that he enjoyed it more than any of the big affairs that he attended. I have always considered him a wonderful man. Our first child was born some sixteen months[9] after we were married and was named Catherine S. Killman[10] after the barkentine that her mother had already made many voyages in.

After finishing with the Santa Fe, I took a cargo to San Francisco and chartered to take a cargo to Mexico. The day before I was to sail I was told that Captain Winslow Hall[11] wanted to see me. I went to his office although I knew the man only by sight, and was given a welcome handshake on my arrival.

He started out by saying, "You are the man I want to see. The captain of the schooner *Lyman D. Foster* was killed by the cook on the way to Shanghai. I want you to buy the master's interest and command her, but you may have to go to Shanghai after her."[12]

"Well, Captain Hall," I answered, "I don't know as I can do that, as my ship will be ready for sea tomorrow, and I have not got the money. I own a large share in the *Catherine Sudden*, but I don't know whether I could sell it or not, and I must take the ship to Puget Sound."

I asked him how much money it would take to buy the interest in the *Foster*. The captain owned more than any one of the owners. I was assured that the price would be right and that Captain Hall would attend to it.

"Now," he said, "you go and attend to your ship's business, as I know you have a lot to do, and let me know tomorrow morning. But you must take the *Lyman D. Foster*."

When I told him that he might be buying a pig in a bag, he said, "That is all true, but I know what I am doing."

I met a friend of mine and told him about the offer, and he said he would let me have what money I needed if I wanted to take the ship. I then went to the office of S. H. Harmon, the agents for my vessel, and told them what I was going to do. They assured me that they could not blame me, but were anxious for me to stay. I gave them a power of attorney to sell my interest in the *Catherine Sudden* for a certain amount, if they could, and asked them to have a man relieve me as soon as possible after my arrival in Puget Sound.

I had some cargo on board and had to clear, and the Spanish manifest had to go in the ship, but I got everything ready for sea that day and ordered the tug for ten in the morning to tow me to sea. I went to Captain Hall's office in the morning and told him that I would take the *Lyman D. Foster* on her return to the Sound, and if he wished I would go to Shanghai and bring her home. Accordingly, we made all the arrangements in regard to paying for the interest when the price was made with the captain's widow, and I got everything in writing from Captain Hall.

I left and went to sea, my wife joining me with our little girl, then only a few months old. Arriving safely at my loading port, I found that S. H. Harmon had sold my interest in the *Sudden* and the new master was there to take command,[13] so I took my wife and little daughter to Port Townsend. On arrival there I received a letter from Captain Hall saying that he had had a cable stating that the mate of the *Lyman D. Foster* was capable of taking the ship back to the Sound and that I need not go after her, but was to take command as soon as she anchored in Port Townsend. She soon sailed from Shanghai and had a very good voyage home.[14]

This was the first time that I had ever seen the *Lyman D. Foster*. She was without doubt a very fine ship. I might say she was the pride of the Pacific, as there was no better than she. I must say that I was very proud of my new ship and of my employers, too, for Hall Brothers built the best wooden ships that were built on the Pacific Coast. And they were fine to work for. I should know, for I stayed with them for twenty years.

10 Trouble on the Yangtze

The captain that brought the *Foster* home stayed mate with me. We went to Port Hadlock to load back for Shanghai again, and after finishing loading went to Port Townsend to get a crew.[1] After shipping the crew, I cleared and towed to sea, taking my wife and baby with me.[2] We sailed the last of June and had fine weather until we neared the China Coast, where we had a typhoon that blew very hard. I kept the ship on the outside circle of the storm, but we shifted our deckload, giving the ship a very bad list to port.

After the storm was over we had fine weather again and in a few days were at the entrance to the Yangtze River. The pilot came on board some six miles from the river and remarked that by the looks of the ship we had had a typhoon. I told him that we had a very severe gale and that my ship did not handle well with the heavy list. I thought we had better go a short distance up the river and anchor. The Ningpo boat would report us in the morning, and a tug would come down and tow us to Shanghai.

He said it would be a waste of money, as we would be at Woosung at anchor before morning. He seemed to be very attentive to his business, as when supper was served he said he would have his on deck. This gave me more confidence in him, so I let him go on.

The first few hours we did not go very fast as the tide was running ebb, but as soon as the tide turned the wind was very strong, and we sailed along very fast with all sail set. At eleven-thirty p.m. I went below. My feet were paining me badly, for I had been on deck for many hours, but as I could see the lightship a long way off on the starboard bow I thought if I could put them in cold water for a few minutes they might feel better.

A moment before I went back on deck I heard the second mate using some very loud talk. I had told him a few days before to stop it, as I did not want any of the men with any marks on them at our arrival, but I did not think anything about it. Then I heard the topsails banging so ran on deck. We were only a few yards from the lightship, and the pilot was shouting to let go both anchors. I stopped that and brought the ship up into the wind, but we struck the lightship.[3]

She was a big teak-built vessel with a bowsprit which struck us just abaft the main rigging and cut through several 12 × 12 timbers before it broke off at the knightheads. The lightship went down forward fast, and I thought sure that we were going over her. Her bow went under water some three feet, the stern standing almost directly in the air and the crew howling something awful.

All at once the chain parted, and the ship came out of the water like a rubber ball, swinging alongside with her spare anchor coming up into our deckload. I jumped to the after companionway to tell my wife to get up quickly, as the lightship was aft nearly to where I thought she was asleep in her berth; but she was up and had our little girl in her arms fast asleep.

As soon as the lightship was clear of us, I let go my anchor. Our sails were banging and slapping, so I got them down in a short time. Then I called the first and second officers aft, the pilot, too, and asked my officers why the ship should be so close to the lightship. They told me that first the pilot was going on the starboard side of the lightship but did not give the ship time to pay off when he shifted his wheel. The ship had started to pay off, and when he shifted the wheel to go on the other side of the lightship it took time before the ship could come around enough to clear the lightship. It was no fault of the ship but was an error on the part of the pilot.

I then turned to the pilot and asked him what he had to say for himself. He said, "I have nothing to say, as the officers have told it as it was."

I was very mad and made a jump at him, but he pleaded that he had a wife and two small children. I stopped, but told him to get out of my sight. I knew that the lightship was badly damaged and did not know how badly my ship was hurt, and being new in the employ it was no little upset. I owed a lot of money, and how I would get out of the trouble and how much it would cost me remained to be seen.

When I went below my wife had dressed and wanted me to tell her all about it, so I did, but I was very blue. She told me that I was smart enough to win, but I wasn't so sure, because the lightship belonged to the Chinese government. However, I would do my best and wait to see what happened.

At two a.m. the steamer from Ningpo went by. He stopped and asked me if I was all right and if there was anything he could do for me, so I gave him the ship's name and asked him to notify the tugboat company that I wanted a tug. At noon a big tug came and took me in tow. When I was close to Woosung a big launch came alongside flying the Chinese flag, and a gentleman came aboard in full uniform, to serve papers on me that I would be held responsible for all damages that had been done to the lightship. There were so many papers that I never did read them all.

I asked him if he thought that I would be hanged or imprisoned for life. He laughed and said he did not think it would be that bad, but that I had a very hard man to deal with. He left and we went on, but they would not let me go to my berth and anchored me a mile or more below where I was to discharge. It was late in the afternoon before I was at anchor, and I knew all business houses would be closed, so I did not go on shore that night.

At eight thirty p.m. I got a letter from Captain A. M. Bisbee the head man of the coast defense, who had full charge of the harbor, all their coast defense boats, and the pilots. I also received mail from the American Consul's office telling me that the coast defense ship would go to the lightship, leaving at four a.m., and advising me to go and see what I must pay for. He, Lloyd's representative, and the dock manager would also be there. Otherwise, everything was attended to, my ship did not have to enter the customs, and she would be berthed, ready to discharge, the following day. I talked it over with my wife, and of course I must go and see my fate, but I made up my mind that I would fight hard before I would hold up my hands and say that I had had enough. I would say very little until I had seen the American Consul General, and possibly he might help me if I needed help.

There was a guard at the gangway of the ship when I arrived at four a.m. I told him my name, went on board, and was met at the head of the gangway by the commander. He asked my name, and when I told him he shook hands with me and said he was very sorry to see me in trouble, then lowered his voice and said that I had a hard man to deal with. I assured him that I would make the best of it.

Just at that time a cutter came alongside, and Captain Bisbee came on board. I had gone aft and was walking up and down the deck on the starboard side, and Captain Bisbee came aft and walked on the port side. After the ship's anchor was up and she was steaming down the river, he came across to me and asked if I would like a cup of coffee. I replied that

I surely would have a cup of coffee for him if he was called to my ship at this time in the morning. He then walked away and in a few moments told me to come with him.

We went to his saloon, which was very nice. There were two cups and a plate of toast on the table. He turned to me and in a very low voice said, "Will you have a whiskey first?"

We went to his room, which was large and fine, all in teakwood, with furniture all the best. After locking the door he said that he had to be very careful and strict. We had a drink and then went back and had our coffee and toast. Not a word was spoken. We both went on deck, I taking the starboard side and he the port side, both walking back and forth.

After a while, he came across to my side and asked me what part of the states I came from. I told him that I was born in Maine on the Penobscot River.

"Yes," he said, "I was born in Massachusetts not far from there."

Then he turned the conversation to the West, asking about Puget Sound and San Francisco, and what I thought of the Pacific Coast. Of course I was getting a living there, and there was nothing too good that I could say.

After some time he said to me, "All the men that are on this survey are on board, asleep. Now, Captain, I am going to tell you what to do. Don't say one word. Look wise, and I will look out for your interest. It won't cost you anything. The Chinese government will have to pay for it. The lightship has got to come in before long for an overhaul. The only thing is that I have no other ship to take her place, which means that I will have to go to Japan and tow one from there and back again. That would be very expensive, and you would have to pay for it."

"Oh, no," I said, 'you can have my ship as a lightship for so many days. That would be much cheaper for me."

"We may overcome that. We will see," he replied. "Are the lights all broken?"

I told him that they were and that most of the glass was on my deckload, but he said that there was a full set of spares on board and that they should be able to get them up that day.

"We will pull the lightship off the beach at high water," he said. That was all that was said about it at the time.

We got down to where the lightship was on the beach and came to an anchor. We then had breakfast, where I met all the gentlemen that were to survey the ship and bid on the repairs. They started to ask me questions about running the lightship down, but I told them that I was in no position to answer any questions, as I had to see my Consul and it was possible that I might have to have a lawyer.

"You are right, Captain Killman," they said. "We should have thought of that."

So that was settled, and as we went on the deck of the lightship Captain Bisbee got a chance to speak to me and said, "You did fine when they started to ask you questions. Your brain acts very quickly."

As soon as we got on board, the captain of the lightship came to Captain Bisbee, giving him a list of everything that was broken, and I never will forget the reception he got. Captain Bisbee said, "Have you not a full set of everything onboard that is required so that the lights will be burning at sundown tonight? Why are you not at work at it? You have some twenty men under you, and if those lights are not burning at sundown you will lose your job. You had better get to work damn quick. What are you passing me a list of things for?"

He took the list he had in his hand, tore it up, and threw it overboard.

"Come, Captain," he said, "let us join the men forward."

We went forward then where they were writing down what would have to be done to put the ship back in good condition. There was a lot to do. Everything had to be teakwood.

The only thing I said was, "Gentlemen, if I have to put all this back in teakwood, I suppose I can have the old bowsprit to remember the Shanghai River by?"

They all had a good laugh, and Captain Bisbee said that he would see that I got all the old teakwood. After they had taken all the measurements they wanted, we returned to the ship, but before we left Captain Bisbee gave the captain of the lightship one more going over. The crew of the Coast Defense ship was taking measurements for a place to anchor the lightship and plant a buoy a short distance from where she was before, so that they could drag for the cable and anchor lying on the bottom.

At high water they pulled the lightship off the beach and anchored her. The lights were already being put up. Two officers from the Coast Defense ship took charge of the work, and I heard them tell Captain

Bisbee that they would be ready for use before sundown. We left them there and on our way back met another Coast Defense ship going down to drag for the cable and anchor.

We arrived back at Shanghai early that afternoon, and they set me on board my ship. She had been moored and the discharging had started at one o'clock that day, so I was very well pleased. I had made a contract with a stevedore the day before. Before leaving the Coast Defense ship, Captain Bisbee asked me to come to his office the next day at noon and have lunch with him. He wanted to see me on business, too.

After the doctor had been on board the next morning, I went on shore, saw my agents, and entered the customs. Then I went to the US Consul General's office, left the ship's papers, and had a long talk with the Consul General. He knew all about my trouble. I told him how I had gotten along with Captain Bisbee, and he was very much surprised.

"Well, Captain," he said, "it is a great surprise to me, as Bisbee is a hard man to get along with, but it looks as if you handled him the right way. I will not advise you, as I think you are able to do your own business without any help, but if you need any I will surely do all that I can for you.

"I want you to come here every day and tell me how things are."

He also told me that he wanted to see Mrs. Killman and my little daughter but said, "You must be very careful, as it is very unhealthy here. I have given orders that none of the crew can come on shore. You can allow the officers to come ashore twice while you are here if they will behave themselves."

It was very hot there at the time, and men on board the ships were dying every day with cholera. Strong able men, sick only a few hours, would pass away. I at once got a nurse for my wife, so she could get away, and a very good one she proved to be. She was a Chinese woman, and one dollar a week was all that she asked. But my wife, I am sure, gave her much more than that, for she became very fond of her. She took very fine care of the little girl.

The next day I went to Captain Bisbee's office, and we had lunch together. After lunch he told me that the bids for the repairs to the lightship would not be in until the next day, and that as it was not my fault he would not ask me to pay any of them.

"Now, Captain," he said, "what are you going to do about the pilot? He is very much afraid that he is going to have his pilot's license taken from him. If you give it to me in writing that you want him tried, I will have to do so, but I cannot take his pilot's license away from him, as he has never before had any trouble, whereas the lightship has been in trouble many times. That is what she is there for, as it is a bad place and the current is very unreliable. I could take his papers away from him for sixty days, but that won't help you or repair the lightship."

The pilot had given a written statement to his office, and Captain Bisbee gave it to me to read. The pilot had taken all the blame himself and said he was sure that it would not have happened if I had not gone below a few minutes before and that I had told him that the ship did not handle well with the heavy list.

"I have not seen him myself," Captain Bisbee continued, "and he won't come here until I send for him, but I am sure that he is very much worried about the whole affair and will do almost anything for you that he can. You know he has a wife and two boys, so you do as you think best about it. I know that it is causing you a lot of trouble, and you don't know if your ship's bottom is damaged or not. It would be expensive to dock here. It is worse because your ship is new, you might say, and a very fine vessel."

"Well," I said, "it will do me no good to file a complaint against the pilot, so I will talk it over with the Consul General and see what he thinks about it. I will come here tomorrow morning and let you know what steps I am going to take."

I went to the Consul's office and related to him the whole affair, and after he had heard it all he said, "Captain, it would not do you any good to have his papers taken away from him for sixty days, and it surely would make his wife feel very badly. You ask Mrs. Killman what she thinks about it, and I am sure you will not make any request to have them taken away from him. You are surely getting out of it very cheap, and I am surprised that Captain Bisbee is repairing the lightship without trying to make you pay for the repairs. He must have taken a great liking to you, as he is a great fighter for the Chinese government. You know, also, it is expensive to retain a lawyer, even if you win, and it was sure in my mind that you would have had to pay part of the repairs."

I told him that I would let the matter drop, as I was more than pleased that I did not have to pay, for it probably would mean a lot of money.

The next morning as I came on shore the pilot was waiting for me, and he did look as if he didn't have a friend on earth.

He asked me what I was going to do about him, and I said, "Well, Pilot, what do you think I should do? Put yourself in my place. You know the lightship is badly damaged and has to be repaired. I am a big owner in my vessel, so it hits me very hard, and I don't know how the rest of the owners will take it. And, you know, this is my first voyage in the company. I may be relieved when I get home.

"Now you have the whole thing. It is sure that they can't make you pay for it, but it is possible that you might lose your pilot's license. You know Captain Bisbee better than I do. He has full swing, so I am told by the Consul, and I think he knows what he is talking about."

"Now, Captain Killman," he replied, "if you won't ask Bisbee to take my license away from me, I will do anything for you that is in my power. I have a few hundred dollars in the bank, and I know that I can get more from one of the pilots, because he told me that he would let me have what money I might need."

I told him that he must have one good friend. He said, "Yes, but how much will it cost me?"

I looked at him, and there were tears in his eyes, and I had to smile.

"I don't want your money," I said, "and your pilot's license will not be taken away from you. You may get a good talking to by Captain Bisbee, and I think that will be this afternoon, if I am not mistaken. Now I am going up town."

So we both went uptown together in rickshaws. As we got up to the largest and best tailor shop in Shanghai, I said that I was going to stop there and get measured for a suit of clothes. He stopped with me, and we both went in. He had his clothes made there, and they carried a large assortment of materials. I picked out the piece that I wanted, and they measured me and asked me to come in the next day to try it on. When I came ashore in the morning, my wife came with me in a carriage by herself, for she wanted to see if the clothes I was having made were a good fit.

In the shop I tried on the suit I had ordered, and then the tailor came with two more suits for me to try on.

"I only ordered the one suit," I said, and he replied,

"No, pilot come back, and he get these for you. He say you very good man."

We had a good laugh and went away. When I went to get my suits I wanted to pay for the one I had ordered, but they were all paid for and had been sent on board the ship.

The pilot was very thankful for what I had done for him, and his wife called on Mrs. Killman and offered to do everything for her while we were there. I never did learn how much it cost to repair the lightship. I did not think it my place to ask Captain Bisbee, although we were great friends and I liked him ever so much.

The American Consul General could not make the whole affair out, knowing Captain Bisbee as he did. Before I sailed for home he said that it would be one thing we would have to drop out of our lives unless I could explain it, but I couldn't, unless it was the way I had met Captain Bisbee that morning on the steamer. I was feeling very down-hearted and was anything but agreeable, as I could see a big bill to be paid and could not see any way out of it, since a pilot only gives his local knowledge, and the master of any ship can take the command out of his hands at any time.

After finishing discharging, I sailed for Port Townsend for orders and had a fair passage home.[4] I was ordered to Port Blakely to the shipyard there owned by Hall Brothers for repairs. Arriving there late in the afternoon and after entering the customs and paying off the crew, I found that H. K. Hall[5] was off sick, so I went to his home to see him. He told me to engage the drydock at Quartermaster Harbor, as he was sure that the bottom of the *Lyman D. Foster* had been badly cut by the lightship's cable and that the keel must be damaged. I told him that I didn't think so, but I had no more to say and left for my ship.

By this time, I must say, I was getting mad, and if I got drydocked and there was nothing wrong with the ship's bottom it would mean a big loss of money and time. So I made up my mind that I would put the ship on the beach at high water and see if there was anything wrong. I made arrangements for men to work that night, got copper paint to paint the ship's bottom with, and had everything ready to clean and paint her if the bottom was not damaged.

At high water we hauled her on the beach. As the tide went, we cleaned the ship ready for painting. It was a fine night, the wind from the north and very drying. When the tide was out, I found that her bottom had not been damaged one bit, and I was able to get her painted and dry. When the tide came in, I listed her over the other way, cleaned the other side, and painted it. I then hauled the ship alongside the wharf, as I was having some new gaffs made and was getting my stores at Port Blakely for a long voyage to Fremantle, Western Australia.

After I had gotten alongside, Mr. Hall came to my cabin where I was with my wife, and we were glad to see him getting better. After he had been there some time, he turned to me and said, "Killman, you and I were both in a bad frame of mind last night, but you won, and I am glad to know that you took the affair in your own hands, as you saved us a lot of money. You always come out on top."

It was never referred to again, and I went to Port Hadlock to load. Several days after I arrived there I got a letter from Mr. Hall's brother, Captain W. G. Hall, who was the manager of the ship. He said that he had gotten a letter from his brother, saying that I had saved the owners a lot of money. He didn't know which one of us was in a worse frame of mind when I arrived at the shipyard, but that I had won and deserved a lot of credit for what I had done.

11 A Court Case

After loading, I started on my long voyage to Fremantle, arriving there after a fair passage of one hundred and ten days.[1] It is one of the hardest passages, I think, to make. I got to Bass Strait in the dead of winter. The wind is strong from the west, the course is due west, and heavy seas and a strong current are against you all the time. My ship was very able and had the best of sails, but it wanted a lot of courage to know how much they would stand, and meant driving them all the time. I arrived all safe after taking off some of the deckload and had to go to Owen Anchorage, some seven miles away.

It was very dangerous there in the winter months, and there had been several ships go on shore in the heavy westerly gales. While I was there the Swan River was opened, making a fine harbor, and they had a big banquet on board the steamer *Sutton*,[2] the first steamer to enter the river after it was opened officially. I had an invitation but did not go to the dinner, but with my agent went down about three in the afternoon and went on board. The captain saw us coming and invited us to his room. We both knew him and had a glass of champagne and something to eat.

"Now," he said, "suppose let's go down to the dining room, and you will see that they had a good time."

We went down, and there were at least twenty guests that had slid under the table and were asleep. We had a good laugh and went ashore.

Fremantle is a large city now, and a lot of business is done there. Coal freights had dropped to such a low price to the Hawaiian Islands that we could not afford to go to Newcastle, so my owners cabled me to say nothing about where I was going but to go to Westport, New Zealand, buy a cargo of coal, and go to Honolulu and sell it.

So after I was discharged I sailed for Westport,[3] arriving there the fourth day of July. It was bitter cold, and no tug had come out for me, so I had to stand out to sea again, but the next day I got in after a very quick passage and went alongside the coal bunkers to load. Westport was a small place, and everything was very cheap. Yet we had a good time there, because there were some very fine people.

After I was loaded, I lay several days, bar-bound, before I could get out, as it is a bad bar for a ship drawing the draft of water that my ship was, but I finally got away. Of course I was glad to get to sea, as all shipmasters are, always trying to get to their next port as quickly as they can. I tried to go through Cook Strait but got in about one-third of the way when the wind came from the other way, blowing strong. So I turned and ran out, going around the north end of New Zealand.

After getting off the north end, we had a most heavy gale from the east and a heavy sea, so heavy that it looked at times as if the ship could not stand the amount of water that was going over her, and it was twenty-four hours before one could get forward or aft. After the gale moderated I got the sun at eight-thirty a.m. I always wound the chronometer at eight in the morning. At eleven-fifteen the sun came out, so I thought I would take an ex-meridian. I went to the chronometer; it had stopped, and I at once found that the main spring had broken.

"Well," I said to my wife, "we will have to find Honolulu without a chronometer, and that is all there is to that, because I will not put in to New Zealand."

She looked at me and said, "I am sure you will be able to, because you always do what you make up your mind to do, but it will give you many nights on deck, for you won't trust anyone, and your officers you say are very unreliable."

We kept on, and when we were anywhere near land I stayed on deck all night, and we had no trouble. I wanted to make any of the islands in the South Pacific to get a new departure, so I went out of my course, yet made a fair passage to Honolulu. Captain Hall had sold the coal cargo to Sam Elin at a good price, and the ship made a very good freight out of it.

Captain Godfrey, the president of the Inter-Island Steam Navigation Company,[4] owned a piece of the *Lyman D. Foster*, and I was very well acquainted with him. He came on board and asked what I was going to do about my chronometer, because there were none there that I could get.

My reply was, "You own an interest in this ship, and of course if you object I will have to wait until I can get one from San Francisco, but if you do not, I am going to Puget Sound without one."

He said that he had no insurance on his interest and did not want any as long as I was master, and he was sure that I would get to Port Townsend in good time without any chronometer.

So, as soon as I was discharged, I sailed without a chronometer and made a fine passage, having no trouble. My dead reckoning was not but a little out, but of course I was very careful, and weather conditions favored me, it being clear with a fair wind. A few days before arriving, I was running with a very strong fair wind, well aft, with a heavy press of canvas on the ship. I was at work in the carpenter shop when I looked out. The ship was paying off and the booms nearly coming over.

I sang out to the man at the wheel to look out for his steering, and he replied that if I didn't like the way he was steering to come aft and steer myself. I went aft slowly, thinking the whole thing over. It would only be a few days more before I would be in and they would all be paid off, but as I was crossing the after house he drew his knife.

"I will cut your heart out if you come over here," he said. "I always have wanted to kill an American, and you are the one I am going to kill."

I told him to keep still, as he could not kill anyone, and to put the knife away before I got there, which he did. I then called the first officer, Mr. Hall, well known by hundreds of shipmasters as Bob Hall, to look out for the steering while I went below to get a pair of handcuffs, as I was going to put the sailor in irons.

I went below and got them, and as I came close to the sailor he drew his knife again very quickly and made a strike at me. I stepped aside and struck him with the handcuffs. He fell unconscious. By this time, I was very mad. I put the handcuffs on him and drove him, when he came to, forward . . . [At this point most of a page—roughly 1,000 words—is missing from the manuscript. The omission no doubt was deliberate. On 5 November 1897, on the schooner's arrival from Honolulu, an ordinary seaman named John McDonald swore out a warrant against Captain Killman and Mate Hall at Port Townsend charging that he had been beaten and locked up for several days. Captain Killman was found guilty in a trial at Seattle on 10 December and was fined $25 and costs. The mate was acquitted.][5]

12 To The Klondike for Gold

[The *Lyman D. Foster* left Port Ludlow 15 December 1897 with 919,630 feet of lumber and arrived at Hilo 9 January 1898. Here the lumber cargo was discharged and a cargo of sugar loaded: 12,357 bags for J. D. Spreckels & Brothers and 10,200 for Williams, Dimond & Company. The schooner arrived at San Francisco on 9 March 1898, 28 days out. Its sugar discharged, the *Foster* sailed for Port Blakely on 18 March and arrived 3 April. Two charters had been arranged. The first was to carry lumber back to San Francisco. The second was a lucrative charter to the Alaska Commercial Company to take supplies to the Alaska gold fields. Apparently a delay in loading at Port Blakely brought the arrival date of the schooner in San Francisco close to the 13 May cancellation date of the Alaskan charter, but the *Lyman D. Foster* sailed from Port Blakely 1 May 1898 with 950,000 feet of lumber consigned to Renton, Holmes & Company. Killman's narrative resumes at this point.]

. . . to be on board in the morning. I had ordered what few stores I needed and . . . before staying ashore.

The next morning at ten o'clock I bid her good bye and at eleven the tug towed us to sea. The wind was light from the northwest.

During the night it died out calm but before morning I had a fair wind from the southeast. You can imagine how I felt when this favorable wind came but the next question was how long would it last?

I thought the matter over as the time wore on and decided I was crazy to have taken on such a job. The wind held fair and I was shortening the distance fast so by the time the wind swung to the west I was in a position to make Cape Flattery. A tug was there to put a hawser on board and in seven days from the time I sailed from San Francisco I was loading in Port Blakely. They had labor and a letter from Mr. Holmes telling them what must be done for me. The mill management certainly did their part. I was seven days loading. I remember on Saturday night, at dark, I wanted twenty five thousand feet more of lumber for a full cargo but would not lose two days for it as I had a chance to get to San Francisco and get discharged and so make my charter. So I ordered a tug for five o'clock in the morning.

. . . and paid all my bills. At five the tug came, and I started. The tug was very small, but he said that one of the big tugs would pick me up by the time I got to Port Townsend, but we saw no tug, so I told him to keep on. The weather favoring us, we made good time to Cape Flattery. As we got some three miles outside the cape, a fine breeze came from the northwest, and I let go of the tug and set all sails. He blew three long whistles after he had come and taken my mail, and I dipped the American flag three times to him and was soon out of sight of the tug and Cape Flattery. The wind kept fair, a fine breeze but not strong, and in seven days I was in San Francisco again. I went to the dock. It was Sunday and the stevedore was there. I told him that I had nearly one million feet of lumber and laths on board and must be ready to take in general cargo on Friday morning. He said we could do that if they would take the lumber away at the yard there—at Pope & Talbot. I was sure that they would, as I was very well acquainted with them and felt they would do all they could for me in a case of this kind.

Monday morning there was a big gang of men there, and the bow ports came out, the cargo gaff went aloft, and it was not long before the lumber was going ashore from the deckload and out of the hold. As soon as everything was going along fine, I went to the office to see Mr. Billings[1] and get money to pay the crew off with, as I had told them all to be at the ship at eleven o'clock to get their money. Mr. Billings was glad to see me after making such a good voyage, and asked if I was going to make it by Friday morning.

"Yes, sir," I said, "I am; that is, if nothing comes up that I can't see, I will be at the wharf Thursday night ready to take cargo Friday morning, but I will have to work Thursday night to get the hold cleaned out."

I went to the Alaska Commercial office and found out what wharf I was going to and what side would be next to the wharf so I could get the gear ready, as I knew they would want to work two hatches at once. I had a tug fast alongside at the time the last sling load went out of the bow port. We let the apron go in the water as they said that they could get it up and backed out from the wharf.

I had only one hour left to get to the wharf and get to the Alaska

Commercial Company's office to give them written notice that I would be ready to take in cargo at seven in the morning, as my lay days would start at that time and I was chartered by the day.

When we got to the wharf, I had the captain of the tug put the jib-boom over the wharf. I went down on the martingale and jumped onto the wharf, where there was a horse and buggy waiting for me, and got to the office of the Alaska Commercial Company at five minutes before five, giving them written notice that I would be ready to take cargo at seven in the morning, and lay days would start at that date. They remarked that I had had rather a busy month but that it was a great thing to win as I did. They, in the office, had been ready to bet that it could not be done. They were all glad to see me win after I had taken the whole load on my own shoulders, and told me that they would start loading my ship in the morning and expected to do so in as short a time as they could, as they wanted me to get away. I went to the sailors' home and got ten men to come and work that night, sweeping and washing out the hold, and at five in the morning they had it in fine order for cargo, as the bow ports had been open and it dried out quickly. At seven there was a line of big trucks a block long loaded with everything imaginable to go on board, and everything went fine; we were rushing to get the ship loaded as quickly as we could, working three hatches and the deckload going on at the same time. The only delay was that we had to leave the wharf for a short time to go under the shear legs to take a heavy lift on board, that being the boiler and engine of a stern wheel steamer that had been built and knocked down again. We had the whole ship on deck. They notified me Friday that my ship would be loaded Saturday night, so Saturday forenoon I cleared for St. Michael, Alaska.

I went to Mr. Billings' office to sign the bills against the ship. He asked me when I was going to sea, and I told him sometime tomorrow and that I thought I would be loaded about eight tonight.

"Your deckload has to be lashed down," he said, "and it takes several hours, does it not?"

I told him that it does and he said, "You need not go tomorrow. I wouldn't if I were you. You have worked night and day for the Alaska Commercial Company since you started to load, and would they do as much for you?"

I told him I didn't suppose that they would but as my wife was not going with me, I didn't want them to say that I was taking Sunday because Mrs. Killman wasn't going in the ship.

"You do as you wish," he said, "but you don't have to go. You will have to secure your deckload, and the tide serves early in the morning."

"Yes," I answered, "but they are going to keep one of their best tugs waiting to tow me out at any time I am ready during the day, and I am going to tow well outside of the lightship. I have told the Commercial Company that I intend to do so, and they said to, by all means."

I bade Mr. Billings goodbye, and by the next morning we started to secure the deckload as we did not finish loading until eight that night. At ten, the Alaska Commercial came down to the ship with their mail and bade me a fine voyage, but did not ask me if I was going to sea that day or not. I took my wife and daughter to the hotel that she was going to stop at until the boat left for Eureka where she was going to stay with her sister while I was gone, and at one o'clock the tug came and towed me to sea. We had a strong breeze and were soon out of sight of land and once more had to fight the wind and weather to a part of America that I have very little use for.

Before I sailed, the California Shipping Company asked me if I should happen to catch up with the bark *Rufus E. Wood*, if I would tell her captain that the ship *James Nesmith* had arrived and would sail for St. Michael, and he would change ships there and take the *James Nesmith* and the captain of the *Nesmith* would take the *Rufus E. Wood*. I told them that I would, but as she had been away some ten days it was very doubtful if I would catch up with him.[2]

One morning I sighted a bark ahead of us, and as we were hauling up on him fast I was soon able to know that it was the *Rufus E. Wood*. When I got close enough for him to read my signals, I hoisted under the American flag, "Come close, I want to communicate with you," but he made no reply, only set his flag. As I came close to him, he would keep off. I had taken in my light sails. Well, I said, I will talk to you now or I will know the reason why. I then hoisted up "Hold your course," but no reply. I was coming up on him very fast exactly astern of him. As I got close to him, I hauled up across his weather quarter, letting my light sails all run down. I was about fifty feet away from him. I told him what his owners wanted him to know and hoisted my sails up and soon was far away.

We had some sixty passengers on board, going to the Klondike to hunt for their fortune. As soon as I had told the captain what I had wanted to, they gave me three long cheers, and were singing out, "You know how to handle a ship, Captain." I arrived at St. Michael only forty-eight hours ahead of him.[3] It was a great sight there. The harbor was full of ships of all kinds, but no steamers to take the thousands that were there waiting to go up the Yukon, as there had been many stern wheelers leave San Francisco in tow but had all met heavy storms and gone to the bottom. The amount of provisions that were piled up on the beach was amazing: no warehouses to put them in. There were thousands of tons of hams and bacon alone, and everything you could imagine. All kinds of ladies' wearing apparel from calico to silks. It was one busy place if I ever saw one. Ships were lying there full of cargo, but there were not enough lighters. We had four there. One big schooner brought coal, and they discharged the coal as quickly as possible and then loaded her with all kinds of merchandise. The deckload was twenty feet high before they stopped. I did all my discharging at night, paying big, healthy wages to all hands on board. The Alaska Commercial Company paid the bill.

After discharging and putting ballast on board, finishing at eight in the evening, I ordered the tug to take me clear of the shipping. It was the worst day that we had during the time that I was there. A lot of the captains came on board as soon as I set my flag to say goodbye, and they all said I was mad to leave on a morning like that, as I would get no thanks for it. I told them that I wanted no thanks, but if the tug would tow me clear of the shipping, I was going. When the tug came, he said, "You are not going to sea a morning like this, are you?"

"I am if you will tow me out clear of the ships." So I hove up the anchor and bade my many friends goodbye.[4] It was raining, and there was a strong breeze. You could not see but a short distance. At noon the wind jumped to the southwest in a very heavy squall. In a short time the wind fell light and was soon calm. At midnight I anchored, as we were drifting fast toward the beach and were only a short distance off. At eight in the morning it was as smooth as glass, with not a breath of wind. I saw that the beach was covered with white sand. I had the boat lowered, taking one man and the second officer with some sacks to get some sand to clean the decks with. While they were getting the sand, I was strolling around picking wildflowers where Nome is today. I got a large bouquet. They were many different kinds and very pretty, but there was no fragrance to any of them. I went on board, and that afternoon a breeze came and I got under way and left Nome, as it is now called.

I was cleaning the decks beating down the Bering Sea, and I went up aft where the men were working. Where the water was going overboard through the scuppers, I saw gold, or so I thought. I got a small bottle and put the gold in it. I had a very quick passage to Port Townsend[5] where I was ordered to load for Australia. I had the gold tested in Seattle, and found that it was very fine. I told some of my friends that I had a gold mine in Alaska, but did not show them where it was.[6]

After loading I sailed for Sydney, Australia,[7] then went to Newcastle and loaded coal for the Hawaiian Islands. It was a port called Kihei, a new plantation that had just started, and there were no charts of it. My owners sent me a drawing of the place, in Maalaea Bay, and as I had been there years before as mate of a steamer, I did not need a chart, or rather I thought I could find the port without much trouble, which I did. But it was hard to get into, as the wind blew out of it in great force.

I arrived there at night and stood off and on until morning, then I started to beat in. The wind commenced blowing harder as the sun rose, and I had to carry a lot of sail to beat up across it, blowing two jibs away and splitting the mainsail, and of course others had to be bent as quickly as possible, but I soon made the buoy which was to be a stern mooring, and anchored exactly where I was to lie.

The next day I started to discharge coal and it was, without doubt, the worst I have ever seen. They had hundreds of acres of land plowed up, and the dust came with the wind. For hours at a time you could see, at the most, one hundred feet and there would be as much as an inch of earth over the decks every morning. I had to get goggles for the men tending the hatch, their eyes got so bad, and I had to change them and take men from the hold. A ship named the *John C. Potter*[8] had left Newcastle several days before I did for the same port, and one morning, after I had been there some days, she was in sight not many miles away but under easy sail. The manager of the plantation came on board and asked me if I would not put out my big boat and go off to him and bring him in, as he would never beat in under that sail.

I was well acquainted with the captain of the ship and told him I would, so I got the big boat overboard and put ballast into her, as I was going to sail off. As I was about to leave, the ship tacked and came up on the other tack. It would be nearer for me, but she stood too long on that tack, and when she went to tack, she missed staying. The captain put his wheel up to wear around but was too near and sailed bow first onto the reef, going fast at the time. I went down to the ship, and the captain was feeling vary badly, wondering what he could do. She was gone, he was sure of that. Mr. Page, the manager of the plantation, had ridden down on horseback and had a native get him on board, and I told them both that I thought that she could be hauled off, providing she did not fill with water, as she was lying so easy. I had sounded the pumps when I came on board and there was no more water in the ship than usual. Mr. Page went ashore to try to get the *Kinau* and *Claudine*,[9] two steel steamers that traded among the islands, to come and try to pull the *Potter* off, and they arrived about midnight. After getting hawsers on board from the plantation, they tried for some time, but without any success. The *Kinau* went away and the *Claudine* stayed. At five in the morning the wind came off from the land directly astern of the ship, and it would be high water at seven, so I told the captain that he should make all sail, but he told me to do anything that I wanted to, for he was sure that the ship would never come off.

I started to make sail, and I saw that the sailors didn't like for me to boss them, so I called them all aft and after I talked to them a few moments and told them what to expect if they didn't obey orders, there was no more trouble. The steamer gave us the hawser, and the wind had increased to a very strong breeze; in fact, the natives said that they had never seen so strong a breeze from that quarter before.

I got all sail set and the yards trimmed and then told the steamer to go ahead and see what he could do. He went ahead slowly until he got a strain on the hawser, then went full speed, and the ship came off quickly. The steamer stopped, and the ship shot by her, and he had to go ahead or the ship would have hit him, but by so doing, he picked up the hawser in his propeller. It was lucky that the hawser was out through one of the side pipes on the main deck and made fast to the mainmast. The steamer dropped astern, and we were towing him stern first. We were taking in sail and trimming the yards, and the wind was so that we could make the anchorage and did not have far to go, the steamer still astern of us on a long hawser.

When we got to where we were to anchor, we let go the starboard anchor and thirty fathoms of chain, and the chain carried away. Well, we let go the other anchor and that one held. We hauled the steamer up alongside, a native cut the hawser clear of the propeller, and the steamer went away, having done no damage to herself. The ship was leaking some, but after discharging went to Puget Sound before docking, and she made many voyages after being on the reef. She was very old at the time but was well built of good white oak.[10]

13 San Francisco Earthquake, Yokohama Typhoon

Continuing in the Australian trade, I went to Melbourne[1] one voyage, and while discharging there, had the donkey boiler repaired. As soon as I was discharged, I towed out of the river to Hobson Bay. I had shipped all new men in Melbourne, mate and second mate also, and after anchoring, told the mate that I would tow to sea that night, and to have a little steam on the boiler but not to turn the engine over, as I wanted to be there when that was done. I had to go on shore to settle up my bills and remit the freight money home, and had ordered the pilot and tug for eight o'clock. I got on board about seven and asked the mate if he had everything ready for sea, and he replied that he had, so I went to the cabin, had my supper, and changed my clothes ready for work. The pilot came, and at eight the tug came. I then had steam ready to heave the anchor up after getting the tug fast. I locked the windlass and started to heave, and as soon as the engine started to heave, one side of the windlass fell down on deck.

I knew at once what was wrong. They had started the windlass without letting go the compressor. I asked the mate if he had been trying to work the windlass, but he said no. I knew he was lying, and it made me very mad, and would cost money, and how could I work my anchors? I got big blocks up and rove off a heavy tackle along the main deck and knew I could get the anchor up that way. The pilot came to me and asked me if I was going to start without a windlass, and when I told him that I was, he said he wouldn't take me to sea.

"You won't, but the tug will, " I said; "come to my cabin, and I will sign your bill, and you can go ashore. That's what you can do." I started for the cabin, telling the pilot to come along and as we got to the cabin, he said he was very sorry for what he had said and would I let him stay, as it would cause a lot of trouble for him as the Pilot Board would soon know about it. I told him yes, but that he must not try to bluff me because I would not stand for it from anybody.

We got the anchor up in due time.[2] The captain of the tug, being a very good friend of mine and having a very big tug, said he would give me a long tow off if I didn't have a fair wind. When we got outside, there was a strong fair wind blowing so I let go the hawser, after landing the pilot, made sail, and in a few minutes was going eleven knots. It took me to Wilsons Promontory, where the wind came dead ahead. I held the ship behind Gabo Island for eight hours, then the wind came from the west in what they call a southerly bluster. It was very strong, and I had to take in nearly every sail. The ship was diving into the head sea, putting her whole bow under, and I was afraid she would throw the masts over the bow.

As the sea went down, I made sail and had a fine fair wind the rest of the way. I had everything ready to go to the dock and could use one anchor, if necessary. The pilot came on board, and I had a tugboat ahead that had taken me in tow a few moments before. The pilot was an old friend of mine, and I told him my troubles and asked him if he would not send the pilot boat in and tell Captain Newton, the harbormaster, that I had broken my windlass leaving Melbourne and would have to dock. He at once called the boat back and told them to tell the captain in charge of the pilot boat to get in as quickly as possible to tell Captain Newton that the *Lyman D. Foster* had lost both anchors and chains.

"That will wake him," he said, "and he will have a berth ready for you, I am sure of that."

We then set flags for another tug which was there in a very short time, as we were getting in the harbor by this time. He came alongside and asked the pilot what he wanted another tug for, and the pilot told him to make fast on the port side, that it was none of his business as the ship was paying for his services. He made fast, and by that time the harbormaster had a boat off and told the pilot where to take the ship, alongside the American ship *M. P. Grace*, which we did. By the time I was finished with the customs, it was too late to do any business on shore, so I didn't go that day. I had slept only a few minutes since leaving Melbourne.

It was one of the fastest runs that had been made from Melbourne to Newcastle, as the records showed that a German ship had beaten it by three hours.

The next morning I went ashore to attend to business. The first thing, I went to I. & A. Brown's office, as I was to take a cargo of coal from them, and they also owned the tugs that towed me in. By the time I got ashore, everyone knew of my windlass being broken, and the manager of the two boats came and shook hands with me and said, "Killman, you made a great passage. We would not have charged you any more if we had known your windlass was broken."

"Well, safety first," I said to him.

By this time Mr. John Brown came out of his office, and after shaking hands with me, he said, "You not only made one of the fastest passages that was ever made, but you fooled us plenty with your windlass broken. I heard the towboat manager telling you that it would not cost you any more, but I know you did not believe him. You did the right thing, as it would have cost you a fine sum if we had known. Now come in my office and tell me what is broken and I will see if I can't help you."

I told him that the shaft was broken and that it was some job to get the windlass, but he said he would go with me to the machine shop and was sure that it would not cost so much as he would have a talk with the manager. I told him that I must enter the customs and then that we would go, so as soon as I finished, I went to his office and he went with me.

They started at once on the windlass, as Mr. Brown told them that they must have it finished in so many days, as the ship would be loaded, and I must get away, so they got the shaft out that night late, and the next day I went under the cranes to load. It only took thirty-six hours to load, but they worked nights, and by the time I was ready to go to the buoy in the bay, the windlass was finished. I shipped a crew and sailed, after a very quick dispatch, for the Hawaiian Islands, having a good average passage home.

After getting to Port Townsend,[3] I got orders to load for Shanghai, China, and had a good voyage over, arriving there in December.[4] It was very cold while we were there. I was discharged the first part of January, and sailed for Port Townsend. I towed to Woosung, made sail, and sailed out to sea from there. The wind was from the north and west, and by the time we were out of the Shanghai River, it was blowing strong. The next thing was to land the pilot. The pilot boat was some distance to leeward, and I had to keep up to windward or I could not weather the Saddle Islands. The pilot boat was trying to beat up to us, and we were hove to, drifting fast to leeward. At last he got within a short distance from us and launched his small boat to take the pilot off, but he could not quite make us.

The pilot was a fine able man and said he was going to swim for it.

He quickly took off his clothes, all but his underwear, and I lashed his clothes on his back and lowered him over the stern. He made the boat, and I kept away on my course and was soon out of sight, as it was blowing strong by this time.

The next afternoon I passed out of the East China Sea into the Pacific Ocean. It came on to blow hard that night, and I had to single-reef my sails. I had bent all new lower sails, never used, and I did not turn the reefs out until I passed Cape Flattery and carried a strong fair wind to an anchor at Port Townsend. Twenty-four days and eleven hours which, I am sure, is the quickest passage that has ever been made by any sailing ship; if not, I have never heard of one that has beaten it.

I was chartered to load for Antofagasta, Chile, from the British side, which I did and had a good voyage. I arrived back at Port Blakely the morning of the San Francisco earthquake,[5] to load for Yokohama, Japan,[6] and the port was full of ships with no berth for mine. I was to take a cargo of large timber for the Japanese government, and had gotten a survey report from the San Francisco Board of Underwriters that my ship was in good order to perform the voyage that she was about to undertake. I knew it was no use for me to give them notice that my ship was ready for a berth to load and laydays would start at once, as they would send it back to me, since the ship only had so many working days before she would come on demurrage, and it would be impossible for them to get the ship loaded.

I thought for a while, then went to the Post Office and had the letter registered to them with my notice in it. The Post Office was not one hundred feet from the mill office, and the postmaster, an old friend of mine, asked me what I was doing that for. I told him that I only wanted him to get a receipt for that letter, and I would be all set. The manager came to me that afternoon and said, "You are damn smart, Killman. You surely have us in a hole."

My reply was, "The only thing you will have to do is pay the demurrage and look pleasant. I am only working fair for the owners of my ship." They were in a bad fix as I was on demurrage for eight days before I started to load. The timber was 24 × 24 below decks, and on deck 30 × 30, 32 × 32, 34 × 34, 36 × 36, and six big spars. I sailed July the sixth[7] and collected all my demurrage, after the usual amount of trouble. I think demurrage is one of the just bills that causes more hard feeling between masters and shippers than anything else. They always try to frame up some way to get out of it, and as a rule they do if you are not as clever as they are.

My wife and little daughter joined me, as she had been in California at the time of the earthquake[8] and was very nervous after I got to sea. I thought everything over, knowing that I was going to reach the far east in the typhoon season, and it would be impossible to throw the deckload overboard if I wanted to; and if it got adrift, it would take the masts out of the ship. Mr. H. K. Hall, one of the owners of the ship and the man who built her, was more than anxious about the voyage and what I might encounter that time of year. I did not get any word from the managing owner while I was in the Sound on account of the condition of San Francisco, and had taken the spars without his knowing anything about it. Skinner & Eddy[9] had asked me what I would take them for, and I set a price so high that I thought they would laugh at me, but they said that they were more than pleased with my offer, so I had to take them.

The rule to Japan with a sailing ship is to go south of the Hawaiian Islands and go across in the northeast trade wind until nearing the coast, then haul to north up by the Bonin Islands. When I got in the latitude of Yokohama, I hauled due west. I don't think any ship ever tried it before, and I had the finest weather that could possibly be and a leading wind most of the time. I made a splendid passage, fifty-some days,[10] and we moored inside the breakwater on account of the heavy timbers and spars. If the cargo had not been for the government, I doubt if they would have let the ship inside. I let the ship out to stevedores to discharge at seven in the morning, and there were something like fifty who came on board, with a white man as foreman. All had a piece of hardwood pointed out for bars to handle these big spars and timbers with.

I stood and watched them for a while and saw that they would never be able to discharge the cargo that way. My wife and I were going ashore that morning, and I had dressed in a fine white suit, but went below and started to take off my white clothes when my wife asked me what was wrong. I told her that I must get the deckload off, and would not be able to go ashore until it was in the water, but for her to go along, but that she would not do.

I picked out ten of the brightest looking Japs and drove the rest of them into their big sampan, and in a few minutes had one of the big spars overboard. If one of the men got in my way, I would give him a good shove, and it was not long before they saw how things should go, and they couldn't be better. They were all fond of me, so I was told by the Japanese inspector of the cargo, who could talk English.

I put the deckload off in a little less than three days, five hundred thousand feet, rigged the gear to discharge the hold, and then turned my job over to the second mate, as he had gotten on to the way to handle the big timbers. We were nearly discharged when one morning I came on deck and saw that we were going to have a typhoon. None of the men came to discharge the cargo, nor did the inspector. My sampan man came to me and said, "Him blow typhoon by and by." I had most of my freight money, and it had to be registered that day to go in the next mail steamer, so I went and told my wife, who said I must go and do that.

I said, "I may not be able to get back, but I will get everything done before I go, and there is no real danger as the ship has both anchors down and all the chain out, and if she drags, she will only go into soft mud. I would not be able to stop her from dragging if I were here."

I had the sails marled down and everything put in good shape, and told the second mate what to do. I had no mate as I had paid off the one that came with me. It had commenced to rain and blow by the time I was ready to go, and my wife asked me not to worry if I couldn't get back. I told her that I was sure that I would not get back if it kept on this way, but that I could get ashore as the wind was fair, so I went, and got there all right. By the time I was finished with my mail, it was impossible for a sampan to get to my ship so I went to the Pacific Mail office, and tried to get them to set me on board. They said it was most death to undertake it as they had been out to their ship, fast to the buoy, and the boat nearly filled with water going off. It was much worse now, so I said I guessed I would have to wait until it was over.[11]

The brig *Galilee* was to an anchor. She was chartered by the Carnegie Institution, and had four professors on board seeing how much the magnetic variation was changing.[12] They had all come ashore that morning and like myself could not get back. Her captain was John T. Hayes, a San Francisco man whom I had known for years, and we were both very anxious about our ships, and stayed on the dock all afternoon.

It was raining and blowing very hard. Once in a while I could see my ship, always in the same place, which would make me feel much better, but his ship we could not see, as she was outside the breakwater. The wind was coming from that direction and it was impossible to look to windward for any length of time. As soon as it began to get dark, we abandoned our lookout and we were as wet as drowned rats. We went to a hotel where a captain was staying, and we were sure we could get some dry clothes from him as we both knew him well, and he was indeed a fine man.

We got there, and he let us have some dry things to put on. We got a good dinner, the first thing we had eaten since morning, and the woman who kept the hotel took our wet clothes and dried them for us. It blew very hard until midnight, then it started to moderate, so I went to sleep for a short time, but at three o'clock I got up and went away.

It was a lovely morning, and you would have thought it impossible for there to be such a change. I got to the wharf and found my sampan man there waiting for me, and the first thing he said to me was that my ship was all right, but that the other captain's ship on the breakwater had a big hole in it. I got on board shortly after five, and my wife was on deck waiting for me, looking at the *Galilee* through the glasses. I was surely glad to see her. She said it blew so hard that she thought the masts would go overboard, but that the second officer would report to her often that everything was all right and the ship hadn't dragged any, so she had had a good night's sleep. We went below and had coffee and toast, and then went down to the *Galilee.*

She was lying on her port side with the water nearly up to the main hatch and had dragged her anchors some three-quarters of a mile. The mate had gotten out a stream anchor with a hawser on it, but she came directly through the entrance of the breakwater when the wind shifted, and swung broadside on the breakwater. We went on the breakwater and saw a hole in her side large enough to drive a small automobile through. We had a long talk with Captain Hayes and Mr. Peters, the head of the party that was on board, and I told them that the Japs would soon get her off.

In a short time the manager of the drydock was there, and the captain made arrangements with him to float her. That night at four (I was on the survey), she was off the rocks and high and dry on the drydock, and in a very few days was again out to an anchor. They didn't take time to heave the anchors up but buoyed the chains and dropped them off. After boarding the hole over, they had a lighter alongside with very large pumps, and it did not take long to pump the water out of the vessel. As soon as they got the brig afloat, they heaved the anchors up with the steam lighter and were putting the chains back on board again that afternoon, when I was there. It was a wonderful piece of work. Some of the instruments were damaged but were taken on shore, and Mr. Peters told me that they were all made good in a short time.

After finishing discharging, I proceeded to sea, bound for Port Townsend for orders. I found the Japs fine men to do business with, and as the cargo was for the government, I didn't know how strict they would be, but they seemed to be more than pleased with the cargo. The freight money you could have any time you wanted it, and they would render any assistance to you that they could.

I made a fine passage home, completing the voyage in three months, twenty-six days, which was very good, and I doubt if it has ever been beaten by any sailing ship.[13]

14 The Peruvian Oilfields

On my arrival home, I loaded for San Francisco as freights were very high on the coast, and I made a few voyages[1] until the freights fell to almost nothing. I then went to Eagle Harbor to wait for a charter and was not there but a few days when I received orders to tow to Cape Flattery and sail to Grays Harbor to load for Peru.[2]

The schooner *W. H. Talbot* was to take the cargo but did not arrive in time, so I took it. The cargo was to go to Negritos or Sechura Bay, where there were oil fields owned by the London Pacific Petroleum Company, but you had to go to Paita first to enter the customs and pay all dues. I knew that it meant a long passage as there had been several ships to Sechura Bay and Paita with an average of some ninety days, but the distance was not very far. It was in four degrees south of the Line, so I made up my mind that I would go inside of the Galapagos Islands and beat down, as the time of year was right during the southwest monsoons.

I sailed the last of July[3] and had a fine run. As we passed out of the northeast trades, the wind came from the southwest, and we had rain and heavy squalls. I put the ship on the starboard tack and kept her there, and in a few days the wind became light; and with the Equatorial Current setting to the west, it was slow progress, but I was determined to go through with it, if possible. I went between the Galapagos Islands, and made the mainland, standing in close to the mouth of the Guayas River on the coast of Ecuador. I then started beating south with the wind drawing strong up the coast and a strong current setting to the north. My ship was fast, and by taking the advantage of every possible chance there was, I was sure to make it, as up to this time I had done very well. I never left the deck at night, but had a pillow on deck and would lie down if I got too tired. I tacked the ship on a half a point, no matter what time it was. I had a very good crew and always had all hands to tack ship, and it wasn't long before we could tack and have everything set in a very short time, as I had rigged several sails to help the ship go through the water. I made almost forty tacks and anchored in Paita in forty-four days at four in the afternoon.

The customs came on board, but by that time it was too late for me to go on shore. The next morning they sent out a launch for me and I went ashore and entered the customs. The London Pacific Petroleum Company had an agent there who met me at the wharf and congratulated me on the quickest passage that had ever been made, and said that they were not even thinking about my arrival for another forty days. They were not ready for me, as they had not made any arrangements at Negritos, where I was to discharge whole or part of my cargo, and they had telegraphed to find out how much I would charge per day to lie in Paita until they were ready for me. I told them that I would lie for the demurrage that the charter party called for. They wanted it less, but I would not give way. I told them that they could cable my owners at San Francisco, who might do much better, but that I knew Mr. Billings would not have anything to do with it. I knew that he would cable to make all arrangements with the captain, so they decided that they would let the ship come to her discharging port, and that one of the steamers would be in Paita that night with a pilot to help me into Negritos, and for me to bring the mail and some freight that they wanted for discharging. Of course, I was most willing to do so, and the steamer came at eight that night. A Mr. McCallum came on board; he was assistant manager at Talara Bay, and well acquainted, as he had been there for years for the company.

The next morning we got under way and started for Negritos, the distance being short. As we were going in, I had the ship under very short sails, so that I could have a good look at the place, and it did not appeal to me. I was heaving the lead forward all the time. There was a very heavy break on the beach, and when I thought I was far enough, I let go the anchor, but Mr. McCallum asked me why I didn't go a little farther, and I told him that it was far enough for me in that place.

In a short time there was a steam launch from Talara Bay with a steel lighter for the men to live in who were to make the rafts. We put the freight and the mail bags in the lighter, and I had to go ashore to the customs house to deliver the papers that were sent from Paita, and then go to Negritos to see the manager and give him notice that I would be ready to discharge cargo at seven the next morning. I was taking a good look at Talara as we were going in because I was under the impression that the ship would have to go there, as I did not have many laydays, and had a million feet of lumber on board.

When I left, the mate had his cargo gear up, and was taking off part of the deckload lashings. I went and delivered the papers to the captain of the port as he was the only government officer there; then was taken in a small car on a track, hauled by a jackass, to the foot of a big hill. It was very steep, and there was a track laid down the hillside with a small car on the track and a small steel rope attached to it and a steam engine at the top of the hill. I got into the car, they gave the engineer the signal, and he went ahead and hauled the car to the top. Then I got on the engine and we were off for Negritos.

It was a rough road, but the distance was only a few miles. It was dark when I arrived there. The manager, a Mr. Cannard, met me at the little station on the end of the road. I at once went to his home and they were waiting dinner until I arrived. He had a very fine home, and his wife was a charming woman. I was shown to my room and told that it was my room as long as I was in port, and would be expected to stay on shore all the time as their guest. I told them that it was very kind of them, but in a place like this my place was on board my ship.

After dinner Mr. Cannard and I had a long talk about discharging, and he said that everything would go fine, everything would be sent on board that I wanted, and that they had casks to send water off in. He was an excellent talker, and I asked him if it was always as rough on the beach as it was when I came in. He said it was not rough, and that there was no trouble landing lumber as the men were not afraid of a little surf. I couldn't say anything as I had seen it only from the ship.

The next morning we were all up early, and as I looked from the house, I could see there was a heavy surf, but I said nothing. After breakfast, we went down to where the lumber was coming on shore. There was a heavy sea rolling in, and Mr. Cannard said that it was too rough to get surf lines off today, but that it would be all right tomorrow. I told him that I wanted to go on board my ship. She was rolling horridly, lying in the trough of the sea, but he said that it would be fine the next day, and he would like for me to stop on shore until they got started, as I might be able to give them some new way of handling the cargo that would help them out, so I said I would stay until the next afternoon.

He gave me a very fine horse to ride while I was there, and we went all over the oil fields where there were many wells pumping oil, and it was indeed very interesting to me. He also made me acquainted with his staff. They had a fine little club where he put me up as a member while I was there. The day passed away very quickly, and we were invited out for dinner to the assistant manager's, spending a very pleasant evening there.

The next morning when I got up, I saw that they had steam up on board the *Lyman D. Foster*, so I went to the drawing room. Mrs. Cannard met me there, and said, "Captain Killman, I am sure you will be pleased to know that you are going to start to discharge this morning, and you won't want to go on board there after being at sea so long with no one to talk to."

"Mrs. Cannard," I replied, "it is very kind of you, but I don't like the looks of this place, and I see a lot of grief if I have to discharge the whole cargo here, and there's a lot of demurrage to be paid; that always causes so much trouble; but I can assure you that I will collect it if it is due." I knew that she would tell her husband, and I wanted her to.

After we had breakfast, I went down to where they were going to take the lumber on shore. Mr. Cannard was there, and I looked at the sea coming in with terrific force. My ship was putting lumber overboard as they had set the flags to commence to discharge.

"Well, you are going to take lumber on shore, Mr. Cannard," I said.

"Yes, Captain," was his reply.

"How are you going to get your surf lines off?" I questioned.

"That is easy," he answered.

I told him that it was impossible for men to get out through that surf, and if they did, his lumber would be all ruined before he could get it on shore.

He laughed at me and said, "These men will go out through that on the balsas without any trouble," and in a short time they started on their raft to take the surf lines out to the ship. I told him that it was nearly sure death to the three men, but they started, and in a very short time they were all drowned. I turned around and went back to the house, and shortly after that three more men tried it and they went the same way. That was six men that were gone.

Some time after, I was watching my ship, and they stopped work as they had been signaled from shore to stop. Mr. Cannard came to his home, and to me, and said, "I wish I had listened to you, Captain. Six men are gone, and the raft that my men were making alongside of your ship has all washed to pieces, and we will not be able to get any of it."

"Well, Mr. Cannard," I said, "I don't care to see such work. I wish to be set on board at once. This is murder in the first degree."

His wife had heard us talking and asked what was wrong. He told her what had happened, and that if he had listened to me, no one would be gone and the lumber would be on board; as it was, the lumber was gone; also, the men. The tears were rolling down her face as she went to her husband and said, "You should have been guided by Captain Killman as he is sure to know more about it than you do, as he has been to sea nearly his whole life."

We then went to the assistant manager, and talked it over, and they told me they would let me know by noon what they would do. They knew that the lay-days were going on and they didn't want to pay demurrage if they could possibly help it. After we had eaten lunch, he came to me and said that he had taken my advice, and I could take my ship to Talara Bay, as he thought that the demurrage would be greater than the extra expense of getting the lumber around from Talara Bay.

I went on board the steam engine and over to Talara Bay, and the steam launch was all ready. Mr. McCallum was going with me to pilot me into the harbor. It took some time to get the ship ready for sea again, but by night I was ready to start the next morning for my third port. The days were passing by, and nothing done. In the morning I heaved up anchor, made sail, and was soon off Talara Bay, but I had to wait until the wind hauled around so it would allow me to lead into the harbor. I stood off and on, keeping the ship in the proper position to make the port when the wind came up the coast. At two p.m. Mr. McCallum came to say it was all right to go in, but I was in doubt. However, he assured me it was. It was hard for me to doubt his word as he had been there for many years, so I kept off for the harbor.

As we came close, the wind started to fall much lighter, and I told him that I thought we had better stand off for a little while longer, as I didn't think there was any wind inside, but he was sure there was plenty to take us in, as the distance was so short. I kept going, and in a few moments it was flat calm, not a breath of wind, but the ship was going ahead before a little sea. I could see she was setting to the north, and I told Mr. McCallum that I thought we were getting too far to the north, and would soon be ashore; but he said, "No, Captain, we are in mid-channel."

I replied, "I know a damn sight better if this chart is correct. We will soon strike the bank on the port side."

I at once ordered the hand lead thrown on the port side amidship, and there was only fifteen feet of water, and the ship was drawing twenty, but she was still going ahead very slowly.

I dropped the port anchor to hold her bow from going on any more. Mr. McCallum was in a frightened condition as I was telling him how much I thought he knew about Talara Bay. He told me that they had a new ten-inch hawser on shore, one hundred and fifty fathoms long, and he would run it off as I told him that I was sure that it would reach the buoy.

In a short time he had it off to me from the buoy, and I heaved a good strain on it, then heaved up the anchor. In a short time the ship was up to the buoy. She was only laying her bilge on the bank as there was plenty of water under her bottom. I think that he was the worst frightened man that I have ever seen. It did not hurt the ship any.

We lay at the buoy that night and the next day was Sunday. Late in the afternoon a little brig came in, flying the Ecuadorian flag, and she anchored on the other side of the buoy. On Monday morning she made sail to cross my stern and go to the wharf. It was very early, and I went on deck, aft; as she got close to me, they made an error. The captain was forward and told the man to put his wheel a certain way, and he put it the other way; she came into my stern, breaking the spanker boom and the rail aft, also the wheel. I put a line on him and hauled him alongside, keeping watch on him so that he did not get away.

That morning I took the captain of the brig and my mate, as he could talk Spanish, to the captain of the port, and he told the story. The port captain told him that he must pay all damages before he could get his papers, as he was going to Ecuador with a full cargo of brandy and cigarettes, and if he did not pay, I could take his cargo and brig, and he would see that he did not get away. He sent two policemen on board night and day, and that morning I hauled into my discharging berth, still keeping the brig alongside, as she was very small, and started to discharge. They had a large iron lighter that they were loading on the starboard side, and we were making a raft on the port side. It went very fast and by night we had nearly two hundred thousand out. The work went fine, and I sent the spanker boom on shore and had it fitted, so I could go home with it. They sent men to repair all the damages that had been done, and paid me, or the ship, three hundred dollars, which was well paid.

After I was finished discharging, I settled with the company, and everything went fine. Mr. Cannard was a very fine man, and very honest, I should say, and I am sure that he did a wise thing by sending me to Talara Bay to discharge, as he got all his lumber, and if he had tried to discharge at Negritos, he would have lost a lot of his lumber, and a lot more would have been broken.

I turned the ship around and made sail, having a slip line out aft. Mr. McCallam was on board as I was making sail, and I asked him if he was going to show me the way out, but he said that I needed no one to show me either the way in, or out. After I had gotten all sail set, I let go the slip line aft, dipped the American flag three times, and they returned my salute by three long whistles. In a few minutes I was out in the Pacific Ocean with a fine fair wind, bound for Port Townsend for orders.[4] I had a fine passage home, and on arriving paid off the crew for three months and six days. I am sure that that is the quickest round voyage to Peru that has ever been made by any sailing ship, and it will never be beaten. I had gone to three ports, and at the first two I had a lot of delay, as I have explained.

I went to the British side and loaded for Arica, Chile, and made a good round voyage.[5] While in Arica I don't think there was one day but that we had an earthquake, and some of them were heavy; but one got used to them. Arica is the most northerly port in Chile, and was taken from Peru in the war between Chile and Peru. It is a very pretty little spot.[6]

15 Hurricane in the Tropics

In the year 1913 I loaded for two ports in the Fiji Islands in the South Pacific, Levuka and Suva, and made two voyages there without any unusual trouble.[1] The third voyage I loaded at Bellingham, sailed in February, had a fine run to the Line, and had fine trades in the South Pacific. I passed some four miles north of the Friendly Islands, and got a correct position of my ship. There was a strong southeast trade wind blowing. The ship was going fast through the water, and during the night I passed another island, some five miles off. The morning was very fine, and I could see that if the wind kept on, I would easily be in Levuka in forty-eight hours.

At noon the sky commenced to change, the breeze got stronger, and the barometer began to fall very fast. At four p.m. I took in all light sails and had them furled with double gaskets as it looked as if I was going to have a hurricane, although it was not the right season of the year. At six p.m. I double-reefed all the lower sails, also the fore staysail. The wind was on the port quarter, and we were going very fast through the water, the barometer falling very fast, but I was in hopes that it would not amount to anything; as we were going at such a speed, I thought that I might get away from it. But it still blew harder, and at eight p.m. I furled the foresail and heaved the ship to on the starboard tack under a double-reefed main and mizzen sail and a reefed fore staysail.

The wind was increasing very fast, and I was sure that if the wind did not abate by midnight, the spars would go. At eleven forty-five the two double-reefed sails went like dust before the wind, not one piece left. The ropes were all intact, and the gaffs stood up in the air, but not a move out of them. It was raining very hard, and one could not look to windward. Balls of fire would run up and down the wire rigging. At times there would be hundreds of them, and it would be as light as day, and then they would all pass away, leaving utter darkness. At one that morning, the mizzen mast went over the port side, and it came back and went through the port in the first officer's room, and in a few moments the cabins were full of water. The spanker boom broke in the middle, taking the skylights off the cabin, but the man at the wheel got away without getting hurt.

The lights in the cabin soon went out, leaving everything dark, and the first thing I thought about was a lamp locker in the forward companionway. There were three lanterns there, and some matches. The mate got one lit. One of the sailors who was aft was very frightened, and said that he was sure that if I stayed aft, it was the safest place. It was a hard sight seeing all the furniture smashing the cabins to pieces. A large cloth bag of mine came from one of the lockers, and the mate got it. I told him to fill it with canned tomatoes and canned fruit, as I did not know if there would be any fresh water left. I was sure that the main and mizzen masts must go, as by that time the topmasts had all gone over the side.

It was not long before the mizzen mast went, and it was blowing so hard then that one must look out for himself or he would be blown overboard. I was all alone aft, as the mate and the sailor were getting stores, and it was not an easy job as the water was smashing everything in sight. I thought I would try and go forward, for what reason I do not know, but I got on top of the deckload, crawling on my hands and knees. I got along by the mainmast and stopped there. The mast was groaning, and I knew it must break. I moved a little and went down into a hole to my waist, when I saved myself by my hands and got out. The ship gave a heavy roll to port and then back to starboard, and the mainmast went overboard to windward, not two feet from where I was hanging on to one of the deckload lashings.[2]

I then knew that the deckload must go, and I had to try to get off it before it went. It was much nearer to go forward than to try to go aft, but I started aft, getting hold of the deck lashings. I got down onto the break of the afterdeck, and had been there but a few seconds before the deckload went over the side. The ship came up out of the water after getting rid of the four hundred thousand feet of lumber. Only the foremast was left. I had put the foremast in new that time before loading with all new rigging, and I felt sure that there could not be any wind strong enough to blow it over. About three that morning as near as I can say, the wind jumped from the southeast to the northwest in the most violent squall that I ever had seen, striking the ship exactly aft, and the foremast went out over the bow and did not even scratch the decks. It broke off where it went through the forward house. After this squall was over, it settled down to a moderate gale, and as soon as daylight came, we started to clear away the wreckage.

The mainmast was hanging alongside, also the foremast, but we soon got clear of the mainmast, after finding the sailors all down in the forepeak. If anything had gotten over the fore hatch, they would all have been drowned like a lot of rats in a cage. I found one of them with his shoulder broken, but he didn't know how it was done, and I strapped it up the best I could. The medicine chest was gone, and consequently the first thing I went to see was if we had any fresh water left, and when I found a thousand gallons, I can assure you that I was glad, for it might be weeks before there would be a drop of rain again.

I found nine feet of water in the ship's hold and both main pumps broken off even with the deck. I knew that it would only be a short time before the ship would be full of water, and the sea would go over her like a rock at half-tide. I kept the foremast hanging by the forestays, as the wind was blowing me from the land, and with that big spar hanging out forward, it kept the ship's head to the wind, and she would not drift so fast.

I had several cases of canned goods in the afterdeck, and I at once got them on top of the after house, and what else I could think of that I might need. Canvas, twine, ropes, and other things that we won't mention. The boats were all gone. No one saw them go, but one could not see any distance. I had been on deck all the time trying to see everything that happened, but I might say that it took one most of his time to keep from blowing overboard, or from getting hit by falling spars. The mizzenmast had fallen aft over the after house with the trestle trees coming just aft of the wheel box, and the mate and I got the spanker sheet around it and held it there. Next morning we made it well fast, and it made good shelter for us after we got a sail over it.

We got something to eat sometime that day, as we had gotten a lot of canned goods from the cabin, grabbing them as they washed by when the ship rolled. By night we had a lot of stores on top of the after house and had them well lashed so that they would not get overboard. The riding lights and the red lights were in the forward house, and I rigged a short mast aft so I could put up lights saying that the ship would not steer; also kept a watch night and day, in hopes that we might see some steamer that would take us off, but in vain. After getting things straightened up so we could live, we started making rafts with sides and a raised deck that we could put things on to keep them dry. The ship was full of water by this time, with the rudder gone and all the masts; the only thing I had left was the fore staysail boom. I put stays on it and got small sails made out of jibs that were in the sail locker, so when the wind came back to the southeast, I could start drifting the ship back to land. It didn't shift for three days, blowing fresh from the northwest, and how far the ship had drifted in that time I had no way of telling as I had no chronometers, books, or charts. I could only stop and think, but that did not give me the ship's position.

As soon as the wind came from the southeast, I cut away the foremast so the ship would drift faster back toward the land, and we rigged all kinds of small sails on small masts made out of the lumber we had on deck. The largest piece we had was only three-fourths of an inch thick and eight inches wide; however, by lashing several together we made small masts and sails on them, as every little bit helped then. We had to get everything out of the cabin as it had begun to smell bad, and I wanted to see if we could find any of my valuables, a very fine gold watch and chain and some two hundred dollars in gold. I also had a diamond ring that I had told my oldest daughter would be hers when she was eighteen.

Before I sailed, she came to me and said, "Father, aren't you going to give me the ring before you go away, because I will be eighteen before you get home?" But I told her that I thought I would keep it until I got back, but there was no reason why I should not have left it, as I had never worn it. That ring seemed to be the only thing that I felt guilty about, for as to the ship's condition, I had done all any shipmaster could do, but the wind was too strong for any spars to stand. As to my personal effects I did not care, but of course the loss was heavy as I carried the slop chest and had no insurance on any of them.

I had one of the sailors in the cabin on the lee side diving for nails, as I had quite a lot of all sizes in the store room. There were some five feet of water there at the time. The sailor came to me later and said, "Captain Killman, I have found a fine diamond ring, and I am sure it is yours as I don't think anyone else would have one." It was a great surprise to me, and when I got home, I gave the ring to my daughter, who has it at the present time.

Days dragged by very slowly, but we always had something to do to keep our minds from getting the best of us. After sixteen days we sighted land one morning on our starboard bow, and in a short time sighted land on the port; before night I could tell them as the two islands that I was going between when I had drifted back the same way that I had drifted away.

The next day we sighted a steamer some twelve miles away, but he did not see us, the land on each side of him attracting the attention of the officer on the bridge as well as that of the passengers. If he had seen us, we would have abandoned, but he was soon out of sight, and I was sure that we would all get out of the trouble, and that we would soon forget it as one forgets most all trouble.

I had rafts all ready and water bags made and stores all ready to put on them, and had made up my mind that I was going to abandon the wreck when I got in the right place. However, I did not tell even my first officer,[3] and he was a very good man who had been with me for a long time.

The morning that we had been twenty-two days on this hull drifting, we sighted an island. I knew it was the island of Lakemba,[4] so I told the mate to get the rafts over. After they had put the stores on them, I told the mate to go to that island[5] and to be very careful, as it had a solo reef around it, and if he should hit it, it would be sure death to all of them because these islands all have so many sharks around them that one would have very little chance for his life, and not to pay any attention to me as I would be all right.

"You have the best men," I said, "and if you work hard, you should be there before dark, but do not go in after dark. If you can't make it before dark, wait until morning."

After I had gotten my raft all ready, and all hands on it but myself, I went aft and stood on the after house that I had walked for sixteen years, and looked forward, took one look around the horizon and went to the rail. I got onto the raft and told them to let go the line that held us, set the little sail, get their paddles out, and get to work. I felt very badly but did not say anything, only when I gave orders, but steered myself all day.

The mate went away from us fast and was a long distance ahead when I left the ship,[6] and it was not long before he was out of sight. That night about eight o'clock I was close to the island, and was sure that the mate had landed, as there were a lot of lights on the beach. I had the sail taken in, told them to stop paddling, and the cook would give them something to eat as they had had only a little to eat since leaving the ship. After we had eaten, I went in closer to the reef, and it was breaking very heavy at times. I watched it for some time, changing my position by paddling. The lights were very plain on the beach, but it was very dark looking onto that black island; there was no moon, and the sky overcast at times. I thought that they had put up range lights for me, and that in a few moments someone would pick the lantern up and walk away with it. I made up my mind to go in.

I had one Negro sailor. I put him forward on the raft, and told him to look out for rocks and white water, and that if we hit, that would be the last of him. He told me that he would look twenty feet down into the water, so I went ahead slowly and had no trouble whatever, landing close to where the mate's raft lay high and dry. The mate and crew were there, and they all waded out and hauled our raft up on the beach and took everything ashore.

The mate said, "Captain Killman, you took great chances coming in in the night. You gave me orders not to try to land after dark."

"Yes," I answered, "but this is different. I was trying to look out for you, but for myself it does not matter."

He told me that a native girl had swum out and piloted him in, but that they would not go out at night.

There was one white man on the island who kept a store there for the firm of Henry Marks of Suva. He bought all the copra that they raised, and sold food and clothing to the natives. He was on the beach when I landed, and it was a great surprise for me as I was well acquainted with him, he being in Levuka my last voyage. After everything was on shore, we went some mile or so to his store where there was a small village of native huts. We went directly to the store as I was very tired and hungry, not having eaten anything all day.

The crew was all looked out for by the natives. They had had a good supper, and the mate told me that he was going to sleep in the native church, as the natives had put a mat down for him to lie on with a cover to put over him if he should want one. We had gotten very hard, as the mate and I had lost everything we had in the shape of clothes. We had gotten a few things out of the mess from the cabin to cover our bodies with, but they were all torn and tattered; if we got cold in the night, we would lie down in the salt water on the after deck, as it was always washing across there, and the ocean water is always warm in the tropics.

After we got to the store, the first thing we had was a good drink of

Scotch whiskey, and then a fine meal of good food and fine coffee, the first I had had since my ship had encountered the hurricane, and it did taste awfully good.

After we had eaten our dinner, he said, "Now, Captain, you had better have a good sleep, as you look very tired."

"Yes," I replied, "I am a little tired."

He then said that his wife was in Levuka, and that I would have their bed, but I told him that I would lie outside in the sand, as it was warm. He would not have it, so he showed me where I was to sleep in a fine big room off the store. The bed had a fine white spread on it and looked very inviting to me, but when I got into it, I found that there was a mat spread over boards, so hard that I could not go to sleep, and after a while I went outside and lay down in the sand. When the storekeeper came, I was up and told him that I had had a fine night's sleep, and he never knew that I had abandoned his bed for the sand.

I got a suit of dungarees and an undershirt from him in the morning, and after a good wash and some breakfast I felt quite fit again. I sent the mate to the rafts to see if everything was all right. The storekeeper and I went to the top of the island, from which height we could make out the wreck. It had drifted a long way in the twenty-eight hours since we had left her. That afternoon a small sloop came in with some stores from Suva, and after they had gotten them on shore, I chartered him to take us to an island called Lakemba. The storekeeper said that he would pay him, as I had no money, but knew that I could get some from the bank at Suva, and would pay it back to Henry Marks. We went on board that afternoon after bidding them all goodbye, and thanking them for their kindness.

The natives had a fine chicken dinner for the crew and were very good to us all, offering to do anything for us that they could. The island had gotten hit very hard by the hurricane, and thousands of coconut trees had been destroyed. Going to the top of the island that morning, it was a sight one might never again see, those large orange trees lying flat, loaded with oranges, just starting to get ripe. They would be no good, they told me, and the natives depended on them for money as they shipped them to Suva and sold them.

We left there at five that afternoon for Lakemba, where I thought I might get a steamer. There was a small one that called there, but I did not know how often. The distance was some fifty miles, and we got there at daylight the next morning. It was a very pretty island, with palm and orange trees, bananas in abundance, and all kinds of fruit that grows in the Fiji Islands, and everything so green. There was a post office and a large store there, owned by Henry Marks, and the natives wanted to go and wake the manager of the store up, but I told them that I would wait until they opened up.

As soon as the store was opened, some native told them that there was a shipwrecked crew there, and the manager came out, made himself known to me, and asked me to have tea and toast with him, which I did gladly. I learned that they did not know when there would be a steamer, so I made arrangements with the captain of the sloop to take us to Levuka, as that was nearer than Suva. After we had our tea, he asked me if I would not like a bath. I will admit that I looked pretty tough in my new suit of dungarees, but I was clean; however, I had not shaved for twenty-three days, and my hair was long and I am sure had gotten a lot grayer than it was before I struck that horrid hurricane. I told him that it might be a good idea, and he gave me a piece of soap and a towel and showed me to the bathhouse. It was surely a homemade affair and most crude. A big drum that would hold some fifty gallons of water filled from the top of the house; you turned the faucet on and the water ran on you. This was supposed to be a shower bath as near as I could make out, but I don't think it improved my looks any.

I bought sufficient stores from him to take us to Levuka, and got fresh water. At noon he asked me to have dinner with him; I accepted, and he made me acquainted with his wife, a lady from New Zealand. They were very pleasant and asked me so many questions that I thought I would go stale answering them. We were to leave at four that afternoon and I got my bill from him in duplicate. I looked it over carefully and found that he had charged me fifty cents for my tea and bread in the morning, fifty cents for my bath, and one dollar for my lunch. I said it was fine and thanked them for their kindness, and the natives, too, who had fed the crew and been very good to them. They had a big dinner, chicken and all kinds of good things. The mate and second mate told me all about what they had, and I told them I thought I had gone to the wrong hotel.

We left there that evening at five, and at nine that night we landed two natives at a small island. We had a light fair wind all night and I lay on deck what little I did lie down. I had saved one of the *Lyman D. Fos-*

ter's compasses and had it on deck for them to steer by, and there was a small chart in the little cabin of the sloop. I told the captain how to steer, and though I had very little faith in his ability as a navigator, he was a fine native and never left his post. He steered most of the time, but my mate steered some six hours the day after we left.

The next night the wind was fresh, and we were nearing the island of Ngau.[7] It is very dangerous as the solo reef is a long way off. We were steering to go between Ngau and Horseshoe Reef.

At midnight the captain came to me and said, "I am frightened. I think I had better heave to until morning." I told him that I would take charge and everything would be all right. I then called my mate and hauled the sloop's head to the south, saying,

"Now you keep a good lookout and we will pick up the reef in about one hour; we will keep the reef in sight, and by so doing we will get to Levuka early in the afternoon."

In a little over an hour, the captain saw the reef before we could. I steered down close to it so we could see it plainly and then kept off and followed it around. The native captain was pleased; he came and took my hand and said, "Good captain," and then something in his native tongue that I did not understand. When daylight came, we were heading for Levuka, and as the wind is always light in the morning, we made very little headway until ten. Then the breeze came, and at three we anchored close in shore at Levuka.

I had gotten a piece of yellow cloth at Lakemba to set forward, as we were under the same law as though I were in my ship. I must pass the doctor before going on shore. It was Sunday, and we waited and waited, but no doctor came, so I sent the captain of the sloop to tell the first native he saw to go and tell the doctor that there was a shipwrecked crew waiting on him. He came back on board in a few moments, and soon the doctor came down and asked me if the crew was well and had no sickness during the voyage. I told him that there had not been any sickness on board since leaving home, and with that we were told to come on shore.

It didn't take me long to get into the boat, as I wanted to cable home. I found my agent and cabled the managing owner the full account of the disaster. After I had finished cabling, we went to the Union Steamship Company's office, and there I gave them the position of the ship as I saw her last on a certain date, and told them that she was drifting fast to the west. They had one of their ships at the dock discharging coal, and in a few hours she was off for the wreck.

Before this ship got there, the *Foster* was picked up by a small steamer[8] that traded among the islands, and they towed her into a harbor of one of the islands to try to rig a rudder. I had gone to Suva with my crew to be where the steamer came that went to Vancouver, B.C. The Union Steamship Company ship came back to Suva and was sent back with what they claimed was an expert on rigging a jury rudder, to help the small steamer tow the wreck to Suva.

In two days I saw the tow coming, but it looked very doubtful that they would be able to get her in through the passage, as the rudder that they had rigged was of no use. In a short time we could see the house flag of the Lau Traders firm forward on the small mast that I had rigged, and the Australian flag aft on the mast that I had rigged to put lights on. I was at the customs house right at the head of the dock and they were all looking out with me.

I said to the collector, "That is not my ship."

"It certainly is," he said, "and she is flying the British flag aft and the Lau Traders House flag forward."

"I have that ship's papers in my pocket," I replied. "She is an American ship, and I will make someone suffer for setting the British flag on her."[9]

There was a great deal of excitement, and a steam launch was sent off by the customs house to tell them to haul those flags down, and down they came very quickly. As soon as she was anchored, the receiver of wrecks put a man on board. I cabled San Francisco that the *Lyman D. Foster* had been towed into Suva, and was told to sell the cargo, which I did to the original owners, at invoice price plus freight. I knew that the freight money was insured, but I was most sure that there was no insurance on the hull, as I had written to Mr. Billings to cancel my insurance since freights were so low at the time.

Messrs. Kraft and Smith were the owners of the cargo, and very fine men. They tallied the deckload off and took the whole at bill of lading. The Lau Traders claimed the ship and cargo, but I could not see it that way. I got the crew away in one month's time, and it was a great relief. I sent their accounts to the US Commissioner at Seattle, who would pay them off, but of course they had only a little coming to them, as their wages stopped the day I abandoned the ship. If I hadn't left the wreck and gotten her into port, I would have had to pay them three months pay and send them to America; otherwise, the US government has to send all distressed seamen back to the USA.

I was sure that the ship would not be rigged again as business at that time was poor, and the best thing for me to do was to abandon her, and then try to get her into port for the sake of the underwriters. Days passed by, and I could make no agreement with the Lau Traders and the Union Steamship Company. The underwriters in San Francisco kept me in the dark, but at last I got orders to sell the wreck, after giving Sydney, Melbourne, Newcastle, and New Zealand one month's notice, to the highest bidder.

The day of the sale I at once saw that they had all gone together, and that I was going to get but very little for the hull of the ship, which was in fine shape. There were four butts under the starboard fore rigging where the oakum had come out, but that was the only place the ship leaked. There was a small ways at Suva, but they would not haul the ship out for me, saying that they did not have power enough, so the ship went for a small sum to a man in Suva,[10] and the whole thing was framed to beat the owners and the underwriters.[11]

After I had sold the hull and cargo, I was no nearer a settlement than I was before. The Lau Traders and the Union Steamship Company would hold a meeting and I would attend. They would have a set of papers drawn up; after reading them over, they would pass me a copy and ask me to read it. After reading them, they would ask me what I thought of them, and when I said I thought it was fine, they would ask me to sign them. I would sign all three copies "Captain D. O. Killman, subject to San Francisco approval by owners and underwriters."

When they asked me why I signed them that way, I said, "Because I have no other way to sign them as they have not given me orders to do otherwise, and until they do, I shall do as I think best and sign no papers to get myself into any trouble with the underwriters."

I sent the managing owner a cable that I was leaving Suva on a certain date by the steamer *Makura*[12] for Victoria, and in due time received a cable from them to make a settlement, and whatever it was would be most satisfactory with them. As soon as I received the cable, I notified them that I was ready to settle with them immediately as I was leaving for America on a certain date. They called a meeting of the salvors, where I asked them their best terms for a settlement. After some time they said they would settle for seventy-five percent of all. I told them that I would not give them that, but that I would give them my best offer, and if they did not like it, I was sorry, and then they would have the underwriters to deal with, and the court, but as for me I was going to wash my hands and step out of the whole affair.

I had written in the copies that I would give them forty-five percent and take fifty-five for the owners and underwriters. They read it over and went into the air, saying it was impossible. I got up and walked out, telling them that they might change their minds, but that I would wait until tomorrow before cabling San Francisco. The next morning I got a letter asking me to meet them at ten o'clock, which I did, and they accepted my terms; the papers were signed by them, in all three copies. I was glad to get through with it, and at once cabled San Francisco what I had done, and received a congratulatory reply on my success.[13]

Steamship *Arago*, the first steel vessel built on the US Pacific Coast. Like the *Julia H. Ray*, *Arago* was lost on the Coos Bay Bar. Courtesy San Francisco Maritime National Historical Park, Proctor Collection.

Steam schooner *Julia H. Ray*, stranded on the South Spit of Coos Bay, 26 January 1889. Courtesy San Francisco Maritime National Historical Park.

Julia H. Ray, lost on Coos Bay Bar. Courtesy San Francisco Maritime National Historical Park.

Whaling bark *John & Winthrop* off Howard Street Wharf, 1908.
Courtesy San Francisco Maritime National Historical Park, Livingston Collection.

The *Mercury* as a schoolship on Long Island Sound, prior to 1885. Courtesy Norman Brouwer collection

The *Dashing Wave*. Courtesy San Francisco Maritime National Historical Park, Borfeld Collection.

Barkentine *Catherine Sudden*, for which Killman's older daughter was named.
Courtesy San Francisco Maritime National Historical Park.

The *Lyman D. Foster*. Courtesy San Francisco Maritime National Historical Park, Plummer Collection.

Brigantine *Galilee* in the South Pacific. Courtesy San Francisco Maritime National Historical Park.

Henry Hall, owner of the *Lyman D. Foster* and other vessels, in his later years, at home. Courtesy San Francisco Maritime National Historical Park, Hester Collection.

George E. Billings, partner and later manager of the Hall Brothers San Francisco office. Courtesy San Francisco Maritime National Historical Park, Mrs. R. D. Keiler Collection.

16 War in Europe

I left on the steamer *Makura* for Victoria. On arriving home, I sent all the papers to San Francisco and in reply got a telegram from Mr. Billings to come to San Francisco and make up the adjustments to go to Washington, DC. Immediately after arriving home, I was taken sick, so my doctor sent a telegram that I was under his care and it would be several days before I would be able to leave to attend to any business.

The reply was for me to come as soon as possible, which I did. I made all the adjustments and sent them on to Washington DC, and in due time everything was paid. When I was finished, Mr. Billings said to me, "Captain Killman, I have a surprise for you. You told me to cancel the insurance on your interest in the *Lyman D. Foster*, but I had neglected to do so as the policy would soon expire."

And he passed me a check for the amount of the insurance that I thought was cancelled. It looked very good to me. Mr. Billings then said, "Now, Captain, I suppose you are going back home?"

I replied that I would be on the first steamer that left. He continued, "You have been many years in this employ and I do not want you to leave it. The *H. K. Hall*[1] is leaving Sydney in a few days. The *Hall* is the largest and best ship we have, and I want you to take command of her when she gets back."

I told him that I did not want him to put any master out for me, for I was sure I could get another ship as soon as I wanted to, but he said that the captain had been writing to him that he wanted to sell his interest and that now he must leave, and he wanted me to take the interest in the *H. K. Hall*. She was a fine five-masted schooner, large and very modern, and I asked him at what price the captain would value the *Hall*. He said he did not know but would attend to that and see that I was looked out for, so I said I would take her and signed papers to that effect.

The next day I left San Francisco for Tacoma and on getting home told my wife that I was going to have a good rest, as I had never had a moment to myself since we had been married, a little over eighteen years ago. She was glad and said I needed a good long rest, as I was all run down after what I had gone through.

The next morning the phone rang, and I was wanted at the Tacoma Hotel. I went down, and Mr. Thorndyke, the manager of the Globe Navigation Company,[2] met me and wanted me to take one of his ships that had just arrived and was going to load in Tacoma for Callao, Peru. I told him that I could not, as I had bought an interest in the *H. K. Hall*. The captain was there with him and wanted to lay off for a voyage, so they asked me if I would take charge of her while she was there and load her and tend to the repairs that had to be done.

I told Mr. Thorndyke that I would do that for him and took charge of the ship that day, loaded her, and made what repairs I saw had to be made.[3] Each Saturday I went to the bank and drew what money I needed to pay the longshoremen, and I did not see owner or captain until I notified them that the ship would be loaded in forty-eight hours. The next morning, Captain McKay and the managing owner came from Seattle. I had made out a store list for the voyage and also a chandlery list, which they could change to suit themselves. The stores came as soon as the ship was loaded, and I had them all put in their proper places; the officers, cook, and steward came, and the crew was there in the morning.

That night I let go her stern line, and she was off for Callao. I went home and told my wife that I would like to see someone get me to work again until the *H. K. Hall* arrived. This was Friday evening, and early on Sunday morning the phone rang and I answered it. It was a telegram from Mr. Billings asking me to take a schooner to Santa Rosalia, up the Gulf of California, as a special favor, as the schooner was all loaded and would be in Port Townsend that night. The captain, Captain Isaacson, was sick and could not go in the ship, and I would have time enough before the *Hall* would arrive and get discharged. I replied that I would.

There was a steamer leaving Seattle that afternoon for Port Townsend, so I packed two suitcases and that night got to Port Townsend about eight o'clock. The *A. M. Baxter* had arrived during the night, and the following morning the captain came on shore. I told him I was there to take charge of his ship for the voyage only. I changed the ship's papers, shipped a crew, got stores there for the voyage, cleared the customs, and sailed for Santa Rosalia.[4] There was trouble in Mexico at the time, and

Mr. Baxter, the owner of the ship, sent me a telegram that afternoon saying if I did not hear from him to come back to Port Townsend.

I had a very good passage down; likewise a very good dispatch. There was no word from the owners while I was there, so when I was discharged I sailed for Port Townsend, arriving back on the twenty-second day of December, 1913. I would have done better, I am sure, but my chronometer stopped a few days after leaving Mexico. The weather was very bad on the coast, and with no chronometer I had to be very careful making the land and to know what it was after making it.

As soon as I arrived, I sent a telegram to Mr. Baxter, and he answered, saying to lay the *Baxter* up in Port Hadlock and put a ship-keeper on board. I paid off the crew and took the ship to Hadlock. I had gotten a good reliable man to look out for her, and in the meantime I got a telegram from Mr. Billings to take the first train for San Francisco, as the *Hall* was waiting.

I got to Tacoma at ten that night and the next forenoon I left for San Francisco, arriving there at ten in the evening. The next morning I went to the office. The *H. K. Hall* would finish discharging that day and go on drydock to paint Christmas morning. I went home with Mr. Billings that night and stayed all night.

Christmas morning it was raining and blowing a gale of wind, and Mr. Billings said, "I think the *Hall* will be on the drydock by this time."

I told him that she wouldn't if I was master of her. I said, "It is a bad dock to go on when there is as much wind as there is this morning, and they are liable to do some damage and then not get on the dock."

"I will find out," he replied, so he called up the drydock. They had tried to dock her, but she took charge of the tugs after doing some damage. The ship was made fast again and could not dock until eleven the next day because repairs to the dock had to be made before she could go on.

Then he said, "I wish you had been in charge, Killman. This would not have happened."

"No," I said, "I am sure of that, as I would not have let them try to dock her this kind of weather."

The next day, Mr. Billings and I went to the *Hall*. As soon as she was hauled out, I had a good look at her bottom and asked the captain to do some things that I saw should be done. I was well acquainted with him and told him that I wanted to take charge as soon as he brought the ship to San Francisco for ballast and stores. I made out the store list and told them when I would want them. The ship came to the San Francisco side late the next afternoon, the ballast and stores were put on board, and I sailed for the Columbia River to load for Antofagasta, Chile.[5]

I had a very quick passage to Astoria and after loading, sailed and arrived safely at Antofagasta,[6] having the usual dispatch and then a good passage home to Port Townsend for orders. I was sailing up the straits not far from Port Townsend when one of the big tugs came along and asked me if I did not want a tow. The wind was very light at the time, and I was not sure but that it would come from the east fair ahead. The captain asked me if I had heard that war had been declared between Germany and France, England, Belgium, and Serbia.[7]

Of course I had not, as I had not spoken any ships since leaving Antofagasta. I took his hawser at once and was very anxious to learn what it was all about. I was soon in Port Townsend and after passing the doctor went on shore and heard the news about the big war that was going on in Europe. I paid the crew and went to Winslow to have a new rudder made for the *Hall*, as the rudder head was gone. As soon as it was finished, I went to Coupeville to load mining props for Santa Rosalia.

I sailed as soon as loaded[8] with a large cargo—1,700,000 feet—for the copper mines there, owned by France. I was beating up the Gulf of California when I saw a four smoke-stacker coming very fast up the Gulf. I at once knew that it was a man-of-war, and he was soon up with me. I had set the American flag and saw his British flag flying. He lowered a steam launch and was soon alongside.

I had the ladder for them, and one of the officers came on board. We went into the cabin, and he wanted to know if I had seen a German ship, as there was one due for Santa Rosalia. I told him that I had not, and he then told me that the Admiral would like me to come on board the warship,[9] as he would like to talk to me. There would be no danger for my ship, as their launch would be ready at a moment's notice to put me on board again. The wind was very light at the time and we were a long way from land, but I told him that I would be pleased to go if the Admiral wished me to.

I went with him, after telling the mate what to do, and I was soon on board of the fighting machine. The guns were all out ready for action, and they surely meant it. The launch, too, was armed, and every man on board.

The Admiral received me, and we had a long talk. He served liquor and cigars, and when I thought I had stayed long enough I went back to my ship, and he was soon out of sight up the Gulf. Everyone on the warship treated me as gentlemen should, and all looked fine, the officers all with their sidearms on. That fine ship was ready to meet any emergency at a moment's notice. The Admiral was in full uniform, at his left side his sword which looked like gold, but, of course, I am not sure that it was.

In a few days I arrived at Santa Rosalia[10] and found eleven German ships interned[11] there, some of them at the breakwater discharging and those that were discharged lying outside at anchor. I had been acquainted with some of the men for years, and the older ones were feeling very badly and could see Germany's mistake, but the young masters wanted to get home to fight for their country and were sure they could lick the whole of Europe. The only thing that bothered them was if America should get into it—then they did not know what would happen. I let them all talk and said nothing. They all treated me fine, and I also did the same by them.

The director of the mining company was a very fine man and was well acquainted with all the captains, but the Germans had declared war against France, and he must not make any mistakes, as he would get into trouble with his company. They had a steamer lying there which got all the war news that was broadcast every night, but he could not give it to the captains of the ships, so he came to me and asked me if I would give it to them. Every night at eleven o'clock the wireless operator would come to my ship and leave three copies for me to give two to the captains but not to be seen doing it. They came on board every morning to get the war news and talked it all over, more especially the younger men.

There was one ship discharging, a ship that had been built for the Standard Oil Company and sold to the Germans. Her captain was a man nearly sixty, and he would come on board my ship only when he knew that none of the other masters were there, to read the news and talk to me. He had a son and said he was sure that he would never see him again, and he would cry like a baby and say, "The downfall of Germany."

He seemed sure that America would get into the war—that Germany would force her to do so, as they thought that they could lick the world; and he was sure that they would lose in the long run. Their ships would all be taken away from them, and what would become of all the men that depended on going to sea and their wives and young children? He took it very hard, and I always tried to cheer him up; but it did not seem to do much good—he was always very downhearted. His boy seemed to be his greatest grief, and up to my sailing he had not received any mail from his family.

After I finished discharging, I sailed for Portland, Oregon,[12] to load for Lourenço Marques, Portuguese East Africa, a voyage around the world. A big schooner is not the best rig to go around Cape Horn in, running before those heavy westerly gales. We got away in good time.[13] The war was raging in Europe, and I did not know how it was going to be in Portugal, as they were neutral when I left. I had the usual weather to Cape Horn, and when I made Cape Horn Island it was blowing hard, one squall after another with plenty of snow.

After passing Staten Island[14] I got to the north as soon as I could, but the wind would not let me get as far north as I wanted to without hauling the ship up to the wind, and that I would not do, as it would slow her speed down, and I wanted to make a good passage if possible. I sighted many icebergs, big and small, and how near I came to some of them in the night one will never know. We tried to keep the very best of a lookout, but one could see only a short distance. It was raining and snowing and a gale of wind blowing, so I just trusted to luck and went as fast as I could drive the good ship through the water. I stayed on deck night after night if it wasn't fine and clear. I had a very good mate, one that I could trust and very reliable.[15]

I was making fine time, forty-seven days to Cape Horn was good, and if I could cross the South Atlantic in good time, I had a chance to make a good passage. I made the coast of Africa and hauled to the north, the wind fair but light. The weather had gotten much warmer, which was to our liking, and I passed Durban some fifteen miles off, but with the strong current setting south one does not make as much distance, as it holds a ship back. It is very strong at times and is called the Mozambique Current, coming down the Mozambique Channel.

However, one afternoon I got to the entrance of the channel and got a pilot on board just before dark, and we proceeded. In a few moments I had to anchor, as it fell calm, but in a short time we heaved up the anchor and started. We got through the first bad place, but it was not long before we had to anchor again. We kept anchoring and getting under way until midnight, when we anchored. I told the pilot that we would lower down the sails and have a few hours of rest, as I had been on deck for a long time and the crew was all worn out as they, too, had been on deck most of the time for several days.

An anchor watch was set, and the rest went below. We had gotten a long way up the river before we anchored for the night, and as soon as there was any wind in the morning we got under way and once more started on the last lap. We had very little wind and at times flat calm. About eleven a.m. a coast steamer came along. The captain was an old sailing ship master, and he came close alongside and stopped. We had a talk, and he asked me where I was for and how many days I was out.

I told him I was one hundred and six days, and he said I had made a great passage and that he didn't think it had ever been beaten.[16] He asked me if I did not want him to notify the tug to come and tow me the rest of the way. I asked the pilot, and he said no, that he had a good home and that we would get there that night, he was most sure. So we kept going, calm, then light airs, but we were slowly reaching our goal.

At dark we were at the Quarantine Anchorage, and the doctor came off. I had a doctor from Portland as a passenger[17] and had all the papers made out and laid on the after cabin table and had shown him what the boarding doctor would want. The pilot said that we must anchor, but I said that if the doctor would pass us, why shouldn't we put the ship where she was to discharge? It was very dark, but I had a good chart, and the pilot had shown me where the ship must be to unload her cargo of lumber.

I went into the cabin and met the doctor and asked him if everything was all right for me to proceed to where I was to discharge, and he said I might. The two doctors were having a drink and a very sociable time, but I at once went back on deck and told the pilot.

He said, "But, Captain, I don't think I can put the ship in the correct place," but I told him that if he couldn't I was sure that I could. We kept on going, and when we were far enough along I lowered down my sails and asked the pilot if I was not in the correct place, and he said I was just right then. I let go the starboard anchor. The ship was going ahead, slowly, and I let out all the chain, and when she had the chain good and tight I let go the port anchor and then heaved in the starboard chain, letting the port chain run out until I had forty-five fathoms on each chain, both good and tight. I did not have to move the ship until we went away.

After we were all moored the pilot came to me and said, "Captain, I am sure you could bring a ship in here without a pilot."

I laughed, and we went to the cabin to sign his papers before he went ashore. His boat was alongside, and we both had a parting drink. It was the first one we had had, as I don't believe in liquor when there is brainwork to be done and a ship to be taken through reefs, which is not a very good place to come into. I bade him good night and thanked him for his very good work.

The stevedore had sent his launch off and invited me to come ashore for a short time, which I did, the doctor too. We went to his home and stayed a short time, then went back on board. He said that I had made the best passage that had ever been made there from the West Coast, one hundred and six days. It is a long road and a lot of bad weather to go through, and many anxious nights to pass crossing the South Atlantic Ocean.

The next morning, the custom house officer and the owner of the cargo came early,[18] and at one that afternoon I started to discharge in lighters. There were six German ships interned there, all fine steamships, two passenger and four freighters. One was loaded and the balance were empty. The first Saturday night I gave the crew liberty, all but the night watchman. When Monday morning came, I found that I had no crew. Only the night watchman was left; even the steward had gone. I went on shore and found out that one of the Union Castle steamships had come in with hardly any crew and had stolen all of my men and had gone. They were all shipped at a large sum—eighty pounds apiece—to go to England.

I was surely up against it. I knew that the German steamers all had fine crews on board, and as Portugal was a neutral country, as was America, I could take any of them if I could get them. I went to my Consul at once and reported to him, and he said it was no use looking for the men, as they had all gone in the British steamer *Dover Castle*. We went to the agent of the Union Castle Line and found out that they had shipped eight of my men. I asked if he thought it was right, and he said that anything was fair in time of love and war. If your nation was in this war, your men would not have been taken.

I could say nothing, but I surely could think what I wanted to. I asked my Consul if I could get any men from the German ships and if he would ship them. He said, "I will ship any man you want shipped except a Britisher. If the British ships steal your men, I will ship any man but a Britisher."

I at once started to feel out the German captains and found that they were only too glad to let me have men and would pay them off and give me a letter saying that they were paid up to the date that I shipped them, and that there were lots of men among them that wanted to go. I told the Consul that I could get a crew, and he advised me not to ship any of the Germans until I was discharged and ready to sail.

The British Consul had put me up at the British Club and the English Club, but I did not go to either of them. There were at the time a lot of Britishers there from the country, and they were all down on the Americans because they did not come into the big war. I made up my mind to keep away from them as much as possible, for if I kept away from their clubs and away from all war talk, I would be sure not to get into any trouble.

The American Consul came to me one morning and told me that I had offended the British Consul, or the British Consul thought I had. I told him that I was surely sorry if such was the case, but I did not know in what way I had offended him. He told me that the British Consul had come to him about my not going to the clubs after he had put me up at both and sent me a card to that effect. I told my Consul that I did not mean to offend the British Consul or anyone else, but that I had not been to either club and that I was not going. I was not going to be insulted by any Britisher, and I was sure that if I attended the clubs it would not be long before someone would be half drunk and would get after me because we were not in the war, and I wouldn't stand to be insulted by any one of them. So by keeping away, I was out of all harm.

I told the Consul that it was much different with him, and he said he had not thought of it in that way, but he was sure I was doing the correct thing. He told the British Consul why I did not come to the clubs and that no offense was meant. In a few days I got an invitation to dinner at his home, and I intended to reply by thanking him for his kindness but that I would not be able to attend. That day at my Consul's he asked me if I had received an invitation to dinner at the British Consul's home. I told him I had but that I was not going. He said, "You must attend, Captain. I am going and you must go, too, as it is gotten up for you on account of your not going to the clubs."

So I went with the Consul, and it was a very fine affair; some twelve couples and extremely English. The British Consul General made a speech, and I was asked to reply, which I did, but I did not say too much as my nation was neutral. My Consul said that my talk was very good. The party ended about midnight, and I was exceedingly relieved.

When I was discharged, I took eight men from the German ships and signed them, having a letter from each shipmaster saying that they had been paid off and thanking me for giving them jobs.[19] The day after I signed them, the British Consul sent for me, asking if I would call at his office as soon as possible. He was in a very bad frame of mind when I arrived. I sat down, and he asked me if I had not shipped Germans the day before for a crew. I told him that I had.

He then said, "Do you know that you have no right to do so?"

I told him that I did not think he had anything to do with my ship, as America was a neutral nation, Portugal also; but he said that he would show me that he had.

"You are very interested in my ship's affairs, it seems," I said. "If you had so much interest, you might have stopped your *Dover Castle* from stealing my men, and it would have saved you all this great worry."

He replied, "I will see that you don't take them to sea in your ship."

"By what law are you going to do that?" I asked him. "And I would advise you not to get into anything like you suggested because I am going to take them to sea with me, and I defy you to stop me."

He then said, "I will wire Cape Town to the British Admiral, and he will send a man-of-war and take them out of your ship."

I told him that I was surprised that he would think that a British man-of-war would take a crew out of an American ship, but he assured me that I would see. I wished him luck and took my departure. I then went to the American Consul's office, and he said, "Captain, you are having some fun with the British Consul, aren't you?"

I then told him what had taken place, and he continued, "You did exactly right. I knew all about it as soon as you left his office. He called me up and asked me if I had shipped eight men for your ship from the Germans that were interned, and I told him that I had and would sign any man, even a Britisher, after the British steamer had stolen your crew, and that you would not need any men if that had not happened. I asked him why he allowed that to take place, and he said that that was different because we are in war, and a passenger ship must have men. Then I asked him why she left her last port if that was the case, and when he didn't answer I said I supposed it was to make money for the Union Castle Line and hung up."

However, he sent a wire to the Admiral at Cape Town, and I went to sea with the men and did not see any man-of-war looking for eight German sailors in an American ship.

While I was in Africa, I went to Johannesburg. It was at the time the *Lusitania* was put down by a German submarine, and it was a great sight. They burned all the Germans' houses and even their automobiles. There were a lot of fine cars there, and they put them in one of the sewers, poured coal oil on them, and set fire to the mass. They burned big warehouses full of goods, and I could not see why they did not use the goods and get the benefit from them, but they said that they did not want any more of their goods. What a change since then! They are using them now.[20]

17 Arrested for Murder

I had a good passage home,[1] went to Port Townsend for orders, and was ordered to go to Vancouver, British Columbia, to load back to Durban; another voyage around the world. After finishing loading, I came back to Port Townsend to get my stores and ship chandlery for the trip, also a crew.[2] After I had gotten the stores on board and the crew shipped, I cleared the customs and was going to sea the next day. My wife was with me and was going home to Tacoma when I sailed. The last night I made up my accounts to send home and went to bed.

It was very cold at the time, January, and about three in the morning I was awakened by the noise of the sheaves in the blocks that hoisted the small boat up at the stern. I jumped up quickly, put on a bathrobe, and ran on deck. As I passed the mate's room I knocked on his door and told him to get up; that the crew had stolen the little boat and were running away.

I ran aft, but the boat was some way off. You could not see it, as there was a haze close to the water, although clear overhead. I at once told the mate to go and see how many men had gotten away. When he got to the forecastle they were all in their berths asleep, but everything was packed and all ready to put into the boat. There was only one man gone. The other men who helped to lower the boat ran forward as I came on deck, but had planned to take the boat forward, put their things in it, go ashore, and disappear. Then I would have to ship another crew, and it was hard to get men at the time.

I heard someone holler, "Help!" I believe it was the man who was in the boat, but I heard it only once. He must have been trying to get one of his oars shipped, and as the boat had some ice in the bottom of her, he slipped overboard.[3] In the morning I went ashore and reported it to the customs, the U. S. shipping commissioner, and the police. I sent a launch out to look for the boat, and they found it hauled up on the beach. It had been picked up early, and the finders kept it for what they could get for it, making no report. As it had the ship's name carved on it, they knew it belonged to the *H. K. Hall*, then lying in the bay. I gave the man five dollars and was so pleased to get my boat back that I let it go. The police wanted me to arrest the man, but I had something else to do that was more important to me.

I sailed that night and had the usual weather until I got within a few hundred miles of Cape Horn, where we encountered very heavy gales and cold weather. There was no let-up crossing the South Atlantic—it either blew a gale or it was calm. When I was some fifteen hundred miles from the Cape of Good Hope I had a most horrid gale. The sea was something that one cannot express, and the wind from the east, fair ahead. I was under very short canvas, and the ship was laboring very hard with the seas coming from all directions and plenty of water on board in large quantities.

I wore around several times to see if the ship would not lie better, but it seemed that she always acted worse. The first officer came to me and told me that the ship had started to leak badly. I watched the pumps, and the water was gaining on us, so we had to put all hands to the pumps. By so doing, the water didn't gain as fast, but I knew that the men could not stand it for long. The wind started to moderate, and as soon as the sea went down some I started to get a passageway through the lumber on deck so I could get steam to work the pumps.

It was big timber, 18 × 18, twenty-two feet long, and the ship was rolling heavily. It was a hard job, and we had to keep part of the men on the pumps. By the time we had gotten the trench finished, we had nine feet of water in the hold. That made the ship very deep and hard to drive through the water, but as soon as we got the steam on the pumps we could lower the water an inch per hour. Both of our boats had been smashed, so we had no boats to look to, and as there was no ship in that part of the South Atlantic, our only chance was to try and keep the ship as free from water as we could.

I did not have fresh water enough for the boiler, and I knew that it would not be long before the tubes would start to go. After we had run the steam engine on the pumps for twenty-four hours, we had the water down to three feet, but then we had to blow the boiler down and wash the salt out, so we put all hands on the pumps once more. By the time we had steam again, we had eight feet of water, and it looked as if I was up against a big job, but the only thing to do was to keep on and see if we could overcome our hard fate.

In a few days the tubes began going but I was very lucky to have Portland cement to fix them with. We got so we could fix one in three hours, and by the time I reached Durban fifty-two tubes had gone. Everything was working bad about the engine, all the valves worn out, but I was well supplied with most everything.

We had to keep the men on deck most of the time, giving them but little time to sleep, but one could do nothing else. The engine burned a lot of wood to keep steam, and it all had to be sawed from the cargo, but we were getting nearer, and I was determined to reach my port.

I got within sixty miles of Durban, when a fine, big Swedish steamer came along. I was only eleven miles off the coast, so I set my flag and signaled, asking him to come close as I wished to talk to him, which he did. I told him that my ship had eight feet of water in the hold and that the crew were worn out, and asked if he would send a wireless to Durban asking them to send a tug out for me.

He said he would do so. He said, then, that he would take me in tow and land me off Durban, and the Durban tug would tow me into port. I asked him how much he wanted, and he said it would not be much. I saw that I had a smart man, so I said to him, "You are all right, Captain, always look out for yourself first; but I am not going to pay you any salvage, and if you will send that wireless message I will look out for the rest of my troubles."

He answered, "You are all right, Captain, there is no good wasting any more time, but I will send the message for you."

He bade me good-bye and went along on his course north. We lay becalmed for twenty-four hours and no signs of any tug. The current was taking us south fast, away from Durban, but the next afternoon the wind came up strong from the west. Before morning I made the light at Durban, and at eight a.m. I was close to the breakwater. The pilot came on board and told me that the tug had been out looking for me and the harbormaster was on board the tug and very mad for not finding me.

We lay around there until two that afternoon. The ship was hard to handle as the breeze was light in close to land, but at last the tug came and towed me in direct to the wharf where I was going to discharge.[4] The doctor came on board as I was going up the bay, and after looking at the crew and my papers he said everything was in order. He said, "But you don't look too good. You want rest."

I showed him my legs, which had been hurt discharging the deckload overboard to get at the main pumps. "Your legs are bad," he said, "but you have got them on the right side from danger."

I told him that I would go to a doctor as soon as I had finished with the ship's business, and he told me the name of the best doctor, in his opinion, in Durban and gave me his address. As soon as I was alongside the dock, the customs came on board. The U. S. Consul was there, and the customs let him come on board with them, as he had my mail and was ready to render me any assistance that he could.

He said, "Captain, you will have a lot of trouble here, I am sure, but I will do all in my power for you. You must have had a hard time to keep this ship afloat to get here."

I asked him about the war, and he told me that they were all mad there because America did not come in with England, so I could see that I was due to have trouble. He went away, and the rest of the men came looking for business. It was Sunday when I arrived, and there were not so many as there would have been on a week day. The owners of the cargo had a man there to offer any assistance that I might want, and the first thing that I wanted was men to put on the pumps. In a very short time they sent me sixteen Negroes to pump all night, and I thought that they would be able to keep the ship from getting any more water in her than there was, as I was going to start discharging in the morning.

The Consul told me Strong & Sons were the best stevedores, ones you could rely on. As soon as I got through with the ship's business, I got fresh water from the company that I had the cargo for and washed out the donkey boiler, thinking that I might be able to use it until I could make arrangements to have it retubed. After getting it cleaned, I got steam on it, but the tubes went, one after another, as soon as there was forty pounds of steam on it. So I was lost as to steam to handle cargo with, but I had made arrangements with the stevedore to cover all that trouble, and at seven the next morning they started putting off the cargo with some forty-five Negroes.

By night, they had put off some one hundred and five thousand feet, the pumps going all the time and not being able to lower the water any. After I had entered the customs and delivered the ship's papers, I went and had my legs dressed by the doctor to whom I was directed. They were badly swollen, and he did not want me to walk on them any more than was really necessary. When I got back to the ship, the engineer from the plant that owned the cargo came to see me, as I had wanted to have a talk with him. We went to the pumps and watched the men working, and I asked him what power they used at their mills. He told me electric power.

I then said, “Why couldn’t there be a small dynamo put here to work these pumps and stop this heavy expense?”

“Sure there can,” he replied. “I will have it done at once. We can use the mill’s power in the daytime and the city’s at night.”

The next day, by noon, we were pumping by electric power, only having one man to see if everything went right, and then the pumps started to gain some. In four days they had the water all out of the ship and had to pump only during the day, as the ship was coming out of the water fast and the pressure was much less.

I found that I was going to have a hard time to get tubes for the boiler. The government had them, but would not let me have any if I could get them any other place. I went to the engineer and asked him why we could not work my engine by electricity as well as the pumps, and he said, “I will go and see, Captain, and if possible it will be done.”

We went at once. I had looked the whole thing over before going to him and knew it could be done, but it would have to have a much larger dynamo than the one on the pumps and a wheel would have to be put on the drive shaft. He had a look, and I told him what I thought of it.

He said, “I will fix it at once. You can hoist cargo out of your hold.”

The next afternoon we were running our engine by electricity. After I sent all over Africa and could not get any tubes to fix my boiler with, then the government would let me have enough to retube it, so I took the boiler out on deck so that the work would not interfere with the man driving the engine. The motor did good work but did not have as much power as the steam boiler.

I went to the harbormaster to find out about getting the drydock, and he was about as small a man in principle as I have ever met. He told me that before I could go on drydock I must put divers under the ship and try to find the leak and fix it with divers. We had had some unpleasant words before then, and he was mad because he did not find my ship with the tug and was going to try and make me pay a large price for the tug.

I told him that I would not let the likes of him beat me if I could get out of it, but I saw that he had all the big cards in the deck, and I was sure to be beaten as everything I wanted was in the hands of the government. They sent me a bill for the tug, and I went to see them. Hunt,

Leuchars & Hepburn, the owners of my cargo, were a very wealthy firm. They did not like the way I was being treated and stood by me at all times. When I went to see the harbormaster, who had charge of all affairs as to shipping, Mr. Leuchars went with me.

I told the harbormaster that I would pay for the coal and oil that the tug had used, but that all the crew were on monthly wages, and I would not pay for them. The tug had done me no good by the fact that if they had come some thirty miles farther south they would have found the ship. But they only came to where I was when the steamer sent the wireless message, ignoring the strong current that sets south at all times. After a long and hard fight, he would not give in, so I told him to go to the law with it, as I never would pay his most exorbitant bill.

In a day or so he sent me a letter asking me to come to see him. I went to his office, and he had changed; in fact, he seemed to be in his right mind for the first time since I had arrived.

"Now, Captain," he said, "we will talk this all over again and see if we cannot come to some agreement."

I told him that I would do the right thing if only he would meet me half way. I was not with him but a few moments before he said he would settle with me on the basis that I had offered. I told him to have three bills made out and I would sign them, which I did. I paid him only one third of what he wanted at first, and of course I was beaten at that, but I knew that I had to have a lot more to do with him and could not afford to have too much trouble with him, as he had me in a tight place, and I was sure that he was going to get every cent he could out of it.

The only thing that was in his mind was why the United States was not in the big war that was raging in Europe, and he did not forget to tell me what he thought about it. I told him I was not responsible for my country and that I thought I was doing my part, as I was taking great chances of getting blown up, for the coast was mined by a German surface raider and one did not know when he might be taken prisoner and his ship sunk.

"That is all right," he said. "You are doing all you can for us, but we want your country to come into the war."

After I got the ship light enough, I had to put a diver under her to look for the leak. I had to go to the harbormaster, and he sent the diver, and I had to work the air pump. He was there five days and said he could not find the leak. I am sure he was told by the harbormaster not to find it, and I did not forget to tell him what I thought of him. They charged me very heavily for the diver and the balance of the gear that went with him, but he had me and I could not do anything.

I went to my Consul and explained the whole thing to him, but he could not do anything, as much as he tried. He told me that he was doing all he could to help me out, and that I was lucky to have gotten there. The day before I finished discharging, I went to the harbormaster to get the drydock, and he told me that I could have it at a certain time. I gave him a docking plan of the ship's bottom, and he told me that I would have to go and attend to that, as they would have nothing to do with it. I asked him to give me a letter to the manager of the dock, which he did.

I went to the drydock and met the manager, telling him my business and also what the harbormaster had told me. He asked me if I had a docking plan, and I passed it to him.

"Captain," he said, "I will see that this is done as the plan says."

Then he told me that the harbormaster did not know the meaning of a docking plan and was putting me to all the trouble he could because he did not get the ship when he went out with the tug.

As soon as the dock was ready, the tug came for the ship, and in a short time she was high and dry out of water, resting perfectly on her keel. I had bilge shores put in. They were not used to doing that, but the dockmaster was a most capable man and did anything that I wanted done.

In a few minutes after we had the ship shored up to my liking, the harbormaster came in full uniform and wanted me to put up a bond that I would go off the drydock the next day at the same time as I came on, making twenty-four hours. I asked him what he wanted a bond for, and he told me that he would not trust any American. I laughed at him and told him that I was not putting up bonds at that time of day.

"Well then," he said, "I will go to your agent, and they will put up one for you."

I told him that would be fine with me, so off he went, but in a short time he was back again, stating that they could not do anything like that without orders from the master. I laughed at him, and that made him lightning mad. I told him that he had acted like a schoolboy in all the business that I had with him and for God's sake to get out from under foot or someone would throw him overboard.

Then he was raving. He still wanted something to show that I would go off the dock the next day.

I went up close to him, looked him in the eye, and said, "You damn fool! You have full command of this dock, and all you have to do is open the flood gates, and in one half hour the ship is afloat, yet still you want bonds put up! Get to hell off this dock while I am hiring it, or I will smash your face for you!"

He saw that I meant it, as I had thrown my coat off. He left at once and did not come back to see how things were getting along. There were three butts in the ship's bottom that the water was pouring out of, and then I was sure that the diver was told not to find any leak. When I settled up with the harbormaster, I did not forget to tell him that he had not fooled me in the least, but I was in his hands, and there was no way but to do as he had said. I told him what I thought of him in very strong words, most too strong to put in writing.

I put the ship alongside of a big steamer which was condemned, and moored so she could not swing around. Then came the job of trying to get a crew. The ship had a hard name after what the crew had gone through for twenty days. My mate, I think, had the hardest name.[5] They would not let him land, so I put him ashore for safekeeping.

However, there were no men to get, and if a sailor came into port the British or South African Government grabbed him, and he had to go where he was sent. The Consul sent to the American Consuls in all the ports along the coast to try and get men. He got a second mate from Port Elizabeth, and I had my cook and steward and one man. I then wanted seven men and had men searching the whole country, but without any success.[6]

One morning I went to my agent, and there was a letter there from the Crown Prosecutor to come to his office, as he wanted to see me. He was a very smart man, and I had met him before. We shook hands, and he asked me to sit down.

"Well, Captain," he said, "you are having a hard time getting a crew."

I told him that I was, and it looked as if I was beaten.

"Yes," he said, "every man that comes here is grabbed by the government to fill the British ships, as they all come short-handed. They even put them in jail to keep them safe, if they don't want them at the time. But I have a way, and I am most sure that you will be able to get four good sailors from a Swedish ship that were put in jail for ninety days a short time ago for assault on the captain.

"Now, I want you to go to the Governor and explain the position to him and ask him if he won't let you have those men. You will find him a very fine gentleman, and I am sure that you will win. He is not our brilliant harbormaster, Captain."

"Well, I hope not," I said. "If he is I am wasting my time."

Well, we both went out and had a drink, and I went to the Government House. I sent in my card and was received by the Governor and found him a fine gentleman. I told him what I was there for and the position I was in, and that my ship was wanted at that time.

He said, "Captain, I will see that the four men that are in jail are taken to your Consul's at ten tomorrow morning, and you will be there to see that they are signed on. They will go directly to your ship under guard, and I will see that there are police there night and day, so that they don't get away, without any expense to you."

I thanked him for his kindness, and we had a long talk about the war. I got up to go, and he said, "Wait," and he turned a bell and we both had a drink of good Scotch. I bade him good-bye and went to the American Consul's office, telling him of my good luck.

At ten the next morning the men were there and signed the articles and were put on board by the police launch, with a man left to guard them. I picked up the other four men, one by one, after a while. One man that I shipped was a very bad character, as I learned afterward. I put him on board, but the next day he got ashore by some means. I was looking over my account with Strong & Sons, who had done my stevedoring, when this sailor walked in and demanded money for the time he had worked.

I asked him who had given him permission to come on shore.

"I fooled the police," he said, "and I want money for the two days I have worked."

I told him to get out at once, but he was very insulting and would not go, so I got up and walked over to him. My right hand went out, and he was out for a count of more than ten. When he came to, two police took him to the station and locked him up. In a few moments the chief of the Water Police called me up and told me that he was a noted character, and he would keep him in jail until I was ready to go to sea, and then they would bring him on board.

In a day or two I was ready to take my departure. The tug came, also the chief of the Water Police and several other guests, to see the ship get away after so much trouble. I had made many good friends during my long stay, and the steward had the table set in the dining room with lots of fine sandwiches and plenty of drinks for them. The chief of the Water Police took me to one side and asked me if I was well armed. I told him I was not, and he said, "You are taking great chances with this crew, Captain. I am sure that this sailor whom I just brought on board will kill you the first chance he gets, and that won't be long, as he won't lose sight of the land."

"Well," I said, "we will see about that. But he will be very easy to handle as soon as I get to sea."

"Well," he replied, "you be armed at all times and don't take any chances with that sailor. He is a hard case, and he has it in for you. I am sure of that."

Well, the tug had the hawser on board, and it came time when all must leave but the pilot and customs house officer. The tug had some fifty ladies and gentlemen on board, as it was a holiday. The big horse races were that afternoon, and the city was full of people from miles away.

We towed to sea, and as soon as we got clear of the breakwater I started making sail, with no first officer on board. As soon as we were three miles to sea, the customs officer gave me the clearance papers, and the tug blew his whistle to let go the hawser. At the same time, I could see a fine yacht coming very fast, and I knew my mate was on board, as did the pilot and customs officer. Just before she came, the pilot and customs officer got into their boat and pulled clear from the ship. The yacht came close, so the mate jumped, catching the side ladder, and was on deck in a second. He ran forward and went into the engine room to see if the boiler had plenty of water. I, at the time, was on the after deck where I belonged.

All at once, I saw the hard case sailor run up onto the forecastle head and make a dive overboard. I had the wheel put hard down, and the ship came to the wind and stopped her headway. The pilot picked the sailor up, and I told him to fetch him back, which he did. As he got close to the ship, I had a line thrown over the side and told them to bend it around his neck, and we would haul him over the side.

Then I said to myself, "I won't have him on board," so quick as a flash I pointed a big Colt's revolver at the sailor and said, "Dive overboard again or I shoot!" and he went into the water like a seal from a rock.[7]

I ordered the wheel shifted, and the ship started to go ahead. In a few moments all sail was set. I dipped the American flag three times to the tug, and he replied with three long whistles. All the crowd gave three cheers, and once more I was clear of trouble. I can truly say that I never was so glad to get away as I was at that time.

I soon had strong westerly winds running to the east. Some ten days after leaving I had a very heavy gale, and my ship started to leak. The pipes from the main pumps had broken off from the center wall with the swing of the ship, and it looked as if I was up against it. I knew that I could not pump by steam all the way home, as I would have fuel and water to last only a short time. So I told the mate that we would take all the pipes from the steam pumps and put them on the main pumps, and by cutting larger holes in the keelsons they would not break off again.

In some fifteen hours of hard work, we got the pumps fixed. Then it took two days to get the water pumped out, as the ship was running hard with a very heavy sea running. I was sure as soon as I could get by New Zealand and get north in smooth water the ship would not leak so badly.

Two of the sailors went down sick, and it looked as if one of them would die. They had been in East Africa and had malaria fever, and they had taken all the quinine that I had in the medicine chest. Their legs had swollen up to an enormous size. They could not walk and were sinking fast. They were nothing but skin and bones.

I was examining their legs one morning, and I found soft spots on one of the men's legs. The next day I found one on the other leg. They were swollen so badly that they looked as if they would surely burst open, and they were suffering something awful. The next day I made up my mind that I would lance one of the legs and see if there was any pus in it. I took a lance and what things I had with me and went to the forecastle, telling the one who had the soft places on his legs that I was going to lance one of the soft spots and see if there was any pus in it. He was so sick that he did not care what happened, so I cut a hole in his leg just below the kneecap.

Well, I have never seen anything like it. There was more than two quarts of pus in it, also in the other leg. I disinfected them and poulticed them well, and in three weeks he was able to work and get strong. I had to do the same thing to the other man, and he got well also.

At four o'clock one morning I told the mate to set the spanker, as the wind was more moderate. I was hauling to the north, but it was very cold; ice and snow on deck. The crew had no clothes, only what they had bought from the slop chest, and they were not buying any more than they could help, as they wanted all the money to spend when they got to San Francisco. As I was eating my breakfast, one of the sailors came and knocked at the dining room door. The steward opened the door. It was one of the crew.

He said, "Captain, the coon is dead in his bunk."

I told him that was all right; I would come and attend to him as soon as I had finished my breakfast. I went forward and found him dead for at least two hours. I had the body taken onto the main hatch and gave it a good examination, finding no marks of any kind. I had him cleaned up and dressed in his best (such as it was) and sewed him up in canvas to be buried at one that afternoon.

Going aft, I wrote up the official log, called the crew, and read what I had said, and they all signed it. At one o'clock, I read the burial sermon with the ship hove to with the American flag at half mast and committed the body to the deep with heavy weights at its feet.[8]

That reduced me to six men, and two sick made only four to work. With the ship leaking very badly, we had to have all hands on the pumps six hours out of every twenty-four. This also applied to the officers. I would take the wheel while they pumped. As soon as the two sick men got well, it made it much easier for them, and the ship did not leak so badly when we got into fine weather and much smoother seas.

After an average passage I arrived in San Francisco,[9] and after passing the doctor and customs, went to the dock for repairs. The crew were all discharged after the ship was made fast and pumped out and everything in order. The next morning I entered the customs house and made arrangements to pay the crew off at two that afternoon with the deputy shipping commissioner.

The managing owner, the carpenter who was going to repair the ship, and I went over the ship to see what was to be done. We finished and went to the cabin. They were to have lunch on board. I found that I could not stay, as I would not have time to meet my engagement with the commissioner. As I went into the bathroom, Mr. Billings came in and said, "Captain Killman, have you done anything to cause your arrest?"

I was so surprised I looked at him and said, "What do you mean?"

"You are going to be arrested for the murder of two men, one that died in Port Townsend and the man that died on the voyage from Africa."

"Well, what next?" I said. "I have not had enough trouble on this voyage as it is. Do you think that I would be here if I had killed anyone in

Port Townsend, where there was over fifty thousand dollars paid to me and which I cabled to you? I think I would have stayed there for some time and let them look for me."

I told him that I had not put my hand on a man during the voyage, as I did not have any occasion to do so.

"I know what you say is true, Captain Killman," he said and walked out of the bathroom. I went to Mr. Billings' office, got the money to pay the crew off, and went to the deputy shipping commissioner's office. I went inside to talk to the head commissioner. As I came out, an officer in civilian clothing put a large revolver on me and demanded me to put my hands up. I told him that there was not one man living who could make me put up my hands, and if I did not have something more important to do I would make him eat that gun, and to show his papers that I was under arrest, which he did.

Then the commissioner said, "You have gone far enough, and you have not frightened Captain Killman one bit. Now drop that gun unless you want to be thrown out of that window head first."

I stopped at the phone to let Mr. Billings know that I was under arrest, and the deputy marshal again hauled his gun and insisted that I could not use the phone. Then the commissioner said, "I will relieve your pain."

He called the U. S. marshal's office and told them how this deputy was going on and that I had business to attend to and must be there when my crew was paid off. So the marshal said, "Let me talk to him. I will stop it very quickly."

The deputy got orders to keep out of the way and that I could use any phone or go anywhere I wanted to, but I must be at the Post Office building by four o'clock.

After I paid the crew off, I went to my office, the deputy marshal coming too. They all joshed me and asked me when they were going to hang me. I told them that it looked at one time as though my hard case who had served the papers on me would fill me full of lead, and I was so frightened!

Then Mr. Billings stepped out of his private office, saying to the deputy marshal, "I don't think you got very far with Captain Killman. You might kill him, but you could not frighten him or any one else, I am sure of that."

The deputy marshal said nothing.

After I had done what business I had to do, I told Mr. Marshal that I was ready to go with him, and we took our departure for the Post Office building, where the federal court was held. As soon as they had finished with me at the office, a lawyer[10] retained by Mr. Billings came to me, and we went to the court room and asked for bail for me, as I was needed very badly at my ship for they were going to start work the next morning. But the judge said that he could not allow bail on two charges of murder, so I was taken to the city jail by a different officer—a fine man.

We got into the street car, and I remembered that I had no cigars to smoke, so I asked him if he would not let me get something to smoke, and he said, "Certainly, Captain."

So we got off the street car and I got cigars and cigarettes, and we went into a saloon and we had two drinks, which did me a lot of good as I had been very busy all day and had had no lunch. Then we were off for my first night in jail, and for what, I had not learned yet.

After I gave my name at the office of the new city jail in San Francisco, the booking officer said, "Captain, if you have anything in your pockets that is of any value to you, you leave them here. They will be taken good care of, and I will give you a receipt for them."

I had some two hundred dollars in my pockets and the letters that I had got from my family, and I gave them to him, keeping some ten dollars in my pocket. I had an Elks pin in my coat, and he said, "I would leave that Elks pin, Captain, and I am sure you won't be here very long."

"How do you know that?

"I cannot tell you, but I am sure, and it is a shame to see one that is innocent of any crime here, so don't let it worry you."

"It won't worry me, but I have a lot of work to attend to that no one can do but me until I can see them and explain."

"Well, it will come out all right, I am sure of that, and I am sorry to see you have to go to one of the cells that you will be put into with your mate."

I laughed, and I was taken to the cell, and the iron bars closed behind me. It was much different than my lovely cabins in the *H. K. Hall*, but I was there, that was one sure thing, and there I must stay.

I got no supper, but I suppose that they did not serve guests who did not come before a certain time, so I had to go without it. It was a long and hard night. I did not care for myself, but for my wife and daughters. I felt very badly because I knew that the papers would come out in big headlines in Tacoma where I lived: "Captain Killman In Jail For The Murder Of Two Sailors On His Voyage Around The World."[11] I had sent my wife a telegram to come to San Francisco to stay while the ship was there, and I was sure that she would leave at once. Mr. Billings, the night I was put in jail, sent her a telegram saying, "Come at once. Take no notice of the newspaper. You will be met at the train."

The next day they came from the office to see me, and I was told that the commissioner[12] was out of town, and I must go before him to see if I would be tried and for what charges. He would not be back for three days. My wife had left Tacoma by train and would arrive the next night, but I knew that Mr. Billings would look out for her. That afternoon, two friends called on me, and I was taken from my cell and brought downstairs, where we had a long talk. They made me acquainted with the officer in charge of the jail, after which I was taken back to my cell.

I was only there but a short time when they came for me and told me to take what I had there, as I was going to a much better place on the first floor, close to the office. I had a good bed to sleep in and was not locked in until ten at night. One of the men tended to my room, and the food was not bad; in fact, it was good. The next day my wife called with Mrs. Billings. I was taken out in the corridor, and we had a long talk. I told her that it was hard luck, but as I was innocent she could look anyone in the face and tell them to go west.

I was there five days before the commissioner came back, and it was a great experience to hear the crooks talk. They were talking about what they would do when they got out and were all very fine to me and asked no questions whatever as to my being there, and I gave them no information. On the sixth morning I was called for by a deputy marshal and told I was to appear before the US commissioner, as he had gotten back. As I passed the office, I said good morning to the booking officer, and he said, "You won't be here tonight, Captain. It is a disgrace, such work going on. You have got to stay here because there is no one to represent the government, but what can you do about it?"

My reply was, "There is no redress."

The first officer and I went to the Post Office building with the deputy marshal. The commissioner was there, also my lawyer, Mr. Billings, my wife and Mrs. Billings, and all the sailors were there in charge of another deputy. I was put on the stand and questioned by the commissioner in regard to the death of the man coming from Africa. I told him all that I knew about it and showed the official log that I had written at the time of the man's death.

He read it over carefully and said, "That is all at present, Captain."

Then the sailors were called, one by one, and asked to state why I was arrested for the murder of the seaman that died on the voyage.

"Well," they said, "we thought it would make it stronger against the mate."

They all said that they had nothing against me and that I had not molested any of them and that I had saved the lives of two of them, they were sure of that.

"Well, Captain Killman," the commissioner said, "I do not know what you are here for, and Port Townsend has not been heard from. I do not see any case against you, whatever. Your official log is very clear and well written and is signed by the crew, also the US shipping commissioner in Port Townsend. I have nothing to do with the Port Townsend matter, myself, as it was in the State of Washington, and I am sure you will hear nothing more of it."

But he bound the mate over for trial. After the hearing was finished, Mr. Billings took the commissioner, the prosecuting attorney, and myself out to lunch. They told us then that they thought it was one of the worst cases they had ever heard of, but there was no redress. That is what one can expect from the poor, innocent sailor, or at least it has been in my experience. The better you use them, the poorer results you get.

In a few days I got notice from the prosecuting attorney that I could go in the ship to the Columbia River to load when I was ready. The trial of my mate would be delayed until I was back in San Francisco. I would be notified when I must be there for the trial. A few days after my arrival on the Columbia River,[13] I received a telegram to be in court on a certain date. I went to Astoria to take the steamer *Rose City*, and a few moments before I was to sail, I received a telegram not to come, that the mate had taken one year in jail without being tried.[14]

It was all a hoax, I am sure of that, as my official log and my evidence would have cleared him.[15] The sailor died from cold, as he had no vitality. He had been born on the French island in the Indian Ocean, named Madagascar, a little copper-colored boy with no strength. He came on board with no clothes, and the extreme cold weather and storms we had were too much for him.

18 A New Owner for the *H. K. Hall*

After loading, I sailed for Sydney, Australia,[1] with a cargo of lumber. On the way over, in the South Pacific, I passed some fifteen miles from Palmerston Island. About nine in the morning I saw two sailboats coming off. I looked at them for a while, then I gave orders to take in the light sails and heave to, so they could catch up with us. If we had not done this, they never would have caught us. They came at last, so I could see with my glasses that they were natives, with some women and small children among them. They had some green coconuts and shells and three eggs. They could talk good English and were all very religious.

There was one very good-looking young lady named Ann, about twenty-three years old. She was the boss beggar. I took some of them into the after cabin and played the victrola for them, and they asked me to give it to them. I asked one old man who was king, and he said that it was a republic and he was the president. I told him that he was a poor-looking president with the seat out of his pants and barefooted, so he asked me if I would not fix him up.

I gave him two new shirts and pants and a pair of shoes, stockings, and some other things to make a real ruler out of him. I asked him what the King of England would do if he knew that he was president of one of his islands. He said that they did not care what he thought, as the island was theirs. I gave them a lot of food and fish hooks and lines. Ann, the boss beggar, wanted a Bible, but as there was only one on board I could not let her have it. The next thing she wanted was face powder.

Well, I was short of that, so then she wanted perfume. My wife had left a small bottle, and I gave it to her and also gave her a bottle of shaving lotion, and you should have seen her eyes sparkle with joy. I found several things that my wife had left on board and gave them to her, with all of which she was more than pleased. I asked her if she did not wear shoes, and she said she had never had any to wear. Well, I got a pair of mine, but they were too small, so I remembered there was a pair in the slop chest, the largest pair that I had ever seen. They were brogans,[2] size twelve.

I got a pair of socks and made her put them on with the shoes. You would have thought she was the ruler of a mighty throne. I gave her a lot of reading matter and a lot of food. You could have given them everything on board, and they would still want more. I asked them if they had seen any German raiders around, and they said that they hadn't, but a British cruiser had stopped there some ten days before. I asked them if they gave the natives anything, and they said they did not ask the warship for anything, as they knew they would not get it.

Finally, I told the man at the wheel to put his wheel up and the mate to set all sail. You should have seen them fly for their boats. They were soon gone, and in a short time we were out of sight of them and on our way to Sydney. We were taking great chances to stop for any boat, as there had been several ships put down by the Germans in the South Pacific where we were.[3]

After discharging my cargo of lumber, I loaded a full cargo of bulk copra[4] at Sydney[5] for Portland, Oregon. I took the ship to the lower bay after finishing loading, to get a crew. Men were very scarce, and if any were available they were grabbed by British officers and made to go. At last I got a crew on board and was going to sea as soon as the customs had searched the ship for disease.

As I went on board the first mate came to me and said that one of the men refused to go to work and was going back ashore on the first boat that came. I told the mate that I thought he would change his mind and not to have any trouble with him, as I would attend to him as soon as we got to sea. After the customs had searched the ship for at least an hour, they mustered the crew, and as soon as they saw the sailor that was going back on shore they said, "Well, you are here, are you? You are in a good place now, and I would advise you to keep your nose very clean."

When the sailor said that he was going back on shore, they told him that they didn't think he was.

I turned to my mate and told him to heave in the anchor and then called the sailor and asked him if he was going to work or in irons. He said to work, and I replied, "Very well, get forward at once where the work is going on, and don't let me hear any more from you."

We were soon out clear of Sydney Heads, and the tug blew to make sail. In a short time, sail was made, and he then blew to let go his hawser. The pilot and customs officer had gone, and we let go the hawser. He blew three long whistles, and we returned by dipping the American flag three times. In a short time we were out of sight of the shores of Australia, with a fine fair wind sending the ship through the waters of the South Pacific at eight knots.

In a day or two the mate came to me and told me that the sailor who was going back on shore refused to go aloft. Johnson, the mate, was a very fine man, but as I had told him to have no trouble with this man, he came to me. I told him that the sailor was trying to get the mate to lick him so he could get him in trouble.

"You can," I said, "get along without him going aloft, but watch him night and day, for it is hard to say what he will do."

The mate did not like to have to let this sailor get away with anything like that, but he said, "Very well, Sir, I will do as you say."

I watched the sailor very closely but could not catch him at anything. He worked fine on deck and said nothing. We had gotten farther away to the eastward and hauled to the north, and at eight in the evening we were ten miles away from an island. The wind all died out, and it was dead calm all night. I was on deck many times during the night, and the ship was lying with her head to the swell, which was coming from the southeast, the big sails going back and forth as the ship rolled with the swell.

At four o'clock in the morning I went on deck, and in a few moments I saw a stream of fire coming out of the forward ventilator. All hands were at work at once, and the fire was put out. It was a wonder that we were able to get it out, and if it had gotten one minute's more start the ship would have burned to the water, for copra is a most horrid cargo if it ever gets on fire.[6]

As soon as daylight came, I sent the mate to inspect under this ventilator. He crawled in over the copra and found paper soaked in coal oil and pieces of waste that we had been using to clean the engine with, all covered with machine oil. He brought it all up to me so I could look at it, and I knew at once who had done it, but it would be hard to prove. The smart sailor was going to stay on that island until the war was over, as it had some two hundred inhabitants.

At eight o'clock that morning I went down on the main deck and told the mate to call that sailor aft to me. He came, and you could see the guilt in his face. He was trembling with fear, as he did not know what I was going to do. I asked him why he set the ship on fire, and, of course, he denied it. I then put a large Colt revolver in his ribs and told him that if the ship should burn by any means, he would be left on board to burn with her, if I could keep from filling him full of lead, and that he, from that morning, would be spared nothing.

I told the mate to send him up to the mizzen topmast to scrape it down. I would see if he could go aloft or not. You should have seen Mr. Sailor go up that rigging and stay there all day, as I told him that he had imposed on his shipmates, and I would see that he did enough work so that they were even with him. I kept him aloft for days scraping, and he did work. If he slacked one bit I was after him.

Of course we locked everything so that there would be no way to get into the hold. I made a sheet iron band to go around the ventilators, and it was put on every night and locked and taken off in the morning, and the forward hatch was locked all the time. He was a real good sailor, the first at everything, and could he go aloft to those big gaff topsails and shift them over! He could beat any man onboard.

When we arrived in Astoria,[7] I told the mate to watch him very closely, and the mate said he kept his eye on every launch. He expected to see the police come for him any moment, but I knew if I had him arrested it would cause me a lot of trouble, and the darling sailor would be acquitted, so I paid him off at Portland.

When he got his money, I said to him, "You did not expect you would be paid off."

He made no reply but took his money, put it in his pocket, and I have not seen him since. He left Portland that day for some unknown spot in America, as I had the man who furnished crews for ships looking for him, but he could not find him. He must have caught a train as soon as one came along.

We loaded back for Sydney, Australia, and were soon on the deep blue sea again.[8] Nothing but war, the mills were doing their best, and there were plenty of ships to take away the lumber. I had a good voyage to Sydney, and as soon as I got there I received a charter party from Mr. Billings to go to Manila to load copra for San Francisco at seventy-five dollars per ton. As the ship had carried eleven hundred tons the voyage before, the freight on the copra would have been over eighty thousand dollars.

Mr. Billings wrote me that they would not let me go from there light, and he would leave it to me to do the best I could, but if I had to take coal, not to load too deep, as I would be in the typhoon season. In a few days the Consul General sent for me, and as soon as I went to his office he said, "I understand you are to go to Manila."

I told him I was.

"Well," he said, "I have a cargo of jams here for the American government. How much can you take?"

Taking into consideration that Mr. Billings had told me not to load the ship too deep, I told him that I would take fifteen hundred tons, and he said, "That will be fine, Captain Killman. I will give you eighty thousand dollars as soon as it is on board."

So the papers were all made out and signed, and I cabled Mr. Billings what I had done and received a reply of congratulations. As soon as the cargo was out, I at once got the ship ready to take jam, taking some eighty thousand feet of hardwood for a platform in the bottom of the ship and getting all ready to load. I reported to the Consul for a berth to load, and in the Consul's office I received a cable that the US government had taken over my ship, instructing me to line up[9] and load wheat for San Francisco at eighty shillings per ton, the freight amounting to some thirty thousand dollars.[10]

I therefore started to line up for wheat, notifying the shippers at Melbourne as per orders that I was to go under the cranes to load wheat. In the morning I got a cable from San Francisco, "If loaded with wheat, discharge it and take cargo of jams to Manila." I immediately went to the Consul General and told him that I would take the jams. He told me that I was out of luck, as he had chartered a steamer to take the cargo to Manila. I cabled San Francisco and got orders to await further instructions, so I put the ship in the lower bay at anchor, as there were parties looking at the ship to buy her.

In some three weeks I got a cable that the ship was sold, to close all accounts to date, and take orders from new owners. At once I called on Mr. George F. Davis, the man who had bought the *H. K. Hall*,[11] and showed him my cable. He said that he had received one that morning saying the money had been paid for the ship. I told him that I would stop all accounts and pay all bills that I had and would vacate the ship at once for his new master and gladly give him any help, if he should need any, and would remove my first mate, cook, steward, and one sailor that I had on board.

"Why, Captain Killman, what do you mean? I would not have bought the *Hall* if I had had any idea that you would not stay in command of her. You will get two hundred dollars a month more than you have been getting. Of course, you will close all of your accounts up to date, and you will deal wherever you choose, as I know nothing about ship's business."

I then told him that I had a contract with Fenwick & Company for the towing of the ship while in port, but I was sure that they would release me from that, as we were very good friends, and they would see the place that I was in.

"I do not want you to do anything like this," he said. "I want you to stay in the ship, and you must stay, as it is impossible for me to get a master unless I send to California, and then I would not know what I was getting.[12] Your ship is going to load for Vancouver, B. C., with a very valuable cargo, and you must take the ship there."

Mr. Davis was a very fine man and meant every word he said. I had met him several times and, of course, knew that he was trying to buy the ship.

"Well, Mr. Davis," I said, 'you have your agreement drawn up and let me see it before you sign it."

He dictated it at once to his secretary, and after he had finished he said, "Now I will take you to your new agents."

They were Birt & Company, who were agents for all the British transports and did a large business. After he had made me acquainted with the head of the firm, I was introduced to other members that I would have to do business with. We then went and had lunch, and I was asked to be at Birt & Company at two-thirty o'clock, which I was. They passed me a sealed letter, and I asked if that was all, and they said it was. I left and went to my old agents', opened the letter, and read it. It said, "You will have the American schooner *H. K. Hall*, now under your command, at the chrome ore dock tomorrow morning at eight o'clock to start loading chrome ore."

Well, we had a good laugh, as I never had seen anything like this happen to me before in my many years as master of a ship and could see trouble ahead of me. I had a letter typed saying as agents of the *H. K. Hall* you will order a pilot for the said ship and two tugs from Fenwick & Company and let me know at my old agents' what time they will be at the ship. I went on board that evening and had steam in the morning, heaving in thirty fathoms of chain. The pilot came at six o'clock and one tug soon afterwards. We waited for the other tug, but it did not come.

I saw that I would not be able to get to the wharf unless I went with the one tug, and I told the pilot that we would go with the one.

"I will have trouble, I am afraid. It is a bad place to put a ship into," I told him, "but we must go," and I told the mate to heave the anchor up, for I was sure I could put the ship into her berth, if the pilot could not.

We left with the one tug and had no trouble docking the ship. As soon as the ship was fast with the gangway on the dock, the foreman stevedore came on board to ask me about taking the ore and what hatch I wanted it in. I asked him how much he was to put on board, and he said five hundred tons. I did not say anything to him, only telling him where to start.

I started at once for Birt & Company and did not go to Mr. Birt's office but to the man who attended to the cargo, the shipping clerk. He said, "I understand you are at the dock ready for cargo," and I told him I was.

"You shifted with one tug, I learn."

I answered, "Yes, as there was only one, and you wanted the ship there at eight o'clock."

"You know, I suppose, that they always have two tugs to move your ship?"

I looked at him and hardly knew what to say, considering my age and the years that I had been coming to Sydney, so I told him that I didn't think it was any of his damn business, as the ship was there on time.

"I know," he replied, "that it is none of my business, but you are with different agents from those you have been used to, and I am only telling you that if you had had any trouble with the one tug you would have been in wrong with Birt & Company."

I told him that if he only knew how little I cared for Birt & Company he wouldn't waste his time telling me. I was master of the *H. K. Hall* and would be as long as my name was on the ship's register as such. I told him that I wanted to see Mr. Davis at once and asked where I could find him.

He asked if they couldn't answer anything that I wanted to see Mr. Davis about, and I said, "No. Please have me taken to his place of business at once!"

In a short time I was at Mr. Davis' office, and he said, "Well, Captain Killman, I am glad to see you this morning."

We shook hands, and I told him that I had some private business to talk over with him, and he started immediately for the door.

"Now, Captain, what is it you want?"

"Well, Mr. Davis, I came here to tell you that I want you to get a master for the *H. K. Hall* as soon as possible. I will stay and do anything for you that I can, but I will not go to sea in your ship."

"Why, Captain, what is wrong?" he asked.

I told him that they were going to put five hundred tons of chrome ore in the bottom of the ship, and the ship could not stand it, in my opinion, and I would not care to lose the *H. K. Hall.*

"Did they say anything to you about it, Captain?"

"No," I told him, "they did not, and I was hauled over the coals this very morning because I moved the ship with only one tug. I told the shipping clerk how little I care for Birt & Company, and that I am captain of the *Hall* and will be until my name is changed on the ship's register."

Mr. Davis said, "I will go with you at once, Captain. I own that ship, and you are master. You are all that I want, and I want to see that ship arrive at Vancouver safely."

We got into his car, and I could see he was very mad as soon as we got to Birt's office. We went directly to Mr. Birt's private office, and he was there. He received us in due form, but I could see that he had been told what I had said to the shipping clerk. We both sat down, and Mr. Davis asked how much chrome ore he was going to put in the *Hall.*

Mr. Birt told him five hundred tons, and Mr. Davis said, "Did you ask the captain about it or say anything to him about chrome ore?"

"Decidedly not," he replied. "We say nothing to any captain, only asking them to sign bills of lading at certain times of day. We take full charge of what we are going to put on board. We notify our stevedore, and he goes ahead."

"Well, Mr. Birt," Mr. Davis said, "this is one ship that you cannot do with as you have done. In the future you will ask Captain Killman how much of any cargo goes in the *Hall* and where he wants it stowed, as I think he knows more about that ship than anyone living, and if this ship is not loaded as he wants her to be he won't go in her, and what would I do if he should leave? If this does not suit you, I will get another agent and will settle at once with you for what you have done."

You could have heard a pin drop.

"What do you say?" Mr. Davis said. "It is up to you, and I want an answer now. I want you to know also that Captain Killman will not let you or any of your clerks interfere with his business."

It was all over. Mr. Birt was put in his place. I then told Mr. Davis that I would take two hundred and fifty tons of chrome ore and not one pound more.

"You are putting me in a hard place, Captain Killman," Mr. Birt said.

"I am sorry," I replied, "but I do not intend to lose that ship if I can help it."

The shipping clerk was notified, and as soon as two hundred and fifty tons were on board, that was all. There were no more letters written. I was at the office, and they told me I would go the next morning to Darling Island to load general cargo, and I told them to get Fenwick & Company and that I wanted to move at six the next morning.

"We will be there, Captain. We will order the pilot. You needn't bother."

"O.K.," I said.

The assistant manager of the office turned to me and said, "You must have a lot of friends here. They will order your pilot for you."

I told them that it was the custom with the tugs to do all that they could, as all American ships were left to the master to attend to the ship's business, and as there were two tug companies they both looked to get the business.

"It is different with the British ships," he said, and I told him that I knew all about that.

The next morning I moved to Darling Island and was there to go to work as soon as the stevedores wanted to, but there was not much cargo there that day. I had lunch with Mr. Davis, and as we were leaving he said, "Captain, you have a car and driver from now on and take the bill to Birt for payment. Keep it all night if you want it. You lie a long way off, and you cannot make time any other way."

So from then on I had a fine machine at my disposal all the time. They filled the lower hold with coconut oil, and the first thing that they put in the 'tween-deck was one hundred and fifty tons of African cloves in hundred pound sacks; then the hold was filled with rabbit skins, pressed in bales of some five-hundred-pounds and packed in naphthalene. It was very strong, and I wondered how the cloves would taste as they came out, as when you passed the ventilators aft you would get the mothball odor very strong, yet the next time it would be strong of cloves.

On deck we had hardwood and coconut oil, one hundred tons or more sheep casing, and honey in five-gallon tins. The deckload was secured as well as man could, and no money was spared. There were many of the shippers and underwriters on board to see it, and they all said it could never move even if the ship turned upside-down. The cargo was valued at one million two hundred and fifty thousand dollars, and the freight paid on it was one hundred and sixty-two thousand dollars.

Then came the time to get a crew. Well, I had everyone that was available for a job like that, and I talked with the head jailer of the City Jail, who told me to come out and look at some men who were there. If I could use them, he thought that we could get them pardoned and out of the country. I drove out there, and what a hard bunch of criminals! I asked them if they had been to sea, and they all said that they had.

"Can you steer and go aloft? Know a compass? Box a compass?" and they all said that of course they knew all about those things. Yet when I asked them what a compass was used for, there was not one of them who had the least idea. I then left and went with the jailer to his office, and he asked me what I thought of them.

"Well, I think they are in a good place and should stay there the remainder of their lives."

"You are correct, and don't you take any of them, for you will have no end of trouble with them. They only want to get out to get back again."

So I thanked him for his trouble and took my departure. In a few days I got men, such as they were, and sailed for Vancouver[13] with my valuable cargo. It was a fine day, with a light fair wind blowing. The tug towed us some seven miles from Sydney Heads, where we made sail, and the tug blew to let go the hawser. The swell got worse as we got off the land, and the ship was so quick with the chrome ore in the bottom that before night two gaffs had snapped in two pieces.

I at once saw that I had a lot of trouble ahead of me, but I had a good mate, and the second mate turned out well. We had three spare gaffs, and in a short time we had the sails set again, and had fine weather until we got by the north end of New Zealand, where we struck an easterly gale. I reefed the ship's sails before it blew very hard, as I thought the ship was going to act bad.

The sea was getting heavier and the wind increasing, and it was not long before I saw that the deckload was very heavy on the chains that lashed it down. In a few moments the chains started to break and the deckload to move. More than thirty-five big barrels of coconut oil, weighing a ton each, smashed to pieces in a short time; the fife rail around the mainmast was broken, and we could not get to the main pumps.

The green seas were going directly over the ship, and I saw that the big hardwood timbers would get adrift, and if they did they would make havoc out of everything.

I called the mate and told him that we would try to get the ship off and run to the north as soon as I could get headway, and to have the jib ready to pay her head off. In a short time I was going some ten knots to the north, and it was worth one's life to get forward through all that grease—it was all over the ship.[14] We ran to the north until the weather got better, then I hauled to the wind to try to get to the east. It looked as if I would have to go to the westward of the Fiji Islands, but I must go anyway as long as I could keep my ship from getting smashed up. As I got to the north, the wind backed to the south, and I made one of the most easterly crossings of the Equator.

It was some fifteen days before I could get the cargo stowed so we could get to the main pumps, and it was very lucky that the *Hall* did not leak after we repaired her, for if she had we certainly would have gone down. We shoveled thirty-five tons of coconut oil overboard. It was all over the ship, and it seemed as if we would never get rid of it. One was in danger of his life to walk the decks, but at last we were clear of it, and everything was stowed in good shape.

I did not care so much about the cargo that was lost, as it was all put on board at the owners' risk and covered by insurance. We had no bad weather after that, and if we had I do not know what we would have done, as the ship was so quick with that chrome ore in her bottom. We had more than fifteen broken gaffs, but we kept them spliced and were always ready for one to go.

I don't know what we would have done if we had taken the five hundred tons that had first been arranged. Yes, I do know; this story that I am writing would never have been written, as we would all have been drowned off the north end of New Zealand, and the world would have said that I had struck one of the mines that were adrift, placed by the German raider *Wolf*, which put down so many ships and laid mines that added to her toll of death.

I made Cape Flattery, the entrance to Puget Sound, but no sign of any tug to tow me to Vancouver. I signaled every signal station that I wanted a tug, yet none came. The wind was light and always out of the straits, but I was working up slowly. I stood across from the American shore to Vancouver Island, tacked ship, and in five minutes it was dead calm. The flood tide was running up the straits very fast and setting inshore. We passed Race Rocks going at least five knots, and the buoy was in sight not far on the port bow, when we struck a counter current and started for the Rocks.

There was no use trying to anchor, as the water was too deep there. There was not a breath of wind. I had furled the spanker and outer jib a few moments before, as they were banging. The lighthouse keeper came down close on the rocks, I suppose to see the ship land, but did not say one word. I looked toward Vancouver Island, and I could see the wind coming from the island in great force. At the time, the rocks were not more than fifty feet away, and they were so plainly visible under the water that I could see no chance for the ship.

The wind struck the ship, and at once I started giving orders to let go this and that. My mate was very smart and all hands were on deck. The ship's head paid off, and she started to go ahead. In a very few moments we were clear of the rocks that I expected to land on, and the ship was scudding through the water at great speed. The Quarantine Station was not far off, but it was impossible for me to get the sails down, and I could not make it with the wind, so I kept on for Royal Roads. My flying jib had blown away, and I was trying to get the foresail down, but we could get it only half way down when I had to come to an anchor.

I threw the wheel down, and the ship came to the wind. I let go the halyards of the headsails, and as soon as the ship's headway had stopped I let go the port anchor, then shortly the starboard anchor. Having a patent windlass, we kept letting the chain out slowly so as not to carry away the cable. It was not long before we were safe at anchor and the sails down. I had no flags up as we passed the Quarantine Station, but we put them up at once.

"Well, I suppose I am up against it now," I said to the mate. "They will fine me and make me go back to the station."

"That is nothing," he replied. "I was sure the ship was going, and how can you be so cool in a place like that? Your brain works so quickly and always right. The slightest mistake, and the ship would have been gone."

"Well," I said, "we will wait and see what takes place next. There is one thing sure. We are safe at anchor in Royal Roads and made a good passage, seventy-three days, after all that has taken place."

The wind was blowing very hard, and I had to take my flags in as they started to go. In about two hours the mate reported to me that a tug was coming, or the doctor's boat. It was the doctor, and he jumped as the tug passed close alongside, and he was all wet. He was shown to the after cabin and took off his wet things, and the steward hung them up by the fire that was burning in the forward cabin.

"Now, Doctor," I said, "I suppose I am going to get a going-over, so say what you have to say, but it won't help matters any, as it was impossible to stop any ship at the Quarantine Station."

"We knew you could not stop," he said, "and did not expect you to. How did you get clear of those rocks? Did you hit?"

I told him that I did not, but I was awfully close.

"We all thought for a few moments that you were ashore," he said, "but we saw you start when that wind struck you, and we thought that you came off. A pilot started out to board you, but his launch filled with water and was towed back. We are all pleased to see you here, Captain, you have done well to get here a morning like this. I never have seen it blow so hard as it did when you were passing the Quarantine Station. I would like to know how fast you were going through the water."

I told him that I could not say, but she was going too fast to suit me, and I could not get those big sails down, but it turned out all right. We had a long talk about the war, and he got almost dry, called his boat, made a jump for her, and got on board safely. The wind died down that night, and a launch came for me the next morning. I was there three days before I could get a tug to tow me to Vancouver.

After a long wait, I arrived safely,[15] going at once to the dock to discharge the rabbit skins.[16] They went into boxcars of the Canadian Pacific and were taken away. There was an embargo on their importation into the United States, but I am sure that they went to I. B. Stetson in New York.

After I had the furs all out, I went to my agents one morning, the Union Steamship Company, and the manager came to me.

"Your furs all came out without a blemish on them," he said, "and Mr. Davis has notified me to give you two hundred and fifty dollars for their safe delivery," which he did.

Before I was finished discharging the Armistice was signed and a holiday declared.[17] I finished discharging and towed to Portland to load for Sydney again.

19 A Run to Japan in a Shipping Board Steamer

After the ship was loaded, I resigned[1] and came to my home for a rest. I had been in Hall's employ for twenty-one years, but they had lost or sold a lot of their ships and were building none to take their place. After I was at home a few months, I wanted to get back to sea again, so I called the manager of the Pacific Steamship Company in Portland and asked him if there was a steamer for me. He said for me to take the night train for Portland and report to him in the morning, which I did.

I was at once made master of one of the Shipping Board's[2] new steamers, not completed. After some time there became trouble between the Shipping Board and the builders, and I was shifting ships for the company when I took charge of a new steamer and started to load railroad ties for England. After loading I lay for some time awaiting orders, and at last I cleared and was leaving at noon. When I went to the office they told me that I must take another captain to the customs and have the papers changed, as I was to take charge of one of the big new steel steamers that was ready to load and would go on the line in the Oriental trade between Portland, Japan, China, and the Philippine Islands.[3]

I was in Portland three months altogether before I got away, leaving the first of January,[4] my first port Yokohama, then Kobe, Japan. We encountered one heavy gale going to Yokohama, smashing the boats and doing a lot of damage. I was some six hundred miles from the Japanese coast, the engines turning only fast enough to keep steerage way on and the ship keeping head to the sea.

At three in the morning the wireless operator came to the chart room with an S.O.S. call from one of the Japanese steamers running to Seattle and Tacoma, stating that his steering gear was out of order, also the tarpaulins were being washed away from the hatches, and listen. I read the message and put it on file.

The wireless man said, "What does he mean by listen?"

"You go back to your wireless room and listen, and he will let you know what he wants, as soon as he finds out the condition of his ship."

So the operator went to his wireless room, and in about an hour the Japanese ship sent another call, "Captain D. O. Killman, S. S. *Wawalona*. Steering gear no more longer work. Tarpaulins all swept into the sea. Water going fast into holds. Come and save my ship, passengers, and men."

It was a frightful night, and the sea was running mountain high. I called all the officers, also the engine room officers except the one that was on duty, telling them what was in the S.O.S. call. I asked them what they thought about going to the ship that was in distress. They all said they thought that the *Wawalona* would sweep herself clean, and we would be in worse shape than the Japanese steamer was.

When I came to the second mate and asked him what he thought about our going, his reply was, "I think as you do, sir."

I then told the engineer on watch to have a full head of steam, and when I moved the telegram for full ahead to give her all the steam. In a short time he said he was all ready. I watched the seas, and after there had been three heavy seas pass I rang for full ahead and hard to starboard. The ship went fine without doing any harm, shipping only two heavy seas.

We had run some eighteen miles when we got another wireless call saying that his steering gear was fixed, and he was all right and could fix his hatches. I slowed down and hauled my ship back to the westward, the wind moderating, and in a few hours we were going full speed with the weather becoming fine again.

I made the land or light at a point north of Tokyo Bay and went south along the coast. At three in the afternoon I received an S.O.S. call from the S. S. *Deuel*,[5] a new ship on her first voyage from Seattle bound for Yokohama, giving his position ashore and wanting me to come and try to haul him off. I had to go, as he was one of the Shipping Board ships, and I told him that I would come. I could see smoke ahead, so I called the ship and found out that it was the *West Inskip*,[6] another of the Shipping Board ships, and he said that he was going to the *Deuel*. I kept on, and before dark I could see the ship ashore and the *West Inskip* also.

I went up close and anchored. The *West Inskip* had a big steel hawser on board the *Deuel* and hove taut. He had his anchor far out ahead. The captain told me by wireless that he was going to get a pull on the *Deuel* at high water and wanted me to stay. If he could not haul the *Deuel* off alone, we both would have a try at hauling him off in the morning. I had the searchlights on the *Deuel* and knew that it was impossible to haul the steamer off, as his bow was high up on the beach and his stern nearly under water. I watched when the *Inskip* tried to haul him off, but to no avail.

The next morning the mate of the *Deuel* came on board, and the mate met him at the gangway. He wanted to see the captain, and the mate told him that I was in the chart room. He at once came to the chart room and told me that his captain wanted me to put a hawser on board so that both steamers could get a pull on the *Deuel* at the same time. I told him that it would be like trying to haul the Rock of Gibraltar out into the Mediterranean. I asked him how he got there, if it was thick fog, and he said that it was clear. So then I asked him if he knew where the ship lay now, as she was not where they said she was.

I showed him the chart and asked him to tell me where the ship was, and he did tell me where he thought she was. Then I showed him the exact spot, and he was fourteen miles out. I asked him why they did not throw their deckload overboard, but he said they would not do that. I told him that I would see the captain of the *West Inskip*, and he took his departure and went back to his ship.

In a short time the captain sent his boat after me to come on board of the *West Inskip*, which I did. He was a young man and seemed to know his business. After we went to his chart room I asked him if he had seen the captain of the *Deuel*, and he said only at a distance. I asked him to send for him, as I would like to talk to him; so he sent for him, and shortly he was on board.

We received him with all due respect and told him that we were sorry to see him in trouble. "Captain," I said, "you expect to get your ship off from the beach where she now lays, I suppose?"

He replied that he did, and I asked him if her No. 1 hold was full of water. He said it was but that there was no water in No. 2 hold.

"Why do you not throw your deckload overboard?"

He said that he had sent a wireless message to Yokohama asking what to do, and I then told him that I was more than surprised that a man, master of a new ship that cost about one million dollars, would want someone to tell him to throw overboard a deckload of lumber that was worth but a few thousand dollars. I then asked him what he was doing there, anyway, and told him that if his wireless message was correct he did not know where he was. But he said that he did, because his mate had told him.

"Now, Captain," I said, "are you going to throw your deckload overboard or not? It is no use wasting time here, as I can do you no good, and your ship will never come off that shore until that deckload is off. There are some one hundred Japs around your ship that want to work, and you, as master, should at once get rid of that deckload. If you will not start immediately, I will have to bid you goodbye. After the deckload is off, I am sure that the ship that has a hawser on board of you will be able to tow you off if there is no bad weather.

"It would be taking too many chances for me to go below the *West Inskip* with a ship of my size and drawing such a draft of water, and I know that it would do no good for ten ships to pull on you as you now lay."

He said he would not throw his deckload off until he got orders from his agents at Yokohama, and I said goodbye and good luck. Going on board the *Wawalona*, I heaved anchor and sent a message to Yokohama giving the time of leaving the *Deuel* and the time that I would arrive in Yokohama. I arrived that night and went directly to the wharf where I was to discharge a part of my cargo.

Two days later the *Deuel* came in, but the deckload was not there. There were two large holes in her bow after she landed her cargo. From there she went to Kobe, and after discharging she was docked and repaired; but her master was relieved of his command.[7]

After I finished in Yokohama, I went to Kobe,[8] for I had some three thousand tons for there, and the agent had agreed to take three thousand tons of cement from Moji, Japan, to Manila. We had but little time to get there and get it on board before New Year's Day, as they have seven days of holiday in Japan at New Year's. We were working night and day to try to get to Moji in time, and the agent came on board as we were finishing. It was on a Sunday at two in the afternoon, and it had been a very stormy night and still blowing very hard. He came up on the bridge where I was at the time and asked me what I thought of the ship getting out of the harbor in a storm like that.

I told him that I thought it was taking a lot of chances, as the ship's wheel was half above water. No one knew how she would act, and I would advise not to try it. As we were there the pilot who was to take me out came up on the bridge, and the agent asked him what he thought about taking the ship out. He said it was all right, so I agreed that it was possible, but that before we left I wanted them to sign a statement of what I had told them in regards to taking the ship out of the harbor. I went to my room, called the purser, and dictated the statement. The agent signed all three of them, keeping one, although I knew it would not help me if the ship should get into trouble, as the underwriters depend on the captain, not the agent.

The tug came, the agent bade me goodbye, and we were to start for Moji. The tug put his hawser on board on our port quarter and went ahead. When we were as far away from the wharf as we could go, the pilot let go the hawser. I had told the chief engineer to have all the steam that the boilers could stand, and when we ordered full ahead or astern, to give her all he could. He saw the place the ship was in and, like myself, was in doubt as to whether the ship would handle in the heavy gale that was blowing.

The pilot ordered full ahead, helm a starboard, and the ship started ahead but would not pay off the slightest bit. Then he ordered full astern, but the ship would not answer her helm, blowing fast sideways with the wind on the port quarter. He at once said to let go both anchors, but I said that would never do, as we would go down on those new steamers at anchor. The pilot ran off the bridge, the engine going full astern, the breakwater some eighty feet astern, and the ships lying to anchor only a short distance off.

After we had gotten out clear of the breakwater and with plenty of room, I thought I could turn the ship, so I ordered full ahead; but it was no use. I let go the port anchor, and by the time I had one hundred fathoms of cable out the ship had come head to the wind, and the only thing I could do was to wait until the wind moderated some. At four in the morning, I told the engineer and mate that we would have another try.

"Where is the pilot?"

The mate said he was in the dining room lying down, and so I had him called, as I had not seen him since he ran from the bridge. He came to the bridge where I was, and he said, "Captain, we cannot go. Too much wind."

"It was all right yesterday when we laid at the dock, you told the agent, but as soon as you saw that the ship could not be handled you ran away. We will leave now and I think we will be able to get into the Inland Sea, where the water will be smoother."

I told the mate to heave up his anchor, and I was able to get steerage way on the ship, but she would take two points on each side of the course. We got into smoother water, and the wind went down after sunrise, so we started to make good time. The pilot was very frightened that I would report him and that he would lose his pilot papers. I do not know what they would have done to him, as the Japs are far from being scared of most anything that comes along. I told him that I would say nothing, as it would not do me any good, and I was sure it would do him a lot of harm.

We arrived in Moji during the night, and at eight a.m. we started to take in cement. I had until midnight to take thirty-two hundred tons, and I saw that I could not do it, so I called the first officer and told him that I wanted the boatswain. He was a man past fifty years of age who had been second mate with me years before in a sailing ship, and he was all sailor. He came to me at once, and I told him to single the gear on the No. 2 hatch, and we would use a swing gaff as we did in sailing ships, and work from both sides. If it worked, we would single all the gears and would be able to get all the cargo in by midnight.

He did so, and it worked fine. The Japs were looking at it, and without saying one word they singled the No. 1 gear. In a short time we were working from sets of gear on each side, and by eleven that night we had it all in but one hundred tons. There was no more, so we sent our derricks down, and at three a.m. we left for Shanghai, China. It was bitter cold when we got out into the Japan Sea, the wind blowing hard from the north. It was not long before the ship was all covered with ice, but after getting the cement aboard, the ship was able to meet anything.

We arrived at Shanghai in due time. After discharging what cargo we had, we left for Hong Kong[9] and had fine weather down, arriving just in time to get in, as it was a closed port; no ships were allowed to enter after sundown or leave before sunrise. The next morning we discharged what cargo we had and were to take two hundred thousand feet of teakwood logs. The agent told me that they were expecting a strike by the Chinese against the Japs any moment, but to get the logs all in if possible.

Everything went fine, until at a moment's notice there was not a Chinaman to be seen. We had most of the logs in, however, and what was left they came and towed away. We shifted that night to the oil dock, and at sunrise we left for Manila. We arrived at Manila too late to be received by the customs, but the next morning at sunrise we were received and went directly to the wharf, starting to discharge the cement and general cargo that we had. I was frightened that there might be a lot of damage to the cement, but when it was all out they came to me and said it was in the best condition of any that they had had for a long time.

"Well," I told them, "you are easily pleased. I know it is not as good as it should be, but I had to rush the loading to get it on board, and it turned out better than I expected it would."

They sent for me to come to the office, and when I got there they told me that there were a Major and a Captain and his wife from the army[10] who wanted to go to Shanghai in my ship, but that they did not want anything to do with them. I told them that if they wanted to go and if there was any trouble as to their going, they would commandeer the ship, as it belonged to the US government.

They asked me where I could put them, and I said I would have to take the wireless men from their room and give the captain and his wife that room, and the major would have to use the hospital for his. I thought they would be a lot of trouble, so I told the first officer that if any of them came on board to show them where they would be located, but that I would be on shore at all times. They came several times, but I did not see them, as the first officer would tell them that I was on shore.

The day that I was to sail, I told the officer to tell them to come on board that day for supper, as we would get away about eight that evening. After lunch I had to go on shore to clear the customs and sign bills of lading, and on returning to the ship I went directly to my room and put on my uniform. As I came on deck, the captain's wife saw me and at once came to me, saying, "At last I have found the captain of this fine, big ship. My name is Amis Ewell, what is yours, Captain?"

I told her, and she said, "You will come and meet the major and my husband, won't you?"

I did, as they were aft on the deck that my rooms were on, and she made me acquainted with them. We passed the time of day, and I then said that I must go as I had business to attend to.

"Captain, before you go, we have a large pitcher of ice water in our room and some fine Scotch whiskey," said the lady, "and we will all have the first drink to our meeting together. Do come, Captain."

She took my arm, and I went with them. She passed me a glass and the liquor, and I put the slightest bit in the glass, and when she told me it was real good liquor I thanked her and said I had plenty. We drank, and then she passed me the bottle and said that we would all have one more. I answered, "It is real kind of you, but you would not like to see me under the influence of liquor, would you, as I have to take this ship to sea tonight."

"You are right," was the answer, "but we will take one more and excuse you, as I am sure that dinner will soon be served."

They were very fine people, and it was very interesting to me that the lady had been in France as a detective for the United States for a long time before we entered the World War. I made hotel arrangements for them by wireless as at that time it was hard to get accommodations in Shanghai. After arriving, I took them to the US Consul and paid them off, as they had signed the ship's articles, and the lady got a great kick out of it as she said she would have her discharge framed and hung in her living room.[11] I then took them to the Consul General's room, introduced them, and left. They begged me to have dinner with them that night, but I was unable to do so, and we parted, not to meet again.

I left for Kobe[12] after landing some freight and taking some on board and did not go to the dock. The agent came on board, and he was more than pleased to see me, as he had seen the ship go from the dock and go sideways out of the harbor and then anchor, and he could not see how I got the cement in in such a short time. After discharging and taking what freight there was, my papers came on board, with a letter from the agent saying to sail for Yokohama.

I told the clerk that it was too thick fog to sail, and that was what was detaining the Canadian mail boat. He said that her master would not leave until the fog cleared some, and I said I would go when it was safe and not before. In some seven hours, it cleared some, and I took my departure for Yokohama, arriving in due time.

I went directly inside the breakwater and discharged the teakwood logs that I took at Hong Kong and what other freight there was, then sailed for Portland, Oregon. I arrived there safely after making the round voyage five days inside the allotted time, which was ninety days.[13]

Nome
Bering Sea
CANADA
NORTH AMERICA
Seattle
UNITED STATES
San Francisco
Los Angeles
Santa Rosalia
Gulf of California
MEXICO
Galveston
Stockton
New York
Wilmington
Azores
NORTH ATLANTIC OCEAN (THE WESTERN OCEAN)
Hawaiian Islands
Tehuantepec
Martinique
Galápagos Islands
Panama Canal
ECUADOR
PERU
Callao
SOUTH AMERICA
BRAZIL
Arica
Iquique
Antofagasta
Santos
CHILE
Valparaíso
Buenos Aires
ARGENTINA
SOUTH ATLANTIC OCEAN
Cape Horn
Staten Island
see inset
FIJI
Suva
Noumea
New Caledonia
Palmerston Island
Tahiti
Tonga (Friendly Islands)
PACIFIC OCEAN
Cook Strait
NEW ZEALAND
Westport
FIJI
Viti Levu
Ovalau Island
Levuka
Suva
Gau
Lamiti
Lakeba Island
Vanua Vatu
Kadavu Island
Ono Island
Kabara Island

The World

The World (continued)

Maine and the Northeast Atlantic Coast

Indonesia and the Philippines

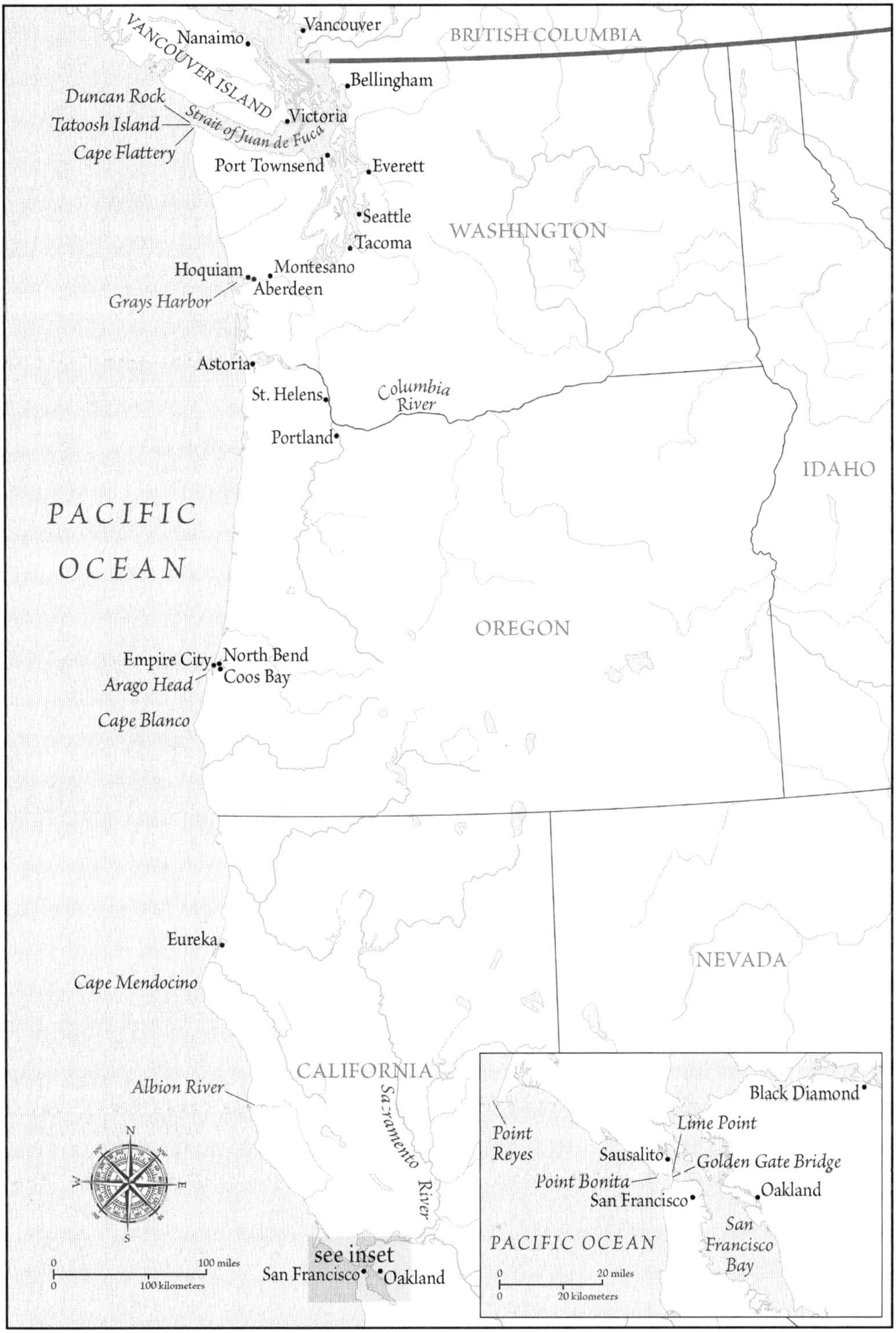

The West Coast from Vancouver, British Columbia to San Francisco

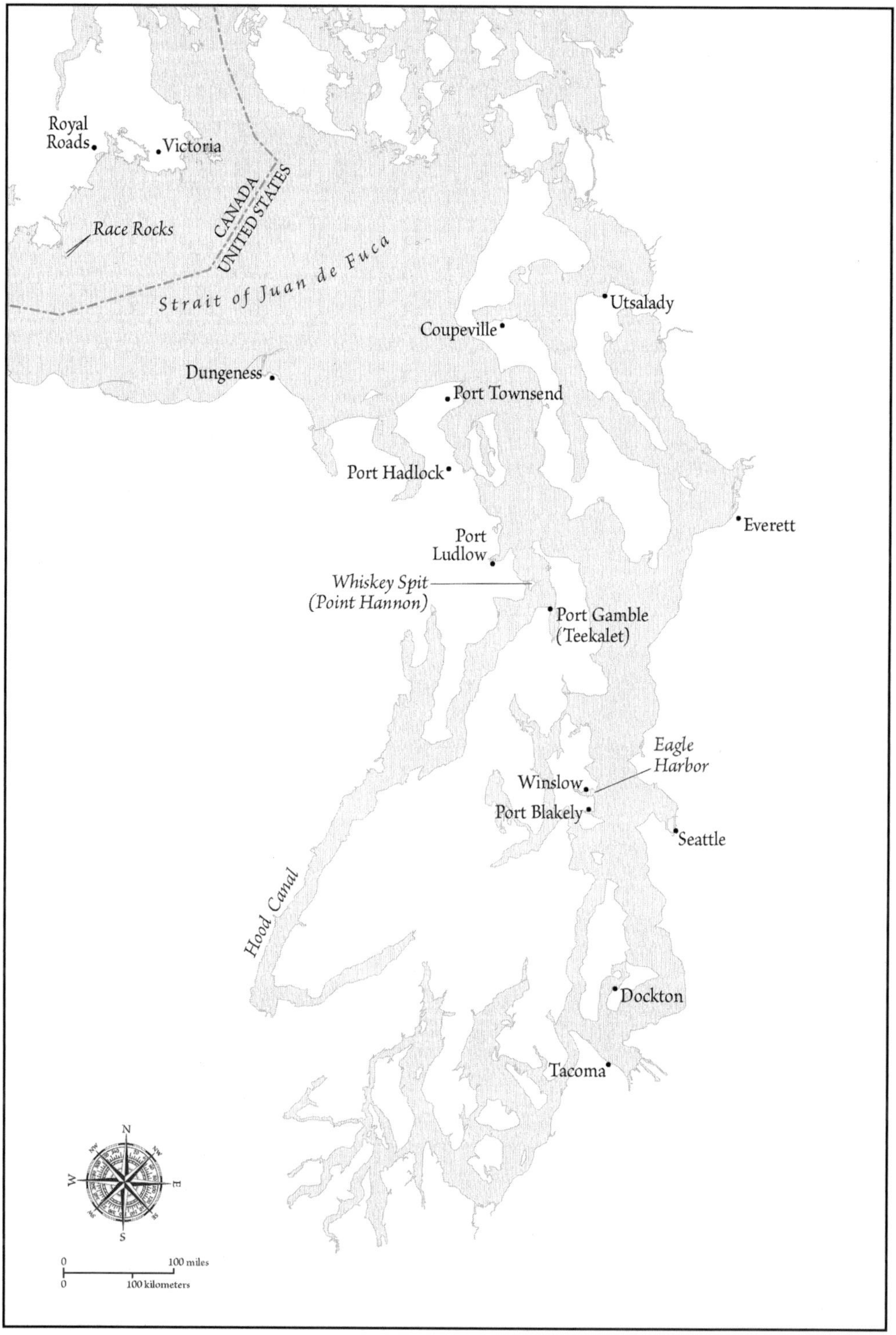
Royal Roads
Victoria
Race Rocks
CANADA
UNITED STATES
Strait of Juan de Fuca
Utsalady
Coupeville
Dungeness
Port Townsend
Port Hadlock
Everett
Port Ludlow
Whiskey Spit (Point Hannon)
Port Gamble (Teekalet)
Eagle Harbor
Winslow
Port Blakely
Seattle
Hood Canal
Dockton
Tacoma
N
E
S
W
0
100 miles
0
100 kilometers

Puget Sound

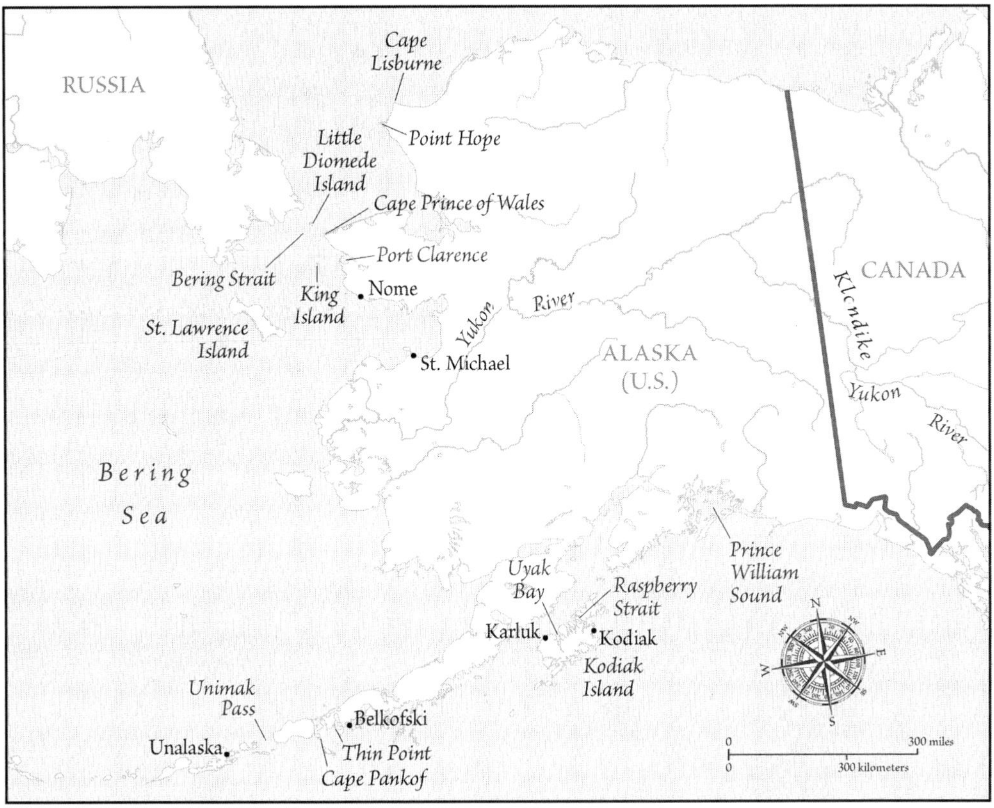

Alaska and the Bering Sea

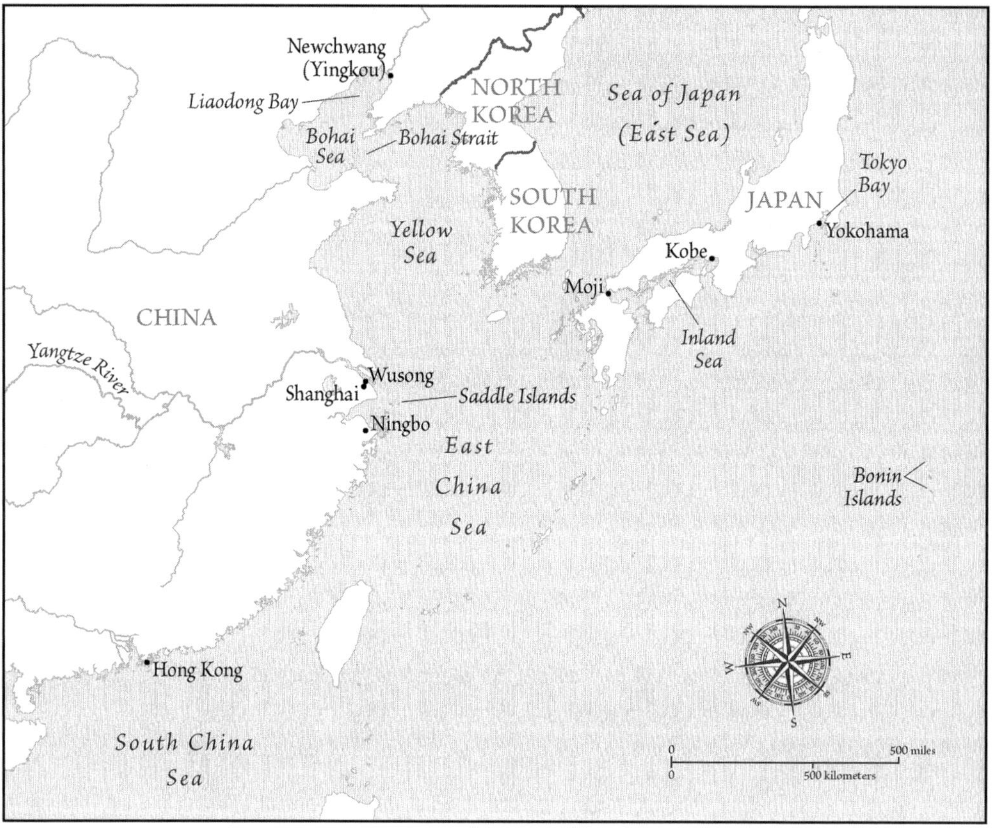
Newchwang
(Yingkou)
Liaodong Bay
Bohai Sea
Bohai Strait
NORTH KOREA
Sea of Japan
(East Sea)
SOUTH KOREA
Yellow Sea
JAPAN
Tokyo Bay
Yokohama
Kobe
Moji
Inland Sea
CHINA
Yangtze River
Wusong
Shanghai
Saddle Islands
Ningbo
East China Sea
Bonin Islands
Hong Kong
South China Sea
N
E
S
W
0
500 miles
0
500 kilometers

The Far East

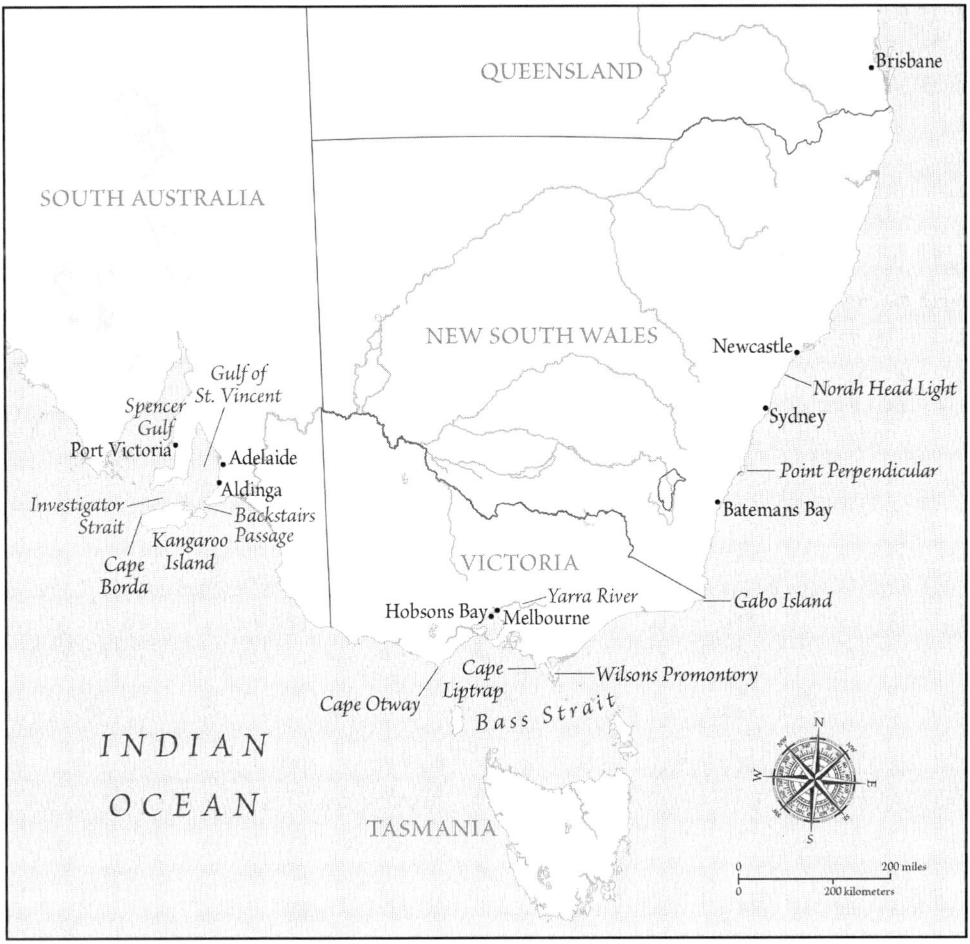

South Australia and New South Wales

20 A Lost Rudder

After the *Wawalona* was loaded, I resigned[1] and went home to Tacoma. In a few days I took command of a new four-masted schooner that had been built at Dockton, a short distance from Tacoma. The *Ella A.*[2] was one of the largest four-masted schooners, over fifteen hundred tons register. When I took command, she had started to load at Everett, Washington, even though not finished, but by the time the ship was loaded she was finished, or was by the time I was ready to leave Port Townsend.[3]

It was very hard to get men at the time, and the law said that I must have so many certificated seamen, but I could not get them. As the ship was getting a large freight, the shippers wanted me to get away. The insurance on the cargo was heavy, and every day counted, so I cleared and paid the fine of five hundred dollars to the customs house. I dictated a letter to Washington, D.C., explaining the whole affair in a very simple way, but stating the truth, and asked the government, if there was any justice to what I had explained, to return the fine.[4]

I sailed, not expecting to hear any more about it, but on my arrival in Adelaide, Australia, I got a letter from Port Townsend, from my agents there, telling me that the fine had been returned and enclosing a letter that the government wished to be sent to me, thanking me for the way that I had explained the case.

I towed to sea to start on a long voyage for Adelaide with a lot of work to be done and one of the poorest crews one could imagine. The ship was very heavy, and the sails were very large and heavy to handle. The ship handled as well as one could expect, but she did not sail very well in light winds, though in strong winds she did very well.

I had a fair passage to the Line, but the southeast trades were light, and the *Ella A.* was not a light weather ship. I made the coast of Australia near Sydney and had made a very good passage, but the hard part was yet to come—to get through Bass Strait, as the wind is mostly from the west and the current as a rule is against you.

After having one gale from the west, the wind came from the east, and I had a fine run through the straits into the Indian Ocean by Cape Otway, and then I had head winds and fog until I got to Spencer Gulf. There I had the wind fresh and fair ahead. I got abreast of the Backstairs Passage, and it shut in thick fog, so I made up my mind to anchor, as I knew where I was. In the morning the fog cleared away. It was still very hazy, but I heaved up the anchor. The glass had gone down during the night, and the wind started to increase. Soon I had to come down to three lower sails, fore staysail, and jib.

At two o'clock it was blowing hard. The haze cleared, and I found I was only some three miles from the beach. I at once saw that I was in a bad position, with no way to get out of it, as the ship would neither tack nor wear around. I would soon be on the beach, with the wind and sea increasing fast, so I said I will anchor.

I called the first officer and told him what to do. The anchor was a patent one, with a large steam windlass, and I had steam on, as I did not know what time I might need it. They took in the foresail and hauled the headsails down, and I brought the ship up to the wind. When her headway was stopped, I let go the port anchor, shifted the wheel, and set a little off the fore staysail, paying off her head and letting go the starboard anchor.

I gave the ship ninety fathoms of chain on the port anchor and eighty on the starboard and furled all the sails, the ship lying fine and not dragging any. I thought I was all right and that the wind would go down some with the sun, but I was wrong. It blew harder, and the sea was getting much worse. The ship was dragging her anchor slightly in the squalls, and at seven-thirty that evening a heavy squall came, and the port chain parted on the windlass. The riding pawl was down, and it was carried away and thrown overboard. It must have weighed fifty pounds, and I saw that I was surely up against it.

I at once got the stream anchor on the forecastle head, with the kedge anchor back of the stream anchor, and bent a new ten-inch hawser and a new six-inch hawser on them and got them overboard. It was very dark, and the anchors were heavy, but we soon had them overboard. The ship was taking her chain over the windlass on the starboard side, as the compressor would not hold the terrific strain when the heavy squalls came, and they came very often, with snow and hail.

We went below in the chain locker and put a fourteen by fourteen piece of timber on the chain, taking two round turns with the chain and lashing the chain together, also the end of the chain to the forward stanchion. It was not long before the ship had one hundred and twenty fathoms of chain out on the starboard anchor, yet still was dragging slowly in the squalls. We put out one hundred fathoms of line on the stream and kedge anchors. It was but a few moments until they got an even strain on them, and the ship stopped dragging.

I felt sure that the ship would ride it out safely. At midnight a very heavy squall came, and the two big lines parted like pieces of thread only a short distance from the ship's bow. Well, I said, this ends the long, long trail. The stream anchor must have hooked a rock, as it took a horrid lot to carry away those two new lines. There was nothing I could do but wait till the ship went into the rocks, as there was a reef of rocks astern, and we were getting closer all the time. Back of them was a cliff one hundred feet high, straight up and down.

I called the carpenter and told him to have a large cold chisel and a big sledge hammer ready, and if we got too close I would cut the bow cable so the ship would go up as high as possible. He did so, and came and told me he was all ready when I gave the order. I had the mate and second mate with the deep-sea lead on the bottom to see how much she was dragging. I went into the cabin and could hear the rudder groaning, and I knew at once that something was wrong with it. All at once it stopped, and I knew it was gone, but there was nothing to be done. So I thought I would write to my wife and tell her how things were with me, and if I had to go on the rocks I would put the letter in a bottle, cork it up tight, throw it overboard, and hope that it might be picked up.

I was sure if it was it would be mailed to her. I could not see any chance for me. Some of the young men that I had might have been saved, but my chances were one in a million.

At three in the morning we had the hardest squall yet. The ship put her whole bow under water, and the green sea came aft and over the stern. There must have been hundreds of tons of water over her. I thought she had struck a rock, but the cable held, and that was the last heavy squall. It started to clear, and I could see stars coming out and the wind getting lighter. We were, say, not more than half a mile from the land when daylight came, but the wind had gone down. Also the sea was not one eighth as bad, and I was sure I was all O.K.

I was thirty-five miles from Adelaide. It is a beautiful country, fine farms and lovely houses. At daylight I set the American flag with the ship's number under it, and I was sure that I would be reported at Adelaide. I said nothing to anyone about the rudder being gone, but my brain was working as to how I could get the ship to Adelaide without a rudder. I had it all worked out if the wind only would come up the gulf, and I was sure it would, since the wind, as a rule, came directly up the gulf.

About two p.m. I saw smoke coming down the gulf. In a short while I could see it was a tugboat. I was more than pleased, as the ship at the time was in a bad position. I was willing to pay a good sum to get her to port, and I knew it would be no easy job to tow the *Ella A.* without a rudder. As soon as the tug came close enough I saw it was one of the Adelaide Steamship Company's tugs.

She came under my lee, and the captain said, "You are in a bad place, Captain. I am getting my big hawser out and will be ready to take you in tow. You have lost one anchor and chain."

I made no reply to that, and he said that it was one of the worst storms that they had had in Adelaide for more than twenty years and had done a lot of damage. He asked if I had steam to heave my anchor up with, and I told him that I had or that it would not take but a few minutes when I wanted it.

"But you want steam very shortly, as I will soon have my hawser ready," he said.

"Will you kindly tell me what you are going to charge to tow this ship to Adelaide?" I questioned, and the reply was, "You don't need to worry about that, you will know soon enough."

"But I must know now," I told him. "I have never ordered a suit of clothes yet unless I knew what it would cost."

"But this is one suit that you are getting that you won't know what it is going to cost for several days, Captain," he said.

I then said, "I think you are mistaken about that. I am willing to pay you a good price, but I must know what it is going to be."

"But you won't know from me what it is going to cost, and that is all there is about it."

"Well, Captain," I replied, "I am past twenty-one, you know."

The reply I got was that he did not care a damn if I was one hundred and one—I would do as he told me to do. That I could not stand, so I made one jump for the cabin and got my brace of revolvers and was back on deck. He saw that I had a large revolver in my hand, and he gave full speed ahead.

I called my mate and told him that I was going to bed, and not to disturb me unless it was necessary and to have no noise around aft. I knew my orders would be carried out. I had been without sleep for a long time, and the mate said, "Yes, sir, I will look out for the ship. You try and have a few hours' sleep."

So I went below and went to bed. The mate told me when I came on deck after sleeping some five hours that the tug came up under the bow, telling him he wanted to speak to the captain. He told him that I was asleep, and he would not disturb me; that he had insulted the captain and everyone on board; and then the mate turned and walked aft. The tug lay around for some two hours and then went back to Adelaide.

After midnight the wind came up the gulf, and I told the mate that when daylight came we would get underway and to have everything ready to make sail, with steam on the boiler. It was a fine morning, and the wind was fresh and fair up the gulf. I set the main and mizzen, and the mate came to me and said, "Captain, suppose the ship casts inshore? She will go into the rocks."

"Well, there will be no trouble for you as it is smooth. You can all get into the boat, and go on shore."

He went away looking as if he had done something that he wished he hadn't. I told him to heave in to thirty fathoms of chain, which he did, and I then set the foresail, hauling it well out over the port bow, as well as the fore staysail. I ordered a man to the wheel and to heave away. The anchor came up, and the ship cast from the danger until she was on the wind and did not pay off any more. I walked aft, looking at the rudder head.

"Well," I said, "the rudder is gone. That will do. You go with the rest of the gentlemen."

I told the mate to shift all the boom tackles to windward, haul the main and mizzen to windward, and set the jib and flying jib. The ship started ahead but would not pay off, going sideways up the gulf. When she got too far offshore, I hauled the foresail well to windward and hauled down the flying jib and jib. Then she would go astern, but drifting fast up the gulf.

I handled the ship all day this way and was making good time sideways toward Adelaide. The wind became fresh with hail and snow in the squalls. I was able to keep the ship exactly where I wanted to. She was nearing her port by going sideways, and at twelve-thirty that night I anchored on the receiving ground at Port Adelaide.[5] There was a strong wind blowing and a nasty sea on. I gave the ship eighty fathoms of chain to be sure it would hold, as when one anchor is gone one cannot take any chances.

In the morning the doctor came on board, and what a reception he gave me! "No rudder, only one anchor, how did you put this ship exactly in the center of the receiving ground?"

I told him that it was not hard to do if you only knew how.

"You should know how, Captain Killman, and you have beaten the Adelaide Steamship Company out of the big salvage that they went after."

He asked me why I didn't take the tug, and I told him that we could not agree.

"He wanted the ship and cargo, I suppose?"

I told him that it looked like it, but that I got mad and it was all off, and that I had gotten there without him and it was much cheaper. He left, and it got so rough that the customs did not come until nearly dark. After I finished with them I went ashore, as a launch came off after me, and my agent was awaiting me at the Semaphore. We went to Port Adelaide, and he had a berth for me. I ordered three tugs to take me up the river, one on each quarter and one ahead, and after cabling my arrival home to the owners, and the trouble I was in, I went back to the ship, as we were to dock the first thing in the morning.[6]

The tugs came, and the pilot to take us up the river, and one of the tugs was the one that came to tow me to Adelaide. After they were fast the captain of the tug asked me if he could come aboard, and when he came he asked me if he could speak to me in the cabin. We went below and I said, "Now, Captain, what is it that I can do for you?"

"I want to tell you that it was not my fault that we did not tow you to Adelaide, and I am very glad that you got your ship here safely. You have done something that no one here has ever heard of."

"Well, I was lucky to have the wind just the right way, too," I said.

"I did as I was told to do from the Adelaide Steamship Company's office," he said. "They had a straight salvage. A ship without a rudder and one cable and anchor gone would have been a lot of money for them. I do not want you to feel hard against me, as I have worked many years for them, but I am resigning tonight. I will not try to put any shipmaster in a hole again."

I told him that I thought it was correct for the Adelaide Steamship Company to send a tug for me, as I was in need of one very badly, and I was willing to pay well for their services, but I well knew what it meant if I took their hawser without a bargain. It was straight salvage, and that was a lot of money, as the ship was fully insured. The cargo also, I am sure. And, on the other hand, if I had made an error and lost the ship after having a chance to get a tow, I would have been to blame, and the underwriters would have barred me from taking charge of any ship again. But as long as I saved them a large sum of money, they will laugh and say that I must be a good sailor.

But the tug captain left the Adelaide Steamship Company, as he said he would.

After I had gotten to the dock and the ship made fast, we sent the gear up to start to discharge. In the morning I had to go to Adelaide to the Consul to deliver my ship's papers, get my mail, and note a protest that would have to be extended. The Consul received me in fine shape and wanted to know how I got the ship there. I told him that it was not so hard if you only knew how.

"You must know how, for there is no one here that has ever heard of anything like it before. I thought the Adelaide Steamship Company would own one half of the ship and cargo this morning, when they phoned me that they had gone after the ship."

I told him that I was more than willing to pay well to get towed, but I got no chance to talk. But when the captain of the tug got insulting, it made me mad, and I couldn't believe him when he said that my owners had sent the tug.

"But, Consul, my troubles have not begun yet," I said. "There is no drydock here large enough to haul my ship out, and I am most sure that the rudder braces have gone from the rudder post. I hear that the rudder is on the beach only a short distance from where I was anchored,[7] and I must go tomorrow to see if the pintles are on the rudder and to get the size of it. It will be an all day job, as I do not know how far we will have to walk. I will take Mr. McFarlane with me, as I was told that he was the best shipwright in Adelaide."

He told me that I had gotten the best man, as he had looked into it, thinking that I might be a stranger, and that he was more than willing to give me any assistance that he could at all and at any time. I then told him that my ship had been chartered to load coal at Newcastle and was getting a big freight. But coal freights had dropped by more than half, and the cancelling date was not giving me but little time, and where was I going to get a rudder stock?

"Well, Captain Killman, you have a lot of trouble ahead of you, I can see, but I am sure you will get out of it. Anyone that has done what you have done will make a way somehow," he said.

"That may sound all right, but I cannot do impossibilities, that is sure, and where am I going to get a cable to fit my windlass?"

"Well, Captain, the only thing that you can do is to leave no stone unturned, and I am sure you will not; but you must not worry too much as you got your ship here without the loss of any lives and went through the heaviest gale that has been here in over twenty years. Your owners and underwriters will surely appreciate what you have done, more especially the underwriters."

"They are my last thought, as I know them very well of old. They take all that they can and give as little in return."

"You are right about that, but we must have them." The Consul was a fine man and was ready at all times to give his opinion if I asked him.

The next day I started for where the ship's rudder was. It was a long ride, and we had lunch after getting down close to where the ship had lain at anchor and where the rudder had gone. We got a man to show us the way to where the rudder lay, high and dry, a long way up from any water. It had been thrown way up on shore by the heavy sea. The rudder pintles were all intact, but some one had started to take them off, as they would sell for a lot of money.

We got what measurements we wanted and got hold of the sheriff of that district, notifying him of what was going on, and he said, "You will have no more trouble, as I will keep an officer there night and day until you have gotten everything you want."

He did so, and we got back late that night and sent men the next day to get the pintles off the rudder. I found a diver locally who was very highly recommended by the Adelaide Steamship Company and others whom he had been diving for, and he went down and reported that all the braces were gone from the rudder post. The first thing was to get a pattern so that we could get new ones made. It took him several days, and to this day I do not know how he was able to get the patterns and have them come correct as he did.

I would talk to him two or three times every day, and he would say, "Captain, I will do a good job and give you a certificate when I am finished."

I told him that would be fine, but I couldn't see what good his piece of paper would do if the rudder braces came adrift, running my easting down in the middle of the South Pacific Ocean. The ship was classed in Bureau Veritas,[8] and their agent in Adelaide was an old gentleman, a very smart and good man. We would talk it over, and the only thing he could say was, "You are the one that would suffer if anything goes wrong; the diver is a government man and has papers to show."

We had to trust to luck; and we did. We sent a telegram to every lumber dealer in Sydney to get a piece of ironbark suitable to make a rudder stock. At last we found one, and it was to be shipped at once on one of the big coal steamers that was coming to Adelaide with a cargo of coal from Newcastle. We sent a telegram to keep it on deck, and the captain got the telegram but forgot to tell his first officer, and he put it down in the bottom of his big hold. Well, you can see how things work—you have framed them out correctly, but someone makes a blunder.

As soon as the diver got his pattern made for the rudder braces, the next thing was to get them made of the correct kind of metal. It was a sure thing that I did not know how, and I couldn't find anyone that did outside of this big machine shop, so I had to trust to his honesty; but he was a perfect gentleman in every way, and his work turned out one hundred percent.

The time was going fast, and I had cabled all the ports in New Zealand and Tasmania, also Melbourne, Sydney, Newcastle, and Fremantle for a cable without any success, as they had none to fit my windlass. The only place that was left was the Navy Yards, and that is a hard source to get anything from, as it would have to go through so many hands and so much red tape.

One morning, I read in the paper of the big French ship *Notre Dame d'Arvor* going ashore at Port Victoria.[9] She was from France in ballast to load wheat. The captain, coming in during the night, made an error, and his ship went ashore. Well, I said, that ship will have just the cable I want. The next day I saw by the paper that she had caught fire and burned. All the masts had fallen, and the wreck would be sold at auction.

The ship was bought by the harbormaster of Port Victoria, so on Sunday morning at four o'clock I started for Port Victoria by auto with two other gentlemen to see if there was any chance to get one of the cables. I had a spare anchor and would be allowed to go home without getting another anchor. I had gotten a stream and kedge anchor at Adelaide.

It was a hard ride, some one hundred and forty miles, and the road was very bad most of the way, so we could not make any time. We had sent a telegram ahead to a little hotel that we would be there at seven-thirty for breakfast, and they had a fine breakfast ready for us. It surely did taste good. They told us on our way back, no matter what time it was, they would be ready to give us some food.

We arrived at Port Victoria at noon, had lunch, and found the harbormaster. He was willing to sell one cable, but it was too rough to go off to the ship to see if the cable would fit my windlass. The harbormaster would have a pattern made of one of the links and take it to Port Adelaide the next day. It was the correct size, although a much larger size link, and I told him to make his price and if it was within reach I would take it. He did, and it was not any more than I expected, as they had me in a hole and there was no way out that I could see.

If I did not take that cable I would have to send home for one, with the expense and delay, and my coal charter would be gone. It looked to me as if I was going to lose it anyway, but I had to try my best to save it. The diver seemed to be doing his best under the conditions, and the water was so muddy I could not see how he could see. After a while he got the patterns made, and then I had to get them cast and see if it would be the correct metal after they were finished. The diver again started his good work and worked very faithfully, as he saw the fix that I was in.

The ship was finished discharging, and one good thing, the cargo came out all correct. I saw that it would be impossible for me to make Newcastle under sail. It could be done only if one had all the fair wind he could use to get there, so I made up my mind to see what I could get towed there for.[10] I went to the Adelaide Steamship Company, and they would not undertake it, as they had use for their tugs. So I went to Huddart, Parker, and they gave me a figure but would not guarantee to get me there in time to save my charter.

I cabled home to my owners, and they replied that the ship was in my hands. It would be three days before the ship was ready, if the rudder would ship and work. I explained to Huddart, Parker that we would have to wait to see how things turned out, and if the rudder shipped they would have time enough to get ready. They said they would and that there would be no delay on their part.

The manager of the Adelaide Steamship Company had sent for me to call at their office, which I did. I was taken to his private office, where he was told by one of the clerks that this was Captain Killman of the American schooner *Ella A*. He got up and shook hands with me, and the clerk left.

"Well, Captain, you look just as I thought you would. You have a very determined disposition, I can see. I want to ask you a few questions, if you don't mind. Are you a man of means, Captain, so that you are independent? Don't you know that you would have gotten a present of twenty thousand dollars if you had let the Adelaide Steamship Company's tug tow you to Adelaide? It would have been a straight salvage job under British law."

"Yes, I know that, and I do know that I would not have gotten any twenty thousand dollars from the Adelaide Steamship Company, as they are not giving one cent to anyone if they can help it; or at least they have had that name in my many years of coming to Australia."

"But Captain, I am the manager of this company and the biggest owner, and I am telling you the truth."

"Well, I got the ship here without your tug. I was willing to pay a good price, but when I was told what I had to do, that I had no voice in the matter, and that my owners had sent the tug out after me, I got mad. I am not used to being talked to that way."

"Captain, we lost a lot of money out of your not taking our tug, and you have lost a fine lot, as you are no more a young man. We are both getting old, and I am sure you know what underwriters are. They don't part with much if they can help it, but you certainly know how to handle your ship, as I have never heard of anyone doing what you have done."

I told him that everything turned out all right, but if it had not, well, I would have been the loser. He wished me good luck in all my undertakings, and we parted.

The day before I expected to get away, I was called to Adelaide. I went to the office of Lloyd's Underwriters' agent, introduced myself, and was at once taken to the man I was to see. He gave me a very warm reception.

"This is Captain Killman. Well, Captain, you look just as I expected you would. You are one of many. You would not let anyone tell you that you had got to do as they wanted. You are a good sample of the old Yankee.

"Sit down. I want you to tell me all about this whole affair and how you handled that ship without any rudder, as I am sure that it has not been done before. I have looked into it, and there is no record of anything like it."

Well, I told him how I did it, and he was more than interested.

"But, Captain, it was a bad night with snow squalls, yet you put that heavy ship exactly on the receiving anchorage."

"Yes, but I had the light to go by, and I had an azimuth bearing to put on my compass, so it was no trouble for me to know where I was by cross bearings, as it did not stay thick very long at any time, and we were not going through the water sideways very fast."

"I know, but your brain must have worked very fast, and you must have known that it could be done, or you would not have done it."

"Yes, I thought I could do it, as I studied on it that day and night, and it worked out exactly as I thought it would."

"Yes, or you never would have tried it. Now I am going to tell you what has been done in Sydney, Melbourne, and here. The underwriters in those cities representing Lloyd's of London have met and have made this report, saying that the underwriters in San Francisco should give you a present for what you have done. You saved them perhaps five thousand pounds, and certainly three thousand."

I told him that it was very nice of them, and I surely appreciated it, but I was sure that I would not get anything, as I was acquainted with them. They would take your money and pat you on the back, but when it came to paying out their money they would fight for one cent. I knew them very well.

"But, Captain, they surely will after they have received this letter signed by the men who have signed it."

"I do not think that they will even thank me."

"Well, we know that Lloyd's would."

He read the letter to me and told me to whom he was going to send it, with a copy to my owners, and after he had gotten what he wanted he said, "Captain, do you ever indulge in a drink of liquor?"

"Yes," I told him, "I came from the State of Maine, and everyone drank even if it had been voted dry before I was born."

We went and had a drink together, and then I went back to Port Adelaide. The rudder was shipped that night after some little trouble and found to work all right. The next day we finished late at night and cleared the customs for Newcastle. I got the ship's papers from the US Consul's office and bade him goodbye. He had done everything in his power to help me along and said, "You are making a hard fight to save your charter and have one chance out of a hundred. I truly hope you are lucky enough to get that chance, as you are deserving of it after what you have done and the way you have worked for it."

We parted, and I went back to Port Adelaide to my ship. I had to take thirty-five tons of coal for the tug on board in sacks, as he could not take enough to tow the *Ella A.* that distance, and that meant going in to some place to anchor while the tug came alongside and we put it on board. The next morning we dropped down to the outer harbor to get the tug to where we were going to make our start from. The tug came up under our bow alongside the wharf where we had made fast. I went forward and looked over the bow to see the tug that was to tow us.[11] The mate was taking a new hawser out of its coil, and I at once saw that he was doing it wrong, and I told him so. He said he knew he was, but that was the way the captain wanted it done.

I said, "I am afraid you will have trouble with it."

It was a water-laid hawser, and they had spliced a large thimble on it and had a fine steel wire to go on it, with a fine big shackle. The shackle to our anchor would not work, being the wrong shape. I lowered the starboard anchor down on the tug, and they shackled the wire onto my bow cable.

The papers of the tug's captain would not allow him to command the tug outside of harbor and bay work. They got a government man to take charge, an old gentleman. He came on board and had a code of signals made out that would apply to anything we would want without looking it up in the signal book and was much easier to use. I asked him if he thought he could make it so I could save my charter, and he said, "It is very doubtful, but you can depend on me to do all that can be done, and I am sure you will do your share."

We started, and it was a fine morning—not a breath of wind all day.[12]

At seven o'clock that evening, one of the men came aft and told me that the carpenter had dropped dead on the forecastle head. I went forward at once and found him in a fit. I had him taken to his room and looked over the bow, finding that the hawser had unlaid the steel wire that was on the end of the tug's hawser.

I signaled the tug to stop, and we had to get the hawser in on deck, take the wire off it, as the wire was ruined, and shackle the hawser to our bow cable. It was dark, and it took two hours before we were ready again to go ahead. I did not forget to give them a piece of my mind and told them that I saw them taking the hawser out of the coil wrong and told the men about it.

We went through the Backstairs Passage, and the next day we had a light fair wind and all sail set to help the tug. We showed our signals to every signal station that we passed, so they would report us in the papers. We got to Cape Otway in fair time, but the tug did not do as well as they expected it would. As we got into Bass Strait we got the wind light from the east, and it slowed us down. I set signals for the tug to shorten the hawser. I had fifteen fathoms of bow cable out and heaved it in, and the tug took in a lot of his hawser, as the water was smooth.

You could see the difference at once. The ship was making one and a half knots faster time. As we got to Wilsons Promontory, the wind came from the west and blew a heavy gale. The tug was shipping a lot of water. I had only a reefed mainsail set, as the tug could not keep away from us. We passed close to the light on the promontory, and the signal station could read the ship's name on the quarter. He waved his hat to us as we passed.

We were making fine time, although I did not know but that the tug would have to take us to an anchor on account of the heavy wind, but as we went to the east, the wind fell lighter. We made more sail and were making fine time; if the fair wind kept on, we would reach Newcastle in ample time. I was most sure that we would have to go into some bay and give the tug more coal, but if the fair wind kept up, he might have enough.

As we passed Gabo Island the wind fell calm, and in a short time was blowing from dead ahead. The tug could hardly make any headway. He blew for us to make sail, and we did set the lower sails. He stood offshore for some hours. Then we went on the other tack until we were close to the land; then offshore again. We were doing better than he could do if towing straight.

When he went back, he signaled that he must have coal. We went into Batemans Bay, getting in there just at dark. I was very careful to see that my compass was correct, and had everything in writing. We anchored, and the tug came alongside. My men worked as hard as they could to get the coal in. The captain came on board, and we went below, as it would take some time to put the coal on board.

"Well," he said, "it is impossible to make Newcastle in time to save your charter."

"It looks like it," I said, 'but I think this wind will come back from the west again before ten o'clock, as the barometer is going up, which is a good sign, and if it does we will have all we can do. But we'll see."

The wind had fallen calm in the bay while we were talking. He told me that his compass was out, and I told him the correct course out, as my compass was correct. In a few moments the wind was again from the west, and the ship was heading exactly out of the passage, so he set his course by my compass. We lost no time, and as soon as the last sack of coal was on board the tug, the anchor was up and we were on our way.

We had a fine fair wind all the rest of the way and at eight in the morning we were taking the pilots on board. It was ten a.m. before we came to an anchor,[13] and I immediately was on my way on shore with the captain of the tug. I went to the Caledonian Collieries office, as they were to furnish the cargo. It was just eleven o'clock when I went into the office. I knew most of the men there, and they all came and welcomed me to Newcastle once more.

I said I wanted to see the general manager, and they asked me if it wasn't the assistant manager that I wanted to see, but I told them I wanted to see the biggest man there and damn quick, as I had not much time left. They went to the manager's office and told him that Captain Killman wanted to see him. I was shown to his office and told him that I was to load coal from his mines, passing him my notice that I was ready to go under the cranes to load.

He looked at me and said, "You are the captain that towed from Adelaide, are you not? I will have to look up my charter party."

"You do not have to. I have one in my pocket that you can look at."

He looked at it and said, "You have your ballast in, have you not, Captain?"

"Yes, sir. I have it all floored over and will let it stay in."

"Your charter expires at noon today. You have done well and have taken a lot of chances. I have heard the assistant manager say that you were sure to lose. Now, Captain, you get your ballast out. I will give you a letter that I accept your ship."

"How can I get my ballast out, as they are all on strike?"

"You wait. I do not want you to lose one cent. You must have paid a big price to get towed from Adelaide, and the extra coal you will take will help pay for the long tow. You let me know every day how you are getting along. I have to cable London to find out what coal they want to put in your ship, and it will be late Monday before I get a reply, as this is Saturday."

I thanked him and took my departure. I at once went to the office of the man who handled ballast and found out the condition of affairs. There was a strike on at the time, but he would put it up to the head of the union to see if they wouldn't put my ballast out. I phoned the pilot office to see if they would move my ship to Stockton, and also phoned for tugs to shift the ship.

The ship was shifted at once to a ballast berth. I entered the customs; delivered my papers to the US Consul; got my mail from my wife, family, and owners; and found everything at home all correct. Monday they put my ballast out, and I reported to the colliery that was to load the ship, going to the manager and telling him that the ballast would be out that night.

He said, "Captain, I will not put your ship under the cranes for nine days. If I were you, I would go to Sydney and stay for at least one week, have a good rest, and get away from the ship."

Saturday night after I had docked, the crew that I had shipped in Adelaide wanted to be paid off, so I paid them all off Monday morning, and at three-thirty that afternoon I took the train for Sydney to get away from the ship, as I had been in one long constant worry and under a great strain. I stayed in Sydney for a week before coming back to the ship. I had no worry as I had a good mate, and in my absence he would not leave the ship.

On my arrival back, I found everything in good order. The mate complained about his ears and that his hearing was getting worse. I at once took him to a doctor that I was well acquainted with, and he said he must not go to sea any more, as if he did he would become stone deaf. So I had to let him go, much as I wanted him to stay, for he was a fine man. He had saved his money and was well fixed.

I got an old German as mate at the last moment. It was nearly impossible to get men of any kind to go in a sailing ship, and what one did get was nearly useless. The mate was in his room over half of the time, getting one hundred and fifty dollars per month, and I had to do his work.[14]

As soon as I got to Iquique, Chile, after a good passage across the South Pacific, I paid him off, and he went to the hospital. I did not see or hear from him for three years. When I came home one Saturday from where I was loading, I received a summons from the Federal Court to appear to defend a suit against me, as the mate had sued me in person for ten thousand dollars. I at once put the case in the hands of my lawyer. The mate had taken the papers out in some small city in the State of New York, and a lawyer in Seattle had the case. He was taken sick and died, and after three years more it was thrown out of court. I expect the mate died in the meantime, or at least he should have, as he was no good on this earth.[15]

I came to the Columbia River from Iquique, Chile, and went to Portland to drydock.[16] The agent of the San Francisco Board of Underwriters was there at the ship as soon as she was drydocked, and the work that had been done by the diver was classed as perfect in every way. In fact, it was as good as could have been done if the ship had been on drydock. The underwriters' agent talked to me about how I got the ship to Adelaide without a rudder and told me that he knew about the letters that had been sent to San Francisco by Lloyd's agent in Australia, and he said that he would like to get the present that I was sure to get.

I laughed at him and said, "I know those tightwads too well."

"You are making a mistake this time, Killman; you saved them a lot of money, and you are sure to get what Lloyd's folks of Australia said. You are entitled to every cent of it and more too, if I know anything about it, as no one has ever done anything like it before as far as I can learn. You surely must have known that you could do what you did before you let that tug go."

"Well, I won't say that I was sure of it, but I had been working the problem over and over in my mind, and I was nearly sure that I could make it. However, I would not have tried it if I could have gotten the tug at a good figure, as I was willing to. I knew that the ship was well insured, also the cargo; but I could not stand for the captain of the tug telling me what I had got to do, and that my owners had sent him out for me. It made me very mad, and then it was all up with the tug.

"I do know that if I had made a slip out of it, the underwriters would have blamed me for not taking the tug; and as I got through without taking the tug they will say we need all we can get our hands on, and let Killman slide."

21 Carrying Coal to Peru

After finishing in Portland, we towed to Grays Harbor to load lumber for Callao, Peru, arriving there on July the second, 1921, and starting to load the day after the Fourth. My manager told me he had gotten the letter from Adelaide and said I was surely entitled to all of what they said I should have. I finished loading a big cargo, but freights had dropped to just a small figure. I went to sea, and did not hear one word from the underwriters, and in fact I did not speak of it, so there were few that knew anything about my taking the ship to Adelaide without rudder and one cable, with three anchors gone and all of my big hawsers.

I made a good passage to Callao.[1] It had been many years since I had been there. A launch came out a long way, but he was not allowed to come on board. He gave me the harbor rules as near as he could. If you were not anchored inside a certain line, you must move in, and if you were anchored too far in, you must move out. Well, you see what one is up against, and all for the benefit of the old tugs that the government owns. I anchored in the correct place, but if the launch hadn't come out, I would have gone in too close, and it would have given the tugs a chance to move me out. One has no comeback, and you cannot go on shore until you have passed the doctor and customs.

The next morning I started to discharge outside at anchor, as I drew too much water to get into the basin. After I had put off some one hundred and fifty thousand feet of lumber in lighters, I went inside. They furnish all the lines to make the ship fast with, and as my ship was very heavy they used all new hawsers. At six o'clock one evening as we were discharging, I walked out the dock. It was very smooth when I went on shore. I was back in a little over an hour, and the ground swell was coming in something awful.

I had a hard time to get on board. The ship was running on the lines very hard, and it was not long before the big springs started to break.

The dockmaster was there with a large crew of men getting new springs out, but as soon as they were out the ship would make a heavy run when a big sea would come in, and they would go. I got my new hawser up, as it looked as if I would soon be adrift.

We lay only some sixty feet from a stone bulkhead, and if I should hit that it would do the ship a lot of damage. It was not long before the big new hawser that was shackled onto our bow cable parted. Then the ship was surely adrift. I got a heaving line ashore, got the hawser fast to the big mooring post, and told them to slack off the line from the offshore quarter, which they did.

I then got a bight of the hawser that was the ship's hawser ashore, and I did not try to haul them taut but only get an even strain on them. The ship would run within ten feet of the stone bulkhead, but the undertow would not let her go any farther. Once every year they have the same trouble, and there has been a lot of damage done to shipping when the ground swell comes, for it does not give out any notice.

It kept on for twenty-four hours, and then it smoothed down again, and we started to re-moor the ship. I got on shore and was presented with a bill for some five hundred dollars from one of the foremen.

"What is this for?" I asked, and he said for lines you have broken, and it is all the ship's fault as your bow cable parted.

"I do not think my bow cable parted, but we will see in a few moments."

The end was under water, and I told the carpenter to heave it up. He went to the steam windlass, and in one moment the end was out of water. My cable had not parted. I went to the dockmaster's office and asked him what the bill was for, and he said it was no use getting mad, that I would pay that bill to him before I left the port, and the less I said the better it would be for me.

"There are a lot of hard men around here, and you are not the man that you were twenty years ago."

"Well, I know that, but it will take a lot of you to frighten me, and I would advise you to pipe down. I am telling you that I am not going to pay you one cent, and I am going to make you look like a damn fool, for you are one if you think you can get five hundred dollars out of my ship," and I walked out of his office.

Then I started to think what I should do, as I was well aware he had a hard crowd. For five dollars they would lay me out, and there would be no redress; only one American gone, and that would be a big name for the man that did it.

I went to the American Consul and told him about the trouble I had had with the dockmaster and his gang. The Consul was a good friend of mine, and a very smart man.

"I am glad you came to me about this, Captain Killman. If anything happens, I will have something to work on, and I want this in writing."

He called his secretary, who took it all down in shorthand, and after it was finished he said he would type it down, after which I signed it.

"Now I am going to see the dock commissioners," said the Consul, "and they will want to see you after they have heard from me. You look out, Killman. Don't let any of these Peruvians get behind you so that they could have a chance to put a knife into you. They never will face you, that is a sure thing."

I told him that I would look out for myself and that I was well armed all the time. The next day I got a letter from the dock commissioners that they wanted to see me at a certain hour. I went, taking an interpreter with me, as I knew that they would talk in Spanish and that I would not be able to understand all that they said. They asked me all about it, and I told them the exact affair. They told me that they would want to see me again at two-thirty that afternoon if it would be convenient for me. I told them I could come, as I had no business to call me away that afternoon.

I was there on time, and in a few minutes the dockmaster came. When he saw me there he gave me a hard look, not knowing what he had to face, but he was as frightened as a little boy when late to school. He was told to sit down and was then told what I had told them, and they asked him what he had to say about it. He did not know what to say.

"You sent the bill to the captain, did you not? Your name is signed to it. Now, we want to know from you what this means. You know that you cannot hold the ship for the breaking of the lines, as he is paying for them every day. You, the one we depend on, we will give you one more chance. If any other complaint comes up in which you cannot prove that you are in the right, we will look for a new dockmaster."

He took his hat and left. They thanked me for what I had done, also for using my own hawser to hold the ship without any damage, and said they would take off dock charges for the days I was detained by the rough weather, which they did. I bade them good afternoon and started for my ship. As I was passing the dockmaster's office, one of his men came to me and said, "The dockmaster wants to see you, Captain."

I went to his office and asked if he wanted to see me.

"Yes," he said, "sit down. Captain Killman, this has all been a big error on my part, and I am not sure but that they will appoint a new man when they find one that they like."

"Well," I said, "the only thing I can say is perhaps that would be a good thing. You thought you would rob my ship out of five hundred dollars. You would have had to divide it among your thieves that you have under you, of course. You would have gotten the big share, and it is worth taking these chances. And as for those hard cases that you warned me against, you tell them for me that if they make one bad move I shall shoot to kill, as you have told me what they will do. Inasmuch as I am sure it is all bluff on your part, I do not care what you do, but take my advice and go straight with me and my ship; that is all I want of you."

"Captain Killman, this has taught me a good lesson, and you and I will never have any more trouble. I am going to ask a great favor of you, and also ask your pardon for what I have done, and I don't want you to hold any grudge against me. I am going to ask you not to say anything about this."

"It is nothing to me," I replied, "the ones you want to get not to say or do anything about it are the big men, the dock commissioners, and you have one chance, and that is to attend to your own business."

I got up to go, and he put out his hand and asked me to shake hands with him.

"Of course I will, and now come on board with me, and I will buy you a drink."

He was ready to go, and we both had a drink. He said, "Killman, your ship will be looked out for while you are here, and you will not have any more trouble with me."

"I am sure of that," I said, and he went to his office and I came ashore. You bet that they saw every line was at an even strain the rest of my stay at Callao. There was no more trouble; everything went smoothly as far as the dockmaster and his men were concerned.

I sailed for Grays Harbor and had a good passage, thirty-three days.[2] After I had crossed the Line and the calm belt, I got fine northeast trade winds, well to the east. The second mate came to the after cabin door and asked me if I would let him have a bottle of liniment. I asked him what was wrong, and he said he had slipped on the ladder going into the lazarette to get the skylight cover and hurt his arm. I gave him a bottle. He went to his room, and at midnight he took his watch on deck.

At four o'clock in the morning, when he reported to me the distance and the course the ship had made in his watch, he said nothing about his arm. At eight in the morning, when he came on duty again, the first mate came to me and told me that the second mate would not go to work. At once I sent for him and asked him what was wrong with him. He said his arm was broken, and I told him to come into the after cabin. I would see if it was broken and would set it if it was. He said he would not let me look at his arm and that I could not set it.

"Very well," I said. "You stay here until I call the first officer and two of the crew."

I called the first officer and told him to bring two of his men to the after cabin, which he did, and the second mate again refused to let me look at his arm and said he would not work any more. I immediately wrote up my official log, read it to the men, and asked him if it was correct. He said it was, and the two men and the first officer signed it, as I did. I had to take his watch the rest of the voyage.

It was blowing hard when I was in sight of the Grays Harbor whistle buoy, and the tug came out two different days, but the wind was so strong that he did not even put a hawser on board. The third day the wind fell light, and the tug took me in tow and towed me in. When the doctor came on board I told him about the second mate, and he called him to the after cabin and examined his arm.

"Yes," he said, "the small bone was broken about four inches below the shoulder, but it has grown together again and is a little out of place."

I asked the doctor if it would bother him, and he said it would not. I gave him a hospital permit if he should want it. As soon as I told the managing owner, he gave him an order to go to the Tacoma General Hospital and also an order for Dr. Whittaker to attend to him; but he did not go. The ship was insured against anything of the kind. I filled out the insurance blank, sent it to the insurance company in New York, and did not hear any more about it for three years.

On my arrival in the Sound after three years, I got a call from the lawyer who attended to the insurance business in the state, asking when and where he could see me, as he knew nothing about the case. A lawyer had taken it, suing the owners in person for fifteen thousand dollars, and the case could not be tried until I could attend. We met, and I told him all about it. It was to be tried in Montesano.[3] He had several pictures taken of the hatch, and when the case was to come up we were there; also my managing owner.

The second mate had a very smart lawyer from Seattle who got all the I.W.W.[4] cases that he could frame. He sued the owners, not the ship, to keep it out of the Federal Court. The case was tried, and the jury granted the poor second mate ten thousand dollars. The last time I saw the insurance lawyer, he told me that the second mate's lawyer had offered to settle for three hundred dollars. I then went away and did not bother to find out the final outcome on my return, as we had insurance against all such claims.

I had been back in Grays Harbor a few days when one evening I was at the managing owner's home. He told me that he had something to say to me, and I must promise to do as he asked me to and not to get mad.

"Very well," I said, "if it is in reason, I surely will."

He took from his pocket a check for me from the underwriters, for five hundred dollars.

"How long have you had it?" I asked him. When he said about a month, I asked him why he did not send it back to them and tell them to go to hell.

"Yes, I know you would have done that, and they would have been more than glad of it. You keep it. It is more than you expected. You surely have their number, Killman, but keep it."

I took the check, turned it over and endorsed it, passing it back to him and asking him to send it to my wife.

22 An Auto Accident

I lay in Grays Harbor some four and a half months and could get no freight that one could come out even on. One afternoon I was in the mill office, and the girl that attended to the telephone said, "Captain, you are wanted on the phone in Portland."

I went into the boss's room, as he was out, and replied to it. It was from the E. K. Wood Lumber Company, saying, "Killman, will you take a cargo of lumber to San Pedro, California?"

"Yes," I said, "if you will give enough so I can come out a little ahead."

"I will give you seven dollars a thousand."

I said, "All O.K.," but I had to take one hundred and fifty thousand per day, and I agreed to start loading at one o'clock the next afternoon at Blagen's Mill. I told the girl to get me Blagen's Mill on the phone, and I talked with Mr. Blagen, who told me where to berth. I asked the girl to say nothing about this to anyone and went away, as I had to get men to move the ship. I jumped into my car and was off.

I found men to come and help move the ship, and ordered the tug. Then I went to the stevedore and asked him what he would load the ship for, and he said he would have to have one dollar and thirty-five cents. I told him that it was too much and I would not pay it. He said I would have to, but I told him that I would show him, that I would load the ship myself.

"You cannot get men," he said, but I replied that I would have a try.

"I suppose I will have some trouble, but that is my maiden name anyway, so here goes for trouble. I might be sorry, it is hard to say, but goodbye—I have lots to attend to, and it is getting late."

I went to the hotel in Aberdeen, got long distance to Seattle, and got the man at once that I wanted to go mate,[1] telling him to take the midnight train and be on board in the morning. I also got a cook and a steward, and they all got away that night. At six sharp in the morning the tug and the men were there, and we at once shifted to the loading berth. When Mr. Shaw came to the mill in the morning at eight o'clock, he saw that the *Ella A.* was not there, and he went into the office and was told that the *Ella A.* was down at Blagen's Mill.

So he got into his car and came to the ship. He came on board just as I was getting up the derricks and asked what this meant. I told him that I was going to San Pedro and that the ship had to go on drydock before she could go on a long voyage, so I would go on while down in Pedro. I told him that I had closed the deal when he was not in the office and that I wouldn't pay what the stevedore asked. I was going to load the ship without stevedores, and I thought I could get men.

"We never had stevedores, years ago, and I am going to try it if you are willing."

My mate came while I was talking to Mr. Shaw; also the cook and steward. I told the mate to go ahead rigging the cargo gear, and that I would resign with thanks.

"Now I will go with you to the mill, if you are going," I told Mr. Shaw. "I want my car; also some breakfast, as I have been to work since five."

I told the mate about the steam winches, and then I went with Mr. Shaw. When we got to the mill office, we soon got hold of men by phone, and they said they would have a good gang of men at one o'clock to go to work, as the stevedore hired men from Hoquiam only when he did not have enough Aberdeen men. I reported to Mr. Blagen's office that I would be ready to start at one o'clock. They told me that they didn't think I could take in one hundred and fifty thousand a day, but I told them that this ship was different, with much larger hatches and different loading gear.

At one we started working two hatches, and at five that night I had taken in one hundred and three thousand. The next day I took in one hundred and ninety-eight thousand. Mr. Blagen came to me and said, "Killman, you have beaten me. I am most out of lumber, and I want to know if you will go back to your own mill for today, as there is a big steamer coming in. I will pay all the bills moving both ways."

I told him that I surely would, and the next morning I went back to where I had been lying and lay two days; then back to the mill to load. The men that had been working came to me and said that they were told not to work any more on the *Ella A.*, for if they did they would get into trouble. I told them to go to work and I would see that they would not get into any trouble on that dock.

I went to Mr. Blagen's office and told him that it looked as if they were going to take my men away, and I was sure someone would fall before I would.

"I will stay with you, Captain Killman. I own this property, and I will see him."

He called the boss stevedore and told him that he wanted to see him at once. The man came, and Mr. Blagen sent for me. I went to his office and asked the stevedore what he meant by telling my men not to work on the *Ella* and that they would get into trouble if they did not quit.

"I am afraid *you* will get into trouble if you don't stop," I told him. "Now I am giving you warning, and you take my advice. I have as much right to hire men in this country as you or anyone else, and I know how to load a ship with any cargo much better than you do, and you well know it. That is all I have to say to you."

Then Mr. Blagen told him that if he bothered my men in any way he would do all in his power to protect my interests; that he had no business around his mill unless he was loading a ship there; and that he would notify the police and have men there at once, which he did. I had business up town shortly afterward, and the boss stevedore came to me.

"I am very sorry that this has happened," he said, "and I don't want you to think that I was going to try to stop you from loading your ship yourself if you wanted to."

I told him he was a damn liar, and all I wanted of him and his gang was to stop at once. If he did not he might get into serious trouble, as I had big backing.

He said, "Captain Killman, you will have no more trouble. It has taught me a good lesson, and as I have known you and your disposition for so many years I will do no more."

"That is all I want," I told him, "but I advise you to go to Mr. Blagen and try to square yourself with him, as he is very mad."

"I will go at once." And he did.

When I got back to the ship, Mr. Blagen told me that he thought there would be no more trouble as the stevedore had been to him and asked his pardon. "But if there should be any more talk to your men, you can depend on this company to the last moment."

That was the last of it. None of the men were spoken to, and the loading went along fine.

One evening I met a friend of mine and asked him if he did not want a ride, and he said, "Sure, I do." We started for Aberdeen. Just as we passed out of Hoquiam into Aberdeen, we saw a fire engine a short distance to our right. The men were all standing around the engine, and it appeared they were out for practice, as there were no signs of fire. I had slowed down to about seven miles per hour, and we were close to Park Street. It had a wide parking space in the center of the street and a one-way road on each side. There was a gas station on the corner that obscured the street until you were abreast of it.

All at once I saw the hood of the fire truck coming at the rate of forty-five miles an hour. At that rate it would take one and a half seconds to hit me. There was nothing I could do except step on the gas. The fire truck was not blowing its siren, and it struck me just where I sat. The car was driven forty feet. It struck a tree in the center of the parking some three inches through and broke it off, and the fire truck's front wheels were up on top of my car's hood with me underneath.

My friend was thrown over fifty feet, and the only thing wrong with him was that his face was scratched slightly on one side. The fire chief was there in a moment with his men. The car was pressing into my left side and the battery was running into my face, but I was unable to move. The car caught on fire, but it was put out at once by the fire department. They got a sack over my face so I would not get burned too badly.

They had to jack the fire truck up first; then they had to jack my car up before they could get me out. The fire chief said he was sure it was a shipmaster by the language I used. They jacked the car on the wrong corner, and it was forcing the car down through my side.

I hollered, "You damn fools, jack on that starboard side!" The chief had been to sea and at once did as I said. By the time they got me out, many of my friends were there from Hoquiam, including my managing owner and several doctors. The ambulance was there, and they took me and laid me down in the ambulance. I asked them where they were going to take me, and they said to the Aberdeen Hospital.

"You are not!" I said, and I got up very quickly. My boss was there alongside of the ambulance and asked where I wanted to go. I said to take me to the Hoquiam Hospital, which they did. My clothes were burned from the battery acid, and I was in some mess. I had no control of my left hand; it simply dropped.[2]

After the nurses got some of the dirt off me, and the doctor dressed the cuts, as I had many, I told them to let me alone until morning, for I was in awful pain. I knew that my ribs were broken, and the shock was awful. I nearly froze all night. They had a special nurse for me, and she did all in her power for me, but I suffered more from shock than anything. I could not lie down, and they bolstered me up and put my left arm in a straight bar so the hand lay out straight.

The next morning the doctors all called on me, as they were all friends. At nine that morning Dr. Ahlman[3] came to my room to give me a thorough examination. He wanted to see if he could not do something for me, as he was aware that I had had a hard night of it. I told him that the shock had gone some, but there was plenty left.

After he had gotten through, he said, "Your ribs are all broken on your left side, so I will strap you up, and it will relieve you some. Your hand, I think, will come out all right in time as the spinal nerve is not killed altogether, but it will take several months before you will have much use of it. There is no medicine that I can give you that will do you any good. You must stand the pain. Have you slept any?"

The nurse replied that I had not closed my eyes. She said, "I wanted to give him a sleeping powder when the marine doctor left, but he refused to take any."

"Well, that is best if he can stand it, and he has a lot of stamina and will power. I'll be in again before long, Captain. Try and eat something so you don't lose your strength."

I told him that I had drunk a quart of good whiskey another doctor brought me.

"That is good, Killman. That is better than drugs."

My wife arrived from Tacoma that morning, and I really felt better when she came into the room.[4] She put her arm around my neck and said, "Daddy, are you in awful pain?"

I told her that I did not feel too good, but I would not be there very long, as I had a lot to attend to. I had night and day nurses, but they could not do anything to ease my pain, and as for the food they served, I could not eat it, so my wife brought me my food, and I was able to eat a little. My first officer came and told me every day how everything was going on board and how much lumber he was taking in. He had to stop for lack of lumber at times. He brought the payroll to me, and my wife checked it over to see that it was correct. When Mr. Shaw came to see me that evening I gave it to him and told him that he had better send one of the men from the office to pay off the longshoremen the next day.

"You have a good mate, Captain, that has been years with you. I will take the money to him, and I am sure that he will do it better than anyone I have."

I told him that would be all right, and I was sure everything would be in order. He took the money to the mate, who brought me the receipts and the amount of lumber that was in that night, and I found that I was loading the ship at less than one dollar a thousand. The deckload we would take on at much less cost than below decks. I really think that did me more good than anything I could get at the hospital.

The fifth day after my wife came, I told her that I was going to my ship, as I would never get well where I was. When I told the nurse that I was going to check out, she said I could do nothing of the kind until the doctor told me I could. I asked her who in hell there was there that could stop me, as I was going.

"I cannot stop you if you are determined to go, but I would advise you to wait until your doctor says if it will be all right for you to do it."

"I will not wait for any doctor. I am going to my ship."

When she asked me if I knew I was very weak, I told her that this was a damn fine place to get strong. I asked my wife to get my clothes, and I would dress. I found, after I got my clothes on, that I was so weak I could not walk without help, but my wife helped me. I got into the elevator and went downstairs, saying nothing to the man at the office, and stepped out on the sidewalk.

As I did, the gentleman who had been in the wreck with me came along, and I asked him to get a car and take me to the ship. He said he surely would, and he got a car and drove very slowly, and in a few minutes I was in my lovely cabins. The mate and my wife helped me up the gangway and into the cabin. It was so refreshing to get into the cabin, I went to bed, and it was not long before I was sound asleep and slept for three hours. It was more sleep than I had had for the five days I was in the hospital.

The owners came to me and told me that they did not think I should go to sea in the ship. They asked if I could get a master to take the ship to San Pedro. I told them that if I was not able to go my mate would take the ship, and they said that would be fine. I could go home and stay until the ship was nearly discharged and then go down and see to docking the ship and settling all the bills. If I did not want to come back in the ship, I could come home and let the mate fetch the ship to where she was going.

My wages would go on just the same, and they would pay all the travel bills. I told them I would see how I felt and let them know in ample time.

The day before I was to finish loading, I sent for my doctor, and he and his wife came to the ship in the evening. He had a good look at me, and I told him that I had gotten much stronger and that I was going in the ship.

"You are doing the right thing, Captain. It is summer and the weather is fine this time of the year. You have a good mate, one that knows you well, and you will be much better off on your ship. If you go home, you will be worrying all the time. By all means, go in your ship."

The next morning, when Mr. Shaw came to see me, I told him that I had made up my mind to go.

"That is fine, Captain, but don't go unless you feel well enough."

I told him I would be much better off in my own cabin than I would be any other place. My wife was there, and she told Mr. Shaw that she thought I was doing the correct thing, as she knew me better than anyone that lived.

"Then if you think it is the best thing for him, I am sure it is. I will send a good easy riding car for you, Captain, and a good driver. You keep him until you go away, as you have a lot to attend to."

I was finished loading the next night, and a full crew came on board and started to get the deckload lashed down and the ship ready for sea.[5] I finished all my business, kissed my wife goodbye, and at high water I took the ship to the lower harbor, as she drew too much water to go out the same day. The tide would be falling before we could get to the bar, and we wanted all the water there was at high tide. The next day the tug came, and we hove up the anchor and proceeded to sea. I stayed on deck until the tug had gotten us out over the bar and had let go the hawser, and we had all sail set with a fine fair wind.

I set the course, had the patent log put out, and noted it in my book in the chart room. I called the mate and told him that I was going to bed and to look out for the ship, as I would not be on deck for a few days unless it was necessary.

"You go to bed, sir, and I will look out for everything and keep you posted all the time."

My mate was a good navigator, and I knew he would do all in his power for me. The fair wind kept up, and we were making fine time. He figured out the exact cost of loading and brought it to me to see if it was correct. I told him that it was, as I had had it done in the office. I had loaded the ship for seventy-three cents per thousand, and the stevedore had wanted one dollar and thirty-five cents, a saving of sixty-two cents per thousand. As the ship had one million six hundred and forty thousand, that was a big saving.

We kept going with a fine fair wind until we were almost down to the Santa Barbara Channel. I had not been on deck but was feeling much better. In the morning I went on deck when the sun was about eight degrees high and took a number of sights to get the correct position of the ship and to check the mate's work, which I found was correct. I also got a good latitude at noon, so I was sure of the ship's position.

That afternoon the wind got much stronger, and as the sun went down it shut down thick fog. When I had run my distance, I hauled the ship in to go between Santa Rosa and San Nicolas Islands. The ship was going fast through the water all night. The mate did not leave the deck, as I was able to stay on deck only a short time before I had to lie down. As daylight was coming I went on deck. It was still thick fog, but I could tell that we were between the islands, as the water had gotten much smoother and somewhat lighter.

It cleared away for, say, one minute, and I just saw the top of the island for a second, but no one else saw it. They were all looking, but they did not get it. I then steered for a buoy some few miles from San Pedro. I had the ship under easy sail, so I could handle her very quickly. I came right up, head on, to the buoy. One of the men saw it first through the fog.

I kept off, and in a few moments the fog cleared, and a tug was coming out after me. I took his hawser, and soon we were anchored inside San Pedro breakwater, seven days and a few hours from Grays Harbor. It was Sunday afternoon, so I did not go on shore, but told the captain of the tug to send a launch out after me in the morning, which he did.

I went to the E. K. Wood office, and they told me where I could berth. I called up the tugboat office, and they told me what time they could berth me. I then went to town, and as I went along the dock Mr. Maher saw me going very slowly. He came out and shook hands with me. He was the president of the First National Bank and had a big stevedoring outfit. I asked him what he would discharge my ship for, and he told me. I told him that it was too much, and he said he knew it was and asked why I didn't do it myself with my crew and hired men, and if I failed he would come to my rescue.

"Well," I said, "I will see. My crew might not want to work cargo, and if they want to be paid off I shall let them go, as I am not able to have any trouble."

As soon as we got to the dock and the ship made fast and everything ready to start in the morning, the crew all came aft and asked for their money, as they did not want to work the cargo. I told them I did not want them to, and to pack and get out at once. At ten o'clock in the morning, if the shipping commissioner would be ready, I would pay them off with pleasure.

I at once sent my mate to the shipowners' slave market, as I named it, to see what men he could get. He came back and said he had a full gang for the morning. In the morning we started putting out cargo, and everything went fine. I went to the bank, drew what money I needed, and went to the US shipping commissioner's office. The crew were all there, and he said, "Captain, you need not pay these men off if you don't want to."

I told him that I was not able to bother with them, and they would not do anything if they wanted to go. They had only ten days' pay coming to them, and I was glad to get rid of them, also the cook and the boy. The mate and second mate stayed, and the second mate kept steam on the boiler. We had no trouble. I had to fire only one man while I was putting out the cargo, and discharged for seventy cents, saving fifty cents on every thousand. It amounted to over eight hundred dollars.

As soon as I was finished discharging, I went to the Los Angeles Shipbuilding & Drydock Company, and I never have had better service than I had there. The morning I came off the drydock, I got a telegram from my managing owner to go to San Francisco and try to charter the *Ella A.*, which I did. After being in San Francisco some nineteen days, I finally chartered the ship to go back to Grays Harbor and load for Sydney.

I had a very good passage back,[6] the ship made a very paying voyage, and the owners were more than pleased with my good luck. I had recovered from my auto smash, and my hand had gotten so I could use it some, although it took a year before I had proper control of it.

23 A Finnish Sailor Bests Five Peruvian Police

I had a good voyage to Sydney, and after finishing there I went to Newcastle and loaded coal for Valparaiso, Chile. It was midwinter when I arrived there.[1] It is a fine place in the summer, but in the winter it is very bad. You have to have three anchors out ahead and one astern. We had fair weather until we were half discharged.

One Sunday the wind came from the north, and in a few hours it was blowing strong. All the steamers that were there heaved up their anchors and went to sea. Two Chilean warships left at three in the afternoon, and the lifesaving crew came off with the lifeboat and wanted me to leave the ship. I refused, saying I was O.K. They took the men from several of the hulks that were there, and at four that afternoon the old bark *Independence*,[2] once an American ship, dragged ashore and went to pieces. In a short time they had taken the men out of her, and once more before dark they came off to me and wanted me to leave with my crew, but I refused.

At nine that night it started to moderate, and we only dragged a short distance. The green seas were coming over the ship, and one would have thought her a rock at half tide. The main deck at times had hundreds of tons of water on it. One had to watch his chance to get forward, I can assure you. I was glad when the wind started to fall light, as it looked to me at one time as if the ship had only one chance in a thousand, and possibly not that.

The next day it was so rough that no boats could get off, but the day after that we were able to start work again. The day before I finished discharging I learned from one of the W. R. Grace men that my ship was under charter to them to go to Iquique and load nitrate for Honolulu. I had to get dunnage, and as soon as the last tub of coal was out, I started putting in the dunnage, finished at three that afternoon, and towed to sea that night. The weather looked bad to me, and I wanted to get out before there was another norther.

I had a fair wind leaving, but the next day the wind came from the north and blew hard. I did not think anything about it, only that I was glad to be at sea. I had a fine run to Iquique. After the north wind let go, it came strong from the south and took me right to an anchor at my loading port. As soon as I went ashore I learned that shortly after I left they had one of the worst northers at Valparaiso they had had for many years, and it had done a lot of damage to the shipping, mostly ships that were laid up there.

The U. S. Consul sent me the papers with pictures showing the ships going ashore. If I had not gotten away that night, I am sure the *Ella A.* would have been left there in Chile, as the Consul wrote me that I could not have gotten away the next day. My ship would surely have gone on the rocks, and there was no show for anyone to be saved. I had gotten my floor laid in the hold on the way coming from Valparaiso, and as soon as I was moored we started taking in nitrate.[3]

I never had had a nitrate cargo before and knew it was very bad on a ship like mine without laid 'tween-decks, but I was sure I could stow it so the ship would be easy. After finishing, I went to sea and found out I was wrong, as I never have seen a ship roll like the *Ella A.* did. The water was smooth nearly all the way to Honolulu,[4] but the ship rolled and banged something awful. I made a good passage, although I sailed hundreds of miles out of my course to favor the ship. The owner of the cargo said it was one of the best cargoes of nitrate that he had ever had, hardly a bag broken; but I was glad to get it out of the ship.

From Honolulu I went to Puget Sound,[5] and after chartering the ship I loaded part cargo for New Caledonia and the balance for Sydney. New Caledonia is a French island in the South Pacific on the other side of the dateline. France used to send convicts there years ago. I made a good passage there, sailing to an anchor. It is a bad port, as the island has a most dangerous reef all around it. The day before I got in, I sailed many miles only a few miles off the reef. Lying on the reef could be seen ship after ship that had been out in their positions and had landed, never to get off again.

I arrived there on a Sunday afternoon and passed the doctor.[6] It was too late to go ashore, so I went the next morning, called on the agent of the cargo, and entered the customs. That afternoon I went to the dock to discharge. There were two small tugs owned by a company that operated a big smelter there. They came with a pilot to berth me. I asked how much water there was at the wharf where I was to lie, and the harbormaster told me, knowing how much my ship drew.

The southeast trade winds are fresh in the bay in the afternoon, going down at night, and the morning is calm. We got close to the wharf and let go the starboard anchor, ran a six-inch line ashore, and took it to the steam windlass to heave back into the berth, giving the ship chain all the time.

All at once, the ship brought up on the bottom, and a big piece out of the keel came to the surface. I at once hove on the windlass, letting go the stern line, and hove the ship off. The harbormaster was on the wharf, and I asked him what he was trying to do. Didn't he know how much water there was at the wharf? He was all dressed up for the occasion with a lot of gold braid on his coat sleeve and brass buttons.

"You have given me your draft wrong."

I asked him if he knew who he was. I knew that the draft I gave him was correct, but he did not know how much water there was at the wharf. They had to shift a steamer that was there from France, discharging mostly wines. I at once lowered my boat, and the pilot and I sounded and found there was not enough water for my ship by three feet. The harbormaster did not know what to say when the pilot told him the exact water there was, and the worst of it was that it was a ledge of rock. We had only to go ahead fifty feet, and there was plenty of water.

I had a good dispatch there and found it a very cheap port in every way. The French there hated the Americans so badly that I got a lot of pleasure out of telling them that they surely did love us when we went into the war to keep the Germans from eating them. They would surely sling their arms around and say, "You did no good! Your men could not fight like the Frenchmen."

I laughed at them, and that made them still madder.

After getting discharged, I moved at once to a buoy in the harbor. The next morning I went ashore, and my agent told me that if he was not wrong I was going to have trouble with the owner of the cargo. I was surprised, for I had shown them how to lay out their lumber yard, as they were a new company. This was the first shipment they had gotten, and I told them how to pile their lumber, saving them a lot of money.

"What is wrong?" I asked him.

"You know, Captain, your charter party called for only fifty thousand feet per day, and you have averaged almost ninety thousand per day, and Mr. Huet is going to claim dispatch money."

"I am surprised, after what I have done for them. I have saved them thousands of francs, and they have told me as much. If they did not want any more than fifty thousand per day, they should have stopped when they had received that amount or asked me if I wanted it by dispatch. And they should have collected it day by day, as demurrage is collected, as there is no clause in my charter party. I think Mr. Huet is out of luck, and it will not take me long to settle with him. If he says much, he is liable to go home with a black eye to his little French wife." I then said to my agent, "Has he stopped the ship from clearing the customs?"

We got the papers all ready, and went to the customs house and cleared for Sydney, Australia. When we got back there was a letter awaiting me, saying that Mr. Huet would see me at one-thirty that afternoon at my agent's. After we came back from lunch, I went into the private office, as it was nearing the time when Mr. Huet was to collect his dispatch money.

He was very prompt. He came in and asked for me. My agent told him that I was in his private office, and to go in. He came in, and shook hands with me.

"Well, Captain, I have come to settle with you for the dispatch money."

"Dispatch money you want? Is there any clause in the charter party that you can claim dispatch money? You got your cargo, and I have a receipt for it in full. I am surprised at you that you don't know any more than you do, after what I have done for your firm."

I jumped up and threw off my coat. "Now I give you all the dispatch you want, if you don't get out of here damn quick."

He was gone so quickly that one could hardly see him running up the street. My agent, Mr. Johnson, came in laughing and said, "It did not take long to settle that dispatch claim, Captain Killman, but I was in hopes you would give him one black eye. It might have taught him a good lesson."

However, I am sure that it would not have helped him any, as I then learned that he was a very crooked person. After I had settled with my agent and had all my bills paid ready to go to sea the first thing in the morning, my agent got a phone call asking us to come to the office of the secretary of the lumber company. He was a very large man and good natured, who owned a large wholesale store. I had been to dinner with him the Sunday before and spent a most enjoyable day. He could not talk any English.

When we got to his office, he put his arms around me and slapped me on the back, laughed, and said, "Dispatch money!" He said in French, "You are a very good man, Captain. I told Mr. Huet that he might have a lot of trouble before he settled with you, as the company was not entitled to anything. You had taught them how to pile lumber and how to handle it, and had saved them a lot of money. Instead of dispatch money, they should pay you!

"But I am glad you settled so easily with him, although I wish you had landed one good one, so he would have had two black eyes. Now, Captain, we are going to drink champagne, as I had some put on ice as soon as I heard about how you paid Mr. Huet."

In a few moments after having had a glass of champagne I bade him goodbye.

While I was in Noumea they had a prize fight between a big New Caledonian and a Frenchman. The Frenchman had been a good man in his day but, like all prize fighters, had passed out of the picture after a certain age. The New Caledonian man was six feet tall, black as coal, with the longest arm I ever saw on a man. He weighed something over two hundred pounds and was young. The Frenchman was some thirty-five years old.

They came to me and asked me to referee the fight. After some time I told them that I would. I arrived at the arena a few moments before the fight was to start. It was a very swell affair, all the Four Hundred[7] being there, the ladies and most of the gentlemen in full dress. The arena was finely decorated, with a bar at one side and two waiters to serve the members. There were two amateur fights before the main event. When the two main eventers came, I looked at them and said to myself, "If this young colored man knows anything about fighting, the Frenchman has little show."

I called them into the center of the ring and gave them their instructions, and soon the bell sounded, starting the big fight. I soon changed my mind about the outcome. The big fellow rushed the Frenchman, striking out with both rights and lefts, but the Frenchman was not there, and he failed to hit the Frenchman. The second round was the same.

The Frenchman did not try to hit his opponent. I could see at once what he was doing: he was finding out how much he knew.

The third round, the Frenchman started at him like a wild tiger, hitting him every time where he wanted to, although he did not have strength enough to put him out. The fourth round was the same, and the New Caledonian was looking bad—one eye was closed and the other badly cut. The fifth round lasted only a short time when I stopped the fight, as the Frenchman was hitting his eye repeatedly, and I was afraid he would lose it if I did not stop it. The young man was in bad shape. The ladies made a great fuss over the Frenchman; he could have bathed in champagne if he had wanted to, but he had only one drink and left.

The next day the Frenchman came to the ship to see me. We had a long talk. He had had many fights in his day but said he was outclassed as age had gotten the best of him. They came to me and wanted me to take one hundred francs for refereeing the fight, but I declined and told them I was only too glad to be able to serve them.

I bade Mr. Johnson goodbye and went to my ship, saying to myself, "This, I trust, is my last voyage to this port," as it was anything but a pleasant port to make or get away from. The next morning at eight o'clock the tug came. I gave him a hawser. We let go from the buoy and started for Sydney. I dipped the American flag three times. Many flags had been hoisted on shore, and they all returned the salute. The big smelter also blew three long whistles. We had a long way to go to get out into the Pacific Ocean, the tug had very little power, and the *Ella A.* still had one million feet of lumber on board. We had very little wind all day and at all times one could see the dangerous coral reefs either on one side or the other. At five p.m. we were nearing the Pacific. The sea was breaking heavily on the dangerous coral reefs. I had all the lower sails set to help the tug all we could, but the wind was almost ahead and so light the pilot on board the tug kept off so the ship's sails would draw and help as much as possible.

We were close to the north reef, the last passage we had to go through, when the hawser parted. They had let it chafe on board the tug. At once I hauled the jibs down and put the wheel down, hauling aft the spanker sheet. The ship came to some three points, and I was looking over the side at that white coral expecting her to strike any moment, but she went clear just by inches. The tug came back, we gave him the hawser again, and he towed us some three miles from the dangerous reefs. By then the breeze had freshened, and we were off by our own power. He let go the hawser, came alongside, and the pilot said, "Captain, you did some wonderful work. I thought you were gone. If you had ever struck that coral, your ship would have been a total loss."

But we did not strike. We bade them goodbye, and they turned back toward home. I dipped my flag to him; he blew the usual three whistles and was soon out of sight.

We had a lot of bad weather going to Sydney but arrived all safe and well. After finishing discharging I went to the buoy off Mort's Dry Dock. When I got to my agents' they told me that the Navigation Department wanted me at once at the customs house. "Well, what's wrong now?" I said.

"You can never tell, Captain, what this Labor government will want you to do," was the reply.

I went to the customs house and to the Navigation Department office. There I made myself known as master of the American schooner *Ella A*. "You are going to Newcastle, Captain, to load coal for Callao, Peru, I understand?" I told him that I was unless some unforeseen thing stopped me. "The Commonwealth Government has passed a law that we are to cut a Plimsoll mark on each side of your ship, and that will be your loading mark."

I said nothing until he had said his piece. I then said that I did not think that they could make a law whereby they could cut any marks on an American ship's side. He was in a very bad frame of mind and at once told me that they were going to cut the Plimsoll marks on my ship's side. I then told him that he was not as long as I was master, unless the owners gave instructions to that effect. He said he cared nothing about the owners or me; they would do as they wished while the ship was in the Commonwealth Government. I then told him that he could not carve, cut or engrave anything on my ship's side. They could chalk if they wanted to. "I am giving you warning now and if you want I will give it to you in writing."

"No," he said, "I care nothing for you."

I then told him I would shoot the first one that made a mark in my ship's side. "So govern yourself accordingly. I am giving you fair warning." I then went out.

That night when I got on board I told the first officer what they said they were going to do, and in my absence by all means not to allow anyone to cut any mark on any part of the ship. The next morning at eight a.m. two men came on board and asked for lines and planks to rig a stage over the side. The first officer asked them what they were going to do. They told him that they were going to measure and cut Plimsoll marks on each side of the ship. The first officer reported it to me at once. I went out and told them that they could not cut any mark on the *Ella A.*'s sides.

"That is orders from the Navigation Manager," they said. I told them that I would not allow it under the penalty of death if they cut one mark on the ship's side.

"Well, Captain, we are not going to get into trouble, that is one sure thing; and we do not think that they can pass a law whereby they can cut Plimsoll marks on an American ship's side. We will report back to the office."

That afternoon I was again called to the office of the Navigation Department and asked if I had stopped the men from cutting the Plimsoll marks on the ship's side. "I had," I told him, "and what are you going to do about it? Perhaps you had better come and do it yourself. I would like to have you come on board and cut marks on the *Ella A.*

"Goodbye," I said, and walked out. I heard no more about it. As soon as I had finished drydocking the ship I towed to Newcastle and at once went under the cranes to load.[8] Again the Navigation Department gentlemen came on board, came to my cabin, and told me who they were.

"You are going to cut the Plimsoll marks, I suppose?" I asked.

"No, Captain, we are not. We understand that they tried that in Sydney and failed. We will measure and mark with chalk your loading mark, and we trust that you will not load deeper than that."

"O.K.," I said. "We will see where you put them."

After they had put the marks I told them that the ship would be at least one foot lighter than those marks. I then said, "How much will this cost me?"

"Well, you will get the bill at the customs house when you clear."

"It is very kind of you gentlemen to take such an interest in the welfare of my ship and crew."

After I was finished loading, they again came on board. The ship was fourteen inches lighter than their marks but it cost the ship fourteen dollars. I laughed at them when they passed the bill to me and I paid it. "We do not blame you, Captain Killman, after all the years you have been coming to this port, and they start telling you how deep you can load. If they had stopped the old tubs years ago under their own flag that went down with all hands, it would have been some good. It is a great law, but what can we do?"[9]

I got away after a hard struggle getting a crew, and such men! The sailors have all gone, or if there are any they go in steamers. I don't blame them, for it is a hard life at the best. We had a fair passage to Callao, Peru, with the usual amount of bad weather down in 43 south latitude, but arrived all safe and all hands well.[10] As soon as we got to the dock and gave the crew money, they were all drunk and wanted to be paid off. Some were paid off and some ran away.

As I was getting discharged I started to find a crew. I found six young Italians that wanted to go, and the Consul signed them the day I finished discharging. I also shipped two Russian Finns and had engaged the tug and pilot to take the ship out from the dock to an anchor in the roads where I could get underway after settling up my accounts and clearing. The next morning at five a knock came at the after cabin door. I went to the door. The pilot was there, all excited.

"Well, Pilot, what is wrong this morning?"

"One of the sailors that you shipped yesterday afternoon has beaten up a lot of the police."

"Well, " I said, "that is fine. Where is the sailor?"

"He is on board, I am most sure, but you get your gangway in as quick as possible, as they are coming to take him out of the ship."

"That they cannot do, as he is an American now, since I have signed him on my articles, unless they get the proper papers from the US Consul."

I told the mate at once to see if the crew were all on board. He reported in a few moments that they were, and I told him to take the gangway in at once, which he did. It was not long before a gang of police came down to the ship's side demanding the gangway be put out. I told them it was impossible, as I was going into the stream in a short time, but I was very sorry that I could not oblige them.

They soon went away, and we went into the stream to an anchor. As soon as we had anchored the police launch was alongside demanding that a gangway be put out. I told them it could not be done, and not to attempt to come on board. "What do you want?" I asked them.

"We want one of your sailors!"

"What do you want one of my sailors for?"

"He beat up five police last night."

"Five police?" I said. "Real live police? He must be some man, or you police are not up to much." I told them I was real sorry, but they could not come on board unless they got the proper papers from the American Consul first, as the men that I had signed on yesterday were under the protection of the American government.

I went ashore in the tugboat and at once went to the Consul. "Well, Captain Killman, that last man I signed last night had a fine time—if one would call it that. As reported to me, he licked five police, tore the clothes off from them, and three of them are under a doctor's care. Some sailor! I thought all the hardcase Western Ocean packet rats were gone, but there must be one left. We will go and see the chief of police."

The chief had a long, hard story to tell. After he had held the floor for some time, I asked him if my one sailor had really beaten five of his police officers all at one time. "Yes," he said, "he did, and three of them are in bed under the doctor's care with their uniforms all torn to pieces."

"And your policemen are well armed. He must be some man or your police are not up to much."

The Consul talked to him and told him that he would go aboard the *Ella A.* and see what he could find out about the fight and who was to blame. The next day being Sunday, the Consul came on board for lunch. After lunch he said, "Now, Captain, if you will have the Finn sailor sent aft we will see what we can find out about the affair."

The sailor came to the after cabin, and the Consul asked him to tell him all about the fight. He said he was coming aboard after midnight. When he got to the dock gate the police stopped him and asked him where he was going. "I told them that I was going to my ship, the *Ella A.* They told me that I could not go on board. I told them that I had signed the articles and my clothes were on board, and the ship was going out of the dock early in the morning and I must be on board. But they said I must not go on board. I started to go, and they grabbed me. I had been drinking a lot of Pisco, and I think that I knocked them both down and went straight on board.

"I lay down in my berth and went to sleep. The next thing I knew, there were a lot of police trying to tie me up. I do not know what I did, but they did not get me. I went back to bed again and know nothing more until I was called to take in the gangway. Then I saw that the table was all broken to pieces, and the place was all over blood.

"I would not have had any trouble if I had not been drunk."

We then had the rest of the crew aft, but they could not give any information that amounted to anything, as they had all come on board under the influence of liquor. They had heard some noise but paid no attention to it.

The next morning the Consul and I interviewed the chief of police. The Consul told him what he had heard from the crew and what he had seen, and in his belief the police were in the wrong. The affair must stop, the Consul told him, as they had no claim on the sailor or the ship. In the first place, his officers should have reported to the master or chief officer before going forward in the *Ella A*. The chief of police had sent a bill of something over one hundred dollars, but I think they are still looking for the money.

I at once went to my agent and told him I wanted my ship cleared for Port Townsend. I then went back to the Consul and told him that I had cleared and that I would sail at three p.m. if there was any breeze. We had lunch and went to the office of the chief of police. He wanted his bill paid, but I told him that I wanted the mess room repaired. "Well," he said, "you will not leave this port until you have settled with me." Then he picked up the phone and called the customs house, telling them not to clear the *Ella A*. They told him that the ship was cleared and the Captain had all his papers.

He looked at me and said, "You win! I was too late."

"Well," I told him, "if there is any breeze this afternoon I will pay that bill with the main topsail."

After lunch the Consul went on board with me. I at once told the mate to set the lower sails, as there was a breeze coming. In a short time we went on deck, and I gave orders to heave in the chain to twenty fathoms. As soon as that was done, I set the jibs with the staysail and foresail to windward and then hove up the anchor, and we were off.[11] The Consul got a great kick out of seeing a sailing ship get under way. He bade us goodbye and took his departure. I had the flag dipped three times for him, and in a short time we had lost sight of Peru.

On our way home once more, the sailor that was such a hard case turned out to be a very fine man, and the six Italians that I had shipped learned very fast and did fine. Some six months later I was towing to sea off Tatoosh Island when a fishing boat came alongside, and there were two of the Italian boys that had come from Peru with me. They said, "We are going to give you some fine fish, Captain."

I had a line thrown to them, and they bent on three fine, large salmon.

24 Saving the Charter of the *Ella A.*

When I got back, freights were so low that the ship was laid up. After some six months the owners told me to charter the two ships and have the *Elinor H.* repaired, as the planking had gotten wormed. I soon chartered them, and after repairs they went to their loading berths to load for Melbourne, Australia.[1]

The *Elinor H.* got away first, but it took some time to get a crew for her.[2] Sailors for sailing ships had almost become a lost art. In the meantime I had chartered the *Elinor H.* and the *Ella A.* to load coal at Newcastle, Australia, for Callao, Peru, giving them ample time, as I did not expect to be held up for crews. After the *Ella A.* was loaded I was some fifteen days getting a crew,[3] and such men! I went to sea[4] once more knowing that it would be a schoolship. Three could steer, and that was about all they could do, but one must try to teach them.

After we got to sea one of the men came aft to me and wanted some salve to put on his leg. After I had looked at it, I asked him what he had come in this ship for. He said he had to ship to get something to eat. He never did any work during the voyage, and every day I dressed his leg. I was afraid he would not reach port, but he did and was paid off. I saw him around the street, drunk. Being an American, he was sent back by the Consul.

On my arrival I found that the *Elinor H.* had lost her charter by one day,[5] and it looked as if I would not be able to save mine. I left nothing undone that could be done to save the charter, but the labor conditions were so bad that one could not do much. In fact, they tried to hold my ship back.

On my arrival I paid off my Chinese cook. He was an old man and had been a very good cook, but his health failed and he was not able to work any longer. I put the matter before the Consul General. He told me that he would attend to it. He called the Chinese Consul General, and the arrangements were all made. He was going to be sent to China. When he was paid off, the Consul General was there, also the Chinese Consul General. "Now, gentlemen," I said, "you know more about this Commonwealth law than I do, but I don't want any trouble about this, and I am not going to pay one hundred pounds for this Chinese."

"You will not hear anything about it, Captain Killman," was the reply.

The Chinese Consul took the cook's money, and I had every reason to think that it was all finished. Three days later, as I was passing the customs house, one of the customs officers was standing outside. I greeted him. "Captain, you will be in jail before one o'clock today if you don't pay that one hundred pounds into the customs house for paying off your Chinese cook. Don't you know you can't do that?"

"Well," I said, "I know that, and I am not going to be in jail, and I have paid off my Chinese cook."

"But you will," he told me.

I put my hand in my pocket and took out a five-pound note, saying, "For five pounds I will not."

He at once took out a large roll of notes. "Make it one hundred pounds, if you are so smart."

I told him that I did not have that much money on me. I at once got into a taxi and went to the Consul General's office. I told him what had been told me by one of the customs officials. He was angry in a moment. "I will see if they can run America and China!"

After he had settled down, I said, "Now, sir, it looks to me as if there has been something crooked about this. You put on your hat and coat. I have a car outside. You go to the Collector General, and he will soon straighten this matter out."

"You may be right, Captain," and at once we went away. When we got to my agent's, I stopped the car and asked him to call for me when he was on his way back, as I did not want to appear in the affair. Before long, the driver called for me, and I went to the car and back to the Consul's office. The Collector had heard nothing about the affair. The Chinese Consul General had been to the customs house and offered to put up the money as a guarantee, but they told him it was not needed.

"You will hear no more about this," the Collector told the Consul, "and the Captain will not be arrested, but some of my staff will hear from me."

The cook was sent to Brisbane and took a steamer there for China. I was passing by the customs house shortly afterwards and met the customs officer who had told me I would be in jail before one o'clock. I stopped and said, "I have not been in jail yet, nor have I paid a hundred pounds to your government."

"Yes, I know you have not, but I have lost my job."

"What!" I said, "You got fired over the China cook? Well, it is too bad. You come with me to the Grand Hotel, and I will buy you a drink. That will help soothe your sorrow, and in the future you keep clear of these old American shipmasters, as they are a hard lot."

"I don't think you are right, Captain."

"Well, never mind. I will leave you in a few days and soon be forgotten."

The American Consul General asked me to call on the Collector General, as he wished to see me. I went to his office, sent my card in, and was received by the Collector General. He was very sorry, he said, that this should have happened, and he did not think anything like it would occur again. He gave me credit for the way I had handled the affair. I bade him goodbye and left.

I heard no more about the affair until the Chinese Consul General called me up and asked me to call on him at my leisure. I went to his office and he showed me where the Chinese cook had gone to Hong Kong in the mail steamer from Brisbane. He was a very fine gentleman.

The discharging of my ship was going very slowly, and there was no way that I could make it go faster. It was the horse-racing season while I was in Melbourne, the Caulfield Cup, the Melbourne Stakes, and the biggest race of all, the Melbourne Cup. That day was declared a holiday; everything closed. I had the *Ella A.* fumigated, as it must be done before sailing. Of course it cost three times as much, but I saved one day by so doing. I went to the three big races, and there were some very fine and fast horses. On Melbourne Cup day there were one hundred thousand or more people there. It was a wonderful race, won by a horse by the name of Trivalve by only five inches.

The day that I was discharged my crew had all gone. Some had been paid off and the rest had deserted. I went to the Consul in the morning to see what men they had on the waiting list. They said they thought they would have a crew signed on by noon. I went again at three p.m. and found that they had only five signed. I told them that I would be back at four-thirty and would they have my papers ready for me, as I had cleared the ship for Newcastle and would be discharged some time that night and must get away in the morning. If I was short of men I could sign them myself after clearing.

"Yes, Captain, you can do that, but where are you going to get them?"

I told him that there must be some bums on the wharf that were hungry and would take a chance to get something to eat. I went back to the Consul after my papers. I was told that the Consul General wanted to see me, and I went to his office.

"Well, Captain, are you discharged?"

"No, sir, I will be about eight tonight."

"And you expect to get away the first thing in the morning?"

"Yes, sir, I am in hopes to."

"And you are three men short, they tell me. Have you settled up with your agent?"

"No, sir, but I will tonight, as he will come back to his office at eight-thirty p.m."

"Well, Captain, you expect to get the rest of your crew in the morning?"

"I am in hopes to."

"You are surely taking a lot of chances in trying to save your coal charter, and I surely hope you are successful, as you have done all anyone could do." He wished me all the good luck that I had worked hard to receive, and we parted. He was one of the finest men that I ever have met. I got my papers and bade him goodbye, and went back to the ship. We were discharged at seven p.m. After I had my dinner I went to my agent's and settled with him. He was to bring all the accounts to the ship in the morning.

The mate, Mr. Hansen, came to the after cabin early, telling me he had three men that wanted to sign on. I told him to bring them along. I signed them, asking if they had any clothes. They replied that all they owned they had on, which was O.K. with me. Then the agent came with the papers. "Captain, if we find any errors we will let you know, and you do the same."

"I sure will."

In a few moments the two tugs and the river pilot came. The mate had the derricks down by this time. After getting the tugs fast we let go our lines. I looked on the wharf, and who was getting out of a machine but the Consul General! I greeted him and he said, "You are off, Captain Killman. Did you get the men?"

I told him yes.

"Good luck to you, and I hope that you make your charter."

Down the river, you must stop at Port Melbourne where customs and police come on board to see if everything is O.K. As soon as they came to my cabin I told them what time was to me, slipped each one a pound, and signed their papers. They each took a big drink of whiskey and ran for the gangway, saying, "Good luck, Captain Killman. Come back soon."

The pilot had come aboard, and the river pilot came and shook hands with me, saying, "I hope you will be able to get out, Captain. You have not got much time, but the captain of the tug is an old friend of yours, and he told me he would do all he could." He went into his launch and away.

As we got down Hobsons Bay, a light fair wind came along and the pilot wanted sail made. In a few moments we had sail set, but it soon died out calm again. We helped the tug all we could when there was any breeze. The pilot was worrying. He said to me, "Captain, we may not be able to make it. The tide will soon turn flood."

As we got in the worst place the ship stopped for a short time. He came to where I was watching a range that I had. "We will have to turn back, Captain."

"No," I said, "she is starting to go ahead."

The black smoke was billowing from the tug's smokestack, and the safety valve was throwing out steam.

"He will make it. I am sure now," I said.

"Yes, you are right. He is gaining ahead fast now."

In a few moments we were out into Bass Strait. The big steam pilot boat came close, lowered their small boat, and took the pilot off. He shook hands with me, saying, "You will soon have a fine fair wind, Captain Killman. Good luck to you, and I hope that you may make Newcastle in time to save your charter."[6]

"Well, that is hard to say. I will not stop trying, that is one thing sure."

The tug towed me some four miles off and blew to let go the hawser, which I did. It was flat calm. What a night I had! There would be a little breeze for a few moments. I always had to wear around, getting nearer the beach all the time. Then it shut down thick fog and rain. The lights were all obscured. My only guide was the lead, and I hardly left the deck during the night. When daylight came, it cleared and we were very close to the beach. Then there came a light breeze. I had all sail set and was laying a course just clear of the beach. The pilot boat came close and told me if the wind did not haul so that I could lay clear they would haul me out a few miles. "Have a hawser ready."

"O.K.," I told them, and that was the last I saw of them. I had to keep going on that tack until I was abreast of Cape Otway. I was well clear of danger, and then it died out calm again. I lay there all night looking at Cape Otway Light. As the sun came up, a breeze came from the west. All sail was set at once, and I steered for Cape Liptrap. We had a fine breeze all day, but as we got abreast of Cape Liptrap it died out calm again. I could see very little show left, as time was going fast. We lay there becalmed some twelve hours until a fair wind came along, and that night I had passed out of Bass Strait.

I thought I would surely have a chance, but in a short time it died out calm, and the next morning the wind came from the north, fair ahead. In a short time it was blowing hard and a nasty sea running. I was driving the ship very hard, knowing that as soon as the wind came from the north there would be a strong current setting south. The worst of it is when the wind is from the north. It becomes so hazy one can see but a short distance, even though there is not a cloud in the heavens.

I stood to the west and tried to see the land, but I could make out nothing. I was heaving the deep-sea lead and knew that I was but a short way off. For twenty-four hours it came from the north. Then it died out calm. I had but forty-eight hours left. In the afternoon there came a light breeze from the west. I made all sail and called the second officer aft, telling him I was going to lie down as I had been on deck most of the time since we left Melbourne, and for him to watch the weather in the west and let me know at once if there was any sign of a change.

I had been below but a few minutes when the second officer came to the after cabin door, saying, "You had better come on deck, sir, as I do not like the looks of it."

I was on deck as soon as he was. "Call all hands," I told him. The mate was out in a moment.

"Take the raffee and squaresail in, and let the second mate take in the spanker topsail and spanker."

We got them in, but it was a job to furl that big spanker, for the wind had struck us in terrific force, and I had never seen it hail so hard before. One could not look to windward. Everyone was covered with blood, as the hail would cut like a knife. I could not leave the man at the wheel. The fore, main, and mizzen gaff topsails were set, and I knew that as soon as the halyards were let go they would go to pieces. So I let them stand, but they soon went, one at a time. There was two feet of hail on the lee side of the main deck.

After the sun went down, it stopped hailing, and the wind moderated to a very strong breeze; all one could wish for, but so black over the land one could not judge how far we could see. We were making fourteen knots by the patent log. At eight a.m. the first officer came on deck. He at once came to me and said, “Captain Killman, you must go below and get some rest. You have been on this ship’s deck four days and nights; in fact, you have had very little rest since we left Melbourne. My eyes are good, and I will look out for the ship. You go have some rest.”

He took the reading off the patent log, and I went below. It put me some few miles north of Point Perpendicular. I went on deck again and told him where I placed the ship, although my reckoning might not be correct, as I could not judge the currents. He should keep a good lookout and let me know if he saw any lights. The light on Perpendicular Point was a good one, so he might see it. I went below and lay down on the lounge.

In a short time Mr. Hansen sang out down the after companionway, “Light-O!” I jumped on deck. It was a bright flash, but we did not see it again. At midnight he came to me and gave me the distance the ship had run. I was hauling off from the land some few degrees to be sure. I placed the ship on the chart again and thought I would have another hour’s sleep, but I could not, so I put on my coat and took the deck. As soon as it began to break daylight I told the mate to get them all out and get some of the topsails bent, as I should want them. At eight a.m. I jibed over and steered for Norah Head Light. At eleven a.m. the head came in sight, also the lighthouse. At two p.m. we kept off for the Nobbys, the entrance to Newcastle harbor.

It was not long before we made out a tugboat coming out, diving into the seas, and the spray was going clean over him. I took in the light sails and spanker, as we were coming up on him fast. It was the tug *Champion*, J. & A. Brown’s largest tug. When he came near us, I asked the captain, an old friend of mine, what he wanted to come out here for, as I was sailing much faster than he could tow us.

“It was orders from the boss, your old friend Mr. Brown. There will be a tug ready to come alongside as soon as we get to the Nobbys, and you will go straight to the dock on the Stockton side.”

"O.K.," I said, "we are all ready."

We took his hawser on board, and I can assure you that I was feeling a lot better, as my lay days expired the next day at twelve o'clock. We slowed to take the pilot on board some three miles before we got to the Nobbys. The pilot was also an old friend of mine. He put his arm around me.

"Well, Killman, you are a wonder. You have saved your charter. It has been the talk of all the shipping men. Most of them said you could not make it. We knew when you passed Wilsons Promontory, and we knew there had been a strong north wind off Gabo Island until yesterday afternoon when the wind came strong from the west. Well, I told them that you would be here today, but one of the pilots said you could not make it. So we bet a new hat on it. I do not care for the hat, Killman, but I am mighty glad you saved your charter, as I hear that they are anxious for you to lose it."

We went direct to the dock on the Stockton side.[7] As soon as we had gotten alongside, there were a lot of my friends there with cars to take me to Newcastle. The captain of our schooner the *Elinor H.* was there. He had lost his charter by one day. After the ship was fast and the gangway out, they all came on board to welcome me back once more. I called Mr. Hansen and told him to start early in the morning to paint the ship's sides with copper paint.

I then left for Newcastle, went to the Consul's and got my mail, and sent cables to my owners and to the Consul General at Melbourne. It was seven p.m. then, time for dinner and a night's rest. The captain of the *Elinor H.* came to Newcastle and told me he had six sailors and two officers on board. I told him that we would go to the ship at six a.m. and get his crowd to work painting on my vessel, so she would be painted by noon. We were away early in the morning and got his men and officers to work on the *Ella A.*, and at two p.m. the ship was all painted, ready for cargo.

I went to my agent, Mr. Patton, at eleven-thirty a.m. He was glad to see me, as he was an old acquaintance. "Well, Captain, you are pretty late, aren't you?"

"No, I have one half hour left yet."

"Yes," he said after looking at his watch.

"I had a good sleep this morning, as I really needed it."

"I am sure you have had but very little since you left Melbourne."

I gave him my notice that I was ready to receive a cargo of coal as per terms of the charter party.

"I will put you under the cranes at one o'clock, Captain Killman." He reached for the phone and called the pilots' office.

"Can you put the *Ella A.* under Crane Number Twelve at one p.m. today?"

"Yes, if they have steam on their boiler."

"Have you steam, Captain?"

"No, I have not, but we have a large gas engine."

"How long will it take you to get steam?"

"Two hours," I told him. He told the pilot in charge.

"That won't do. You will have to wait until tomorrow." Then to me, "We will have to wait until tomorrow, Captain. But you and I will go to the Hotel Northern and have a drink on your good luck, and then you will enter at customs."

"That will be just fine," I told him, all of which we did. After I was finished I went to the ship and found the painting was all completed. I told the first officer, Mr. Hansen, that we would go under the cranes at one p.m. tomorrow and to be all ready with steam. I had seen the pilots earlier and told them what I wanted.

"O.K., Killman, don't have steam and we will not move you."

One day, before I sailed, as we were going to the Northern Hotel for a drink, Mr. Patten said to me, "You got your ship painted all O.K., Killman?"

"Yes, I certainly did. It was well done.'

"Leave everything to you, and it will come out right side up." We had a good laugh. I told him that I would pay for the drinks. He did not care; he was only doing what was right. He must load the ship, yet W. R. Grace did not want the coal, as they had chartered a big steamer that was going to Chile for nitrate at half what they were paying the *Elinor H.* and *Ella A.*, and they had more coal than they wanted in Callao.

We went under the cranes the next day and started to load at once. As soon as the ship was fast all the men that I had shipped in Melbourne came aft and told me they were done and wanted their money. It seemed that after they had gotten full of good food, work and they fell out. Well, I told them that I would love to pay them off, as they were no good to me, if the U. S. Consul was willing. I would see him during the afternoon and let them know. The Consul said, “Yes, Captain, if you don’t want them I will pay them off at ten a.m. tomorrow.”

With that settled, the next day I paid the sailors off and was glad to get rid of them. That afternoon I received a cable from the managing owner to charter the *Elinor H.* if possible, as soon as my ship was loaded. I left her in charge of the first officer, and the captain of the *Elinor H.* and I went to Sydney to try to get a cargo for the *Elinor H.* It was impossible. I stayed a week and then came back and cabled the owners that it was impossible and advised sending the ship back in ballast. I at once got an answer to send the *Elinor H.* home in ballast to Port Townsend for orders. The next afternoon the *Elinor H.* sailed in ballast for Port Townsend.[8] I then got a crew for my ship after some trouble, as sailors are a thing of the past, settled all my bills, and cleared for Callao, Peru.

25 The Last Voyage of the Schooner *Ella A.*

At 1:30 p.m., December 6, 1927,[1] two tugboats came, the *Champion*, J. & A. Brown's largest tug, and the *Commodore*, to assist while in the harbor; also the pilot. My friends, who came to see me off, bade me goodbye and a good passage. The bow cable was let go from the buoy, and the tug *Champion* went ahead, as also the *Commodore*. In a few moments we were moving down the harbor. I ordered the American flag dipped three times, as I had done so many times before. I could see many of my many friends waving their hats as I was passing down the harbor. In a few moments the ship was outside the harbor. The tug alongside let go, blowing a goodbye whistle, and returned to his dock. In a few moments the pilot came. "If you will sign the papers, Captain Killman, I will bid you one more goodbye, and be sure to come back."

I signed his papers, we had a goodbye drink, and he was off. The pilot boat *Ajax* blew three long whistles, which I returned by dipping my flag three times. Little did I think of what was in store for me on my last voyage. The tug *Champion* towed me off some eight miles and blew his whistle to let go the hawser. It was flat calm at the time. We set the big lower sails and jibs but soon lost steerage way. The tug came back after hauling in his hawser, saying the usual things, "You will soon have a fair wind, Captain. Good luck to you, and a fine run across the South Pacific." He blew three long whistles. I dipped my flag to him three times, the last time after so many years in and out of the port of Newcastle, and I can say that I liked Newcastle better than any foreign port that I have ever been in.

We were becalmed all night, drifting slowly south. The lights of Newcastle were all very bright, as I was on deck most of the night looking for a breeze of wind. As the sun came up in the morning, a light breeze from the east came at the same time. The ship was put on the port tack, and we slowly went south along the land. At eight p.m. the lights of Sydney were bright. Then calm all night, then came a light fair wind, and we soon lost sight of the Island of Australia. We had light east and west winds until we passed the north end of New Zealand, off which we had been a long time, but one cannot control the winds and weather. Then we had strong east winds with rain and thick fogs.

On January 4, 1928, latitude 36°15′ S, longitude 177° W, we had a very heavy gale from the southeast. At four a.m., I gave orders to haul the main jib down. After it was down I went into the cabin. In a few moments I heard men running on the after deck, and I knew that something was wrong. At once I went on deck and learned that my best man had been washed overboard. I saw him once as he came to the surface, then he went down and was not seen again. They had thrown a life buoy to him, but he did not try to get it. He had on long-legged rubber boots and oilskins, and his chances were very slight. I know that if I had lowered a boat with the men that I had, it was sure death to them. So I said gone where many have gone before him.

When the weather got better, I wrote the official log and called part of the crew with the officers to witness it. He was paid off at Honolulu, and what money he had coming to him was sent to Finland, where he came from.[2]

The next day we found that the ship was leaking slightly, which I thought nothing of, as a wooden ship is bound to leak some in such weather as we had then. After that storm we had light east winds. On January 19, 1928, we had a very heavy gale from the south southeast. The seas were very heavy, running mountain high. I reefed the ship's lower sails and made her go as easy as possible. At ten p.m. I left the deck; it was blowing hard, raining in torrents, and very dark. At midnight Mr. Hansen reported to me that there was no change, but it was nearly impossible to do any pumping, as there were such heavy seas coming across the main deck.

I told him to be careful that none of the men got washed overboard, and as soon as daylight came I would start the gas engine; it would not take but a few moments to pump out what water there was in the ship. I went on deck and took a good look at the weather. It was not blowing any harder than it was at ten, when I left the deck, but I think the sea was somewhat worse. I went below again but could not go to sleep. I was tired and needed sleep. At two a.m. I went on deck. It seemed that the ship did not have the right motion, but I said nothing. There were very heavy seas going across the main deck. I told the second mate not to let the men go to the pumps, as I was afraid some of them would get hurt.

Day would break by three-thirty a.m., and we would start the gas engine, which had very fine pumps.

I started it at three a.m. At daylight, after the gas engine had been going over half an hour, the ship still looked very deep to me and I thought she did not have the same motion. I told the second mate to watch his chance and go forward to sound the pump well. He was off, and in a short time was back, saying, "There is eight feet and four inches in the ship, sir!"

I told him to call all hands and to go down forward into the chain locker and see if there was any water there. He did so, and came back to tell me that the water was only two feet from the between deck beams there. Mr. Hansen came aft. I told him that I was going to try to get the ship off before the wind. He was to have the jib loosed and when he saw me give the signal to have all hands hoist it up, and to look out that no one got washed overboard.

I watched the sea for some time, and when the correct moment came I had the wheel put hard a starboard. The ship started to pay off; then I had the jib hoisted. I did not know whether the ship would get so much water on that large main deck that the hatches would be broken in. If so, it would be good night to all hands on board. Some heavy seas came on board, but the ship kept paying off and soon had the wind on the starboard quarter. I then gave a course to steer, called the mate, and told him to get steam on the boiler so we could get the big steam pump working.

It took some three hours before we were ready to start the steam pump, but when it was working it surely was pumping some water! The gas pump was running all the time, and as soon as the men could stay at the main pumps, both of them were going. When I started to get the ship off before the wind, I could see only one chance in a million, but I had to take that chance. The sea was one of the worst that I ever have seen, but it looked as if our time had not come. If I had not gotten the ship before the wind, in a short time she would have been full of water, and that meant sinking with all hands as it was impossible to get the boats out and they could not live in that kind of weather.

After all the pumps were going, we soon saw that we were gaining on the water in the ship. We were going nine knots, and the wind in some twelve hours commenced to get lighter, with the sea going down. It took three days to get the water out of the ship with all the pumps running. I had to stop the steam pump, as we would not have fresh water enough, and to put salt water in the boiler only meant that in a short time the tubes would start to blow out.

I had made up my mind to try to make Tahiti, if possible. The wind fell light, hardly enough so the ship would steer, where I should have had good southeast trades and the water was as smooth as a lake. I then could keep the water out of the ship by pumping three fourths of the time with the main pumps and two hours per day with the gas pumps. I had the boats all ready if needed, with water and bread on board. We were making very little distance, as the wind continued to be very light, but I was sure that if the ship started to leak worse we could make some of the islands in the boats and save the crew.

At last we made Tahiti. I had a fine breeze that day. I called the mate to my cabin and told him that I was going to try to get the ship to Honolulu, for if we went into Tahiti, what could we do? There was no drydock; in fact, there was nothing that we wanted. He said, "Captain, you will reach Honolulu, I am sure."

So we kept on, and in a few hours we were out of sight of Tahiti. Then the wind fell light, the ship making only twenty miles per day. Tahiti is in latitude 18° south and Honolulu 21° north. We kept on day after day, and no change. When we got to 5° south, we struck the current setting west. I told Mr. Hansen that we would surely get the wind from the southeast on the other side of the Line, and we could make what easting we would need to weather the Hawaiian Islands. But it did not come, and it was sure that I could not make the Islands without beating. If I had to go to leeward of the Islands, I then would have to go into the Northeast Trades and go north to get to the east. The Northeast Trades are strong, with a bad sea, and I was sure that we would not be able to keep the ship afloat. So I started beating. The gas was commencing to get low, and our food was also getting short. Water had to be measured out. The flour at last gave out, forty days before we reached port. Our potatoes lasted one hundred days. We had plenty of beef and pork, salt fish, and canned vegetables, but with flour, potatoes, rice, and cereals gone and the weather very hot and working the pumps and handling the big sails, it became very hard on the men.

After beating for several days, I anchored off the Barking Sands, three miles from Waimea, Kauai Island, at 7:45 p.m.[3] It was very dark at the time I anchored, and the wind was light. As we drew close to the land I was heaving the lead all the time. The first mate said, "Thirty-five fathoms, sir."

"That will do," I said, "Haul the jibs down." I gave orders to the man at the wheel to put his wheel hard down. The ship came to the wind, and I told the mate to let go the anchor. After forty-five fathoms of chain were out, and the sails lowered down, I told the mate to have the lead put over the side. "I want to see how much water there is here."

I watched the lead as it brought up on the bottom—eight fathoms. We were a long way off, and it was very dark and hard to judge distance looking at a dark background of low land. The ship then was drawing twenty-three feet.

The next morning at sunrise I had the flags set forward for the doctor and the American flag aft with the ship's signal letters underneath. I waited until noon, but no signs of anyone coming off, so I had my big boat lowered and manned with four seamen and the second mate and went to the wharf at Waimea.

I had been there a few times before as mate, but forty-odd years before. I went ashore, telling the second officer to lay well off from the wharf and allow no one on shore, and wait until I came back. I walked up the dock and met a Hawaiian at work. I asked him where the sugar mill office was, and he showed me. As I was going to the mill office, an automobile came along and stopped. The driver asked me if I was from that ship lying at anchor down the coast. I told him that I was the master. He then told me that he was Captain William G. Gorham, manager Kauai Railway Company, deputy collector of customs, and harbormaster.

"You get in here, Captain Killman, and I will render you any assistance you want." I told him that the first thing I wanted was to send a cable to my sick wife, not knowing if she was alive. I was sure that Lloyd's had posted the ship as missing, and if she still lived she would be the first one to see it, as the shipping news was the first thing she looked at and no one could cut anything out of the paper. She was bound to see it.

I at once sent a cable home to my wife and daughters, then to the managing owner, telling them that all hands were well and where the ship was. I then cabled Alexander & Baldwin to be my agents and to see what arrangements they could make to have the ship towed to Honolulu. Then I cabled the collector of customs that I had landed against the law. He at once replied, saying that it was quite in order as I was in distress, but not to let any of the crew go on shore. In a short time I received a cable from Alexander & Baldwin saying the Inter-Island Steam Navigation Company would tow the ship to Honolulu for a certain sum of money for a certain amount of time and after that it would be so much per hour. There was no doubt in my mind that if they sent a good tug the ship could be towed to Honolulu easily in the time stated. So I accepted the offer, and they replied that they would have a tug there the next day at one p.m.

I then ordered my badly needed stores and had them sent to the wharf. Then I told Captain Gorham that I would go on board and try to get a little rest. As we were coming to a bank that I had seen, I asked him what bank it was. He told me it was a branch of Bishop's Bank in Honolulu. He stopped at the bank and said, "We will go in, Captain. I want you to meet the manager. It is after banking hours, but we can get in."

We went in and he made me acquainted with the manager and the other members of the bank staff there. "Now, Captain Killman, isn't there something I can do for you?"

I told him that I thought the only thing I needed was a lot of money.

"Why, Captain, I will give you what money you want to pay your bills here."

I replied to him, "You may never get it back."

"Well, I do not care, Captain. The bank will not lose it and as it will be for a good cause I never would care." I told him that I did not need money at the present time. He looked at me. "Captain, you need a lot of rest. You are only working on strong will power."

"Possibly," I told him. "But now comes the worst of it all—my friends the underwriters to cope with."

"Yes," he said, "but look out for yourself."

I only quote this as it is only once in a lifetime you meet a man like him. A few days later I received a long wireless message from him, asking me how I was getting along and if I was taking good care of myself. I replied thanking him for his kind thoughts.

I then went on board. The stores were all on the dock. We put them in the boat and I bade Captain Gorham goodbye, thanking him for his kindness. The next day at one p.m. the tug *Lehua*[4] came, a large wooden boat. He said only, "Stand by the hawser," as he passed. We took the hawser on board, and in a very short time the anchor was up and we started on the last lap of our voyage. I soon saw that the tug was all hull and no power, as we were not moving over three knots. The water was very smooth and no wind, and I could see that he would not be able to do anything with the ship when he started to cross the channel, as the northeast trade winds were strong and a heavy sea running.

At seven p.m. he started to cross the Kauai Channel. In a short time the trade winds came, also the sea, and the ship would hardly steer. At eleven we lost steerage way, and the ship lay in the trough of the sea. The sea was piling on board, but the steam pumps were running and keeping the water down. Shortly after midnight he started the Morse Code, telling me to let go the hawser. I replied that the hawser had two ends. He could let go his end; mine was fast.

At six a.m. he turned the ship around after some time and started back with a fair wind. At ten a.m. we anchored at Port Allen. Captain Gorham came on board with a cable from my daughter Katherine, saying her mother was fine and for me to come home. Captain Gorham told me he had communicated with the Inter-Island Steam Navigation Company and that the steamer *Kinau*[5] would come to the assistance of the *Lehua*.

At one p.m. the *Kinau* came, and at two-twenty p.m., after getting the hawsers on board, we once more hove up the anchor and started for Honolulu. After a hard tow we arrived at Honolulu at nine-thirty p.m. on the sixth day of May, 1928.[6] The doctor came on board very early on the seventh of May, finding the crew all well. The ship was at once fumigated, and as soon as we were finished two tugs came and put the ship at the Inter-Island coal dock. Before the ship was fast Mr. Kennedy, vice president of the Inter-Island Steam Navigation Company, came on board to see me. He asked me not to request them to be agents for the ship, as it would look better if I appointed some other firm, since they were the only ones that had a dock to handle the coal cargo and also owned the drydock and thus were the only ones who could repair the ship. I told him I was well aware of that, and I would try to have Alexander & Baldwin act as agents.

"That will be fine, Captain."

Alexander & Baldwin had their man there to receive me. I went to their office and they said they would act as agents. We then went out and entered at customs. I had a long talk with the deputy collector and shipping commissioner. I told them that it was most sure that all hands would demand their money that night and would want a certain amount of it, but I would not have any for them, but would pay them all off as soon as affairs were arranged and I got money to my credit from the owners.

"They will have to wait, Captain, as you are here in distress."

"Yes, that is true, but they will get all kinds of advice, which will not amount to anything, and put me to all the trouble they can."

"I will do all I can for you, Captain Killman. You will handle the affair properly, I am sure of that."

That afternoon when I went on board the crew all came aft and told me that they were done that night and wanted to be paid off at once and wanted so much money that night. I told them that I would pay them all off as soon as I got the money and that they had better stay on board and work until arrangements had been made and that I had no money for them.[7]

"The same old story," was their reply. "We will get all the money we want, and you will get into trouble over it."

I told them to go ahead and do all that they could and to get forward out of my sight. I was sure that they would all leave. I made up their accounts that night. The next morning I was up at four a.m., as I had to start the gas engine to pump the water out of the ship. The cabin boy came to me and said all hands had left, officers and cook with the sailors. "I will have your coffee in a few minutes, sir."

I went on deck and sounded the pumps, finding that the ship was not leaking so badly. I started the gas engine, and the pump was soon going and throwing a lot of water. In three hours I had the water all pumped out. At nine a.m. I was at Alexander & Baldwin's office. I sent a cable to my owners that I wanted so much money at once. The same afternoon I got a cable from the owners saying what do you want money for? The cable was in code. After I had taken it from the code book I showed it to the manager.

He read it, looked at me, and said, "Captain, it is strange. Can you make out what they mean?"

I was lost for words. I sat down to think, as I was so well acquainted with the managing owner. His name was not signed to the cable. In a few moments they came to me and said that they would not act as agents for such owners.

"Sending such a cable to a man like you, Captain, after you have worked for them for so many years."

I told them I could not make it out and asked them to act and that I was sure everything would come out all right; that there must be some mistake, or the manager is out of town and some clerk sent the cable.

"No, Captain, we are done. You must look for some other agent. We will do anything we can for you, but we want nothing to do with your owners. That is final."

Well, there was only one left, the Inter-Island Steam Navigation Company, so I went to them. After a long talk with the president and vice president they said they would act, but there must be a certain amount of money placed to my credit, and more if it was needed. So they had learned from Alexander & Baldwin of the cable that was sent me, and as it would take thousands of dollars to repair the ship, they must be sure of their money. I told them that they surely were right, but we would have to wait until we saw what the underwriters were going to do, and that wouldn't be long now.

I then sent another cable saying I must have money at once or the ship will be libeled to pay off the crew. The money was cabled that night. At eight a.m. the next morning, as I was standing on the break of the after deck while the gas engine was pumping the water out of the ship, a man came down the dock, stopped abreast of me, and said, "Are you the captain of that ship?"

I told him I was.

"I am the assistant district attorney. Why don't you pay that crew off?"

"Is that any of your business?"

"I'll soon show you that it is." He went on until I lost my good disposition. I told him to come on board and talk like that, and he would soon go to the hospital or the morgue. I told him I did not know if he was crazy or a damn fool. He went up the dock saying what he was going to do.

I went to the Inter-Island office at nine that morning. There was a cable from the underwriters saying the Bishop Insurance Company was appointed to be their agents and to call on Mr. Burg at once. More trouble. My friends the underwriters! Well, we would soon know what they were going to do.

I went to their office, was received by a young lady, and gave her my name, telling her that I wished to see Mr. Burg. "Yes, Captain, they are expecting you."

I was taken to his office, and the young lady told him who I was. I was received in due form and asked to take a seat. He extended his sorrow for my bad luck, saying that I surely needed rest.

I passed him the cable that I had received.

"Yes, Captain, I am to represent the underwriters. I have appointed Mr. McKay as surveyor and will have him here at a certain time to meet you."

"I will be here to meet him. Now, Mr. Burg, I want to say a few words to you, so you will know how I feel about underwriters. I think they are without doubt more unjust than any people living in this world. They take your premiums, pat you on the back, give you a cheap cigar, and smile and say come again, but when it comes to paying a claim of any kind, they can crawl out of the smallest hole for five cents."

He looked at me. "Why, Captain, you don't think I am that kind, do you?"

"I do not know, but if the shoe fits you, wear it with honor. But, Mr. Burg, I am going to give you a run for your money, and I am looking forward to a lot of trouble."

"You will have no trouble with me, Captain Killman. I will act fair and honest in every way. If I send a cable or write a letter to the underwriters, you shall read it first and have a copy. I will give you a copy of all cables and letters I may receive from them."

"That is fair. I don't expect any cables or letters from them. If I do, I will show them to you. Mr. Burg, the first thing I must do is to extend my protest at once, as I am going to pay all hands off, and we must have a certain proportion of those names on it."

"Yes, Captain, you are right. Mr. Scott is very good at it and is a Notary Public." He made me acquainted with Mr. Scott.

We at once went to the ship and got the mate's logbook. The mate was there and I asked him if he and the boatswain and two of the sailors would be there at a certain time that afternoon to sign the protest. He said he would have them on board at the time I wanted them. We then went and extended the protest and got the required number of names of the crew on it. I met the appointed surveyor, Mr. McKay, and he asked me if I would be on board at seven p.m. I told him I surely would, as I had a long spell of pumping to do.

Mr. McKay was there at seven. After the ship was pumped out, he asked me if I had any objections if he sealed the pumps up for twelve hours. I told him no, but I did not think anyone would put water in the ship or pump any out, but he said that the underwriters would want it done.

"Yes, I suppose so. They will try to make out that the ship was all right but the damn fool of a master got cold feet."

He said nothing to that. We then sounded the pumps and sealed them up. "I will be here at seven a.m., Captain."

"You had better, as I will start those pumps at seven a.m."

He was on board at six-thirty a.m., and at seven we went and broke the seal on the pumps. I gave him the sounding rod, and he dropped it down to the ship's bottom and hauled it up, then turned to me and said, "Can this be right, Captain? Thirty six inches?"

"Yes, it is six inches less than the twelve hours before. The holds are filling up here."

"I do not know how you got this ship here."

"Well, she is here."

"You will have to discharge and go on drydock and caulk all over."

"I will send the owners a cable at once to that effect, if this is final."

"Mr. Burg, I am sure, will notify San Francisco as soon as I make my report to him."

That afternoon I went to the drydock and had a long talk with Mr. Mack, the manager of the dock. We came to the agreement that we could leave one thousand tons of coal[8] in the ship without harming her any, if it was taken out so as to leave her on an even keel and leveled down the whole length of the ship, and the dock could lift that much without doing any harm.

26 Bound for Home

As soon as the owners cabled "Repair the ship," I started to discharge her. We left one thousand tons in her and then went on the drydock. The ship was placed on the dock in very fine shape and lifted, one of the best docking jobs that I ever have seen. We started to caulk at once, but we had only five men, as wooden ships had nearly gone out of existence. I was allowed to place the best men where it needed them most.

Mr. McKay tested the tubes in the boiler, and they had to be replaced with new ones. I called for bids from the Honolulu Iron Works and the Inter-Island Steam Navigation Company, and found that the drydock would do the job much cheaper. As soon as the ship's bottom was caulked up high enough so that the rest could be done from stages, we came off the drydock. I had claimed that the coal would be dangerous after being put back into the ship, and that the ship would be in great danger of catching on fire. So Mr. McKay took some of the coal to the Honolulu Fertilizer Works, where they had a testing laboratory. After it was there for a few days, I was called to Mr. Burg's office. Mr. McKay had a report made out, which was read to me, and I was asked to sign it. It stated that the coal showed no signs of heating. I told them that I did not believe their test amounted to anything, as the coal had to be put back into the ship, and the grabber they handled the coal with broke a lot of it, so there would be a lot of fine dust going back into the ship. When the ship got to sea and got in motion, the dust would all settle to the bottom of the hold. As the coal there had been wet for weeks and was wet at the present time, it would cause a firedamp,[1] and the ship was very likely to burn up.

"Will you sign this report of Mr. McKay, Captain?"

"Yes, under protest as I have signed all his reports, and no other way."

"Very well, Captain Killman," Mr. Burg said, "I well remember what you told me the first time we met, and you are surely looking out for your ship and yourself."

"Mr. Burg, I am not going to give the San Francisco Board of Underwriters any chance to say 'that damn fool of a captain did so and so.'"

"Now, Captain, I want to know if, when the ship has finished her repairs, you will take her to Callao, Peru."

"Mr. Burg, I do not think that has anything to do with you or anyone else. The underwriters can refuse to take a risk on the ship if I would stay. Then the owners would have to put me out. I do not know as yet what I may do if the ship takes the coal to Peru, or starts with it. I will let my owners know in due time if I am resigning, but I do not think that the coal will leave here for Callao after the underwriters see that I protest this statement of Mr. McKay."

"Captain Killman, I am going to ask you one more question. Have you engaged a lawyer here to help you from time to time? Sometimes I think you must have, as you are so quick with your decisions."

"No, sir, I have talked with no one in regard to the ship's taking the cargo to Peru, or what I was going to do, as I think I have no right to discuss the underwriters' doings beyond this office and my agent's."

I then went to my ship to watch the work. That afternoon Mr. McKay came into my cabin. He asked me what I thought of the work that had been done. I told him that everything had been done very well, and I was sure the ship would be as good as she was when she was new. He at once said, "Then you will go to Callao, Captain, in the ship?"

"Why should you be interested in my affairs? You look out for your own business, and I will attend to mine!

"Now, Mr. McKay," I continued, "I want to say a few words to you. We will admit that the ship will be strong and seaworthy to meet any kind of weather when she is finished and goes to sea with this cargo of coal that you stated to the underwriters will not heat or fire. The *Ella A.* goes to sea, and is never heard of again. The opinion of those who are interested will be that the ship caught fire and burned, and all hands were either drowned or starved in the boats. How will you feel, with the blood of fourteen men dripping from your fingertips? Will you be able to look your wife in the face again after the *Ella A.* is posted as missing? Will you ever look at the Pacific Ocean again without the fear that one of those poor sailors might come out of that ocean and ask you if you were not the man who said that coal cargo was safe?

"I would rather you would make that statement than myself. But, Mr. McKay, I do not believe that cargo of coal ever will leave Honolulu for

Callao, Peru. In a very short time, we will know. I am positive in my own mind that they will not take the risk, as I think it is too great. But we will see."

In a few days I got a cable that the cargo of coal was sold to the Inter-Island Steam Navigation Company. "Discharge the balance, and when finished with the repairs sail for Port Townsend for orders." We went to the coal wharf when we came off from the drydock and finished discharging the balance of the cargo. Then we finished the repairs. As soon as they were completed and the accounts made up, I signed them, and I will say that the repairs were well done and that the Inter-Island Steam Navigation Company did their very best at all times.

Then came the trouble to get men to man the *Ella A*. I got a young man to go mate, and a young Danish boy who came from Newcastle in the ship came up to me on the street and asked me if I would not take him back, as his money was all gone and he had not had anything to eat for two days. I told him to go on board at once and keep his eyes open, as there were so many bums around who would steal anything they could get their hands on.

I got all kinds of men, anyone that would sign the articles to go in the ship. I made the young Danish boy boatswain, and the next day I was ready to take my departure from Honolulu. I had bade Mr. Burg goodbye.

He said, "Captain Killman, you are glad to get away, I am sure, as it has been nothing but trouble for you, but I am sure you have looked out for everything, and no one has put anything over that you have not seen. You still have the average adjusters to contend with, and W. R. Grace, and the balance."

"Well, Mr. Burg, I am still going to try and see that the ship gets a fair and just settlement."

"I am sure, Captain Killman, you will attend to that."

The next morning when the tug came, I was one man short. I told the US Shipping Commissioner that I would go short.

"You have got the hardest looking lot of men that I have ever seen, Captain. I do not know how you are going to get along with those men. I think there are two that can steer, and that is all."

"Well, I think I can teach some more of them, and it is a fine time of year. I will get home some way." I bade him goodbye.

"I wouldn't like your job! But you will get through some way; I am sure of that."

As the tug was coming a man on the dock asked me if I had all hands. I told him I wanted one man. I saw he was a sailor.

"Will you give me a sailor's job?"

"Where are your clothes?"

"I have only what I have on."

Two police were on the dock, and I asked them if the man was wanted for any crime there. They looked him over and said, "Take him away, Captain."

As he came on board I saw he was half drunk. I told him to go to work after I had signed him on the articles. The lines were let go, and in a very short time we were outside Honolulu.[2] After a while, I got sail on the ship. The tug blew to let go the hawser, which we did. He blew three whistles, and turned back for Honolulu. I dipped the flag three times to him, and if ever I was glad to get away from any port, I was glad to leave Honolulu.

We had fresh northeast trade winds, and at dark we were out of sight of the Hawaiian Islands. The next morning the mate reported to me that the sailor whom I took from the dock before sailing was not able to work. I told him to send him aft. He said he could not lift his right arm but did not know how he had hurt it. I strapped his shoulder as he said it was there, but could not see anything out of place. He did not do any work during the voyage except keep lookout.

I had a fair passage home for the time of year. The morning I towed in by Cape Flattery, it was clear with the sun shining bright. I set my flag and the ship's number so as to be reported, and as I looked up that wonderful sheet of water with all of its beauty, I could not but think of the great changes that had taken place since I first had passed in by Cape Flattery. I have counted at daybreak twenty-four ships and barks all beating, trying to get inside that cape, watching for a tug to come. The one that was ahead would be served first. Some of the finest sailing ships in the world were among them.

What a change time has made! Now you see a cloud of smoke coming down the Sound. You know it is a steamer, and you pay no attention to her. She is operated by machinery and has no charms for anyone. Well, sailoring is a lost art, or nearly so.

On arriving at Port Townsend,[3] I entered customs, paid the crew off on board, and at once left for Eagle Harbor where the ship was to be laid up, there being no freights that would pay. I had the sails all unbent and put away, saying to myself, "I think this is the last time that I will ever have this to do," as I could see that the strain had been too much for a man of my age, and I had gone through too many storms.

Arriving at Eagle Harbor, the tug came alongside so that I could place the ship's anchors. The boss rigger, Mr. Fisher, came off with a large boat to take the big wires on shore and make them fast for me. As soon as they were fast, he came on board to see me. We shook hands, as I had known him for many years. "Now, Captain Killman, I will finish this for you, as I am sure you want to go home and you have not got too much time."

I called the mate and told him that Mr. Fisher would finish mooring the ship. I went below to get ready to go home. After the ship was moored, Mr. Fisher came to my cabin, telling me that the ship was well moored and how much chain was out on each anchor. "Well, Captain Killman, as you know, I have seen a great many crews of men. But this is the worst that I ever have seen. How did you get this big schooner here? There is no one that knows anything. It is time to give it up, I think."

I told him that I thought it was very hard, as there were no more sailors for sailing ships, or if there were I did not get them.

The captain of the *Elinor H.* came after me to take me on shore, as I had not much time. He was to look out for the ship while I was gone. The crew all went to Seattle in the tug. We went on board his ship to see his wife. I was not there but a few minutes before a boy came from shore saying my daughter Katherine was on shore with a car to take me home, and that there was not much time to catch the ferry at Port Blakely.

I at once went on shore, and we soon started after a good hug. In two hours I was at my house, and my dear wife put her arms around my neck and the tears ran down her cheeks with joy. "You look bad, Daddy," she said and no more.

The next day one of the owners came for me, and we went to Seattle to the average adjuster. After they had talked for some time, he said to the adjuster, "I must go. When will you want me again?"

"I will not want you again. Captain Killman is the only one that knows anything about this, and he is surely able to handle it."

The average was settled in some six months. I saw the adjuster often. On the last day of February 1929 I resigned so as to be with my wife, as she was slowly becoming worse, and on the 4th day of May 1931 she passed away. Her troubles were all over; no more gales of wind to worry her, as she had always worried if the wind blew, thinking I must have the same weather. It was a hard blow for me, but I knew that I would soon be by her side, with no more storms, no more Cape Horn to contend with, no calm belt to get across; that it would all be sunshine and fair winds.

Will the beautiful sailing ship ever come back? I think there is nothing that can compare with a full-rigged ship under full sail, with three skysails set, gliding through the water.

I wonder—I wonder.[4]

The *A. M. Baxter*. Courtesy San Francisco Maritime National Historical Park, Scott Collection.

The *H. K. Hall*. Courtesy San Francisco Maritime National Historical Park.

Schooner *Ella A.*, which Killman managed to get into the port at Adelaide, South Australia, after losing the rudder in a storm. Courtesy San Francisco Maritime National Historical Park.

INCOMING MAIL
FROM THE COAST
Wilhelmina, today, p. m.
FROM THE SOUTH SEAS
Niagara, May 18, a. m.
FROM THE ORIENT
Pres. Jackson, Friday, a. m.

The Honolulu Advertiser

Hawaii's Territorial Newspaper

YEAR NO. 14,800.—14 PAGES — HONOLULU, TERRITORY OF HAWAII, TUESDAY MORNING, MAY 8, 1928. — PRICE FIVE CENTS.

CHOONER ELLA A ARRIVES FROM NEWCASTLE AFTER FIVE MONTHS VOYAGE

The four-masted schooner Ella A. was towed into port yesterday after nearly five months at sea. The vessel was bound for Callao, Peru, from Newcastle, N.S.W., with a cargo of coal, but was blown off her course and sprang a leak, forcing her to put in here for repairs. Food and water supplies were at a low ebb when the ship arrived.

At left are members of the crew, snapped by Al Williams, Advertiser staff photographer, just after the vessel tied up at Pier 27, the coal dock. Upper center is a snapshot of Capt. D. O. Killman, master of Ella A. Center shows the schooner entering the harbor, while at the right are the two mates, the top one being S. Hansen, first mate, who has been with the ship since she left her home port in Puget Sound last June 10.

Tugs Tow Four-Master in; Crew Shows Wear and Tear, Leaking Ship Looks Trim

Exactly five months after leaving Newcastle, N.S.W., with a cargo of 2280 tons of coal for discharge at Callao, Peru, the four-masted schooner Ella A., whose home port is Hoquiam, Wash., under command of Capt. D. O. Killman, arrived off port in tow Sunday night and was brought into the harbor and docked yesterday morning for repairs. The schooner was first sighted last Thursday afternoon off Kekaha, Kauai, where the captain went ashore in a small boat and reported that his vessel had made heavy weather after leaving Newcastle and had sprung a leak, forcing him to alter his course and seek smoother seas.

At times there was as much as eight feet of water in her holds, requiring all hands to man the pumps day and night. Fearing that the ship would go down if he attempted to make Callao, Captain Killman decided to make for Honolulu where repairs might be obtained. The run from Newcastle to Callao should have been made in about 40 or 50 days or 70 at the longest.

When the schooner reported off Kauai the Inter-Island tug Lehua was sent from Honolulu to tow the vessel here. They left Friday afternoon but were forced back by heavy weather to Port Allen where the Kinau went to ...

Why Such a Spectacle in Broad Daylight?

At the head of Fort street, not more than 500 yards from the center of town, between the hours of 2 p.m. and 5 p.m. these days, traffic is brisk and well directed.

Traffic that defies the law and violates the law.

Houses of prostitution on Fort and Kuakini streets, wide open and catering to men. An officer in uniform, perchance a graduate from the United States Naval academy, at the head of several special police, keeping order.

Broad daylight, that all may see who wish to see. And those who come there to see, are school children of the neighborhood—little children and older boys and girls. They sit, in large groups, on fences, on the curbs, stand around, idle about, watching the throng—watching young men in white uniforms enter and leave these houses.

Now, by some quirk or decree of Fate, or Nature, or otherwise, it may be necessary that men in the service visit such places. We are not entering into the merits of such an argument. The question arises: Why such a spectacle in the broad light of day?

Why carry on so brazenly and openly? Why defy the conventions of a supposedly circumspect, law-abiding community?

If these men must visit these houses, why not arrange it for the dark hours of night? If the community must wink at the spectacle, why not relieve the community of the obligation during daylight hours?

One of the reasons, it is claimed, that the sailors are not given shore liberty at night, is because of the menace offered by Honolulu houses of ill repute. If this is true, then why permit them to operate in daylight—and especially under the direction of special and local police, where the parade becomes a passing show for the children and the community?

Joy Zone at Fair Dreary; Wheels Know When to Stop To Keep Prizes On Shelf

They called it the Joy Zone in some of the advertising, and the Wikiwiki Way in other announcements. "Something doing every minute," was one of the trite phrases employed.

And what was the Wikiwiki Way at the Territorial Fair? Several gambling concessions, a merry-go-round, Ferris wheel, ice cream stand, waffle stand, a "circus," a Samoan village, the mirror hoax, trained monkeys and parrots, and two devices for "thrilling" rides. Probably a few other concessions, but the foregoing, in the main, provided the attraction.

The prevailing "games" were operated to the tune of some sort of a wheel. The wheel, apparently, is endowed with magic. It whirls to suit the customer as well as the owner. At least, the customer is so informed. Sometimes the customer twirls it for luck and loses his luck.

A makeshift with-in-the law practice was in order. To avoid being openly charged with conducting gambling devices, some of the concessions offered "something" with every turn of the wheel. Walk up and lay down your dime. Walk away with a ribbon or a buttonhole flower, or whatnot. Walk up and lay down your dime expecting to pick off a prize ham. Spend a dollar, walk away with several ribbons and buttonhole flowers.

SOME CAN'T AFFORD IT

We merely use these as illustrations. The "big sport" from Wai-

(Continued on Page 3, Col. 2)

JAPANESE TO BLAME AVERS SOUTH LEADER

Chiang Proposes To Expose Brutality Of Japan

U. S. WILL NOT JOIN FORCES

(United Press by Navy Radio)

SHANGHAI, May 7.—Responsibility for the recent clashes between Chinese and Japanese troops at Tsinanfu, Shantung province, was placed squarely upon the Japanese by General Chiang Kai-shek, supreme military leader of the Nationalists, in telegraphed messages received here today.

"Japanese troops challenged the Chinese," General Chiang Kai-shek's message of explanation said. "They fired upon our soldiers and then upon our civilians.

TO EXPOSE BRUTALITY

"As a revolutionist I cannot bow to such bullying. I propose to expose the deliberate brutality of the Japanese to the world."

Meanwhile unconfirmed reports received here from the Shantung war area state that Japanese officials at Tsinanfu have issued an ultimatum

(Continued on Page 2, Col. 6)

RUMANIAN SITUATION GROWS TENSE

...000 Peasants In March On Bratianu's Headquarters

...POL PLANS TO TAKE COMMAND

CONGRESSMAN FLAYS ARMY OFFICERS HERE

Criticizes Policy Followed in Handling Land Exchanges

(United Press by Navy Radio)

WASHINGTON, May 7.—"Army officers in Hawaii have conducted themselves as leaders of conquering forces in a subdued nation," Representative Louis C. Cramton, Republican of Michigan, declared from the floor of the house of representatives today.

The statements attacking army authorities in the Territory were made by Representative Cramton during debate on a bill introduced by Representative W. Frank Jones, Republican of Michigan, authorizing acquisition of land at Fort Kamehameha for use as a flying field.

Representative Cramton vigorously criticized the policies followed by army officers in Hawaii in conducting and handling land exchanges. Enthusiastically he endorsed the position taken by ...

INDIANA NAMES CHOICE TODAY AT THE POLLS

Outcome Will Determine Strength of Hoover as Candidate

(United Press By Navy Radio)

LONDON, May 7.—Without a record vote the house of commons today passed a bill extending the franchise to all English women over 21 years of age.

Experts estimate that the bill will make 2,000,000 more women voters than men in England in event they exercise the franchise fully. Men are greatly outnumbered by women in post-war England.

CONTROVERSY ON SIDEWALKS TO BE REVIVED

Board to Receive Report of Survey Made by C. R. Welsh

Revival of the Manoa sidewalk controversy is expected tonight when Captain Charles R. Welsh, engineer with the city planning commission, submits to the board of supervisors his recommendations as to what streets in the valley should have the cement walks.

Although Welsh's report had not been completed yesterday it was learned that in all probability the city planning engineer will recommend the construction of sidewalks on more streets than those named in the original resolution.

Several weeks ago when the sidewalk controversy was at its height ...

TAX LEAGUE TO CANVASS ENTIRE CITY

Residents of All Sections Listed to Further Organization

The committee of the newly formed Taxpayers' league held its first meeting last night at Liliuokalani school and mapped out plans for making the organization city-wide in its scope.

Ed Towse was named permanent chairman of the new organization; A. R. Kroll, vice president; J. R. McLane, statistical secretary, and Harry T. Mills, recording and corresponding secretary.

Names of representative persons in all sections of the city were listed and these will be canvassed in the move to increase the radius of activity. Waikiki, Kalihi-uka, Kalihi-kai, Manoa, Puunui, Kakaako, Diamond Head and Kahala beach will all be enlisted in the move for tax reform. The secretary was instructed to get into communication with these various districts through the persons agreed upon at the committee meeting. These persons, in turn, will unite into a central organization covering Honolulu proper.

Rural districts are not being considered at this time. It is the plan ...

Fleet Chapter Of De Molay to Install Class

All De Molays and master masons in Honolulu are invited to attend the first installation of members of that order at the Scottish Rite Cathedral at 7:30 tonight. The Battle Fleet chapter of De Molays will install a number of candidates from the ships at the meeting.

The De Molay is an organization composed of young men between the ages of 16 and 21 and is sponsored by the masons all over the country. There are a ...

Mussolini Lauds Organization He Founded in Italy

SPORT HIGHLIGHTS

The *Honolulu Advertiser* of 8 May 1928 heralds the arrival in port of the *Ella A.*, on her way from Australia to Peru. Courtesy San Francisco Maritime National Historical Park, Captain Klebingat Collection.

Wilder's Steamship Company Dock, Honolulu. Inter-island steamers *Claudine*, *Kinau*, and *Helene*. Courtesy San Francisco Maritime National Historical Park.

Elinor H., sister-ship to the *Ella A.*
Courtesy San Francisco Maritime National Historical Park, Gordon Jones Collection.

Attendees at Captain Taylor's Navigation School.
Courtesy San Francisco Maritime National Historical Park, Max Lembke Collection.

The steamer *Kinau* in drydock on Marine Way, at the foot of Punchbowl Street in Honolulu, about 1890. Courtesy San Francisco Maritime National Historical Park.

Afterword

For me it was the stuff of legend—the autobiography of Capt. Daniel O. Killman. I had heard about the Killman manuscript from Karl Kortum off and on for years after he hired me as librarian in 1972 at the San Francisco Maritime Museum. The books were not catalogued or even clearly separated from manuscripts, so I set to it. In time it occurred to me that the Killman manuscript was not there.

Overflow books were stored in "the cage," a former bathroom in the basement that had water on the floor following rain and when the lawns were watered. No Killman there either.

Karl's special place for storing his most precious books and documents was a small closet under the double stairway to his third-floor office overlooking the Aquatic Park Lagoon and the historic ships he had rescued. Odd shaped and difficult of access was this closet, with two "rooms," one about four feet deep, the other about five, both fifteen feet wide.

Karl made use of every inch of that odd closet. He had learned this skill when sailing three-quarters of the way around the world on the square-rigger *Kaiulani*. There, in extremely limited space, he had repurposed what was available into what he wanted. Eventually I got into this sacred space. Among projects from across the world were manuscripts and documents, including the triple-elephant-sized folios he made in an effort to sell the city on transforming a dirt parking lot into a gas-lit park as context for his Victorian-era historic ships. Everything was there. Except Killman.

Karl told me bits and pieces about Killman's manuscript. I learned, for instance, that his nickname was "Crazy" Killman. But Karl never talked about its content. Whenever he got close to that, it seemed somehow beyond expression. All I gathered was a sense of hushed awe.

Nor was Karl the only one impressed by this manuscript. It had captured the "devout attention" of other founding figures of West Coast maritime history: Dr. John Lyman and Capt. Harold Huycke.

Who were these three, and what gave them such standing?

- Karl Kortum, uncomfortable with having downrigged the last American Cape Horn sailing ship in 1948, wrote to Scott Newhall, editor of the *San Francisco Chronicle*. The product of that letter is the San Francisco Maritime Museum. In the ensuing decades, Kortum and the museum became the nexus for West Coast maritime history collections, research and exhibitions. And while building the museum, Kortum kept tabs on surviving square-riggers throughout the world. He was instrumental in the rescue of a dozen historic ships worldwide—from Australia to Great Britain. In Britain, Frank Carr, chairman of the World Ship Trust, said Kortum was "the world's leading exponent and expert on historic craft preservation," and called him "a genius." But among all his maritime relationships, the longest and probably most productive were with John Lyman and Harold Huycke.
- John Lyman was an oceanographer for the US Navy whose avocational interest since college had been West Coast maritime history. In the 1940s he established his foundational place in West Coast maritime history with his publication of summaries of the careers of West Coast ships in *Marine Digest*. As a decades-long research associate of the San Francisco Maritime Museum, and in his personal work, he continued to advance his standing. His periodical, *Log Chips*, contained more substantive information than any other maritime periodical I have seen. One example of his research prowess has always impressed me: Karl said that after "research in the national archives, and . . . I don't know how," Lyman came up with an estimate of the total number of square-rigged ships that sailed around Cape Horn to San Francisco between the onset of the Gold Rush, in 1848, and the opening of the Panama Canal, in 1913: ten thousand.
- Harold Huycke, another long-term research associate of San Francisco Maritime Museum, also began his West Coast maritime research in the 1940s. Over the decades he corresponded with seafarers from the ages of both sail and steam, many of whom sent him written reminiscences. From

among the drifting material of seafaring history, Harold salvaged numerous first-person accounts of West Coast maritime history, including Captain Killman's remarkable autobiography. Harold is best known for his definitive *To Santa Rosalia: Further and Back*, a study of German square-riggers held in Baja California during World War I, reputed to be the only Mariners Museum publication to sell out.

The "devout attention" of Lyman and Huycke, as detailed by Rebecca Ellison, consisted of extensive research and vetting in 1975 and 1976, during which time they worked together to confirm names and dates pertaining to ships, ports, and people. Their notes are nearly a quarter the length of the autobiography itself. And beyond simply verifying facts, they provide interpretations and conclusions, such as this from chapter 25, note 1: "The use of exact dates and positions in this chapter indicates that, for the first time, Captain Killman was writing from records and not solely from memory. Here he probably was referring to the schooner's log for a copy of the protest he made on his arrival in Honolulu."

No doubt Kortum's high regard for the manuscript was grounded in his extended experience as both an Able-Bodied Seaman before the mast and as mate in a square-rigged ship. Such experience would have included not only his work but also his treatment both by others and of others and his exposure to accounts and yarns by older deepwater square-rig sailors. And if his opinion was grounded in square-rig experience, it was modulated, refined, and further informed by extensive study of the period of bucko mates, particularly Andrew Furuseth's *Red Record*, an inventory of brutalities and oppressions practiced upon seamen by officers and shoreside thugs, and of the square-rig experience in general in the period 1849–1935.

What is very clear is that the Killman autobiography is a West Coast story, fostered by Karl Kortum and carefully vetted by two preeminent West Coast maritime historians.

Once I picked up the manuscript I could hardly set it down. My friend Steve Hyman, rigger extraordinaire, responded similarly. Picking up the manuscript late at night, he read the entire account straight through, at the cost of a night's sleep.

The autobiography raises some fascinating questions. First, how accurate are voyage books? Many of these "yarns" are spun from the imagination, but others are actual reports, often prefaced by a statement such as, "This is what happened, and no shit!" One periodical run that Kortum charged me to review was *Sea Stories Magazine* (1922–1927), a pulp publication whose contributors were exclusively seafarers. The contributions were indeed sea stories, but each was based on its author's experience—which raises a second, related, question. Because librarians whose knowledge of seafaring and its writing style might be questioned classify many seafaring titles as fiction, one must ask which of these titles are more fact than fiction and therefore are untapped sources of history.

A third question: What in this autobiography so captivated the giants of West Coast maritime history? We might begin by considering Killman's family history. He was named after his father, who was named after his father, both of whom were masters of square-rigged ships. The Killmans were a long-established and well-respected Maine family. Daniel was heir to a tradition of success at sea. Most American clipper ships, the apex of sail, were built just down the coast, and they were succeeded by Maine down-Easters, whose masters upheld the reputation of American ships as "the pride of the ocean." Born in 1860, Killman went to sea when Americans were turning their attention from the sea to westward expansion. As a consequence, crews consisted primarily of foreigners who had no place else to turn, men hardened by persistent misfortune. Hardcases—drunk, intractable, ignorant of the sea, often shanghaied—they made motley crews. When our author went to sea, man-bashing bucko mates were well established, but the backlash against brutal treatment afloat had just begun.

To be sure, cargo was "king" and had to be delivered. And consistent with the reputation of American ships as "the pride of the ocean," their cargoes were delivered not only speedily but also in ships that presented a "fine" appearance in harbor.

Which was Capt. Daniel O. Killman, A or B?

A. Might makes Right. He had no sympathy for others, his only concern being his own success and that of the ship. In spite of his intent, his own account reveals the motivations, rationalizations, and actions of the Bucko Mate.

B. Might in the service of Right. His guiding light was to do good and to make good. His logbook writing style—"I was merely doing my duty. These are the facts."—shows his pride in seamanship. His account demonstrates his ability to save ships in dire predicaments, gain contracts, and protect the business of owners, all the while behaving as a professional seaman, even though a gruff one, who would not and could not tolerate fools.

Perhaps he was a combination of the two.

Or does Killman's story embody the dilemma of Everyman: sometimes our efforts to do good as we understand it go horribly wrong?

Perhaps further study will reveal not only what made this man tick, but also how Kortum, Lyman, and Huycke related to one another in their individual readings of this landmark autobiography.

After Harold's death I met with the Huycke family in their home near Seattle regarding their donation of Harold's collections to the San Francisco Maritime National Historical Park. It was then I learned that the Killman manuscript was safely stowed in his basement office.

In 2012, two years after that meeting, I had a telephone call from Rebecca Huycke Ellison. She was preparing the Killman manuscript for publication and, having seen a poster about the Karl Kortum Award for Maritime History in her father's office, thought that might be a good starting point and called me to ask about it.

The Kortum Award, sponsored by the Friends of the San Francisco Maritime Museum Library, is limited to unpublished manuscripts in specific fields of West Coast maritime history. A primary purpose of the award is to bring worthy manuscripts to the attention of publishers.

The Killman manuscript was the most important submission for the Kortum Award in its nineteen-year history, joining at least two other oral histories of Killman in the J. Porter Shaw Library. The eighth award was presented to Rebecca Ellison in 2013. Now that *Forty Years Master* is in print, six of the eight Kortum Award manuscripts have been published.

Many voyage books recount coastwise and deepwater sail experiences on and from the West Coast. Some are by shipmasters, those who analyze risk and give orders. But none that I know recounts with Killman's degree of detail and clarity the events in this critical period. Even so, "Crazy" Killman's story might have been forever in the shadows of western American maritime history. Instead, thanks to good fortune and hard work all that changed. When Rebecca submitted the manuscript to Texas A&M University Press, their acquisitions editor Thom Lemmons and his colleagues, to their great credit, recognized gold. And now, after eighty years, the autobiography has found the light of day.

—David Hull,
Principal Librarian, Retired
J. Porter Shaw Library
San Francisco Maritime NHP
July 2015

Notes

INTRODUCTION

1. The progenitor of this "bottom up" maritime history is Jesse Lemisch, in his seminal article, "Jack Tar in the Streets: Merchant Seamen in the Politics of Revolutionary America," *William and Mary Quarterly* 25, no. 3 (July 1968): 371–407. Sailors and working-class activism figure in Peter Linebaugh and Marcus Rediker, *The Many-Headed Hydra: Sailors, Slaves, Commoners, and the Hidden History of the Revolutionary Atlantic* (Boston, MA: Beacon Press, 2000), and Marcus Rediker, *Between the Devil and the Deep Blue Sea: Merchant Seamen, Pirates, and the Anglo-American Maritime World, 1700–1750* (New York: Cambridge University Press, 1987). An overview of this historiography is contained in Matthew Raffety, "Recent Currents in the Nineteenth-Century American Maritime History," *History Compass* 6, no. 2 (February 2008): 607–26.

2. A model for this sort of even-handed treatment of shipmasters is Margaret S. Creighton, *Rites and Passages: The Experience of American Whaling, 1830–1870* (New York: Cambridge University Press, 1995), especially chapter 4.

3. Much of the history of the maritime labor movement is covered in Leon Fink, *Sweatshops at Sea: Merchant Seamen in the World's First Globalized Industry from 1812 to the Present* (Chapel Hill: University of North Carolina Press, 2011).

4. Technological transformation is covered in Alex Roland, W. Jeffrey Bolster, and Alexander Keyssar, *The Way of the Ship: America's Maritime History Reenvisioned, 1600–2000* (Hoboken, NJ: John Wiley and Sons, 2008).

5. Roland, Bolster, and Keyssar, *The Way of the Ship*.

CHAPTER 1

1. According to Mrs. Charles M. Clements of Belfast, Maine, whose great-grandfather's sister Margaret was Killman's grandmother, his parents were Daniel Odam Killman (1816–79) and Martha Ann Grant. Both were from Prospect, Maine, which is on the west bank of the Penobscot River, below Winterport (Frankfort until 1860) and above Stockton Springs (Stockton until 1889), and they married there 12 September 1840. Killman's father was the son of another Daniel Odam Killman (1781–1859), whose parents were Samuel and Abigail Killman and who married Margaret Heagan, daughter of John Heagan and his wife, Betsey Stinson. Killman's mother, born 11 August 1823, was the daughter of Capt. Japheth Grant and his wife, Judith (letter to Harold D. Huycke Jr. from Mrs. Charles M. Clements 29 February 1976).

2. Killman's younger sister, Amber, was born in 1866. Bourgeois is apparently Bourgeois Inlet, on Lennox Passage, Cape Breton Island, Nova Scotia, Canada.

3. George Savary Wasson and Lincoln Colcord, *Sailing Days on the Penobscot:*

The River and Bay as They Were in the Old Days. With a Record of Vessels Built There (Salem, MA: Marine Research Society, 1932), 436–40, lists twenty vessels built at Frankfort by Treat & Co. between 1855 and 1872. According to Richard V. Palmer, Director of the Penobscot Marine Museum, Killman's father was master of the Treat & Co. bark *James M. Churchill*, built in 1855 (letter dated 15 March 1976). The *George Treat*, 639 tons, was built at Winterport in 1866 by W. H. Brown. Her first document, Register No. 1, issued at Frankfort, Maine, 10 February 1866, gives her owners as James and William Treat of Winterport, with 1/32; Edward D. Peters & Co. of Boston, with 20/32; and Edward Sweasey of Boston, with 11/32. Her master was Daniel Killman, but George W. Ginn became master by October 1867.

4. According to information received from Richard Palmer, from Roger Dubose, a volunteer at the Penobscot Marine Museum, and from Robert B. Applebee of Stockton Springs, Killman's father had earlier commanded the 174-ton brig *Clara Ellen*, built at Stockton in 1846; the 199-ton brig *Kate Foster*, built at Bangor in 1851 by Crosby Bros.; and the 721-ton ship *Gibraltar*, built at Frankfort in 1854 by Daniel Williams. (Letter, Palmer, 15 March 1976. The Dubose notes are undated; those from Applebee are untraced.)

5. The 1860 census for Prospect lists only six of Killman's eight older siblings: Thomas W., age eighteen; Annie, sixteen; Henry C., fourteen; Charles, eleven; Fred, six; and Margaret, two. Killman himself did not arrive in the world in time to be enumerated.

6. Killman's mother's tombstone gives her death as occurring in 1871. Killman would have been eleven (not seven).

7. Killman's father married Miss Emily J. Curtis of Stockton in Prospect on 12 June 1873. Mrs. Clements located her in the 1860 Census as the four-year-old daughter of Lincoln and Mary Curtis, with older brothers who were seafarers. Thus she was only seventeen when she was married and (as Mrs. Clements comments) "probably entertaining standards of behavior a 13-year-old boy would find impossible."

8. The 495-ton bark *Courser* had been built at Stockton, Maine, in 1862 by Mudgett, Libbey & Co. In 1874, Alvah P. Blanchard of Brooklyn, New York, owned half of her, with several individuals in Stockton owning the other half. Andrew Dickey then was her master. The endorsements of change of master have been torn off her last register, so it is uncertain when Killman's brother took command, but the 1877 *American Lloyd's Register of American and Foreign Shipping*, which records a survey at Boston in October 1876, gives the master's name as Killman. Casualty reports in *Mitchell's Maritime Register: A Weekly Journal of Shipping and Commerce* (London: William Mitchell, 1856–1884) state that the *Courser* encountered heavy weather on 9 May 1877, in 52° S, 104° W, on a voyage from Auckland, New Zealand, toward New York. She lost spars, sails, rigging, boats, and

deckhouses, started leaks in her deck, and had five men washed overboard. The *Courser* put into Valparaiso on 17 June 1877, still leaking badly, and on the 30th was discharging her cargo into a hulk. Repairs were estimated at $12,000. Early in October she was sold locally for $5,000.

9. The 539-ton bark *Masonic* was built at Stockton in 1864 by Stowers & Staples. On 14 March 1878 she arrived at New York with a cargo of sugar from Havana, Cuba. Alvah P. Blanchard then bought her from Booth & Ward of New York and put Thomas W. Killman in command.

10. Daniel Killman was born into a family with a history of seafaring. In addition to his father and both grandfathers, at least three uncles commanded their own vessels, as did two of his brothers. Throughout the family tree can be found names connecting the Killmans through marriage to other seafaring families. According to Robert P. Applebee, in *Searsport Sea Captains: A Collection of Photographs Compiled by Colonel Frederick Frasier Black with Brief Biographical Sketches, Including the Ships They Commanded* (Searsport, ME: Penobscot Marine Museum, 1960), the town of Searsport, less than ten miles from Prospect, "furnished more masters to the square mile than any other community in the United States." It is no surprise that young Dan Killman would expect to go to sea.

11. The *Masonic* sailed from New York for Nagasaki, Japan, 18 May 1878. Thus Killman was a month and four days short of his eighteenth birthday when he first went to sea.

12. Killman's affliction with seasickness at the start of each voyage must have become particularly vexing after he married and began taking his wife to sea with him. His daughter stated that her mother was never seasick. (Taped interview, 2 September 1975, Mrs. Sydney Killman Pierce and Harold D. Huycke Jr, Tacoma, WA. San Francisco Maritime National Historical Park Research Center Oral History Collection [hereinafter OHC UCC], 139a.)

13. The *Matilda* might have been the 627-ton Canadian bark built at Summerside, Prince Edward Island, in 1874. Apparently she was not classed with *Lloyd's Register*. Possibly for this reason *Mitchell's Maritime Register* did not record any casualty involving her in 1878. In contrast, the *Masonic* is listed as having put into Manila on 5 November 1878.

14. The 24 March 1879 *San Francisco Chronicle* reported on the crime as follows:

In the case of Edward Bertrand, who arrived in this city by the *City of Peking* on last Friday, and is charged with the murder of Captain Thomas W. Killman of the bark *Masonic* on the 14th of November, 1878, it appears that Bertrand was the cook and steward when the vessel sailed from New York on the 17th of last May. The trouble between the cook and the Captain does not seem to have commenced until the day previous to the murder. Bertrand was before United States Commissioner O'Beirne last Saturday afternoon for preliminary examination, and was held to answer before the Grand Jury. Following is the testimony of two eye-witnesses of the homicide:

Frank Swenson, a sailor, testified that on the 14th of November, 1878, the Captain asked him where Bertrand was, and going into the galley saw the defendant, kicked and swore at him, and continued doing so for some time. The cook begged the Captain not to maltreat him anymore, but he continued his abuse. Bertrand then jumped up from the galley floor, where he was lying, and picking up a knife stabbed the Captain, the blade protruding from his back. The Captain fell before he could reach his cabin, and was carried thence and died about 2 o'clock the next morning, and was buried at Manila the same day at 4 o'clock p.m.

Benjamin F. Farrell, second mate of the *Masonic*, testified that about 6 o'clock on the afternoon of the 14th of November he heard the Captain say to the steward that he had made a poor complaint to the American Consul in saying that he (the Captain) had refused to give him money. The steward give [sic] the Captain the lie. The Captain struck at the steward and shoved him on to the deck. The witness also stated that he saw blood on Bertrand's shirt and beard, and also that the Captain had told the men not to allow the steward to sleep below. About half-past 9 o'clock witness saw the Captain on deck holding his hands on his abdomen, and calling out that he was stabbed. The cut was four or five inches long, and there was a wound on the back that looked as if the knife had gone through the body. On the conclusion of the testimony the prisoner was held to answer before the United States Grand Jury.

A month later it was reported that Bertrand "was found not guilty, the evidence showing self-defense" (*St. Paul Globe*, 25 April 1879 via chroniclingamerica.com).

15. Manly S. Genn of Prospect, Maine, assumed command of the *Masonic* at Manila on 18 November 1878, and she sailed again for Nagasaki on 12 December. On 2 January 1879 the *Masonic* once more put in at Manila, having suffered in bad weather in the China Sea. While making port she struck San Nicolas Shoals, and the surveyors recommended that the cargo be discharged and transshipped. Osman S. Nichols of Searsport, Maine, replaced Genn as master on 2 February. While the cargo was being transferred to the bark *Mount Lebanon*, it was found to be twenty-two cases short, whereupon (over the protest of the US consul) the *Masonic* was seized by the Spanish authorities, condemned, and sold. Evidently the case was pursued for several years: the bark's register was not surrendered until November 1886.

16. The 644-ton bark *Elmiranda* was built at Stockton, Maine, in 1874. Isaac Lanpher (who also had been the first master of the bark *Masonic*) owned 1/16 interest in her. This item establishes Stockton, Maine, as Killman's birthplace.

17. The *Thermopylae* sailed from Shanghai for London 27 November 1878 in company with the *Salamis*, which was bound in ballast for Australia. In *The Log*

of the Cutty Sark (Glasgow: Brown, Son & Ferguson, 1928), 173–75, Basil Lubbock records that the *Thermopylae* passed Anjer Point on 19 December and *Salamis* on 29 December, while the rest of the fleet was "still struggling to leeward of Thwarttheway." Thwarttheway (from the Dutch "Dwars in den weg") is the island in the middle of the narrowest part of Sunda Strait, now called Sangiang.

18. Guano, a natural manure composed of the excrement of sea birds and bats, is found chiefly on islands near the Peruvian coast.

19. The Spanish bark *Teodora*, Lopez, bound from Saigon with rice for Cienfuegos and Havana, Cuba, put into Batavia, Dutch East Indies (now Jakarta, Indonesia), 4 January 1879 having lost her foremast in a collision in Sunda Strait with the ship *India*, Patterson, which proceeded on her voyage. The *Teodora* had to jettison part of her cargo and on 11 January was being discharged. So reported *Mitchell's Maritime Register*. The *India* was a 1,294-ton ship, built at Bath, Maine, in 1868.

20. The *Elmiranda* left Manila 26 November 1878 and arrived at New York 17 April 1879 with a cargo of sugar and other Philippine produce consigned to Brown Brothers & Co. She was made into a barkentine in September 1894 and was abandoned at sea 14 November 1904 on a foreign voyage from Jacksonville, Florida. The British steamer *Horsa* rescued the crew and landed them four days later at Bermuda.

21. Killman's father was born in 1816, died in 1879, and is buried beside his first wife and their son Henry C. in Prospect Cemetery. Probably this Henry C. was their second son. Born in 1845, he lived only a year and a half. A second Henry C., born to them in 1849, is buried in California. (See chapter 4, note 9.)

22. Killman's grandmother was the Margaret Heagen mentioned in chapter 1, note 1. Mrs. Clements and her grandmother were each named Margaret for her. Mrs. Clements provided the following stories from the *Belfast Republican Journal* telling of Margaret Killman:

Prospect. There was a very pleasant gathering at the residence of J. H. Killman on the 2nd Inst. to celebrate the 95th birthday of Mrs. Margaret Killman. There were present of the family Mrs. Abigail Thompson, Mr. Richard Killman, Mr. J. H. Killman, Capt. Robert Killman, Mrs. U. Marden, Mrs. Sarah Lane, Mrs. L. Lane. The eldest was seventy-three and the youngest forty-eight. Mrs. K. has lived to see her family of eleven children grow up and marry, and could visit all of them in one day. There were twenty-one grandchildren and six great grandchildren present, and she has two great-great grandchildren. Her only living brother, Gen. S. S. Heagan, was present. The day was enjoyably spent in conversation, and at noon the company, numbering 65, sat down to a well filled board. Eight sat at one table, whose united ages were 629 years, average 78-1/2 years. Mrs. Margaret Killman is an intelligent woman, interesting in conversation, and very active for one of her years. Many younger women are not a match for her in her favorite work of spinning and knitting. She spun, doubled and twisted 30 skeins of yarn in 5 days last summer.

Rev. H. G. Carley was present and made an impressive prayer. At a late hour, after wishing Mrs. Killman many years of health and prosperity, the company separated, all feeling that they had spent a pleasant day. [10 April 1884]

Prospect. Mrs. Margaret Killman, now on a visit to her daughter Mrs. Sarah Lane is probably the oldest person in this county. She was ninety-six years old last month. She tried her hand at spinning, the work she always liked, last Saturday, and will spin a fine skein of yarn yet. She retains her memory remarkably for one of her age. She was married and the mother of two children in the War of 1812 and can remember events of the war. Mr. Killman was posted on the river when the English came up the river. One English vessel went ashore on Packard's Point and some of the soldiers ran away. Two of them, Jimmie McKan and Owen Quinn, came to Killman's house, left their guns, changed their military clothing and tried their luck in America. Mr. Killman was the first settler on the second tier of lots from the River, and it was all woods from Mosquito Mountain to Cape Jellison Harbor at that time. Wild animals were prowling about, and the Killmans lost their hogs by bears when they first settled. [21 May 1885]

23. On 2 April 1889 the *Boston Daily Globe* carried an account of Mrs. Killman's 100th birthday celebration:

She Comes of Sturdy Stock. Margaret Killman, Whose Father Owned a Whole Mountain in Maine, Celebrating Today the Centennial of Her Birth. Bangor, Me., April 2. – One hundred years ago Mrs. Margaret Killman of Prospect first saw the light of day. At this time this venerable lady, surrounded by her children, her grandchildren, great-grandchildren and great-great-grandchildren, is celebrating in the happiest manner the centennial anniversary of her birth and within sight of the same noble river upon the banks of which she was born. Mrs. Killman is beyond doubt one of the oldest people in New England and the oldest in Maine, and her longevity is remarkable, for, like many other hardy women of the Pine Tree State, she did work enough before she reached the age of 20 to have killed an ordinary mortal.

A few hours passed with the venerable lady are sufficient to convince one of her knowledge of the history of our country and that her intellect has not been dulled by time.

Mrs. Killman comes of sturdy stock and her people were nearly all long-lived. She was the daughter of John Heagan, who was born on the lovely Anowsic [Arrowsic] island, off the western coast of Maine. He was a man of rare ability and energy and in early life he came to the shores of the Penobscot and settled 18 miles below Bangor, in Prospect. Before his death he was one of the largest land owners in eastern Maine, and widely known. The large mountain on the right bank of the Penobscot was one of the possessions of this energetic old pioneer, and was named for him, Heagan's mountain. Mr. Heagan was the father of five sons and three daughters, and all but one or two of them passed four-score years. Mrs. Killman is the last of this famous family. Her brother, General S. S. Heagan, who was 10 years younger, and the most prominent of all the children, died about two years ago at the age of 88 years. He was widely known, and held many State offices during his life.

Margaret, who is 100 years old today, was married 80 years ago to Daniel Killman of Brewer, whose widowed mother left Boston with him and his three brothers the very day that the patriotic bean-eaters filled Boston harbor full of tea.

It would seem as if the incident fully instilled courage and manliness into the mind of Daniel, for Margaret Killman now draws $12 per month from the government at Washington for the good services of her husband in the war of 1812. When the couple were married they commenced life after the true style of the pioneer of the olden time, by settling upon a tract of wild land, and their lives was [sic] devoted to clearing and converting it into a fine productive farm. They had 10 children, six sons and four daughters, and with the oldest son, James H. Killman, who has already reached three score and 10 years, the aged lady now resides. Four of the sons followed the sea and rose to the command of as good ships and barks as ever ploughed the Atlantic, being known far and wide for their integrity and seamanlike qualities.

Three sons and three daughters of Mrs. Killman's large family now survive, the oldest being a daughter, who is 78 years old. All of them live within a radius of a few miles of their aged mother, and today they surround her, and are as proud of her as if she were the ruler of a mighty domain. The old lady has 27 grandchildren now living. Of her great-grandchildren there are 20 living while of the fifth generation there are now six representatives. Besides those living in Maine, there are others scattered through Massachusetts and Connecticut, and some have gone to California. The husband of Mrs. Killman died in 1861, at the age of 79 years, and after a happy married life of half a century. Mrs. Killman has always known hard work, and throughout her life spinning, weaving and milking were her regular duties in addition to her usual household work. Some of her spinning feats have been remarkable, and not the least among them was performed two years ago, when at the age of 98 years she walked to the house of a son who lives more than a mile away and spun 45 skeins of yarn in a week, and then walked back, unaccompanied. Her general health has seemed quite good until a few days ago, when she felt the effects of the changing weather and has been somewhat ill. Her intellect is remarkable, and one could not find a more interesting aged lady. Her memory is good and her knowledge of local history seems unlimited. She remembers when, in 1812, the British squadron sailed up the Penobscot river, and the alarm occasioned among the inhabitants by the unwelcome visit of the red-coated marauders. There are still houses along the river which she remembers were hit by balls from British cannon. She has a distinct remembrance of Washington's death and the reverence in which the people of those times held the "Father of his country."

Mrs. Killman gives every evidence of living a number of years to come. (Article courtesy of NewspaperArchive.com, provided by Everett, Washington, Family History Center).

24. The 383-ton half-brig *David Owen* was built at Bath, Maine, in 1866 by B. L. White for Goss & Sawyer. Her master was Charles G. Chadbourne. W. A. Baker covered her history in *A Maritime History of Bath, Maine, and the Kennebec River Region* (Bath, ME: Marine Research Society of Bath, 1973), 528–30. The dates of Killman's service in her are closely approximated by the dates on which an enrollment was taken out at New York (14 October 1879) and exchanged for a register at Pensacola (16 December 1879). Readers familiar with stories of the careers of British shipmasters at this period will notice the contrast with the American system. A British lad had to go to sea for a full four years as an apprentice (or as a foremast hand for an even longer period, embracing 1,460 actual days at sea) and then pass stiff oral and written examinations before he was eligible to serve as a second mate on a foreign-going vessel of 100 tons or larger. Killman, on the other hand, served as second mate of the *David Owen* after only about sixteen months of sea experience.

25. Many years later, in February 1912, the *Aberdeen Herald* reported that Killman dove into the Hoquiam River to save his young daughter Sydney, who had accidently walked off the deck of the *Lyman D. Foster* in the darkness during a storm. (*Aberdeen Herald*, 19 February 1912, courtesy chroniclingamerica.com)

26. Santos is a port city in Brazil.

27. The *Grace Bradley* had been built in 1873 at Thomaston, Maine, by Samuel Watts for his own management. Originally 438 tons, she had been enlarged to 557 in October 1879. She arrived at Portland, Maine, 1 February 1880.

28. "Pogy" is a common name for menhaden, a fish in the herring family. Pogy scraps, used in Killman's day as fertilizer, are now called fish meal, a highly valued component of swine and poultry rations.

CHAPTER 2

1. The *Louis Walsh* was a 1,556-ton full-rigged ship, built at Belfast, Maine, in 1861 by White, Connor & Co. Her history has been detailed by F. C. Matthews in *American Merchant Ships* (Salem, MA: Marine Research Society, 1930), 1:198–200. When Killman sailed in her she was owned by members of the Pendleton, Carver, and White families of Searsport, Maine, with Augustus S. White as master and owner of 11/48ths.

2. In the 1870s and 1880s most crude oil came from Pennsylvania. With very little refining it could be used as lubricating oil. In the 1930s, when Killman was writing, highly refined (and hence basically colorless) lubricating oil made from

Texas or California crudes often had a blue "bloom" added to it to imitate the color of Pennsylvania oil.

3. The *Louis Walsh* cleared customs at New York on 15 June 1880 and sailed the next day for Bristol, England, where she arrived on 26 July consigned to M. Whitwell & Co.

4. The original manuscript called it the Carlton Bridge. A Carlton Bridge spans the Kennebec River in Maine, but the bridge spanning the Avon River near Bristol, England, is the Clifton Bridge, which was completed in 1864.

5. The *Louis Walsh* left Bristol 20 August 1880 and arrived at Saint John, New Brunswick, on 22 September, according to *Mitchell's Maritime Register*.

6. The *Louis Walsh* was loaded for Liverpool by W. M. Mackay of Saint John and cleared that port on 1 November 1880.

7. Historically "St. George's Channel" encompassed all the waters between Ireland and Great Britain.

8. *Mitchell's Maritime Register* reports that the *Louis Walsh* arrived at Liverpool on 6 December 1880. There is no mention of any damage on the voyage.

9. Killman's promotion to first mate once more contrasts with the British system, in which an aspiring officer again had to face examinations after serving a full year as second mate. Killman had served about two months as second mate of the *David Owen* (service that would not have counted in Britain, where a half-brig, or brigantine, was not considered a square-rigged vessel) and less than five months as second mate of the *Louis Walsh*.

10. The date of leaving Liverpool on the return voyage was 21 January 1881, and the arrival at Saint John was on 9 March, which does not agree well with Killman's memory of a nineteen-day passage! Luke Stewart was the consignee of the salt cargo.

11. The *Louis Walsh* cleared customs at Saint John on 11 April 1881, loaded by R. & A. J. Stewart with 645,559 feet of deals, 132,424 feet of scantling, 12,142 feet of boards, and 12,274 pieces of paling. She arrived at Liverpool on 16 May, and *Mitchell's* reported that on the 17th she parted her cable, losing the anchor and 75 fathoms of chain but bringing up without injury to the vessel.

12. Clearly Killman's memory was faulty with regard to another round trip to Saint John. He sailed in the *Thomas M. Reed* from Birkenhead Dock, Liverpool, on 29 May 1881, just twelve days after the anchor incident in the Mersey.

13. The second vessel of that name, the 1,988-ton ship *Thomas M. Reed* was launched 13 May 1880 by Arthur Sewall & Co., Bath, Maine. Her master, Abel E. Work of Brooklyn, New York, owned 1/8 interest in her, Arthur Sewall 1/16, and Thomas M. Reed 1/4. Her history is given by Matthews in *American Merchant Ships* 1:322–23.

14. The *Thomas M. Reed* arrived at San Francisco 21 October 1881, 145 days from Liverpool, with 2,750 tons of coal consigned to Williams, Dimond & Co. Cap-

tain Work reported speaking the *Maritime Union*, bound from Hull to San Francisco, on 29 September in 12°17' N, 120°30' W. The *Maritime Union*, a 1,500-ton ship owned in Saint John, New Brunswick, was abandoned on fire on 11 October, and the crew of twenty-three were landed at Astoria, Oregon, on 25 October by the American bark *Emma T. Crowell*. The *Oregon Daily Astorian* recorded Captain Perry of the *Crowell's* report in the 27 October 1881 issue as follows:

At 7:30 p.m., Oct. 11th, sighted a ship leeward, ensign set, union down; bore away for her; found it was the *Maritime Union*, from Hull, bound for San Francisco, 145 days out, with cargo of gas coal on fire; smoke coming up through the hatches in great volumes. The captain and crew did not think it safe to stop by the ship, so I took them on board my vessel and laid by. Shortly after we left the ship she burst into a flame, and at 9:30 p.m. she went down in lat. 28 deg. 50 min. north, longitude 125 deg. 7 min. west. Arrived off Columbia bar Oct. 224 [sic]; made Disappointment light and stood off for daylight.

15. On 11 November 1881 the *San Francisco Chronicle* reported that the grand jury was looking into a charge of arson against Henry Scott, a seaman from the *Thomas M. Reed*, and that another seaman, William Ozier, was being held as a material witness and for battery on a US marshal. According to Matthews, in *American Merchant Ships*, Scott was convicted.

16. The *Thomas M. Reed* burned at her dock in Liverpool 4 February 1888, and the charred hulk was sold to local owners.

CHAPTER 3

1. The 1,450-ton *Carrollton* was another Sewall-built ship, launched in 1872 and owned between 1873 and 1886 by Howes & Crowell of Boston (Matthews, *American Merchant Ships* 1: 57–59). Her master was Elnathan Lewis of Yarmouth, Maine. She had arrived at San Francisco 30 September 1881 with 8,819 steel rails consigned to J. N. Knowles, 140 days from Liverpool. She was chartered to take wheat at the rate of £3.17s.6d per long ton to Cork and cleared customs on 9 November with 47,941 centals valued at $79,000. A long ton is 2,240 lbs., a cental 100 lbs., and a bushel of wheat 60 lbs. Thus, with the pound at the gold standard of $4.86, these figures correspond to a total freight of about $40,300 on 2,140 tons and a price of wheat at San Francisco of $0.99 per bushel.

2. The *Carrollton* sailed from San Francisco on 12 November 1881 and arrived at Le Havre, France, on 9 March 1882, a 117-day passage rather than the 101 Killman recalled.

3. The *Carrollton* arrived at Philadelphia in ballast from Le Havre 11 May 1882, consigned to Workman & Co. Killman's hasty departure to New York is documentary confirmation of many forecastle rumors concerning the inability of seamen to bring Yankee mates to justice after mistreatment on a voyage. Captain Lewis also left the ship, putting up at Plumer's American Hotel. On 6 June 1882, when the

Carrollton was cleared for New Tacoma, Washington Territory, he was relieved by S. H. Thatcher.

4. The 1,155-ton ship *Norris* was built for her own ownership in 1874 by Metcalf & Norris of Damariscotta, Maine. Her master was J. G. Barstow.

5. The *Norris* was cleared at the Philadelphia custom house 10 June 1882 by Sutton & Co.

6. The *Norris* arrived at San Francisco on 7 November 1882, 146 days out, with 1,505 tons of railroad iron consigned to John Rosenfeld, Sutton's San Francisco agent.

7. The *Norris* was cleared at San Francisco on 18 January 1883 by T. Bell & Co. and sailed four days later.

8. The *Ida Lilly* was a 756-ton ship built at Richmond, Maine, in 1860. She was owned in 1883 by James W. Elwell of New York.

9. The Tehuantepec Railway served the American-Hawaiian Steamship Co. from 1904 until 1914, but Mexican reaction to the US landing at Vera Cruz in April 1914 caused the route to be abandoned.

10. The *Norris* returned in ballast to San Francisco 11 May 1883, 30 days from Salina Cruz, consigned to J. F. Chapman.

CHAPTER 4

1. The 427-ton steamer *Planter* sailed with 200,000 feet of lumber to San Francisco under the name *Camilla*, arriving 17 August 1883. Her engines were made by E. B. Deacon of San Francisco, and she ran her trial trip on 3 October. She left San Francisco 9 October 1883 and took 11 days to reach Honolulu.

2. Mr. Foster doubtless was Thomas R. Foster, a prominent Honolulu shipping man.

3. A Polynesian word meaning "people" or "person" sometimes used disparagingly by outsiders.

4. The later career of the steamer *Planter* is covered on pages 235–37 of *John Cameron's Odyssey* by Andrew Farrell (New York: Macmillan, 1928). Captain Cameron lost her on Niihau, Hawaii, 28 January 1886.

5. King Kalakaua was the last reigning king of the Kingdom of Hawaii (1874–93).

6. Killman's memory again seems to have faltered with regard to the *Discovery*. The barkentine in question was the *Eureka*. Because both vessels were run in the same line by the same owners and had been built by Charles Murray (the 295-ton *Eureka* at Eureka, California, in 1868 and the 415-ton *Discovery* at Port Discovery, Washington, in 1874), the confusion is understandable. Moreover, "Eureka" ("I have found it") means almost the same in Greek as "Discovery" in English. Both barkentines were owned by John Kentfield of San Francisco, and both ran in Williams, Dimond & Co.'s Hawaiian Line.

7. Under Capt. John Lee, the *Eureka* arrived at San Francisco 15 April 1885, 21 days from Honolulu.

8. Killman likely means that because the ship's cargo was so heavy, its decks went below the water line when it rolled.

9. Killman's brother Henry arrived in San Francisco in the *Arkwright* on 25 April 1885, nine days from Port Ludlow with lumber to Pope & Talbot. Henry Killman's sea career has not yet been traced, but apparently he was mate of the ship *H. L. Richardson* in 1880. Milton A. Dalby in *The Sea Saga of Dynamite Johnny O'Brien* (Seattle: Lowman and Hanford, 1933), 136–37, tells of the ship *Alice C. Dickerman* furnishing supplies at sea to the *H. L. Richardson* early in 1880 and obtaining a receipt from her mate, "a Dan Killman, for nearly half a century later to be a noted Pacific Coast shipmaster." Since, as we have seen, Dan Killman was before the mast in East Coast schooners at this time, it must have been his older brother. Henry Clay Killman's death is reported in the *San Francisco Call* as having occurred 7 September 1910 at his home in Alameda. He is reported to have been ailing since the prior February, "when he returned from Africa to New York and underwent an operation in that city." Family history indicates that the cause of death was a cancerous infection of the jaw. The *Call* identified Captain Henry Killman as sixty-one years old at the time of his death, a master mariner, and a native of Stockton, Maine. His funeral service was conducted under the auspices of Oak Grove Masonic Lodge No. 215 of Alameda.

10. The 1,266-ton *Arkwright* was originally a full-rigged ship, built as a transatlantic packet by G. Raynes at Portsmouth, New Hampshire, in 1855. She ran to Liverpool first from Boston, later from Philadelphia, and finally (until 1868) from New York. Pope & Talbot bought her in 1872, converted her to a bark rig, and put her under the ownership of their Puget Sound Commercial Co. of Port Townsend, Washington. Capt. Henry C. Killman took command of her in January 1885.

11. Pope & Talbot was one of the major Puget Sound sawmill operators. The firm was organized in 1862 by Andrew Jackson Pope (1820–78) and William Chaloner Talbot (1816–81), natives of East Machias, Maine, who came to San Francisco in 1849 and 1850, respectively. Pope was married to Talbot's sister Emily. In 1862 Pope & Talbot took over W. C. Talbot & Co., sales agents for the Puget Mill Co., which the two partners also controlled. Talbot owned a half interest in Pope & Talbot, but Pope at first shared his interest with five brothers in the East. By 1866 Pope had transferred all his Atlantic interests and $230,000 in notes and cash to his brothers, in return for which he acquired their interest in Pope & Talbot. (See E. T. Coman Jr. and Helen M. Gibbs, *Time, Tide and Timber* [Stanford, CA: Stanford University Press, 1949].)

12. It was the custom on the West Coast to bestow identifying nicknames on captains when there was more than one with a given surname. Daniel Killman was distinguished in this way from his brother by being known as "Crazy" Killman. No

doubt this designation originated after incidents like the one he describes with the *Arkwright* helmsman.

13. Cyrus Walker (1827–1913) was a native of Brunswick, Maine, who started out in 1852 for the Australian goldfields. A chance meeting in New York with E. S. Brown, a millwright from Bangor, Maine, who had been engaged by Capt. W. C. Talbot to build a sawmill on Puget Sound, diverted him to the West Coast. In 1862, having risen from timekeeper to superintendent of the Pope & Talbot mill at Teekalet (later called Port Gamble), he was permitted to buy a one-tenth interest in the Puget Mill Co. for $30,045 and was designated manager of the Puget Sound operations. In 1913 his stock was worth well over a million dollars.

14. The Australian voyage commenced with surrendering the *Arkwright*'s enrollment and taking out a register at Port Townsend 6 June 1885. The bark was in port in Australia on 31 October 1885, when she paid a £64.10s fee. The US government issued certificates of enrollment to vessels of 20 tons burden or more engaging solely in coastal or fishing trades and certificates of registration to vessels engaging in foreign trade (René de Kerchove, *International Maritime Dictionary*, 2d ed. [New York: Van Nostrand Reinhold, 1961]).

15. The 693-ton barkentine *Kitsap*, built by J. J. Beaton for the Puget Sound Commercial Co. at Port Ludlow in 1881, was lost on Palmerston Island, in the central Pacific, on her return voyage from Melbourne, 23 May 1886.

16. The *Arkwright* exchanged her register for an enrollment at Port Townsend on 26 March 1886. She left Port Gamble, Washington, for San Francisco on 17 April with 912,000 feet of lumber and arrived at San Francisco eight days later.

17. William Talbot (1860–1930), son of Capt. William C. Talbot, controlled San Francisco operations of the lumber empire for forty-nine years after his father's death in 1881. (See Gibbs, *Time, Tide and Timber*.)

18. On 1 May 1886 D. O. Killman was endorsed on the *Arkwright* enrollment as master in lieu of H. C. Killman at San Francisco. The next day (Sunday) he sailed for Port Gamble.

19. The San Francisco Bar is a horseshoe-shaped area of shallow water outside the Golden Gate. Running down its middle is the main channel for shipping. The North Bar, also called the Four Fathom Bank, stretches from the main channel to land.

20. H. C. Killman again assumed command of the *Arkwright* at Port Townsend 24 May 1886, and he remained in her until relieved by H. E. Jones at San Francisco 19 September 1887. It is evident that Killman's statement "we went back to San Francisco" is incorrect, as it generally takes over a month for a sailing vessel to complete a round trip between San Francisco and Puget Sound, counting loading and discharging times.

21. The 867-ton *Atalanta* was another old-timer, no longer insurable for carrying perishable cargoes but still able to haul lumber. She was built as a ship at

Amesbury, Massachusetts, in 1851 and bought by Pope & Talbot in 1867. The *Daily Commercial News* of San Francisco for 8 June 1886 carried the following: "Port Townsend, 1 June. Bark *Atalanta* which has for the past two years been laid up in Ludlow Creek, was taken to Port Gamble where she was put on the beach, her metal cleaned, topsides caulked and she is now loading lumber for San Francisco. Mr. Killman, brother of Captain Killman, of the bark *Arkwright*, will command the *Atalanta*."

22. The *Atalanta* arrived at San Francisco 16 June 1886 with 650,000 feet of lumber, six and one-half days from Port Gamble.

23. The *Atalanta* was back at Port Ludlow by 20 July and on 23 August was registered at Port Townsend for the Honolulu voyage, sailing the next day with 635,000 feet of lumber.

24. The *Atalanta* was back at Puget Sound by 12 October 1886, having made the voyage in 49 days, which is even better than Killman's recollection of 53 days.

25. The 1,186-ton *Emerald* was originally a ship, built at East Boston, Massachusetts, in 1855 by G. & T. Boole. She ran for a time between Boston and Liverpool in the same line as *Arkwright*.

26. Displayed the flags upright and with the union at the top left.

27. The 316-ton tug *Tyee* was built in 1884 at Port Ludlow by Hiram Doncaster and William Augustus McCurdy for the Puget Sound Commercial Co. Her compound engine by the Union Iron Works of San Francisco developed nearly 1,000 horsepower, making her the most powerful tug in the country. Her captain was William Gove, born in Maine in 1834.

28. The *Guide* (like the *Daily Commercial News*) was a daily shipping paper published in San Francisco. Both papers featured lists of vessels en route to and from various Pacific Coast ports.

29. According to Frederick Hokanson, Killman's grandson-in-law, the captain suffered from edema (an excess accumulation of fluid in the tissues of the body).

30. Pope & Talbot's port captain in 1885 is named Leech in Gibbs's *Time, Tide and Timber*. Probably he was the G. W. Leach listed as master of the *Atalanta* when she was enrolled at Port Townsend 2 March 1885.

31. The *Atalanta*'s failure to deliver her cargo in Hawaii would have been a financial disaster to a vessel not owned by a big lumber company. In addition to their export business, however, Pope & Talbot maintained a large wholesale lumberyard at Third and Berry Streets, San Francisco. Thus they had no problem both disposing of the *Atalanta*'s cargo locally at a profit and dispatching to Honolulu, in another of their ships, a duplicate cargo from one of their Puget Sound mills.

32. D. O. Killman relieved Henry Tibbetts as her master at San Francisco 18 January 1887 and sailed for Puget Sound two days later. Captain Tibbetts in turn took command of the *Atalanta*, sailing 23 January.

33. Cyrus Walker married W. H. Talbot's sister Emily in June 1885. His Port

Gamble home burned that year, and the Walkers built a new home at Port Ludlow, completing it in 1887.

34. Killman doubtless meant the Strait of Juan de Fuca rather than the Puget Sound.

35. Because Port Townsend was the Port of Entry for Washington Territory at this time, ships would stop there to clear customs.

CHAPTER 5

1. The full-rigged ships *Bonanza* and *Palmyra* were among the finest in the Puget Sound Commercial Co. fleet. The two ships were of nearly the same tonnage, 1,356 and 1,359 respectively, although *Bonanza* was 10 feet longer. *Bonanza* was built in 1875 at Bath by William Rogers and was bought brand new by Pope & Talbot. They kept her in the Cape Horn wheat trade until 1882. She was then laid up until 1885, when lumber ports were cut into her bow and stern and she became a lumber carrier. *Palmyra*, built at Bath in 1876 by Goss & Sawyer, was bought by the Puget Sound Commercial Co. in June 1887. (See *American Merchant Ships* 2:44–47, 258–59.)

2. The four-masted schooner *Kitsap*, which replaced the barkentine of that name in the Puget Sound Commercial Co. fleet, was built at Port Ludlow by E. B. Wright. He was later in partnership at Alameda with Alexander Hay. Hay & Wright built several fine four-masted schooners there at the turn of the century. Named for a county in the state of Washington, the *Kitsap* grossed 791 tons, cost just over $50,000, and carried a million feet of lumber.

3. Killman was relieved by Alanson Ford in the *Emerald* 27 October 1887. The *Kitsap* was launched 1 November 1887 and received her first papers at Port Townsend on 28 November. The second *Kitsap* also had only a short life: she was wrecked on Borodino Island, Japan, on 6 September 1891.

4. Arranging for Captain Killman to rig the *Kitsap* not only saved her owners the expense of sending a professional rigger up to Puget Sound from San Francisco but also ensured that Killman as master would have no complaints about how the rigging job had been done. Except for an aberrant converted barge named *Victoria* in the 1860s, the first four-masted schooner on the West Coast was the 592-ton *Novelty* on Coos Bay in 1886. She was followed in 1887 by the 585-ton *Volunteer* at Hoquiam, Washington, the 473-ton *Wm. F. Witzemann* on Humboldt Bay, and the 791-ton *Kitsap*. So *Kitsap* was not only the first four-masted schooner in Puget Sound but also the largest on the West Coast in 1887. Rigging her was far from a routine task.

5. West Coast tides generally are semidiurnal with strong diurnal inequality. That is, each day there are usually a "high low" and a "low low." In Puget Sound the difference between these two tides is about six feet—the height of a deckhouse.

6. The foremast of a four-masted schooner is generally an inch or two thicker

than the other three. Thus, even though the *Kitsap*'s masts were all the same length, the foremast was the heaviest.

7. In a 30 October 1887 column titled "Schooner *Kitsap*: Some Facts Concerning the First Four Masted Schooner Built on Puget Sound," the *Seattle Post-Intelligencer* noted:

Her registered length is 1882 feet; registered breadth 405 feet; registered depth 160; gross tonnage 791.15 tons; registered tonnage 755.84 tons.

The *Kitsap* is the pioneer vessel of that build, on Puget Sound, but there can be no question but that four masted schooners are destined, within a few years to enter largely into our coasting trade. She is a fine looking craft and remarkable for strength of build, and the fine quality of lumber used in her construction. With her immense breadth of beam she will carry a tremendous deck load and no doubt will float off close to a million feet of lumber each trip. . . .

Heretofore the lumber carrying trade of the Sound has been done principally by old worn out barks, or ships, with a few three-masted schooners thrown in, but the era of the old lumber droger will, in a few years, be a thing of the past. Some of the advantages of four-masted schooners for lumber carrying over ships and barks are as follows: A four-masted schooner costs less to build than a ship, and on account of being able to stow away so much on deck, will carry as much lumber as the largest ship. Again, the schooner is a faster sailer than the ship, does not require nearly so large a crew, and is much more easily handled. Men who can read the signs of the times declare that in twenty years fully two-thirds of the lumber shipped from Puget Sound will be carried by four masted schooners.

8. The only vessel on the West Coast in 1887 named *Sycamore* was a 34-ton schooner built at San Francisco in 1850.

9. *Goliah* was a walking-beam side-wheeler, built at New York in 1849 by William H. Webb and reputedly the second vessel built in the United States as a tug. She had come out to San Francisco in 1850. Her tonnage was 235. Pope & Talbot bought her in 1871, and she lasted until 1899.

10. The southern extremity of the Marin Headlands, on the north side of the Golden Gate Strait, about three miles west of the present-day Golden Gate Bridge.

11. *Lady Mine*, a 58-ton schooner, was built by Hall Brothers at Port Ludlow in 1880.

12. A point of land beneath the north end of the present-day Golden Gate Bridge.

13. Meigg's Wharf, located where Fisherman's Wharf now stands, was San Francisco's legacy from Henry Meiggs, a pioneer sawmill and real-estate operator who absconded from the city in October 1854.

14. Killman was relieved in the *Kitsap* by Henry Tibbetts at Port Townsend on 29 May 1888. His service in her lasted only six months, not fifteen.

15. At about this time Killman joined Masonic Lodge No. 5 of Port Gamble, Washington Territory. In a letter dated 15 August 1976, Secretary Berger Carlson of the Franklin Lodge of Port Gamble, wrote: "Captain Killman was initiated an Entered Apprentice, 31 March 1888; passed to the degree of Fellowcraft, 19 May 1888 and raised to the Sublime Degree of a Master Mason, 21 May 1888. The Master Mason degree was conferred at a Special Communication. . . . 21 May being a Monday it appears the Lodge needed a special dispensation to meet and confer the degree. Their regular meeting night was Saturdays of the full moon."

CHAPTER 6

1. Killman took over the *West Coast* from Emil Liebig on 30 June 1888. That steamer, a vessel of only 179 tons, was built by C. G. White at San Francisco in 1885. She first was owned by the West Coast Steamship Co., of which Charles Montgomery of San Francisco was president. In July 1887 her ownership was transferred to a group of seven individuals, chief of whom was C. A. Hooper with a full half interest. Hooper's half was acquired by Henry Garthwaite of Oakland in October 1887.

2. Killman's comparison of the *West Coast*'s sailing qualities loaded and light may seem paradoxical until it is explained that most of the year there is a northwest wind along the California coast. Thus the ballast passages were made with a head wind whereas there was generally a fair wind when the *West Coast* was headed down the coast with a lumber cargo.

3. The 144-ton *Benicia* had been built at Martinez, California, in 1881 by James Henry (who also was her captain until 1885) for Paul Shirley of Martinez and L. B. Mizner of Benicia, California. Capt. A. A. Polhamus took over her command on 2 July 1888, and on 18 July 1888 she was redocumented at San Diego under the ownership of the San Diego & Coronado Ferry Co.

4. Captain Banning must have been one of the sons of Gen. Phineas Banning, who died in 1885 leaving them in control of an extensive transportation business between Los Angeles, San Pedro, and Catalina Island, including management of the Southern Pacific wharf at San Pedro.

5. Capt. Christopher Nelson (1823–93) was a native of Vedbeck, Denmark. Christened Christian Lars, he Americanized his name after he began sailing out of New Bedford in 1839. In 1851 he was shipwrecked in the Fiji Islands, where he met Charles Goodall. The two captains went to San Francisco and established a partnership operating coastwise steamers. Later they were joined by George C. Perkins. In 1876 Captain Nelson left the partnership and subsequently established the Oregon Coal & Navigation Co. to exploit the coal deposits of Coos Bay.

6. The *Arago*, a steel steamer of 827 tons, was built and engined by the Union Iron Works of San Francisco in 1885 for the Newport Coal Co. In May 1887 she was transferred to the Oregon Coal & Navigation Co. Besides carrying passengers

both ways between Coos Bay and San Francisco and freight north, she generally carried a coal cargo as well as a lumber deckload to San Francisco. She was lost with thirteen lives on Coos Bay jetty in October 1896.

7. Killman's reference to his papers not being "large enough" reflects the US practice of endorsing officers' licenses with restrictions as to tonnage and geographical area. As he mentioned at the beginning of chapter 4, Killman had a 600-ton endorsement at this time.

8. F. E. Morley relieved D. O. Killman as master of the *West Coast* on 7 September 1888, and the latter in turn relieved J. H. Mountfort of the *Arago* on 12 September. Mountfort had previously commanded the steamer *Arcata* and had taken over the *Arago* 27 March 1888.

9. The new ship referred to here was the *Ajax*, a diagonally strapped wooden steamer of 835 tons built for the Oregon Coal & Navigation Co. in 1888 by Boole & Beaton of San Francisco. Captain Holt is credited with designing her.

10. Killman's attention to the compass in this, his first steel vessel, is typical of care he gave to details of navigation.

11. Captain Holt died 1 May 1889.

12. The *Julia H. Ray*, 296 tons, was completed by Charles G. White at San Francisco in March 1888. W. S. Ray (who also owned 3/16 of the *West Coast*) owned 5/16 of her, and Henry Garthwaite owned 1/8. Killman replaced George W. Jenks as master of the *Julia H. Ray* on 2 January 1889. An earlier *Julia H. Ray*, of 177 tons, had been built in 1884 and lost in Coos Bay in 1885.

13. George Marshall, formerly of the *Arcata*, relieved Killman on the *Arago* 7 January 1889.

14. The *Annual Report of the US Lifesaving Service* for the fiscal year ending 30 June 1889 printed on pages 193–94 the following account of the loss of Killman's steam schooner, prepared in Washington by a professional writer from data submitted by the local station-keeper:

About 4 o'clock in the afternoon of the 26th of January, the steamer *Julia H. Ray*, of San Francisco, California, loaded with general merchandise, and having on board two passengers and a crew of fifteen men, in attempting to enter Coos Bay during a strong ebb tide and rough sea, grounded on what is known as the north spit, several miles northeast of the Cape Arago Station (Twelfth District,) coast of Oregon, losing her rudder and springing a leak. No regular crew being employed at this station, the keeper got the Lyle gun out on the bluff and fired it a number of times to attract the attention of the bay tugs, the nearest of which was eight miles off towing a schooner that had swamped in going out over the bar. Meanwhile the steamer worked off the spit, but without a rudder was unmanageable in the breakers, and soon stranded on the south spit, some five hundred yards from the shore. In response to the keeper's signals two tugs arrived on the scene, but too late to save the vessel; nor could they approach near enough to take off the emperiled

[sic] people. Seeing that no assistance could be rendered by them, the keeper set out for Empire City, for the purpose of securing a volunteer crew to man the life-boat, it being impossible to use the beach-apparatus, as the vessel had stranded abreast of a steep bluff, covered with a dense growth of brush. About midnight he got back with a force of nine men. On the way he picked up three men who had left the wreck on a life-raft soon after she struck. They were provided with dry clothing and otherwise properly cared for. At 4 o'clock in the morning (27th), the life-boat, with a crew of ten men, reached the bar, where, by previous arrangement, a tug was met who took the surfmen in tow for the scene of disaster. The weather was bitter cold with a strong wind and rough sea. The slack of the towline fouled the life-boat's rudder and split it in pieces, but the keeper soon got the boat under control again with a steering oar. At Coos Head the line was cast off and the surfmen pulled in towards the steamer. Her stern being seaward she afforded no lee or sheltered approach. The life-boat had to be kept head to the sea, and several times the keeper tried to drop down alongside, but in every attempt was carried past his objective by the strong flood tide. The boat filled to the thwarts more than a dozen times, but promptly freed herself. After many attempts a line was gotten aboard the vessel and an attempt made to haul up to her bow, but the breakers rolled in with such force, sweeping the lifeboat fore and aft, that the keeper ordered the line cut. Fearing that some of the shipwrecked people would become alarmed and try to land, the keeper put two surfmen ashore, who, by means of a line fastened to a tree, let themselves down the bluff on to the beach, and fortunately just in time, as three men leaped from the vessel's bow and struck out for shore. They were all pulled safely out of the surf, although one had injured his leg and was nearly exhausted. An hour later, at slack water, the life-boat succeeded in getting up to the steamer and took off two passengers and seven seamen, the captain and the chief engineer refusing to leave the vessel although urged by the keeper to do so. The surfmen then pulled away, narrowly escaping accident from the furious seas, and in tow of the tug that had been waiting in the channel, proceeded to land the rescued party. At low water in the afternoon, the captain and engineer seeing it would be useless to remain longer on board, jumped off the bow and succeeded in reaching the shore. Later in the day most of the baggage that had been left on deck was brought ashore in the lifeboat. The vessel and cargo became a total loss.

On pages 338–39 of the same report, the value of the cargo was given as $8,000 and of the vessel as $45,000, all a total loss.

CHAPTER 7

1. *John & Winthrop* was a 338-ton bark built in 1876 by Goss, Sawyer & Packard. She made two successful sperm-whaling voyages out of New Bedford and then a rather unsuccessful one, arriving at San Francisco 20 December 1888. J. N. Knowles and Millen Griffith of the Pacific Steam Whaling Co. then bought her

from her New Bedford owners, each taking a half interest. Her new papers, with D. O. Killman as master, were taken out 26 April 1889.

2. The *Robert L. Belknap* and the *America* were big full-riggers. The 2,251-ton *Belknap*, built at Rockport, Maine, in 1884 by and for Carleton, Norwood & Co., was commanded by Horace Staples of Stockton, Maine. The 2,054-ton *America* was built at Quincy, Massachusetts, in 1874 by George Thomas. After being wrecked at San Pedro, California, in February 1887, she was repaired at San Francisco under the ownership of the Pacific Steam Whaling Co.

3. Capt. Josiah N. Knowles (1830–96) was a native of Eastham, Massachusetts, who had made a great name as a shipmaster before retiring from the *Glory of the Seas* in 1876 to become a shipping merchant in San Francisco. An early investor in steam whalers, he became general superintendent of the Pacific Steam Whaling Co. when it was incorporated in 1883. He also managed the subsidiary Arctic Oil Works.

4. The bark *Mars*, 256 tons, originally a brig built at Newburyport, Massachusetts, in 1823, was rebuilt in 1868. She was owned in 1889 by William Lewis of New Bedford and commanded by Leroy S. Lewis. The bark *Cape Horn Pigeon*, 212 tons, was built at Dartmouth, Massachusetts, in 1854. She was owned by J. & W. R. Wing of New Bedford and commanded by Thomas Scullan.

5. The Diomede Islands are in the Bering Strait with the Chukchi Sea to the north and the Bering Sea to the south. The islands are separated by an international border. Big Diomede Island is the easternmost point of Russia.

6. The *Thrasher* was built at Bath in 1883 by Goss, Sawyer & Packard for the founders of the Pacific Steam Whaling Co. She was one of the largest American whalers, grossing 671 tons. Her master was Charles E. Weeks.

7. The *Grampus* was the next-to-newest addition to the steam whaling fleet. Her hull was originally built at Boston in 1874 as the revenue cutter *Richard Rush*. The *Rush* was rebuilt at Port Blakely, Washington, in 1885 by Hall Brothers, who put her engines and other fittings into a new hull. The old hull was re-engined at San Francisco for the Pacific Steam Whaling Co. as the 326-ton *Grampus*, making her first voyage in March 1886. Besides these two, in 1889 the Pacific Steam Whaling Co. had the steam whalers *Balaena*, *Narwhal*, *Orca*, and *Beluga* and the sailing whaler *Wanderer* in the Arctic.

8. In his manuscript, Killman refers to the master of the *Jesse H. Freeman* as "Captain Freeman." Clearly this was a lapse of memory. In 1889 she was commanded by M. A. Baker.

9. Captain Griffith was Millen Griffith, a Fortyniner, a founder of the Shipowners' & Merchants' Towboat Co., and later one of the founders of the Pacific Steam Whaling Co. The *Freeman* had been built at Bath in 1883 by Goss & Sawyer as a steam-auxiliary three-masted schooner. Measuring 516 tons, she made her first whaling voyage in 1888 as the newest addition to the steam whaling fleet.

10. The *Thetis* herself was originally a whaler, having been built at Dundee,

Scotland, in 1881 by A. Stephen & Sons, from whom the US government bought her in 1884 for the relief of the Greely expedition (a scientific expedition to the Arctic that ended in tragedy). After that mission was accomplished, she was transferred to the Pacific. As a warship she retained her bark rig. Her commander was Lieutenant Commander Charles H. Stockton (not Lieutenant, as Killman calls him), a Naval Academy graduate of the class of 1865.

11. It is not possible to identify the small schooner with whose skipper Killman had the altercation. The *James A. Hamilton*, 78 tons, the *Alton*, 89 tons, the *Mary H. Thomas*, 99 tons, and the *Nicoline*, 69 tons, were all in the Arctic in 1889. The *Nicoline* can probably be eliminated, as she did not leave San Francisco until 2 July.

12. The *Little Ohio* was actually named *Ohio*, but because she was only 205 tons she was so called to distinguish her from the 363-ton *Ohio* built at Rochester, Massachusetts, in 1833. The smaller *Ohio* was built at Baltimore in 1830. Both were lost in the Arctic within the space of eight months, the *Little Ohio* at Point Hope 3 October 1888 and the other on Nunivak Island 1 June 1889.

13. Lieutenant Commander Stockton of the *Thetis* sent a report to the Navy Department concerning the loss of the *Little Ohio*. According to the *Los Angeles Daily Herald* on 21 September 1889, the report included a letter from a John Kelly, an employee at Hope, giving details of the loss:

The letter states that October opened with a fresh northeast wind; the ground had frozen, the temperature ranged from ten to twenty-two degrees, and the land was white with snow. Just before the blizzard began the *Ohio* was off Cape Lisburne, land being plainly in sight. Two barks were near and hove to. Massive rollers struck the vessel with great violence, lifting her up and throwing her closer in, the spray leaping clear over the lower yards. Captain Allen had ordered the mast cut away, but a man could not stand anywhere without holding with one or both hands. A few men went up the main mast and several up the mizzen. Many sought shelter about the cabin tops and between the galley and cabin entrance. The house fell in, trapping the men underneath, and then the ship broke in three parts about the mizzen and just abaft the tryworks, and except for part of the bow, the *Ohio* disappeared. Thirteen men were carried ashore by the waves, through flying debris, and three men came down on dry land from the mainmast when it went over. The men sought shelter with the natives, who agreed to care for them until a ship would take them off. Two flags were set to attract the attention of passing ships. Captain Bayne, at the whaling station, let the men have a whale boat and all the clothing and blankets he had. Ship after ship passed without noticing the colors. On October 12th the steamer *Belvidere* passed twelve miles out. Seven men took the whaleboat and tried to intercept her, and were never heard of again, their boat probably being swamped. Late in the evening the steamer *Narwhal*, Captain McGregor, came along, saw the flag, luffed up under the point, waited a little while and then kept off. If the whale boat had not been gone the men could have saved themselves. Captain Bayne moved his stores outside and took the men into the station, and clothed and fed them as well as his resources would permit. Six of the men were taken away on the *William Lewis* in July, and three others were taken by the United States steamer *Thetis* on the same day.

14. The laws to which Killman refers were R.S. 1433 and R.S. 4577–79. R.S. 1433 gave the powers of a consul to the commander of a warship; the others related to the return of destitute seamen from foreign ports. The vessel was compensated at the rate of $10 per man for a voyage up to 30 days, and if a man proved unable to do duty according to his ability, additional compensation was payable upon application to the comptroller of the Treasury. Killman was correct in stating the law was still in effect. (See Title 46 USC 679.)

15. The *John & Winthrop* returned to San Francisco 9 September 1889.

16. The arrival in San Francisco of the *John & Winthrop* was reported in a short piece under the headline "Disemboweled," stating that the vessel entered port with her flag flying at half-mast. On board was "a scene of excitement and confusion. The men were running to and fro and the Captain seemed more excited than his men. Several sailors were bending over a shipmate, who was bleeding from a terrible knife-wound in the abdomen. The intestines protruded from the gaping cut and the man evidently was in a dying condition." The sailor had been stabbed by another outside the Heads after a lively row. Frank Darrow was turned over to the police after stabbing shipmate Albert Hodges. (*Sacramento Daily Record-Union*, 10 September 1889; *Arizona Weekly Citizen*, 14 September 1889. Both articles courtesy chroniclingamerica.com)

The "Heads" is a reference to the headlands—Marin Peninsula on the north and San Francisco Peninsula on the south—that separate San Francisco Bay from the Pacific Ocean.

17. J. A. Cook replaced Killman on the *John & Winthrop* document 9 December 1889. (See John A. Cook, *Pursuing the Whale: A Quarter-Century of Whaling in the Arctic* [Boston: Houghton Mifflin, 1926], 15ff., or Captain John A. Cook and Samson S. Pederson, *"Thar She Blows": Experiences of Many Voyages Chasing Whales in the Arctic* [Boston, MA: Chapman & Grimes, 1937], 23ff.)

CHAPTER 8

1. *Hattie Gage* was an 80-ton steamer built at San Francisco early in 1889 for the Aleutian Islands Fishing & Mining Co., of which Henry W. George, a San Francisco merchant, was secretary. She was taken over by the Alaska Packers Association in May 1893 and after a long career in Alaskan waters was sold in October 1917 to the Smith Navigation Co. of New York. On 29 June 1918 she was wrecked at Nags Head, North Carolina. The endorsements of change of master have become un-

pinned from her early enrollment, so the dates of Killman's service in her cannot be verified from this source.

2. Rosebury Strait is most likely Raspberry Strait, of the Kodiak Island Archipelago. (Courtesy Denise Sproat, kodiak.org.)

3. The bark *Hope* was owned from February 1889 to January 1891 by the company that owned *Hattie Gage.*

4. *Gertie Storey,* 73 tons, was completed by C. G. White a week or two before he delivered the *Hattie Gage.* She was owned by the Central Alaska Co., H. W. George, secretary. She passed to the Alaska Packers Association in May 1895 and was dismantled at Alameda, California, around 1931.

5. Black Diamond, California, is now called Pittsburg. Both names recall its function as a loading port for coal from the Mount Diablo mines, most of which were abandoned by the early 1900s (courtesy Sheila, Walnut Creek Historical Society).

6. Thin Point is the western headland of Cold Bay, on the south side of the Alaska Peninsula very near its tip. Unalaska is about 160 miles southwest.

7. *Jeanie* was a steam auxiliary four-masted schooner, 1,071 tons, built at Bath, Maine, in 1883 by Goss, Sawyer & Packard. She was owned from about 1887 by the Pacific Steam Whaling Co., which at this period was branching out into salmon canning.

8. Killman's statement of the pack at the two Thin Point canneries can be compared with figures published by J. F. Moser in the "Bulletin of the United States Fish Commission 1898," 51–52:

	1889	1890	1891	1892	1893	1894	1895
Thin Point Pkg. Co.	25,161	2,401	4,206	Closed	Closed	dismantled	
Central Alaska Co.	. . .	7,000	4,089	Closed	Closed	Closed	dismantled

A great investment of San Francisco capital in new canneries in Alaska in 1889 resulted in an increased output of canned salmon, which temporarily glutted the market. To some extent in 1890, and to a greater extent in 1891, canneries that had competed pooled their operations in a given area in the manner described by Killman at Thin Point.

9. Belkofski is a small settlement a little to the east of Cold Bay.

10. Cape Pankof is the southeastern tip of Unimak Island.

11. The episode with the fishermen is perhaps better understood if "union organizer" is substituted for his term "ringleader." At any rate, within a few years the Alaska salmon fishermen had become unionized under the wing of the Coast Seamen's Union. Likewise the formation of the Alaska Packers Association put the

canneries in better financial hands after 1893. (Many operators had been under-capitalized commodity speculators.)

12. Edward B. Pond, a shipping and commission merchant, was mayor of San Francisco at this time. (He died 26 April 1910.) His son, who was involved in salmon packing in 1891, possibly was the individual J. H. Cobb describes in "Pacific Cod Fisheries," *Report of the United States Commissioner of Fisheries for the Fiscal Year 1926* (Washington, DC: US Government Printing Office, 1927), 410–11, as follows:

One of the most picturesque figures in the industry, and one who cut a wide swath while in it, was Edward Pond. Beginning in 1902, with apparently no end of money, he sent two vessels to Bering Sea. In 1905 his fleet had increased to three vessels, two of which fished in the Okhotsk and one in the Bering Sea. Prices for fish were low in 1906 and 1907, and when the two vessels he had sent to the Okhotsk Sea in the latter year returned virtually empty, having been driven from the sea by the Russian authorities, he was forced to the wall, and his stock of fish on hand and to arrive was taken over by the Union Fish Co.

13. Of all the incidents described by Killman in this book, the stranding of several dozen fishermen does him the least credit. He seems to have felt that, having beaten their spokesman in a fistfight, he was fully entitled to leave them over the winter without medical attention or the opportunity either to communicate with their families or to earn a few dollars.

14. The *Gertie Storey* arrived in San Francisco in ballast from Thin Point 3 October 1891.

15. The concluding sentence of this chapter is a masterly understatement. If Killman thereafter had set foot on any vessel carrying fishermen to Alaska, they probably would have thrown him overboard.

CHAPTER 9

1. The *Mercury*, 1,156 tons, was built in New York in 1851 for the Boyd & Hincken line of Havre packets. After eighteen years of carrying emigrants from Havre to New York, she was used for a time at New York as a reform school with naval discipline. She came to the West Coast about 1885. Killman took command at San Francisco 14 December 1891. The ship was nine years older than he.

2. The *Dashing Wave*, 1,054 tons, was built at Portsmouth, New Hampshire, in 1853. Some authorities rate her a medium clipper, but *American Lloyd's Register* for 1862 describes her as a full model. She entered the coast lumber trade in 1870 under the ownership of the Tacoma Mill Co. (See Octavius T. Howe and Frederick C. Matthews, *American Clipper Ships, 1833–1858* [Salem, MA: Marine Research Society, 1926], 115–19.)

3. Tatoosh Island, Washington, lies one-half mile northwest of Cape Flattery, the southern headland of the Strait of Juan de Fuca. Cape Flattery Lighthouse is

actually on the west end of Tatoosh Island. Duncan Rock is a mile northwest of the lighthouse, but sunken rocks limit the passage between Tatoosh Island and Duncan Rock to a width of less than half a mile.

4. Killman handed over the *Mercury* to William Colby 9 May 1893. On 11 October 1893 he recorded a purchase of 1/16 of the *Catherine Sudden* from John Thomsen, and on 28 October he relieved C. H. Attwood as master. Built in 1876, the barkentine was of 386 tons and carried 475,000 feet of lumber. Since April 1887 she had been owned by the S. H. Harmon Lumber Co., which sold a substantial interest to J. M. Weatherwax of Aberdeen, Washington. After resigning from the *Mercury* and before taking command of the *Catherine Sudden*, Killman took command of a two-masted schooner, the 141-ton *Wing and Wing*, which had been built at San Francisco in 1881 by C. G. White for A. M. Simpson. Although he mentions no trip in her, the *San Francisco Call* carried a story dated 21 July 1893 headed "Lost to Sight; The Mystery of the Wing and Wing; No News for Forty Days":

On April 19 last the *Wing and Wing*, in command of Captain Erickson, and with a crew of six men all told, set sail from Santa Cruz, in ballast, bound for Coos Bay, where she was to take on a cargo of lumber. Two days later she put into Port Harford and reported having had one of her rudder-braces carried away. Repairs were made and on the next day she started again for her destination. She has not reached there yet. Thirty-seven days later, or forty days from the time she left the harbor, she arrived at Santa Cruz again. Captain Erickson reported that owing to head winds, light and baffling winds and calms and fresh northwest gales, he could make no headway to the north, and telegraphed to A. M. Simpson, the managing owner in this city, to send down a tug to tow the vessel up here. The managing owner was wrathy when he received the dispatch, and, instead of sending down a tug, he went to the ship-owners' shipping office and engaged a new captain and crew for the vessel and took them down to Santa Cruz by rail. Captain Erickson and his crew were then deposed and the new crew took possession, and on June 10, or forty-one days ago, the *Wing* made another start for Coos Bay. Where she has been from that day to this, or where she is now, no one on shore knows. The fact remains that she has not yet arrived at Coos Bay and has not been spoken since leaving Santa Cruz. . . . At the non-union shipping office it was learned that the following are the names of the crew who sailed on the vessel when she sailed the last time: Daniel Killman, captain. John Williamson, mate. W. Nelson, Max Freisland, George Williams, C. Anderson, seamen. Captain Killman, or as he is familiarly called on the front, "Captain Dan," is about 38 years of age, a native of Maine. He is known as a good careful seaman; but as Captain Monroe says, "a devil to crack on." He was until recently captain of the ship *Mercury*, and was master of the steamer *Julia H. Ray* when she was lost up the coast. . . . The *Wing and Wing* is very bluff in the bows, and is known as being anything but a fast sailer, and the general opinion among seafaring men is that Captain "Dan" is meeting with some of the bad luck that befell Captain Erickson, and that he will yet turn up at Coos Bay safe and sound.

The *Wing and Wing* arrived at Coos Bay from Santa Cruz 24 July 1893. Later she was owned by the Union Oil Co. as a barge, her register being abandoned in 1921.

5. The principals in Inman & Poulsen were Robert D. Inman and Johan Poulsen. Their mill was on the riverfront at East Carruthers Street, Portland.

6. At the time Sutton & Beebe were agents for the sailing-ship line E. B. Sutton & Co., which regularly dispatched chartered square-riggers from New York and Philadelphia to West Coast ports. The senior partner was Allen M. Sutton, a son of E. B. Sutton, who was located in San Francisco; the junior partner was Charles Francis Beebe, 16 N. Front Street, Portland.

7. Redondo, now called Redondo Beach, is on Santa Monica Bay in Los Angeles County. The Santa Fe built a lumber-handling pier there about 1890.

8. The marriage certificate of D. O. Killman, age 34 years and Minnie Campbell, age 23 years, states that they were married on the 14th day of August, 1894, in Los Angeles. A society announcement in the *Los Angeles Herald*, reporting the wedding date as the 15th, informed readers that the ceremony was performed with a few intimate friends in attendance, including Capt. F. A. Perry of the barkentine *Argo*, J. B. Mullen, S. B. Hall, and Mr. and Mrs. F. K. Parke (the assistant auditor and his wife). "The house," said the *Herald*, "was elegantly decorated and the presents were numerous and costly." (Courtesy newspapers.com.) Six years later, at the time of the 1900 Census, Minnie and her daughter Catherine were living at the home of her brother-in-law and sister Henry and Martha (Campbell) Lane, hotel keepers in Rohnerville Township, Humboldt County, California, while her husband was sailing on the *Lyman D. Foster* between the Hawaiian Islands and Australia. Minnie, her sister, and presumably other siblings were born in Canada, had emigrated to North Carolina for a brief period, and from there had made their way to California.

There are variations on the spelling of their elder daughter's name. Captain Killman's original document spells it "Catherine," "Katherine," and "Kathryne." In the 1900 Census it is "Cathrine": in later census records, "Katherine." Her sister, Sydney, spelled it "Catherine."

9. The 1900 Census identifies "Cathrine Killman" as having been born in October 1895.

10. Catherine Killman was still living in 1976, but it was not possible to interview her in the course of editing the Killman manuscript. The Killman's second daughter was about ten years younger and was named for Sydney, Australia. "Catherine and I used to discuss this," she said. "She was always so glad that she hadn't been named after the *Dashing Wave*. And I was so glad I hadn't been named

Newcastle" (taped interview, Harold D. Huycke, Jr, and Sydney Killman Pierce, 2 September 1975, OHC UCC, 193a.).

11. Winslow Hall (1832–98) was one of five brothers (in a family of fifteen siblings) who came to California from Cohasset, Massachusetts. From 1864 to 1869 he was skipper of the 71-ton schooner *John D. Sanborn*, which he owned with his brothers Samuel and Abraham. In 1874 he formed a shipbuilding partnership, Hall Brothers, with his brother Isaac and, later, another brother, Henry. Winslow managed the San Francisco office of the firm, which expanded into ship owning as well as shipbuilding.

12. The 777-ton four-masted schooner *Lyman D. Foster* was a big step upward from the *Catherine Sudden*. Completed by Hall Brothers at Port Blakely in October 1892, she had been named for the son of Samuel Foster, a provision merchant of San Francisco who invested in vessel property. She cost $49,500, so the 3/32 share of Capt. Philip Dreyer, a native of Marstal, Denmark, represented an investment of some $5,000. The death of Captain Dreyer at the hands of Lin Gew was reported in successive Friday issues of the *North China Herald & Superior Court and Consular Gazette* in March 1896 as follows:

20 March, page 433: On Wednesday morning the American schooner *Lyman D. Foster* was boarded by Cheap Jack's boat off the Tungsha lightship, when the mate reported that in the course of the voyage from Puget Sound to China the Captain had been shot and killed by the cook.

27 March, page 477: At the US consulate on Monday afternoon the affidavits of the mate and others belonging to the *Lyman D. Foster*, with reference to the murder of the captain, were taken. It appears that the vessel left New Whatcom [one of four communities that merged in the early 1890s to form the city of Bellingham, Washington] on the 22nd of December, for Shanghai. On the 25th of February, the ship being in lat. 17° N and long. 160° E the captain went into the donkey-room for some purpose, when the cook, a San Francisco Chinaman, attacked him with an axe. The steward who was close at hand endeavored to get the axe from him, when the cook suddenly drew a revolver and shot the captain twice in the left breast. In the meantime the mate had procured a revolver and a pair of handcuffs and went forward to try to secure the cook, who had taken refuge in the galley. The mate fired two shots into the galley and then rushed in and secured the cook, who was immediately handcuffed and lashed to the mainmast. He had previously saturated the galley with kerosene and set fire to it, and while the crew were engaged subduing the flames he managed to free himself and, before he could be secured again, jumped overboard and was drowned. The captain survived until the following morning, when he died and was buried at sea.

13. On 9 May 1896, Killman turned over command of the *Catherine Sudden* at Seattle to F. E. Mathiesen, the purchaser of his shares (which had increased to one-eighth).

14. The *Lyman D. Foster* passed Tatoosh (a small island among a small group of islands about one-half mile northwest of Cape Flattery) on 16 May 1896, 36 days from Shanghai.

CHAPTER 10

1. On 16 June 1896 Killman officially relieved the *Foster*'s former mate, A. Anderson, as master of the schooner at Port Townsend. The next day he put to sea with 942,000 board feet of lumber, loaded at Port Hadlock, at a freight rate of £2.7s.6d per thousand.

2. Years later, Catherine's hometown newspaper, *The Tacoma Times*, featured her in a piece about the faculty and students of the local school where she taught. She is identified in a group photo as "Katherine Killman."

From uncertain life at sea on a sailing ship to the calm of a schoolroom was a transition in the life of Catherine Sudden Killman, fourth grade teacher at Sherman school. For the first 14 years of her life, Miss Killman sailed the high seas with her father and mother, Capt. and Mrs. D. O. Killman.

"Catherine Sudden" were the names given Miss Killman by her parents at the time of her birth in Fortuna, Calif. She was named after a sailing ship, the "Catherine Sudden," which her father owned and commanded. Before she was one year old, Miss Killman started a voyage to the Orient on the ship after which she was named.

After his daughter's first voyage, Capt. Killman took command of the *Lyman D. Foster* and in this ship Miss Killman was to spend most of the first 14 years of her life and visit many lands. She recalls that she made five different trips to Australia and at the age of eight witnessed a bull fight at Mazatlan, Mexico.

While at sea, Miss Killman was instructed by her father, who she says was a hard taskmaster and compelled her to study a great deal.

Many experiences of storms at sea and an encounter with a typhoon on the ocean are firmly imprinted on Miss Killman's recollection. The trip to Australia usually took from seven to eight months.

Although life at sea was interesting, it was very lonely, Miss Killman recalls. She is satisfied that life on the mainland is best [the *Tacoma Times*, Saturday, January 25, 1930].

3. The *Foster* arrived at Shanghai 26 August 1896. A typhoon that swept Kobe, Japan, on 18 August might have been the one that shifted the schooner's deck load. The casualty to the lightship was not mentioned in the *North China Herald*.

4. The *Lyman D. Foster* arrived in Port Townsend 10 November 1896, 49 days out of Shanghai.

5. Henry Knox Hall (1830–1909) was trained as a shipwright and for a time was associated with his older brothers, Isaac and George, in a shipyard at Cohasset, Massachusetts. During the Civil War he became a foreman at the Boston Navy

Yard and then was transferred to the Mare Island Navy Yard on San Francisco Bay. He joined with his brothers Winslow and Isaac in their shipbuilding partnership in 1875. After Isaac's death, in 1879, he continued to manage the shipyard, which moved from Port Ludlow to Port Blakely in 1881.

CHAPTER 11

1. The *Lyman D. Foster* left Puget Sound for Fremantle, Western Australia, 18 December 1896 and arrived 24 April 1897, which is 126 days after allowing for the day lost crossing the International Date Line.

2. The *Sutton* was a 2,526-ton British tramp steamer. *Lloyd's Register* shows her as completed in May 1897, so she must have been on her maiden voyage.

3. The *Foster* sailed for Westport, New Zealand, on 12 June 1897.

4. The president of the Inter-Island Steam Navigation Co. at this time was Capt. William B. Godfrey. Because he was not a resident of the United States at this time, his equity in the schooner was disguised, but in 1911 Carrie E. Godfrey, William's widow, owned 1/16 and D. O. Killman owned 1/32.

5. Following indictment by a grand jury at Walla Walla, Killman was tried at Seattle before Judge Cornelius H. Hanford. He was prosecuted by an assistant US attorney named Claypool and defended by A. R. Coleman of Port Townsend and Gen. J. B. Metcalfe. McDonald and four other crew members testified for the prosecution. Killman and Hall testified in their own defense, and a customs inspector named Loftus and a prominent Seattle real-estate man named Fred E. Sander (an in-law of the Hall Brothers) were character witnesses. The judge instructed the jury that Killman and his mate could assault or imprison a man if it were necessary to bring about discipline but that the law prohibited beating or imprisonment "through hatred or malice." (In this instruction, the learned judge was ten months behind the times. On 3 March 1897 the law had been amended to omit those words, although the language "without justifiable cause" remained.) After about two hours of deliberation, the jury returned to ask the judge what the penalty would be in case of conviction. Judge Hanford informed them it was a fine up to $1,000, imprisonment up to five years, or both, and then scolded them for asking the question. Following about three more hours of deliberation, the jury acquitted Hall, convicted Killman, and then recommended the "utmost leniency of the court."

The *Seattle Daily Times* covered McDonald's court case in the 10 December 1897 issue as follows:

The fate of Capt. D. O. Killman and Mate Robert Hall of the American schooner *Lyman D. Foster*, who are charged with cruelty on the high seas, went to the jury shortly before noon today. The trial has occupied the best part of two days in the Federal Court and has attracted the attention of many seafaring men. The prosecuting witness in the case and the man upon whom the cruelty is said to have been practiced is John McDonald, an ordinary seaman on the *Foster*.

McDonald's story is to the effect that on October 26 of this year, while the vessel was returning from a cruise to Westport, Australia, the Captain ordered him to keep the schooner up in the wind. McDonald says that he replied that he was doing the best he could, whereupon the Captain rushed upon the deck and struck him a fearful blow in the mouth. Then McDonald says the Mate took a hand and that the two beat him (McDonald) until the blood flew in all directions. After they had beaten him a while he says the Captain went below and secured a pair of handcuffs. Returning, he claims that the Captain assaulted him with the handcuffs, finally felling him to the deck, after which they kicked him. He says he shed tears and begged for mercy but that none was shown him! He says that he dragged himself to his bed, where he was confined for several days. While he was in bed he alleges that Capt. Killman frequently assaulted him and threatened him.

McDonald exhibited to the jury several ghastly scars which he claims were the result of the assault upon him by Mate Hall and Capt. Killman.

Albert Brazier, cabin boy on the *Foster*, and three members of the crew corroborated McDonald in essential particulars. Then the Government rested its case and the defense opened. Mate Hall was the first witness for the defense and he told an entirely different story from that told by McDonald and his witnesses. He claimed that on the day of the trouble McDonald was at the wheel. He was not doing his work in a proper manner and Capt. Killman urged him to keep the vessel up in the wind. Hall says that McDonald with a curse that reflected on Capt. Killman's maternity yelled out that if he didn't like the way in which he was doing his work to come up and do it himself. The Captain started to do so, and when he came within a few feet of the wheel McDonald drew a knife and told him not to come any further or he would cut his heart out. While the Captain was urging McDonald to behave himself, Hall says, McDonald struck the Captain in the face. Then the trouble began. Hall says that both of them attempted to stop McDonald from doing the Captain injury and that in doing so McDonald was thrown down and that the Captain struck him. Finally he was let get up and he made a break to get away. He was promptly captured and placed in irons.

Capt. Killman went on the stand and corroborated Mate Hall in every essential particular. All of this testimony was taken yesterday, after which the Court adjourned until this morning. At this morning's session of the court Fred E. Sander of this city went upon the witness stand for the defense and testified that he had known Capt. Killman for twelve years, and during that time Killman had been a peaceable, even-tempered man. In fact, Sander gave Killman and Hall the finest kind of a reputation. Customs Inspector Loftus was another character witness and corroborated Mr. Sander. Then the Government presented some rebuttal testimony and the argument commenced. Col. Claypool's argument for the Government was very brief and A. R. Coleman for the defense made a logical, clear-headed and eloquent argument for his clients. He was followed by Gen. J. H. Metcalfe, also for the defense, who made an extremely eloquent and logical argument, emphasizing the fact that McDonald was insubordinate and that if any assault was committed at all that it was justified. Gen. Metcalfe pointed out that at the time of the alleged assault Capt. Killman's wife and children were within ten feet of him and that no man who loved his wife and daughter would act in a brutal manner and use vile and profane language.

Col. Claypool was a masterpiece of sarcasm. He ridiculed the testimony of Killman and Hall as unworthy of belief. At times Col. Claypool grew very eloquent, and he presented his case in a manner that indicated that as a prosecuting officer of the Government he will be a decided success during the four years which he will hold his present position.

After Col. Claypool closed his argument Judge Hanford instructed the jury, who at once retired to their room. A verdict will be rendered some time this afternoon.

At 2:15 o'clock this afternoon the jury returned and asked Judge Hanford what the penalty is that the law prescribes in such cases.

Judge Hanford told them what it was and then proceeded to speak of the uselessness of asking such questions.

In addition to the difficulty with seaman McDonald on the return voyage, Killman had had trouble with his mate on the outward voyage to Fremantle. The mate, Nils E. Hindsgaul, libeled the schooner after she returned to Puget Sound, and the suit was heard in the same courtroom as that in which Killman and Hall were tried for assaulting McDonald. In answer to Hindsgaul's complaint, Killman filed an affidavit, parts of which were published in the *Seattle Times* Tuesday, 7 December 1897, as follows:

That on December 27, 1896, while the said schooner was on the high seas on its said voyage and about 240 miles south of Cape Flattery, and while said schooner was lying to, close reefed and in a heavy gale and in the track of all north-bound sailing vessels, and while said Hindsgaul was on duty as first mate, affiant went on deck and found said Hindsgaul asleep without anyone performing his duties. That affiant had heretofore, and just prior to said Hindsgaul going on duty, cautioned said Hindsgaul that said schooner was then in the track of all north-bound sailing vessels, which would come up flying, running before the wind, and that the said schooner was helpless to avoid collision with north-bound vessels, and that he must keep the keenest lookout for north-bound vessels and burn the torch lights prepared for him to signal and warn approaching vessels. That affiant then and there reproved said Hindsgaul for such conduct and told him not to let it occur again. That because of the conduct of said Hindsgaul aforesaid, to wit, sleeping while on duty, affiant thereafter was compelled to keep the closest watch on said Hindsgaul to see that he properly set the sails and generally performed his duty. That on January 23, 1897, while said schooner was on the high seas affiant went on deck while said Hindsgaul was superintending the greasing of the mast. That he was doing the said work so carelessly and negligently that he was using a pot with a hole in the bottom of it and the grease was running through on the mainsail and had materially damaged the same. That affiant then and there reproved said Hindsgaul for such negligence and carelessness, using proper language in so doing. That said Hindsgaul became insolent and abusive toward affiant and struck affiant. That affiant then and there caused said Hindsgaul to be placed in his room and off duty. That no more force was used than was necessary in so removing said Hindsgaul to his room. That said Hindsgaul was not confined in his room or elsewhere, but was allowed to go about the ship whenever and wherever he pleased. That said Hindsgaul remained off duty until February 8, 1897, when affiant ordered him to return to duty, which he then and there refused to do, giving as an excuse that he was sick and unable to perform duty, all of which was false as far as affiant was able to judge from his appearance and conduct, and more especially as said Hindsgaul was then eating as heartily as any seaman on board said schooner and continued so to do. That notwithstanding affiant did not believe said Hindsgaul was sick and unable to perform his duty, he did not resort to force to compel him to return to duty, but informed him that he could have any medicine he wanted from the medicine chest of the ship, and affiant sent the medicine books of the ship to said Hindsgaul in his room.

"That said Hindsgaul thereafter remained off duty until the said schooner arrived at the port of Fremantle, West Australia. That on April 24, 1897, while the said schooner was coming to anchor in the said port of Fremantle affiant went under the forecastle to see how much chain went over the windlass, and generally to superintend the anchoring of the said schooner. That said Hindsgaul was then standing near the windlass; that it was then a little dark and affiant did not recognize said Hindsgaul, but seeing a man standing in an improper place, called out to him to stand out of the way. That said Hindsgaul then and there and without the slightest provocation struck affiant with great violence, knocking him down and cutting a fearful gash under his right eye, which had to be stitched by the health officer when he came aboard the ship at said last named port, and the scar of said wound still remains. That said Hindsgaul immediately after striking affiant, as aforesaid, seized an iron bar about two feet long and weighing about nine pounds and used to lock the windlass and viciously assaulted affiant and attempted to strike him with said bar of iron. That affiant then had his marine glasses in his hand, and they being the only thing about him or near him with which he could defend himself from said assault, struck said Hindsgaul with said glasses, using no more violence than was necessary to defend himself from said assault. That if affiant had not properly defended himself in the manner aforesaid said Hindsgaul would have struck affiant with said iron bar and would have inflicted great bodily injury, and in all probability would have killed affiant, which affiant feared he would do. That immediately thereafter affiant went ashore at the said port of

Fremantle and reported the said assault upon him, last aforesaid, to the United States Consular Agent at that port, Edward A. Mayhew. That the said Consular Agent then and there caused the said Hindsgaul to be arrested for said assault and taken before a local magistrate for said offense. That said Hindsgaul testified upon said trial in his own behalf and had a number of the crew of said schooner subpoenaed in his behalf, who testified, and all corroborated the testimony of affiant, and thereupon said Hindsgaul was found guilty and sentenced to twelve weeks in jail at hard labor. That all the wages due said Hindsgaul at the time of his arrest and trial aforesaid were paid to the said Consular Agent, and there is now nothing whatever due said Hindsgaul on account of wages or upon any account whatsoever from the respondent. That the said vessel sailed from the said port of Fremantle on July 15, 1897, as shown by the ship's logbook, while the said Hindsgaul was still in jail serving out this said sentence. That the payment of the wages of said Hindsgaul to said Consular Agent aforesaid is shown by the official endorsement of said Consular Agent on the original shipping articles. That other than as herein stated affiant had no difficulty or trouble of any kind whatever on said voyage with said Hindsgaul. That affiant never used abusive language toward said Hindsgaul, and never used greater force and violence toward him than was necessary to enforce his proper orders and in the defense of his person. That said Hindsgaul was at all times impudent, insulting and abusive toward affiant and was utterly incompetent in any position and for any purpose whatever."

The outcome of the suit is set forth in the following, quoted from *Federal Reporter* 85:987–89, with the three headnotes omitted:

THE *LYMAN D. FOSTER*

HINDSGAUL v. THE *LYMAN D. FOSTER*

(District Court, D. Washington, N.D. March 5, 1898.)

This was a libel in rem by Nils E. Hindsgaul against the schooner *Lyman D. Foster* to recover wages, expenses, and damages for an assault alleged to have been committed upon him by the master.

P. P. Carroll, for libelant.

Metcalfe & Jurey, for respondent.

HANFORD, District Judge. The libelant was employed as first mate of the schooner Lyman D. Foster, for a voyage from Port Townsend to the port of Freemantle [sic], West Australia, and return to a port of the United States on the Pacific coast,—the voyage not to exceed 16 months,—and was to receive wages at the rate of $50 per month. Within a short time after sailing from Port Townsend there was trouble between him and the captain, in consequence of which the libelant was deposed, and the captain himself performed the duties of mate. After the schooner had entered the harbor of Freemantle, and when she was about to drop her anchor, the captain went forward to oversee the running out of the anchor chain, and, meeting the libelant near the windlass, ordered him to get out of the way, and immediately there was a fight between the two. Blows were struck by each. The captain was knocked down, and received considerable injury. There is a conflict in the testimony as to which was the aggressor, but, in the view I have taken of the case, it is unnecessary for me to decide this question. When the captain went ashore he reported the occurrence to the consular agent of the United States, who thereupon lodged a complaint with a local magistrate, charging the libelant with the commission of an assault upon the captain. The record of the proceedings in the case in the Australian court has not been produced, but from the testimony I find that the libelant was taken before the court, and the witnesses to the occurrence on board the schooner in the harbor were summoned. One was sworn and gave testimony on the part of the prosecution. Three others, called at the instance of the libelant, were sworn and testified in his behalf. The magistrate or judge before whom the case was tried then refused to hear the testimony of other witnesses called at the instance of the libelant, for the reason that the three who did testify corroborated the testimony of the one witness for the prosecution as to the material points in the case. And, on the testimony taken, the court adjudged the libelant to be guilty as charged, and sentenced him to be punished by imprisonment for 12 weeks; and he was detained in prison under said sentence, having yet several weeks to serve, when the schooner was ready to leave the port. Before sailing from Freemantle, the captain gave to the United States consular agent a sum of money for the libelant, equal to the entire amount of his wages, at the rate agreed upon, for the time he was in the schooner, without making any deduction for the time he was off duty. The consular agent paid the costs and expenses of the criminal prosecution against the libelant, and gave him the balance. In this suit the libelant claims the balance of his wages for the entire voyage, and his expenses incurred at Freemantle and in returning to the United States, and also damages for assaults and abuse which he alleges were committed by the master.

Admiralty Rule No. 16, prescribed by the supreme court, precludes the libelant from maintaining a suit in rem against the vessel to recover damages for the assaults and injuries alleged to have been inflicted by the captain.

Libelant's counsel has presented his case upon the theory that a court of a foreign country does not have jurisdiction to punish an American seaman for an offense against the laws of the United States, committed on board of an American vessel; and it is his contention that the imprisonment of the libelant at Freemantle was wrongful; that the captain violated his duty in sending the libelant ashore to be imprisoned in a foreign country, and that, having by his wrongful acts prevented the libelant from completing the voyage, he should be held estopped to dispute the right of the libelant to recover wages for the entire voyage, according to the terms of the contract; and that, having left libelant in a foreign port, the schooner is also liable for the amount of his expenses incurred while there, and in returning. I assent to the proposition that the courts of one country have no jurisdiction to punish a seaman for any offense committed at sea on board a merchant vessel under the flag of another country, nor to punish a seaman for an offense committed within its territorial jurisdiction, for an act made punishable as a crime by the laws of the country to which his ship belongs, unless such act is also a crime under the laws of the country where committed. But the jurisdiction of a court to punish infractions of the local law committed within its territorial jurisdiction may not be denied on the ground that the offender is an alien in the country, or that the act was committed on board of a foreign ship. The act of which the libelant was accused at Freemantle is malum per se, and presumably punishable as a crime in all civilized countries. The prosecution of the libelant was conducted according to forms of procedure designed to insure fairness and to promote justice, and he was convicted upon testimony of a witness against him, which was corroborated by witnesses called at his instance. Whether the judgment against him was just or unjust is a question which the courts of this country are not competent to decide, having no power to review the judgment of a court of competent jurisdiction of a foreign country. I hold that the detention of libelant at Freemantle was not an unauthorized interference on the part of the local government, nor a wrong done to him at the instigation of the captain, but that he received British justice, at the hands of a British court, for a violation of British law committed within British territory. As a necessary consequence of his imprisonment, he was rendered incapable of fulfilling his contract and earning the wages which he is now suing to recover. By placing the amount of his wages for the time the libelant was in the schooner in the hands of the United States consular agent, for the libelant, the captain fully performed his duty towards the libelant as to payment of his wages. From that time the consular agent became responsible to the libelant for the money, and is liable if he misapplied any of it, but the schooner is free. Under the circumstances, there could be no formality observed in discharging the libelant from the service of the schooner,—the actual condition of things effected an actual discharge; for the captain would not have been justified in detaining the schooner, on expense, in a foreign port, for several weeks, for the mere sake of receiving on board a subordinate officer detained in prison as punishment for an aggravated assault. He pursued the right course in going to sea when the schooner was ready to sail, and leaving all the money which the libelant could legally claim in the hands of an accredited representative of our government. A decree will be entered dismissing the suit, with costs.

CHAPTER 12

1. Mr. Billings was George E. Billings (1851–1929), a native of Cazenovia, New York, who came to California in 1868 and married a niece of the shipbuilding Hall brothers. He joined Winslow Hall in the San Francisco office, taking over its management after the latter's death, and also expanding into marine insurance.

There was a persistent rumor that Killman and Billings were brothers-in-law (see for example Gordon Newell, ed., *The H. W. McCurdy Marine History of the Pacific Northwest* [Seattle, WA: Superior Publishing, 1966], 450), but this is incorrect.

2. Killman sailed from San Francisco in the *Lyman D. Foster* on Sunday, 29 May 1898. The *Rufus E. Wood*, Captain McLeod, had sailed 21 May.

3. The *Lyman D. Foster*'s arrival at St. Michael, Alaska, was reported as 10 July 1898 and the *Rufus E. Wood*'s three days earlier.

4. The schooner sailed from St. Michael on 21 August.

5. The *Lyman D. Foster* arrived at Port Townsend 21 September 1898.

6. The great Nome gold discovery in the beach sand was made late in the season of 1899. (See Elmer Green, ed., *Adventures of Carl Rydell* [London: Edward Arnold, 1924], 238–39.)

7. Before going to Australia in October 1899, Killman made two more voyages to China. He sailed from Port Blakely 27 October 1898 for Shanghai with 930,000 board feet of lumber with a freight rate of £2.8s.3d per thousand, arriving there 27 December. The record return brought him to Port Townsend in ballast 20 February 1899, 24 days from Shanghai. He reached Port Blakely on 22 February, and on 28 March left Port Gamble for Newchwang (now called Yingkou) with 922,000 board feet of lumber at £3 per thousand, passing Port Townsend the same day and arriving out 21 June. He sailed on the return voyage on 24 July 1899 and arrived at Port Townsend 11 September. The greater freight rate to Newchwang (713 miles by steamer from Shanghai) reflects the time and risk involved in sailing across the Yellow Sea, through Bohai Strait, and across both the Bohai Sea and Liaodong Bay. In the period between 21 September 1898 and 11 September 1899 (just 10 days short of a year), the *Lyman D. Foster* had grossed $24,300 with these two cargoes.

Freights were high, but seamen were scarce, and Killman was back in federal court as a consequence. Suing as paupers, three seamen (D. McLean Brown, Martin F. Lundquist, and Chris Brock) alleged that on 29 March 1899, while the *Lyman D. Foster* was still lying off Port Townsend assembling a crew for the voyage to Newchwang, Killman employed an individual named Wright to procure sailors for the schooner. Their story was that Wright had brought the three to Port Townsend, where they were compelled to go aboard the *Foster* and at 11 p.m. on the 29th were compelled to sign articles with advance notes of $13.33 each, after which they were confined in the forecastle. Although they requested to be set ashore the next morning, they said, Killman, using a Winchester rifle, had herded them into the forecastle, preventing them from communicating with the shore, until the schooner was at sea. Then they agreed to go to work, they said, and Killman promised to cancel the advance notes. From 29 March to 12 September 1899, the three said, they worked as A.B.s, for which the prevailing rate of pay at Port Townsend was $40, and because the forecastle was wet and cold and proper clothing was not available each was "damnified" to the extent of $500, although Killman had offered them $20 per month at pay-off.

Killman was served with papers in this case on 22 September and had to post $1,500 to release the schooner. Judge Hanford's decision, handed down on 15 December, was that the men had not been shanghaied or coerced. Yet they should have been signed on ashore, and although they had a legal right to leave, the captain had detained them. He accordingly disallowed the allotment notes and awarded the three claimants $30 per month less the slop chest accounts and cash advanced at Newchwang, so each was awarded between $139 and $142 plus interest, at 7 percent. The lawyers for the plaintiffs were M. M. Madogan and George Johnson (National Archives Record Group 41, Correspondence File 124016–N).

Killman meanwhile had sailed from Port Hadlock, Washington, on 11 October 1899 for Sydney, arriving there 10 December with 796,000 board feet of lumber at £2.3s.9d per thousand. The lower rate of freight for the longer voyage reflects the availability of coal as a return cargo whereas the return passages from China were in ballast. He sailed from Newcastle on 4 or 5 February 1900 and arrived at Kihei, Hawaii, on 12 May.

8. The *John C. Potter* left Newcastle 22 February 1900; her arrival date at Kihei was reported both as 15 May and 17 May.

9. The *Kinau* and the *Claudine* were both owned by the Wilder Steamship Co., which later was absorbed by the Inter-Island Steam Navigation Co. The *Claudine* was built at Glasgow, Scotland, in 1890. When the *Kinau* was built, in 1883, by Cramp at Philadelphia, she was the only iron vessel under the Hawaiian flag and the first vessel to fly that flag in the Atlantic.

10. The *Potter* was made into a barge about 1904 and lasted until about 1929, when she was beached and broken up at Cunningham Island, British Columbia, Canada.

CHAPTER 13

1. The Melbourne voyage was made in 1900, leaving Chemainus, British Columbia, 18 August and arriving at Melbourne 8 November with 887,000 board feet of lumber at £3.1s.3d per thousand.

2. The *Lyman D. Foster* left Melbourne 3 December 1900 and arrived Newcastle, New South Wales, 9 December 1900.

3. The *Foster* left Newcastle 24 December 1900, arriving Kahului, Hawaii, 3 March 1901, then sailed for Port Townsend, arriving 21 May 1901.

4. Killman has reversed the order of this Shanghai voyage and the Sydney-Newcastle-Kihei voyages, which were in late 1899 and early 1900. This Shanghai voyage took place a year earlier. (See chapter 12, note 7.)

5. The San Francisco earthquake occurred at 5:15 a.m. 18 April 1906.

6. Killman is still depending on memory. The voyage from Port Blakely to Antofagasta, Chile, began 25 February 1905. Next he made a voyage to Guaymas, Mexico. Then he sailed from Port Blakely for Yokohama.

7. The *Foster* sailed for Yokohama 10 June (not 6 July) 1906.

8. By the time of the San Francisco earthquake Capt. Killman had two daughters. His second, Sydney, was born in the fall of 1905 and was ten years younger than Catherine.

9. By this time Ned Skinner and John W. (Jack) Eddy had acquired the Port Blakely mill from Renton, Holmes & Co. During World War I this firm was among the first on Puget Sound to undertake steel shipbuilding.

10. The *Lyman D. Foster* arrived at Yokohama 15 August 1906, which is 65 days. The cargo amounted to 898,000 feet.

11. The Yokohama typhoon occurred on 24 August 1906.

12. For an account of the *Galilee*, see the September 1907 issue of *National Geographic Magazine*.

13. The *Lyman D. Foster* arrived back at Port Townsend 4 November 1906.

CHAPTER 14

1. On 1 December 1906, while running on the coast, Killman shipped a second mate named W. M. Coffman at San Pedro. In his autobiography, *American in the Rough* (New York: Simon & Schuster, 1955), 224–26, Coffman describes a fight he had with Killman in the schooner's cabin on Christmas Eve off Cape Flattery. He fully expected to be prosecuted for mutiny, but when paying off at Bellingham on 4 January 1907, Killman merely marked "Fail to Report" under "Character" and "Ability" on his discharge. Coffman proudly reproduces this discharge in his book.

2. Before going to Peru, the *Foster* made a voyage to Valparaiso, Chile, sailing from Tacoma, Washington, 10 December 1907. It was about this time that the Killman family moved to Tacoma, which had a considerably more favorable earthquake experience than California.

3. Killman sailed from Grays Harbor, Washington, 7 August 1908 and arrived in Peru on 20 September with 924,000 feet of lumber.

4. The *Lyman D. Foster* departed Talara Bay, Peru, 25 October 1908.

5. The *Lyman D. Foster* arrived at Port Townsend 12 December 1908, loaded 1,121,000 feet of lumber at Chemainus, British Columbia, sailed 26 January 1909, and arrived at Arica, Chile, 23 April.

6. Upon the *Foster*'s return, the *Vancouver Daily World* reported the round trip as being a series of misfortunes, including unfavorable weather that required eighty-four days to Arica and the loss of two seamen. On 26 January just five hours after the schooner had been dropped by the tug off Cape Flattery, Second Mate J. J. Brennan was swept overboard by a big wave during a heavy blow. M. Mott, a "venerable sailor" died, apparently of natural causes, fifty days out of port. Mott

"was past 70 years of age and had been nearly sixty years at sea, always before the mast. His body was given a sea burial." (*Vancouver Daily World*, 4 August 1909. Courtesy newspapers.com)

CHAPTER 15

1. During 1912 Killman made two voyages to Fiji. He left Grays Harbor 14 March 1912 with 996,000 feet of lumber, arriving at Suva 10 May. Next he left Bellingham 30 August with 1,087,000 feet and arrived 1 November. On this final voyage he sailed 20 February 1913.

2. The dismasting occurred on 15 April 1913.

3. Killman's mate on this voyage was named Cummings. Prior to this voyage, he had crossed the equator in the steel four-masted topsail schooner *Americana*. The *Americana* departed the Columbia River for Sydney 1 March 1913 and probably foundered in the 15 April hurricane. She was never seen again.

4. Lakeba (pronounced "la kemba") is an island in Fiji's Southern Lau Archipelago.

5. Fiji is an archipelago of more than three hundred islands, with more than one hundred inhabited. It is not possible to determine with certainty the island on which the rafts landed, but it probably was not, as here asserted, Lakeba. (Killman subsequently charters a sloop to take him to Lakeba from the island on which the rafts landed.)

6. Killman abandoned the schooner on 30 April.

7. Gau (pronounced "ngau") is the fifth-largest island in the Fijian archipelago.

8. The small steamer was the *Ripple*, Captain T. H. Lippitt, a wooden vessel of 129 tons, with a compound engine, built in New South Wales in 1899 and owned by Lau Traders, of Levuka. The *Ripple* towed the *Foster* to Iloloya, from where the Union SS Co. collier *Waipora* towed her to Suva, arriving 15 May.

9. Since the penalty for hoisting the British flag on a ship not entitled to it is forfeiture, Killman was hardly in a position to make trouble.

10. The *Foster*'s hull lay in Suva until 1917, when it was towed to Auckland by the steamer *Karori* and rerigged with the masts of the *E. B. Jackson* (wrecked February 1917 at Apia, Samoa). As the British four-masted schooner *Lyman D. Foster* she traded for a couple of years between Auckland and San Francisco, part of the time with yards on the foremast as a barkentine. At the end of March 1919 she left Nukualofa, Tonga, for San Francisco, but she never arrived.

11. The cargo brought £4,400 ($21,220); the hull only £280.

12. The steamer *Makura*, 8,075 tons, was built in Glasgow, Scotland, in 1908 for the Union Steamship Co. of New Zealand and ran on the so-called All-Red Route (for Royal Mail Ships) between Sydney, Australia, and Vancouver, British Columbia, where it connected with the Canadian Pacific Railway. The latter's Canadian Pacific Steamship Co. furnished the transatlantic link with Great Britain.

13. The 3 August 1913 edition of the *Tacoma Daily Ledger* carried Killman's account of his encounter with the hurricane.

We left Puget Sound March 1 from Port Townsend in tow of the tug *Lorne*," said Capt. Killman in relating the story of the voyage, "and at midnight, the tow lines were cast off and we were free from the tug about 24 miles southwest of Cape Flattery.

"I would not ask for a better voyage than we enjoyed clear to the islands. We crossed the Line in 23 days, in company with the schooner *Americana*, which has never arrived at her destination in Australia and which, I am certain, was lost in the storm which wrecked us.

"The first land we sighted was April 14 about 6:30 p. m., when we passed to the north end of Vetavetuva, [probably the island of Vanua Vatu, about ninety miles east southeast of Gau] and at 10 p. m. we were about five miles off Latti [likely the village of Lamiti, on the island of Gau]. Another day would see us through the passage between the islands and into the short run leading up to Suva. The night was beautiful. It was absolutely clear with stars shining. About midnight the mate called me on deck. The sky had become overcast and the barometer was at 29.80. With increasing breeze, we furled the stays'ls and the jigger tops'ls. By 7 o'clock in the morning the barometer was 29.90 and the sea was smooth. At 11 o'clock the sun came out and we got latitude, about 29:01 [*sic*]. I slept for an hour after dinner, and when I came up on deck the wind was increasing and the barometer was falling. We furled all tops'ls and at 4 or 5 o'clock the spanker and the jib tops'ls.

"The wind kept increasing steadily into a gale and I knew we were in for a stiff time. At 5 o'clock we double-reefed the fores'l and the mizzen, running under full mains'l and three jibs, but by 6:30 o'clock we double-reefed the mains'l and furled the flying jib. At 8 o'clock we were about 35 miles off the island of Ono and about the same distance from Vetavetuva. We wore the ship around furling all head sails and hove to on the starboard tack, heading eastward. . . .

"From this time the storm increased to a hurricane. At 9 o'clock the fores'l blew away and at 10:30 the first heavy sea swept over the ship, carrying away the small boats from the davits and smashing in the after hatch. We succeeded in double-reefing the mains'l and battening-down the hatches with canvas, when the top of the wheel box was washed away and one of the after companionway doors was smashed in.

"From this time on things were interesting. The hurricane broke in full force and was the worst I have ever seen in all my experience at sea. Shortly after midnight the double-reefed mains'l blew away. It was a brand new sail and went off like a cannon. It seemed to be the signal for a general smashing. I knew right then that unless the wind abated at once no ship on the sea could stand under it and I knew we would be dismasted.

"It was about 10 minutes after 1 o'clock when the jigger mast snapped off about 10 feet above the deckload of lumber, going over the port side. The spanker boom broke in two and came down across the wheel, carrying away the rail over the port side and, carrying away a port, it stove a hole in the mate's room. Nothing could stop the inrush of water and within 10 minutes all of the cabins were filled. The mizzen mast went next and it swung over the house, carrying everything in its path.

"I was pretty mad by this time and must have been inquisitive, for I crawled along on my knees over the deckload to the mainmast and while I was crouching by it it snapped off and went overboard on the windward side. I made my way back and told the mate that we must make an effort to get out some of our stores where they would be accessible. Everything was full of water and in the cabins was a mass of floating wreckage of furniture and fittings. As fast as we would get out stores and canned goods and lift them to the upper deck they would be swept overboard. There were three heavy spars on deck and these, with a big part of the deckload, went overboard next. I was standing in the forward companionway with the water nearly up to my shoulders. The vessel was rolling wildly in the trough of the sea, and the wreckage of chairs, tables and cabin fixtures was pounding out the partitions and adding their wreckage to the mess. With one roll broken chairs and mattresses would come part way out the doorway and with the next roll would crash against the other side of the cabin.

"We were without lights except for a small lantern hanging on a hook high in the cabin, put there for the canary's cage. We had been painting the ceilings of the cabins and I did not have the lamps lighted because I did not want the paint stained. The feeble ray from this lantern was the only light we had and the night was as black as a pocket. . . .

"With the deckload gone, the remaining stump of the jiggermast broke off close to the deck. The next sea which swept the deck carried the broken mast into the companionway and struck me in the shoulder, tearing the flesh and bruising me badly. Had the vessel taken a roll while the mast was in the companionway, I would undoubtedly have been killed. But, as luck would have it, the next sea carried it out again on deck. I heaved a sigh of relief, but it was scarcely out, when back it came, striking me squarely in the chest and knocking me under the water. It went out again with the next sea and was carried overboard. I stood in the companionway in this water for about four hours.

"About 4 o'clock the wind suddenly shifted from the southwest to the northwest and then the foremast went over the port cat head. Daylight found us entirely dismasted, with all of the lifeboats gone and rudder gone and the sternpost shattered. We cut away all of the rigging except the forestays, with which we held onto the foremast for a drag to keep us into the wind. The chain plates and bolts had pulled out when the deckload went overboard and the ship had between seven and eight feet of water in her. We got some canned goods and hard biscuits out of the lazaret and we had about 800 gallons of fresh water in the forward tanks.

"For three days we held to the drag, then, with a strong wind from the southeast, we rigged up a jury mast from a forestays'l boom. We cut away the foremast when the wind shifted and our attempt to drift her back began. There was a heavy swell, which caused the derelict to roll constantly. For 15 days we drifted and once a steamer passed close enough for us to see plainly her cabins and windows, but they did not see us.

"Realizing that our only hope would probably be in abandoning the derelict if we could get close enough to land, we set about constructing two punts from the lumber on deck. The work was accomplished after many difficulties had been surmounted. Every nail, all of the tools and such material the sailors had to dive for in the water. In my cabin I had several valuable articles of jewelry and I lost all of it except my diamond ring. This was brought up with a handful of nails by one of the sailors.

"We used wooden plugs, nails and caulked the boats with rags. Each boat was fitted with a mains'l, jib and squares'l, but they were rather weird looking vessels. The first land we sighted was the island of Ono. We drifted in through the eastern group and saw no land for four days. On the fifth morning we sighted Kimbara [Kabara], to the south. . . .

"About 6 o'clock on the morning of April 30, we abandoned the *Foster*. Mate Cummings set out first with his 'ship,' taking five men with him. I followed later with six men in my clipper ship. Each boat took a supply of dry biscuits and we fixed up canvas bags in which we took a few gallons of fresh water. We sailed for 45 miles in these. I say we sailed, but the greater part of the distance was covered by sculling.

"At 9 o'clock at night, about 500 yards off shore, the mate's boat stranded on a coral pinnacle. The natives had sighted us before dark and there were many confusing lights darting about on the beach. The mate's boat was in danger of capsizing when four native women swam out from shore and helped pull off the stranded craft. The shore was lined with the small reefs and how my boat managed to escape a fate similar to the mate's is a mystery. It was a worn out set that finally landed on the island.

"I slept on the floor of the home of the only white man of the village. Next morning we were treated to a fine chicken breakfast and a supply of excellent fruit. When I saw Mate Cummings I asked him how he had slept. 'Fine, sir,' he said to me. 'I slept in the church, on the pulpit. It was the first time I had been in church in years, and I slept capital.'

"At 4 o'clock that afternoon I set out with one man in a cutter for the island of Lakimba, expecting to get a steamer that would take me to Levuka. I found I would have to proceed to Levuka. I chartered a sloop and we sailed the 130 miles to that port, from which the loss of the *Foster* was reported to the George E. Billings company and Lloyds.

"One of the Union Steamship company's colliers was chartered to look for the derelict. In the meantime, the little steamer *Ripple* had stopped at Lakimba and had gone in search of the wreck. The collier failed to find her, then we got word that she had been picked up by the *Ripple* and towed 70 miles to one of the islands. The collier was dispatched to the place and towed the derelict into Suva. . . .

"The salvage was settled and the remaining cargo sold, and the *Foster* will spend her remaining days as a hulk in the Union company's service among the islands. She was a fine vessel and even with the ragging she got in the hurricane that dismasted her, her hull was sound, and she was not even sprung by the weight of the shifting deckloads against her stanchions."

CHAPTER 16

1. Built at Port Blakely by Hall Brothers in 1902, the *H. K. Hall* was of course named for Henry Knox Hall. (See chapter 9, note 11, and chapter 10, note 5.) She grossed 1,257 tons and was rated as carrying a million and a half feet of lumber. Lyman D. Foster owned 1/64 of the *H. K. Hall.* The master whom Killman relieved was O. Benneche, owner of 1/16.

2. Mr. Thorndyke was George F. Thorndyke, who died at Seattle in 1945 after a long career in shipping. The Globe Navigation Co. was a corporation organized by Great Lakes capitalists (some connected with the L. C. Smith Typewriter Co.), who built a series of large schooners at Ballard, Washington, between 1902 and 1904.

3. The schooner loaded by Killman was the *Alex T. Brown*, which is listed as sailing from Tacoma for Callao, Peru, 9 September 1913.

4. The four-masted schooner *A. M. Baxter*, 516 tons, had been built at Fairhaven, California, in 1898 by H. D. Bendixsen. In 1913 she was managed by J. H. Baxter of San Francisco. She is listed as sailing 11 September 1913 and arriving at Santa Rosalia, Mexico, on 15 October.

5. Killman replaced Benneche as master of the *H. K. Hall* 27 December 1913. His mate on the run up the coast was P. A. McDonald, a well-known shipmaster still living in Santa Monica, California, in 1976. In letters dated 19 February and 10 March 1976, Captain McDonald described how Killman had provided him with a gun and kept the door of the mate's cabin open while he paid off the crew. "I doubt the gun was loaded," he wrote. "Captain Killman's somewhat strange behavior I put down as over-abundance of ego rather than downright viciousness. I had no personal problem." Nevertheless McDonald left the *H. K. Hall* when she was loaded.

6. The *H. K. Hall* left Astoria 15 February 1914 and arrived at Antofagasta, Chile, on 1 May.

7. On the return passage the *H. K. Hall* sailed 24 June 1914 and arrived at Port Townsend 11 September, which is when Killman would have heard the war news.

The assassination of Archduke Franz Ferdinand occurred on 28 June 1914 and was followed by a declaration of war by Austria-Hungary on 28 July 1914.

8. After calling at Eagle Harbor, the *H. K. Hall* loaded at Coupeville, Washington, under charter to the Cie du Boleo. In 1885 this French company began mining El Boleo, a copper mine near Santa Rosalia. She sailed again 19 October 1914.

9. The British warship was HMS *Newcastle*. She was commanded by Capt. Frederick A. Powcett, RN, who doubtless was the "Admiral" described by Killman.

10. The *H. K. Hall* arrived at Santa Rosalia 26 November 1914.

11. The term "interned" used with respect to the German ships lying at Santa Rosalia is incorrect, strictly speaking, although it was also used at the time in reference to German vessels similarly caught in US ports at the outbreak of World War I. All these vessels were actually free to leave port whenever they wished. Only German warships such as the *Geier* at Honolulu and the *Prinz Eitel Friedrich* at Newport News were actually interned. (For a full account of the eleven ships mentioned by Killman see Harold D. Huycke, Jr, *To Santa Rosalia: Further and Back* [Newport News, VA: Mariners' Museum], 1970.)

12. The *H. K. Hall* arrived at Astoria 15 January 1915 under charter to Heatley & Co. at £3.17s.6d per thousand board feet.

13. She sailed 25 February 1915 for Delagoa Bay (today called Maputo Bay), Mozambique. Killman's official log notes the disrating of his second mate, whom on 21 March he "found asleep laying arms on forward companionway while on duty." Killman sent him to the forecastle and promoted a seaman in his place. On 2 April Killman had him placed in irons for "cursing, etc.," but he was released at his request two days later.

14. Isla de los Estados (English: Staten Island) lies eighteen miles east of the Argentinian portion of Tierra del Fuego.

15. Killman's reliable mate was named W. L. Samuelsen.

16. The *H. K. Hall* arrived at Delagoa Bay 14 June 1915.

17. The passenger was Lloyd Irvine, a surgeon, who left the schooner on 3 July.

18. The schooner's consignees on this voyage are given in a marginal note on the manuscript as Hunt, Leuchars & Hepburn, a British firm with branches in London and Durban, South Africa This fact explains the interest of the British consul.

19. The schooner's articles for this voyage show only two desertions at Lourenço Marques (today called Maputo), Mozambique, and two sign-ons: Josef Kalinowski, 25, native of Warsaw, steward, at $25 per month; and Paul Boutin, 27, native of Hamburg, A.B., at the same wages. One conjectures whether Killman simply matched the other Germans against names and descriptions already on the articles, thereby disguising their nationalities. His emphasis on getting letters from their former skippers saying wages were paid up to his sailing date seems to show he was forestalling any attempt for them to collect for the round trip. The unclassified files of the consulate are silent concerning any crew troubles of the

H. K. Hall. At this time US consulates in the British territories in South Africa were handling German and Austrian nationals.

20. The *Lusitania* was sunk 7 May 1915. Killman saw the effects of the rioting, not the riots themselves.

CHAPTER 17

1. The *H. K. Hall* departed Lourenço Marques 27 July 1915 and arrived off Tatoosh Island, Washington, 18 November 1915. The *Vancouver Daily World* reported on 24 December that this would be the first Christmas that Captain Killman spent at home in many years. (Courtesy newspapers.com.)

2. On 9 December 1915 Killman cleared the *H. K. Hall* at Port Townsend for Cape Town via Vancouver. At that time his crew consisted of J. Edwardsen, mate; V.P. Rasmussen, second mate; Joe Takaha, cook; and Sato, boy. Edwardsen was paid off in Vancouver, Rasmussen on return to Port Townsend 10 January 1916. F. Hansen was signed on as mate the same day. The rest of the crew was recruited in Tacoma. The ship was fined $500 for not having the number of A.B.s required under the Seamen's Shipping Act of 4 March 1915 plus $500 for not having enough certificated officers. Before clearing again for Durban on 14 January 1916, Killman executed an affidavit stating there was a scarcity of certificated men (see chapter 20, note 4), and all but $25 of the penalty was remitted.

Effective 4 November 1915, allotments to seamen had been prohibited. Killman, however, signed on Hansen at a wage of "$5 for the first month and $75 for each month thereafter" and the sailors similarly at $10 and $25. Because of the appeal from the fine, the *H. K. Hall*'s crew list was brought to the attention of the assistant secretary of commerce, and on 28 February 1916 he directed a stern letter to the collector of customs at Seattle, soliciting his "careful consideration and attention" to the matter of "bringing this apparent violation of law home to the perpetrators."

3. The crewman who died as the *H. K. Hall* was leaving Port Townsend was named Larsen, as reported by the *San Francisco Examiner* 4 November 1916. (See also chapter 17, note 11.)

4. The *H. K. Hall* arrived at Durban leaking 14 May 1916.

5. The mate, Frederick Hansen ("Fighting" Hansen or Fritz Hansen) was a native of Denmark, 5'11", 234 pounds, born in 1883. In September 1913 he shipped as mate in the four-masted barkentine *Echo* for a voyage with lumber from Grays Harbor to Callao, arriving early in December. Most of the crew deserted in Callao, and on the barkentine's return to Puget Sound some new crew members shipped there claimed they had been shanghaied and then ill-treated aboard the *Echo*. At a trial held at Tacoma 24 April 1914, Hansen freely testified that he had beaten three of the men "because dey vas not gude sailors" and then, not realizing he was a defendant, left the courtroom. He was brought back on a bench warrant to hear

the jury bring in a guilty verdict, and he received a three-month jail sentence. Hansen was in trouble again in the years following his time on the *H. K. Hall*. (See chapter 17, note 14.)

6. In a letter dated 26 May 1916 the vice consul of the American consulate in Durban wrote a letter to the secretary of state in Washington, describing the conditions under which the *H. K. Hall* had arrived in Durban:

Sir: I have the honor to report that the sailing vessel "H. K. HALL" arrived in the port of Durban on Sunday, May 14th, 1916, at 1:15 p.m., in a very leaky condition. The master, D. O. Killman, states he encountered boisterous weather just off Port Shepstone, about 100 miles south of Durban, Natal, and when he found the vessel leaking much, the pumps failing to work properly, and the situation becoming very serious when he saw an opportunity he signaled the Union-Castle Liner "Carlyle Castle" to send a wireless to Durban to have a Government tug sent out to his assistance.

At 2 o'clock on Friday afternoon, May 12th, the Port Captain went out on the tug instructing the Assistant Port Captain to notify the Consulate, and returned about 2 o'clock Saturday afternoon, and reported that he had failed to sight the vessel although he had kept a careful watch by day and had sent out rockets at night, and had done all in his power to locate the ship.

The Vice Consul not being able to get into communication with the Port Captain Saturday afternoon as to what he thought was the reason of not being able to sight the ship, visited him at his residence and learned that it was his surmise that the "H.K. HALL" had got into the Madagascar current and had drifted south. The Port Captain further stated that the wind was favorable from 4 o'clock a.m. Saturday morning and he felt that the distressed ship would get to Durban sometime Sunday morning. She arrived on Sunday morning and was, by the Government tug, towed in alongside the Congella Timber Wharf.

Since being berthed they have been offloading the lumber as rapidly as possible, and as the ship's crew had seen strenuous service during the last days of the voyage and were exhausted, the Master had the discharging done by stevedores. It is understood that pumps have been placed in service connected with the ship's agent timber yard electrical supply during the day, and the Durban Municipal Electric Current at night.

The work is still proceeding, and it is hoped to be able to keep the vessel from settling on the bottom.

The Vice Consul feels it only right and proper to state that from what he has seen and heard of the vessel and Master, D. O. Killman, deserves great credit for his untiring efforts in bringing the ship safely to dock.

I have the honor to be, Sir, Your obedient servant, Hugh S. Hood, American Vice Consul in Charge."

Hugh S. Hood, a native of Ohio, was 52 in 1916 and had been Vice Consul at

Durban since December 1909. Prior to the date of the above letter, he had received written complaints from the Swedish Vice Consul, the Norwegian Consul, and the Amalgamated Society of South African Seafaring Men and Fishermen concerning mistreatment of crew members of the *H.K. Hall* by the first mate. On 25 May he wrote all these authorities that after investigation on board "I am not satisfied that these men have just cause for complaint against the 1st Mate."

Nevertheless, by 7 June Hood was writing the Chief Magistrate of Durban requesting the detention of five crew members as deserters. On 9 June he added the name of the second mate. On 23 June he wrote the Superintendent of Water Police naming four more men. And on 4 July he added another second mate, a man who had been recruited at considerable expense to the schooner from Port Elizabeth and who left, taking the two Japanese cooks with him.

7. According to the schooner's articles, now in the National Archives, the hard-case sailor was Patrick J. Murphy, 35, a native of Dublin, who jumped overboard 7 July 1916. Curiously, his nearest relative was listed as residing in Pelahatchie, Mississippi.

8. The man who died (described as a mulatto by the *Coast Seamen's Journal*) was Raoul Touris, 22, 5 feet 5 inches tall, a native of the Seychelles. His death occurred while the *H. K. Hall* was rounding the south island of New Zealand, 1 September 1916.

9. The *H. K. Hall* arrived at San Francisco 1 November 1916, 116 days from Durban, in ballast.

10. Killman was defended in this case by Theodore Parker.

11. Mrs. Killman would have seen the 4 November 1916 issue of the *Tacoma Daily Ledger*, which carried news of the charges brought against Captain Killman, but by then she had received word from Mr. Billings, as the *Ledger* article makes clear:

CALLS MURDER CHARGE 'FRAME UP'; Owner of Schooner *Hall* Says Accusation Against Capt. Killman Is "Trumped Up"; MASTER'S HOME HERE; Sailors of Well-Known Lumber Vessel Accuse Captain and Mate of Responsibility for Death of Two Seamen.

That the charge of "murder on the high seas" filed against Capt. D. O. Killman of Tacoma, and his first mate Fred Hansen, by sailors of the schooner *Henry K. Hull*, at San Francisco yesterday, is "a trumped up charge that will amount to nothing," is the statement of George E. Billings, owner of the vessel, in a telegram received yesterday by Mrs. Killman, wife of Capt. Killman.

Mrs. Killman was preparing to go to San Francisco to join her husband who is returning from a voyage to South Africa, when she read the Associated Press dispatches from San Francisco. In a short time she received a telegram from Mr. Billings, owner of the schooner, in which Mr. Billings said: . . .

"You have doubtless seen stories today about Dan. Pay no attention to them and do not worry. There is absolutely nothing to it except a trumped-up sailor's story. Do not let it interfere with your trip."

Mrs. Killman will leave this morning for San Francisco. She plans to meet Capt. Killman at San Francisco and accompany him on the schooner to the Columbia river, where the vessel will undergo extensive repairs before proceeding on her next voyage. The *Hall* had a strenuous trip to South Africa and it was due entirely to the skillful seamanship of Capt. Killman that the vessel made port. She was badly waterlogged and at one time it looked as tho the safety of the captain and crew lay in abandoning the vessel. . . .

Capt. and Mrs. Killman and their children have resided in Tacoma many years, the family residence being at 1715 North Prospect street.

"Anyone who knows Capt. Killman," said Capt. W. Frank Andrews, of the Washington Stevedoring company, yesterday, "knows him as a shipmaster who will insist on discipline on his ship, but as far as any brutality or abuse is concerned, it is absurd to believe. It is too thin that a man would be murdered by a captain when a ship was leaving Cape Flattery and nothing be heard of it until the vessel returned home again. There is an American consul at the South African port and had there been any ground for such a charge it would have been made there before him and not on the return home of the vessel. On the face of it, it is a framed-up charge made in a spirit of revenge by sailors."

Following is the dispatch from San Francisco carried by the Associated Press yesterday afternoon:

SAN FRANCISCO, Nov. 3 – The United States district court issued warrants charging murder on the high seas today against Capt. D. O. Killman of the American schooner *Henry K. Hall*, and his first mate, Fred Hansen.

Six members of the crew of the schooner marched to the federal building and exhibiting bruises and other marks of violence, told a tale of horrors aboard ship between Port Townsend, Wash., and Durban, South Africa, and return, which included the murder of two of the crew, they charged.

Capt. Killman and Hansen are charged in one warrant with the death of one man, while Hansen is charged individually in another warrant with the murder of another sailor.

The *Henry K. Hall* arrived here yesterday, 118 days out of Durban. It is alleged that one of the crew died Sept. 1, while the ship was off the Australian coast, from a blow on the head with a knotted rope.

The other man was killed, it is alleged, soon after the ship left Port Townsend last January. The *Hall* reached her outgoing destination last May, leaking badly.

A variation of the report, with the heading "Murder and Brutality Charged on Hell Ship" was printed in the 3 November 1916 *Oakland Tribune* as follows:

San Francisco. Nov. 3. – Bringing tales of cruelties, brutal treatment and wanton murder, which they allege were suffered aboard the "hell" ship *Henry K. Hall*, between Durban, South Africa, and this port during a 118-day voyage, six members of the schooner's crew, which arrived in port today, filed formal complaint against First Officer Fred Hansen with the federal officers. A warrant charging murder on the high seas was issued by Federal Judge Maurice T. Dooling and turned over to a United States marshal for service.

Beatings for alleged trivial offenses, broken teeth, battered faces, gaping wounds alleged to have been caused by harsh methods employed by Hansen, and stories of mistreatment that rival the wildest sea tales of Henty [G. A. Henty, an English novelist and war correspondent] and Captain Boldarold are included in charges of the men. They allege that trouble began as soon as the ship left port on its original trip from San Francisco to South Africa, several months ago.

At that time considerable trouble was experienced in getting men to go on account of the fact that it expected to enter the war zone. A motley crew was finally obtained and the schooner left port. . . .

By the time they arrived on the other side of the water their treatment had been such, they allege, that they refused to sign for the return journey. The alleged shooting of a sailor named Larsen by First Officer Hansen is said to have occurred on the trip out.

On the return trip a crew was finally obtained, say the men, on the understanding that Hansen was to be left ashore. After the schooner had sail up and was ready to depart [unreadable] came aboard, whereupon the [unreadable] trouble commenced. It was on this home trip that the episode occurred, say the sailors, which resulted in the issuance of the federal warrant for murder by Judge Dooling today.

A negro boy, about 19 years of age, known to them only under the name of Louis, was beaten with heavy ropes by Hansen, they allege, until he lay unconscious on the deck. When he did not obey the first officer's commands to rise, the complainants say, Hansen jumped on him with his heavy sea boots and crushed in his chest, causing injuries which resulted in the lad's death a short time afterward. . . .

The body was weighted and thrown overboard afterward, it is claimed.

The sailors do not speak well of Captain T. [sic] O. Killman of the "hell" ship, or Second Officer Larsen, a namesake of the sailor they allege was shot going over to Africa on the out trip. The sailors have asked for a full investigation of all of their charges in addition to swearing to the complaint against their first officer.

United States District Attorney John W. Preston has announced that he will conduct a thorough inquiry into conditions on the "hell" ship and if the allegations of the crew are sustained he will institute federal prosecution. In the meantime deputy United States marshals are engaged in a search for the first officer, who left the "hell" ship as soon as it reached port.

Felix Dymock, one of the crew who made the complaint, exhibited an empty gum where two teeth had been and declared that Second Mate Larsen knocked them out.

"After the vessel reached South Africa, on the trip across," said Dymock, "the crew quit and it was understood that Hansen would not be on board. When he came at the last minute in a launch the new crew was dismayed and one of them, Patrick Murphy, jumped overboard and swam ashore."

North, Dymock and W. Weston described the killing of Louis and declared that the sailor Larsen had been shot as he was attempting to get away from the vessel at Port Townsend, on the trip out.

12. The US commissioner was Thomas E. Hayden. Killman appeared before him on 9 November 1916. The US attorney was John W. Preston. Election Day in 1916 was 5 November, and no doubt Hayden, a Wilson appointee, had been off on the campaign trail. As Wilson carried California (a key state) by a narrow margin in 1916, Killman might be regarded as a victim of history in spending five days in the slammer while due process gave way to practical politics. He was released on $1,000 bail, with the expectation that the homicide charge would be dismissed (which it was), but Hansen was held for the grand jury. Because San Francisco had a Republican administration under Mayor James Rolph (a shipowner), the city police naturally sympathized with Killman.

13. The *H. K. Hall* sailed from San Francisco 1 January 1917 and arrived at Astoria 22 January. On the Columbia River she loaded 1,265,000 board feet of lumber for Sydney at a freight rate of £4.12s.6d per thousand under charter to Comyn, Mackall & Co., grossing (at par) about $28,000.

14. After the *H. K. Hall* episode, Hansen obtained command of the *A. M. Baxter* in May 1918, but he soon was relieved by a man named Hellquist, who lost the schooner in the Fijis, uninsured, in August 1918. In June 1919 Hansen was tried for homicide at Seattle in connection with the drowning of a seaman from the *Edward R. West* in 1918.

We next hear of Hansen as mate of the four-masted barkentine *Rolph* in 1920 on a voyage from Vancouver, British Columbia, to Melbourne, Australia, and then from Newcastle, Australia, to Mejillones, Chile. On arrival at Mejillones, in April 1921, six seamen told a story of mistreatment so striking that the US consul at Antofagasta ordered Capt. A. H. Sorensen to discharge Hansen and arranged to send him by steamer with two of the complaining witnesses to the United States for trial. Hansen, however, simply walked out of the consulate on 10 May 1921 and disappeared. He made his way to Tocopilla, Chile, where he shipped in the Finnish four-masted bark *Mariechen*, sailing 1 June 1921 for Europe via Panama.

Hansen turned up in Seattle a few months later, where he sat for his master's license, receiving it 20 September 1921. This action proved to be his undoing, as it led to his arrest and conviction, and he was sentenced to five years in federal prison. He served at McNeil Island, Washington, from December 1922 until his release on 1 September 1926, with transportation furnished to Aberdeen, Washington. After the *Elinor H.* voyage in 1927, and the return to Honolulu in 1928 on the

Ella A. (see chapter 24, note 2, and chapter 25, note 6), Hansen is last heard of in January 1929, when he had to be paid off as mate of the *Joseph Dollar*, as otherwise the four-masted bark would have been unable to hire a crew. (For more on Hansen, see E. Kay Gibson, *Brutality on Trial: "Hellfire" Pedersen, "Fighting" Hansen, and the Seamen's Act of 1915* [Gainesville: University Press of Florida, 2006].)

15. Although Killman is doubtless correct that the evidence of his official log would have cleared Hansen of the homicide charge, Hansen pleaded guilty to inflicting corporal punishment, which, under the 1915 La Follette Act, was a misdemeanor punishable by imprisonment for not less than three months or more than two years.

CHAPTER 18

1. The *H. K. Hall* sailed from the Columbia River 14 March 1917.

2. A coarse, stout leather shoe reaching to the ankle.

3. Killman's statement as to the risk of stopping is hindsight. When he sailed, the United States was not at war with Germany. Von Luckner in the *Seeadler* sank his first American ship on 8 June 1917, and Nerger in the *Wolf* captured his first, the *Winslow* (named for Winslow Hall), on 17 June.

4. Copra is dried coconut meat.

5. The *H. K. Hall* arrived at Sydney 3 June 1917 and departed for Portland 14 July.

6. Another West Coast five-masted schooner, the *Crescent*, was burned at sea with a copra cargo a few months after the June 1918 incident in the *H. K. Hall*. The *Crescent*, however, was not near an island, and all hands had to sail 1,600 miles in the schooner's lifeboat to reach San Francisco.

7. The *H. K. Hall* arrived back in Astoria 29 September 1917.

8. In early December the *Hall* departed again for Sydney, arriving 7 March 1918.

9. To "line up" for wheat means to provide dunnage under the sacks, so as to keep loose grain out of the pumps and bilge water out of the cargo, and avoid contact between grain sacks and bolt heads and other rust-producing fittings.

10. The profitable charters Killman reports were typical of conditions during 1918. The Australian government put an embargo on the export of grain.

11. The sale of the *H. K. Hall* to George F. Davis is not reflected in any documentation of the schooner now in the National Archives. The US Shipping Board had control of transfers of American ships to foreigners, and in 1918 generally prohibited them. Thus, if Davis was an Australian there was a little hanky-panky taking place. On the other hand, Davis may have been an American residing in Australia. An obscure law dating from 1792 prohibits an American citizen living abroad from owning an American flag vessel unless he is either a consul or a partner in and agent for an American firm, but the practice seems to have been simply to put the vessel in another name.

12. Davis's statement about the difficulty of getting another master was to the

point. He would have had to locate a man who was an American citizen and had a master's license for a sailing vessel over 700 tons. Most schooners trading from America to Australia at the time were under 700 tons.

13. The *H. K. Hall* sailed from Sydney 5 August 1918.

14. Coconut oil melts at about 70° F. In tropical latitudes it is a sticky oil, and in temperate latitudes it is a soft solid; not a good material to have spilled on a ship's deck in either state!

15. The *Hall* arrived in Victoria, British Columbia, 27 October 1918.

16. Rabbit fur is used to make felt. Apparently in America in 1918 other goods took priority over felt hats.

17. The Armistice was signed on 11 November 1918.

CHAPTER 19

1. Killman turned the *H. K. Hall* over to Carl Wikander at Portland, Oregon, 9 January 1919. He had arrived there 20 November 1918 from Victoria. The schooner loaded 1,325,884 board feet of lumber and left Portland 27 January 1919, arriving at Sydney 31 March. The freight rate was £5.15s per thousand. The *H. K. Hall* arrived at Melbourne in July and there loaded a general cargo for London, sailing 12 September, passing the Panama Canal 5 December, and arriving 22 January 1920. On the return voyage, she left London 7 March 1920 and arrived at Melbourne 19 June. G. C. Billings repurchased her from Davis about this time. In 1925 she was sold to Peruvian owners and renamed *Dante*.

2. In 1917 the US Shipping Board established the Emergency Fleet Corporation to acquire, maintain, and operate merchant ships to meet national defense and foreign and domestic commerce during World War I. In 1927 the EFC was renamed the US Shipping Board Merchant Fleet Corporation, and in 1936 the Board and the Corporation were abolished and their functions transferred to the US Maritime Commission.

3. Killman's new command was the *Wawalona*. She was a steel steamer of 6,076 tons, built at Vancouver, Washington, in 1919 for the US Shipping Board by the G. M. Standifer Construction Co. Killman's name appeared on her first register, dated 12 November 1919.

4. The *Wawalona* sailed from Portland on 17 November 1919 (not 1 January) and arrived at Yokohama on 15 December 1919.

5. The *Deuel* was a steel steamer of 5,586 tons, built at Seattle, Washington, in 1919 for the US Shipping Board by J. F. Duthie & Co. She had left Seattle 17 November 1919, and after being aground near Tokyo Bay, arrived at Yokohama 17 December.

6. The *West Inskip*, 5,555 tons, was built to the same design as the *Deuel* by the Southwestern Shipbuilding Co. at San Pedro, California, in 1919. She left San Francisco 14 November.

7. The *Deuel*'s master was William Reed. He was relieved 10 April 1920. The *West Inskip* was commanded by J. K. Tibbetts.

8. The *Wawalona* arrived at Kobe 24 December 1919. She left Kobe 29 December and arrived at Shanghai 3 January 1920. The Shipping Board archives omit the call at Moji.

9. The *Wawalona* left Shanghai 5 January 1920, arrived at Hong Kong 8 January, sailed from Hong Kong 11 January, and arrived at Manila, Philippines, 13 January.

10. On 15 January 1920 two A.B.s and a stewardess were signed on: Everett Roscoe Wilson, 43, 5'10"; John E. Ewell, 41, 6'0"; and Amis W. Ewell, 30, 5'8". A note on Killman's manuscript indicates Major Wilson was in army intelligence.

11. The *Wawalona* left Manila 16 January 1920 and arrived again at Shanghai 22 January. The three passengers signed off her articles the same day.

12. The steamer left Shanghai 25 January and arrived at Kobe three days later.

13. The *Wawalona* left Kobe 30 January and Yokohama 4 February, arriving home at Portland 22 February. Killman thus seems to have been gone five days *over* three months.

CHAPTER 20

1. Killman was relieved in command of the *Wawalona* by Erik G. Troberg 8 March 1920. His daughter gives as his reason for leaving the steamer the amount of paperwork and multiplication of copies involved in the government operation of a steamship line.

2. The *Ella A.* measured 233.4 × 45.7 × 18.5 feet and had a gross tonnage of 1,565. By comparison, the five-masted *H. K. Hall* measured 225.4 × 42.4 × 18.1 feet. The *Ella A.*'s sister, *Elinor H.*, was also a five-master. The *Ella A.* and *Elinor H.* had been ordered by Norwegian owners in October 1917 from Martinolich Shipbuilding Co., of Dockton, Washington. The builders got into financial difficulties, and their plant was sold at a trustee sale in August 1919. The two schooners were completed by John A. Martinolich for Harbor Navigation Co., of Hoquiam, Washington, of which Frank A. Hill was secretary. J. C. Shaw was managing owner. Possibly named for Ella A. Polson, wife of one of the investors in the Harbor Navigation Co., Killman's four-master was launched 9 March 1920, and he documented her at Tacoma 27 April 1920.

3. The *Ella A.* left the mill at Everett on 4 May 1920 and went to sea from Port Townsend a week later.

4. Following is the text of the letter that Killman wrote to Washington:

Port Townsend, Washington, May 8, 1920.

To the Honorable Secretary of Commerce,

Department of Commerce,

Washington, D. C.

Through the Honorable Collector of Customs,
District of Washington,
Seattle, Washington.
Sir:

I, D. O. Killman, master of the American Schooner "Ella A.," hereby apply for relief by the remission of the fine of Five Hundred Dollars ($500.) that has been imposed against the schooner "Ella A." on account for my failure and inability to fully comply with the requirements of the Seamen's Shipping Act of March 4, 1915, which became operative November 4, 1915, relative to the "Manning of Merchant Vessels," Part V, Article 117, of the United States Navigation Laws.

The facts in connection with this technical and unavoidable violation of the Seamen's Shipping Act, which requires my vessel to have sixty-five per cent (65%) of the deck crew provided with certificates issued by a board of the Steamboat Inspection Service, establishing their rating as able seamen, are as follows:

The American Schooner "ELLA A." completed loading a complete cargo of lumber at Everett, Washington, on April 29, 1920, for delivery at Adelaide, Australia. Prior to that date I had ordered my agents to secure a crew to come on board the vessel as soon as the vessel completed her loading; said crew to contain 65% OR more certified seamen.

Finding that no men were available I had the vessel towed to Port Townsend on April 30th. After a delay of eight days I have succeeded in securing a crew composed of seven seamen of which five have been signed as able seamen and two as ordinary seamen. I have been able to secure but one seaman who was properly certified, so that the vessel actually has only 14 2/7% certified seamen. When I found that it was impossible to secure the full per centage of certified seamen I completed the crew with the very best men obtainable in order to avoid a further long and expensive delay for the vessel. I have a crew which I consider competent to properly handle the vessel, and have employed the same number as is usually shipped on a vessel of the same class.

I further state that the present crew was not shipped and signed with any intention to avoid or evade the requirements of the Seamen's Shipping Act.

In view of the above facts, I respectfully pray for relief by the remission of the entire amount of the fine assessed against my vessel.

Very respectfully,
[signature D. O. Killman]
Master American Schooner "ELLA A."
Subscribed and sworn to before me this eighth (8th) day of May, 1920.
[signature H. T. Hayden]

Notary Public in and for the State of Washington, residing at Port Townsend, Wash. My commission expires June 18, 1920.

5. The date of arrival at Port Adelaide was 11 August 1920.

6. On 21 August 1920 the *Adelaide Observer* reported the *Ella A.*'s troubles as follows:

The American schooner, *Ella A*, which was damaged in the heavy weather over the week-end, and which has been at the Semaphore anchorage since Wednesday morning, left at midday in charge of the tugs *Euro*, *Eagle*, and *Yulta* for a berth in the dock, which she reached at 3 p.m. The vessel departed from Port Townsend, USA, on June 11, with 1,500,000 ft. of Oregon timber. Fair weather with an occasional squall prevailed across the Pacific. When the schooner arrived off Cape Borda, it was becalmed for two days, and eventually went right around Kangaroo Island and entered the gulf by way of Investigator Strait. On Sunday, August 8, the wind blew a gale from the southwest, and the vessel anchored off Aldinga. The wind continued to rise, and at about midnight one of the anchor chains snapped, and the schooner lost the anchor and 120 fathoms of chain. A spare anchor was then put over the side. Fortunately, the second anchor held, but on Monday morning the vessel had dragged to within a half-mile of the shore. During the night the greater portion of her rudder was lost, and it was found next morning on the beach. The tug *Euro* arrived alongside the boat from Port Adelaide on Monday afternoon, but her assistance was not required. Steering with her sails, the vessel proceeded from Aldinga on Tuesday afternoon and arrived at the anchorage early on Wednesday morning. The *Ella A.* is a new schooner, having been built only five months. (Courtesy Trove, National Library of Australia.)

7. The place where *Ella A.* had anchored and lost her rudder was Aldinga Bay.

8. Bureau Veritas is a French classification society and register of shipping that was established in 1828. Other principal classification societies included Lloyd's Register, London, and the American Bureau of Shipping, New York. (Kerchove, *International Maritime Dictionary*, 2d ed.)

9. The *Notre Dame d'Arvor* was wrecked off the southwest point of Wardang Island, at the entrance to Port Victoria, 20 March 1920 and burned 1 May. The *Ella A.* arrived in Adelaide in August. Thus the newspapers Killman was reading were several months old.

10. From Port Adelaide to Newcastle is 1,027 miles, a nine-day tow at 5 knots.

11. The tug was the *Eagle*, chartered for £2,000, as reported by the *Newcastle Morning Herald and Miners' Advocate*. (Courtesy Trove, National Library of Australia.)

12. The *Ella A.* departed Adelaide in tow 7 October.

13. The *Ella A.* arrived Newcastle 15 October 1920.

14. The *Ella A.* sailed from Newcastle on Saturday, 13 November 1920. Her new mate was Carl Liedke, 68, who had been sailing as a mate since 1882 but had put in fourteen years as a conductor on the Market Street Railway in San Francisco before going back to sea. He was actually on the articles at $200 per month. By comparison, in 1919 the chief mate of the *Wawalona* was paid $228.75. In an

affidavit prepared by C. Inness Brown, US consul at Iquique, Chile, 30 March 1921, Liedke described several instances when he was assaulted by Killman. Apparently the trouble started the first Saturday at sea. The men had been working from 6:00 a.m. to 5:00 p.m., so the mate gave them Saturday afternoon off. When Killman learned of this, he said to the mate: "You German bastard, trying to make a whorehouse of my ship?"

15. On 12 August 1921 Liedke was admitted to Sailors' Snug Harbor, Staten Island, New York, as an "aged and worn out seaman." There he began writing Washington. The Bureau of Navigation investigated his case, decided that Killman had not kept an adequate log (neither Liedke's injury nor a record of his pay-off had been noted), and computed the *Ella A.* still owed him $903.73, advising him to go to court to collect it. In 1925 Liedke reported his difficulties with a Legal Aid lawyer in New York, and by November he had the case in the hands of James Kiefer of Seattle. He was still corresponding with the Bureau on the subject in July 1927. Liedke died 28 May 1930 at Sailors' Snug Harbor.

16. The *Ella A.* arrived at Iquique 5 February 1921 and left that port 21 March, arriving at the Columbia River and departing Astoria under tow to Portland 17 June 1921.

CHAPTER 21

1. The *Ella A.* sailed from Grays Harbor 2 August 1921 and arrived at Callao 28 October 1921.

2. The *Ella A.* left Callao 13 December 1921 and returned to Aberdeen 1 February 1922.

3. Montesano is the county seat of Grays Harbor County, Washington.

4. Industrial Workers of the World. Labor union founded in 1905.

CHAPTER 22

1. Although Killman does not name his mate, he likely was "French Louie" Huet. At this time the schooner's ownership was changed. Instead of the former corporation, ownership was now vested in J. C. Shaw, Robert Polson, and C. Stuart Polson, all of Hoquiam, each owning one-quarter, and W. H. Abel and Ella R. Abel of Montesano, each with one-eighth.

2. The auto ride took place 1 June 1922. Killman's friend was Charles H. Rychard of Hoquiam. The *Aberdeen Daily World* carried an account of the accident in the June 2 issue:

Captain Dan Killman of the schooner Ella A. was injured, perhaps seriously, and Charles H. Rychard, of Hoquiam, escaped injury when a touring car in which they were riding south on Park street at 7:45 o'clock last night was struck at Market street by a fire truck and hurled 35 feet down the Market parking strip and so completely wrecked that it is a total loss. Captain Killman was pinned under the car when the fire truck carried it down the street, but Mr. Rychard was thrown from the machine, and lighted on the pavement without having received a scratch.

When the two colliding machines came to a stop on the parking strip, the fire truck's front wheels and engine were resting on the smaller car, and the whole fire truck was tilted upwards at an angle of about 25 degrees. Captain Killman, stunned by the collision, was pinned under his machine. Firemen jacked up the wheels of the fire truck, then lifted the touring car sufficiently to allow Fire Chief William Tamblyn to crawl under the car and assist Captain Killman in freeing himself from the wreckage. A short time after the captain had been taken out, the car burst into flames, but the firemen extinguished the blaze with chemicals. Captain Killman was taken to the Hoquiam General hospital, where he was found to be suffering from shock and possible chest injuries. Full extent of his injuries had not been determined today by attending physicians.

Frank Rattie, driver of the fire truck, said Captain Killman was driving along slowly, and apparently had seen the fire machine coming west on Market street. The car, Rattie said, seemed about to stop when it started picking up speed and attempted to cross Market street directly in front of the fire machine. Rattie, who was driving along at about 25 miles an hour, was unable to stop the heavy ladder truck to avoid a collision.

The department was answering a call for a small fire on West Market street when the accident occurred.

3. The original typewritten text omits the doctor's name; "Olman" is penciled in. The doctor referred to must be Eino Ahlman, one of a half-dozen physicians practicing in Hoquiam at that time.

4. Many years later, probably in the mid-1980s, Killman's granddaughter Sally Pierce Hokanson recollected her grandparents this way: "She [Minnie Killman] truly was a sort of goddess—both clever and beautiful. She was a splendid cook, she [did] incredibly artistic and intricate needlework, and was gentle and charming. [Her girls] worshipped her. Grandfather adored her."

5. The *Ella A.*'s papers were changed 9 June 1922. He probably sailed the next day.

6. The *Ella A.* arrived back at Grays Harbor 12 September 1922, having sailed from San Pedro on 15 August. Killman's "good" must refer to the weather, not his voyage time.

CHAPTER 23

1. The *Ella A.* left Grays Harbor 27 October 1922 and arrived at Sydney 18 January 1923. She left Newcastle 25 March and arrived at Valparaiso 5 June.

2. The *Independence* was built at East Boston in 1871 by Curtis & Smith. She was condemned at Bermuda early in 1919 but later that year was sailed to Valparaiso, where she arrived 11 September.

3. Captain Killman had at least a little time for recreation in Iquique, about a year following the car accident in which he damaged his hand and broke several ribs. In a letter from Capt. C. A. Holmqvist to Richard M. Cookson, date unknown, Captain Holmqvist recalled an encounter he had with Dan Killman in Chile:

While the LAWHILL was at Newcastle, N.S.W., in February/March 1923 the American schooner ELLA A., with Captain Killman in command, lay near us. Killman was a New Englander—a real hard case who went under the name of "Crazy Killman." We saw him again at Iquique some months later, still in charge of the ELLA A. Here it was a common sight to see gangs of sailing ship men outside the sailing clubs where the captains used to spend their evenings. One evening a gang came ashore from a Norwegian vessel to see their captain at the Spanish Club and this captain was in company with Capt. Killman of the ELLA A. They acted very uppish and even threatened to fight. Old 65 year old Crazy Killman didn't understand what they said but didn't like their looks either. When he told them to clear out they attacked him—not knowing him as we did. All four were soon lying in the street! The white-haired Killman looked like a Sunday school teacher but had been amateur champion in boxing in San Francisco for 15 years and knew how to fight. He used to say he only met a better man once—and that was his wife!

4. The *Ella A.* left Iquique 31 July and arrived at Honolulu 28 September 1923.

5. The *Ella A.* left Honolulu 13 October and arrived at Winslow, Washington, 21 November. The schooner was laid up all during 1924, apparently at Tacoma. She left Tacoma 19 March 1925 and arrived at Bellingham early on the 20th. In the schooner's cabin at 2:30 that afternoon, the local Presbyterian minister married Sydney Killman to Ward Pierce, a Tacoma bank executive.

6. After loading at Bellingham, the *Ella A.* sailed from Port Townsend 14 April 1925 and arrived at Noumea, New Caledonia, on 17 July (a Friday).

7. A term used to denote the social elite of New York City in the nineteenth century.

8. The *Ella A.* arrived in Newcastle 3 September 1925, having been towed from Sydney.

9. The *Ella A.* was detained in Newcastle more than a month, as a dispute had developed over the use of shifting boards, a new Australian requirement. Killman lost this one, in spite of involving various consuls, but the resulting correspondence fills a fat file (113530N) in the Bureau of Navigation Records. Killman apparently had persuaded R. L. Rankin, the US consul in Newcastle, that he, not the local harbor authorities, had prime responsibility for the vessel, but the US consul in Melbourne, Norman L. Anderson, soon straightened him out on that matter. It was also contended that because the Australian regulation referred to 'tween-decks, it could not be applied to a single-deck vessel such as the *Ella A.* The case ended with "nominal compliance": Killman had to discharge the coal in the square of the hatch, at a cost to him (as he complained in a letter to the Melbourne Chamber

of Commerce) of £135 and fourteen days' delay. On 16 October 1925 he sailed for Callao with 2,257 tons of Aberdeen coal measuring 48 cubic feet to the ton.

10. The *Ella A.* arrived in Callao 27 December 1925.

11. The *Ella A.* left Callao 10 (or 13) February 1926 and reached Puget Sound 4 April.

CHAPTER 24

1. The 12 May 1927 issue of the *Anacortes American* included a notice headed "Local Firm Furnishes Supplies for the Ella A." The local Frye and Co. branch and Roy Graham of Graham's Grocery were reported to have furnished 500 lbs of Wild Rose butter, 60 dozen eggs, 600 lbs of corned beef in brine, 300 pounds of mess pork [barreled salt pork], 100 lbs of beef tongue, 5 lbs of pigs feet, 300 lbs of Wild Rose bacon, 300 lbs of Wild Rose ham, 200 lbs of Wild Rose pure lard, 100 lbs of assorted sausage meats, 2,500 lbs of Yakima potatoes, 300 lbs of onions and a large supply of canned goods and galley provisions.

2. The *Elinor H.* left Port Angeles for Australia 10 May 1927 under Capt. Hans J. ("Poker Hans") Anderson with 1,610,000 feet of lumber. F. Hansen was his mate. It is possible that this is the same Hansen who signed on as Killman's mate on the *Ella A.* for the voyage from Newcastle back to Puget Sound, paying off in Honolulu. (See chapter 17, note 5.) If so, this might explain some of Captain Anderson's difficulty finding a crew.

3. The 10 June 1927 issue of the *Port Townsend Weekly Ledger* offered a tantalizing opportunity for job seekers: "Trip To Australia? Captain Dan Killman of the four-masted schooner ELLA A is still looking for a crew to man his craft on her long voyage to the South Seas and Australian ports. Splendid chance for some adventurous and ambitious would-be travelers. The ELLA A carries 600,000 feet of lumber and has been waiting to complete her crew here for nearly a month."

4. The *Ella A.* departed Port Townsend on 11 June 1927 with 1,558,000 feet of lumber (not 600,000, as reported by the *Port Townsend Weekly Ledger* in the preceding note) shipped by J. J. Moore & Co.

5. The *Elinor H.* arrived at Melbourne 5 September, followed by the *Ella A.* on 10 October.

6. The steamer route from Melbourne to Newcastle is 649 miles.

7. The *Ella A.* arrived at Newcastle 14 November 1927.

8. The *Elinor H.* left Newcastle 2 December 1927 in ballast and arrived at Port Townsend 10 March 1928. In June 1930, after a two-year layup, she was sold for scrapping.

CHAPTER 25

1. The use of exact dates and positions in this chapter indicates that, for the first time, Captain Killman was writing from records and not solely from memory. Here

he probably was referring to the schooner's log for a copy of the protest he made on his arrival in Honolulu.

2. The name of the man lost was E. Hallikos. (See chapter 25, note 6.)

3. The *Ella A.* arrived off Hanapepe, Kauai, on 3 or 4 May 1928, 148 days out of Newcastle. The voyage lasted about twice as long as the average passage between Australia and Hawaii. Captain Killman had been here before in the *Planter* in 1884 or 1885.

4. The *Lehua* was a 360-hp steamer of 204 tons, built at Tacoma in 1918 as the *Ambassador* by the Tacoma Shipbuilding Co.

5. The *Kinau* was an ancient iron steamer, built at Philadelphia in 1883 by Cramp, but her engine was rated at 600 hp, and she grossed 975 tons.

6. The *Honolulu Advertiser* published a front-page story as follows:

Schooner *Ella A* Arrives from Newcastle After Five Months Voyage. Tugs Tow Four-Master in; Crew Shows Wear and Tear, Leaking Ship Looks Trim.

Exactly five months after leaving Newcastle, N.S.W., with a cargo of 2,280 tons of coal for discharge at Callao, Peru, the four-masted schooner *Ella A.*, whose home port is Hoquiam, Wash., under command of Capt. D. O. Killman, arrived off port in tow Sunday night and was brought into the harbor and docked yesterday morning for repairs. The schooner was first sighted last Thursday afternoon off Kekaba, Kauai, where the captain went ashore in a small boat and reported that his vessel had made heavy weather after leaving Newcastle and had sprung a leak, forcing him to alter his course and seek smoother seas.

At times there was as much as eight feet of water in her holds, requiring all hands to man the pumps day and night. Fearing that the ship would go down if he attempted to make Callao, Captain Killman decided to make for Honolulu where repairs might be obtained. The run from Newcastle to Callao should have been made in about 40 or 50 days or 70 at the longest. When the schooner reported off Kauai the Inter-Island tug *Lehua* was sent from Honolulu to tow the vessel here. They left Friday afternoon but were forced back by heavy weather to Port Allen where the *Kinau* went to their assistance and they finally arrived off port about 8 o'clock Sunday night. . . .

When the vessel left Australia there were 13 in the crew, but on January 4 at 4:15 in the morning E. Hallikos, a seaman, fell overboard while reefing the flying jib, when the forestay parted.

The surviving members plainly showed the effects of their five months at sea when they arrived in port yesterday. Several were suffering from boils and other sores caused by lack of proper food, emergency rations having been the order for many days before they picked up Kauai. A few were also in need of a shave.

Alexander & Baldwin are acting as agents here for the owners of the schooner, J. C. Shaw & Company of Seattle. It was stated that most of the cargo will be removed and the vessel will then be placed in drydock for repairs.

When the schooner came into port yesterday morning she showed no outward signs of hardship, except for a little "moss" on her hull near the waterline, indicating she had been at sea for some time. Everything aboard ship was looking spick and span with plenty of evidence of fresh paint at every turn. The decks had been scrubbed and holystoned and everything appeared to be ship-shape. . . .

The *Ella A.* has been away from her home port since last June 10, having delivered a cargo of lumber to Melbourne. The trip to Melbourne from Port Townsend was made in 123 days. The vessel then went in ballast to Newcastle to load coal for Callao, where, after discharging, she was to pick up a cargo for her home port. Whether the vessel will attempt to continue to Peru after repairs here has not yet been decided. Orders from the owners are to remain here until further orders.

Members of the crew are, besides Capt. Killman, the mate, S. Hansen and seamen P. Jansson, J. Grihadsen, D. Simpson, C. W. Hall, J. Johnson, V. Marsters, Askar Ny and Eric Sundgren and cook and mess G. S. Lezardo and M. Torri. With the exception of three, members of the crew were signed on in Australia. The man lost overboard joined the vessel in Port Townsend. He was a native of Finland.

7. U. S. marine law entitles men to draw half their pay at any port at which cargo is handled. Until the coal began to be discharged, therefore, the men had no claim for wages.

8. The entire cargo of coal was about 2,200 tons.

CHAPTER 26

1. Firedamp, as defined in the *Oxford English Dictionary*, is "a miner's term for . . . marsh-gas, which is given off by coal and is explosive when mixed in certain proportions with atmospheric air."

2. The *Ella A.* left Honolulu 13 July 1928.

3. The *Ella A.* arrived at Port Townsend 12 August 1928. On arrival she was fined $30 for having sailed without a valid document, a shortcoming explained by the fact that in 1926 the part owners had sold out to the Eureka Cedar Lumber & Shingle Co. Robert Polson was president of this corporation, which was succeeded by the Polson Lumber & Shingle Co. C. S. Polson was treasurer, and J. C. Shaw was manager. In July 1930 the schooner was sold to Neider & Marcus of Seattle. They stripped her of all useful items and then burned the hulk to recover the bolts that had held her together. These doubtless soon found their way to Japan as scrap iron.

4. Captain Daniel O. Killman died at his home in Tacoma 8 June 1936 and was buried with the Masonic honors of the York Rite. He rests next to his beloved wife.

Glossary of Nautical Terms

A.B. *See* Able Seaman

Aback. When sails are pressed aft against the mast by the force of the wind.

Able (or Able-Bodied) Seaman. An experienced deck-department seaman qualified to perform routine sea duties.

Allotment. A portion of a seaman's wages made payable to a relative or other designated person or to a bank for his account.

Articles. Document containing all particulars relating to the terms of agreement between the master of the vessel and the crew.

Azimuth. The direction of a celestial object from the observer, expressed as the angular distance from the north or south point of the horizon to the point at which a vertical circle passing through the object intersects the horizon.

Backstay. Rope stretching from a masthead and tending aft from the mast. The lower end is fastened to a chain plate on the side of the ship. It serves to support the mast against forward pull. It is named according to the mast it supports.

Ballast. A ship is "in ballast" when it carries no cargo but only heavy material (ballast) placed low to maintain stability, trim, or draft.

Bark. A three-masted vessel, square rigged on the fore and main and fore-and-aft rigged on the mizzen.

Barkentine. A vessel of at least three masts with the foremast square-rigged and the other masts fore-and-aft rigged.

Barometer. An instrument used to measure atmospheric pressure.

Bend Sail. To fasten a sail by means of a bend or knot to the proper yard, gaff, or stay ready for setting.

Bight. The double part in a folded rope; the bend or loop.

Bilge Shores. Short, heavy timbers used in addition to bilge blocks to support the lower part of the hull of a dry-docked vessel.

Bitt. Strong wood or iron post used for fastening, belaying, and working ropes, cables, and the like.

Blood Money. A fee paid by a master to a boarding-house keeper or a crimp (one who illegally detains people to serve as sailors) for the procurement of seamen.

Board. Long, flat slab of sawed lumber; plank.

Boat-Steerer. In a whaleboat, the man who pulls the harpoon oar, darts the iron into the whale, and then steers while the boat-header lances the mammal.

Boatswain. A petty officer who has immediate charge of all deck hands.

Boom. A general name for a variety of horizontal spars or poles for extending the foot of sails, handling cargo, and the like.

Boom Tackle. Tackle leading forward of the boom when a vessel under sail is running before the wind.

Bow Port (also Lumber Port). An opening close to the stem (upright post of the bow) of ships regularly engaged in the lumber trade, to allow long logs to be loaded or discharged endwise.

Brace. A rope used to control the horizontal motion of yards.

Break. The point at which a deck superstructure, such as a poop, forecastle, or bridge house, is discontinued.

Breakwater. A structure or contrivance serving to break the force of the waves and protect a harbor or anything that otherwise would be exposed to the force of waves.

Brig. A two-masted square-rigged vessel.

Brigantine. A brig without a square mainsail. Also a two-masted vessel with a square rig on the foremast and a fore-and-aft rig (no top) on the mainmast.

Bring Up. To come to a standstill because of anchoring, entanglement, or collision (e.g., with the sea bottom).

Bulwark. Raised woodwork or plating running along each side of a vessel above the weather deck.

Bumboat. A small, open rowboat used in carrying supplies for sale to vessels in a harbor.

Butts (also End Joints). Ends of planks that meet endwise exactly and are caulked.

Card Compass. *See* Compass Card.

Cathead. A wood or metal beam projecting far enough over each bow to support a stocked anchor before letting go or before stowing on board.

Charter Party (also Chartering). An agreement by which a ship owner places a ship, or a part of it, at the disposal of a merchant for the conveyance of goods to a particular place for a fee that the merchant undertakes to pay as freight for their carriage.

Chronometer. An instrument designed to measure time accurately despite fluctuations in air pressure, temperature, movement, and the like.

Collier. A vessel designed to carry coal.

Commodore Captain. Courtesy title given to the senior captain of a line of passenger vessels.

Companionway. Steps leading from a companion hatchway to a cabin or saloon below. A wood or steel hood with doors for making weathertight an entrance to the deck below.

Compass card. A circular card with magnets attached to its underside, its face divided on its rim into points of the compass, and resting on a pivot so as to rotate freely.

Crank (also Cranky). Lacking sufficient initial stability; easily inclined by external forces such as wind or the sea.

Crosstree. One of two horizontal struts at the upper end of a topmast used to anchor the shrouds from the topgallant mast.

Davit. Small derrick used for hoisting boats, anchors, and ladders, or handling stores.

Dead Reckoning. Determining a vessel's position by applying to its last well-determined position the run it has made since, using for this purpose its course and the distance indicated by log.

Deal (Great Britain). Fir or pine board cut to standard dimensions.

Demurrage. The detention of a vessel, during loading or unloading, beyond the scheduled time of departure and, by extension, compensation paid for such detention.

Diagonally Strapped Bracing. Beams used in wooden ships to improve the longitudinal strength of the hull. Flat wrought-iron bars arranged in lattice form and fitted diagonally inside the frame timbers.

Dip the Flag. To lower and then raise the ensign as a mark of courtesy to nearby vessels.

Discharge. To unload cargo from a vessel.

Dispatch. The time allowed by a charter party for loading and discharging a vessel.

Disrate. To reduce to a lower rank.

Dockmaster. Officer subordinate to harbormaster who supervises the locking in and out of vessels at docks under his supervision.

Dolphin Striker. A short spar hanging from the outer end of the bowsprit to spread the martingale.

Draft. The depth of water a vessel requires to float free.

Droger. A vessel built for burden, for transporting cotton, lumber, and other heavy loads. On the West Coast of the United States, also applied to vessels engaged in the coal trade.

Drydock. An enclosed basin into which a ship is taken for underwater cleaning and repair. Watertight entrance gates close to permit the dock to be pumped dry.

Dunnage. Pieces of loose wood, matting, or similar material used for the protection of cargo in a ship's hold.

Easting. The distance, in nautical miles, a ship makes good in an easterly direction. Converse is westing.

Equatorial Current. Either of two oceanic currents (the North and South Equatorial Currents) driven primarily by the easterly trade winds and flowing westward on either side of the equator.

Ex-Meridian. The observation of a celestial body to ascertain latitude shortly before or after it has crossed the observer's meridian.

Fathom. A nautical measure equal to 6 feet.

Fife Rail. A semicircular rail at the foot of a mast.

Fill. To trim the sails so that the wind will catch them full.

Flood Tide. The inflow of the tide (as opposed to ebb tide).

Flying Jib. The sail set on the fore topgallant royal stay in square-rigged vessels, used in light winds.

Forecastle (pronounced 'fohk'sul). A short superstructure above the bows generally used as a living compartment for the crew.

Forecastle Head. The extreme forepart of a forecastle superstructure.

Forepeak. Space between the collision bulkhead (intended to keep water out of the forward bulkhead in case of collision) and the stem.

Foul. Said of a ship's bottom when it has a growth of weeds and barnacles on its surface owing to long immersion in sea water.

Fourfold Block. A mechanical device consisting of a casing within which are mounted four sheaves (grooved wheels through which a rope passes) and to which is fitted a hook.

Furl. To roll up or take in sails.

Gaff. A spar for extending the head (upper side) of a fore-and-aft quadrilateral sail.

Gaff Topsail. A fore-and-aft sail set above a gaff.

Gantline. A rope passing through a single block at a masthead, used to send a man and rigging aloft.

Garland. A ring of rope lashed around a spar near its middle when hoisting it.

Gasket. A small line or canvas strap used to secure a furled sail to a yard boom or gaff.

Goose-Winged. Said of a course or topsail whose lower corner is hauled up and lashed to the yard.

Half-Brig. The half brig–half schooner uses the foremast of a brig (yards) and the mainmast (fore and aft) of a schooner.

Halyard. A rope or purchase (arrangement of tackle) used for hoisting and lowering yards, spars, or sails on their masts or stays.

Harbormaster. Officer in charge of mooring and berthing vessels and of enforcing regulations respecting a harbor.

Haul to the Wind. To bring the wind from aft to a point nearer the bow.

Hawse Pipe. A steel pipe near the stern of a ship through which the anchor cable runs.

Hawser. A fiber rope used for towing or working a ship.

Headsail. Generic term for a sail forward of the foremast.

Head Sea. A sea in which the waves oppose a ship's course, so that the ship must rise over or cut through the waves.

Heave to. To position a ship so that the wind acts on the forward surface of the sails, checking its way.

Heaving Line (also Hauling Line). A small line thrown to a dock or approaching vessel by means of which an attached heavier line is hauled ashore or aboard.

Jack. A slightly dismissive term for a laborer; hence, steeplejack and lumberjack—and "Jack tar" for a common sailor.

Jibboom. An extension of the bowsprit.

Jigger. The aftermost mast of a four- or five-masted bark, and the fourth mast of a five- or six-masted schooner.

Jury Rigged. A temporary or makeshift rig set up by a ship's crew to take the place of a rig that has been lost or carried away.

Kedge Anchor. A light anchor used to move a ship from place to place. The anchor is carried a distance from the ship and dropped. The ship is then pulled to the anchor using capstans (machines using mechanical power to raise anchors, hoist yards, and so on) or winches.

Keelson. A center-line girder extending from stem to sternpost above or between the floor plates to prevent vertical or longitudinal movement and to strengthen the hull.

Knighthead. Timber beside the stem (upright post of the bow) that forms the bed for the bowsprit.

Knot. One nautical mile per hour.

Lay Days. Time (not counting Sundays) allowed the master of a vessel for loading or unloading. Parts of days count as whole days.

Lazarette. A small 'tween-decks storeroom.

Leeward. On the side turned away or sheltered from the wind.

Lighter. A broad, flat-bottomed boat used in transporting cargo between a vessel and the shore. To unload goods from ship or shore to a lighter and to convey them from ship to shore or vice versa.

Lightship. A permanently anchored sea-going vessel fitted with a powerful lighting apparatus.

Line, the. The Equator.

Luff. To put a ship's helm down or to increase its sail area toward the stern, thereby bringing its head nearer the wind.

Marl. To fasten, such as a sail to a spar, with a series of hemp-cord hitches.

Martingale. A stay extending from the jibboom to the end of the dolphin striker.

Miss Stay. To fail to go from one tack to the other. When the ship gets its head to the wind, it comes to a stand and begins to fall off on the same tack.

Mizzenmast. The aftermost mast of a full-rigged ship, bark, barkentine and three-masted schooner.

Nautical Mile. The standard unit of measure for marine navigation; about 1.15 miles.

Oakum. Caulking material used to waterproof seams between planks. Its strong, pliable tarred rope fibers swell when wet.

Ordinary Seaman. A member of the crew from the deck department who is subordinate to an able seaman but has learned part of the trade.

Paling. Pointed sticks used in making fences; pales, pickets.

Palm. An instrument used by sailmakers instead of a thimble in sewing canvas.

Patent Log (also screw log). A device for automatically measuring the distance traveled by a vessel.

Patent Windlass. A device designed to increase a sailor's ability to hoist and lower an anchor.

Pawl (also Riding Pawl). One of a set of short pieces of steel hinged at one end to the barrel of a capstan or windlass and whose free end engages with a projection on the barrel to prevent it from recoiling.

Pay Off. To fall off from the wind in consequence of the force exerted on the rudder or the arrangement of the sails or both.

Pintle. Heavy bolt or pin on the forward edge of the rudder frame, by which the rudder is hinged to the rudder post, around which it pivots.

Plimsoll Mark (also Plimsoll Line). A maximum permissible load line painted on a ship's sides.

Protest (also Sea Protest). In maritime law, a notarized statement obtained by a ship's master after his ship enters port following a rough voyage. Its purpose is to protect the ship's charterer or owner from liability for damages to the cargo or the ship, or to other ships in a collision, caused by the perils of the sea (e.g., bad weather).

Punt. Flat-bottomed open boat with flaring sides, raking transoms at bow and stern, and a keel with a slight fore-and-aft curvature.

Quick. Excessively stable; rolls more frequently and with higher amplitude, increasing both discomfort for passengers and crew and risk of damage to ship and cargo.

Raffee. A triangular sail that West Coast schooners set above the squaresail, on the windward side, when running free.

Reef. (a) A portion of a sail rolled and tied down to reduce the area of canvas exposed to the wind or (b) to reduce the size of a sail by rolling or folding up part of it and securing it with short ropes fixed across the sail. Taking a "single reef" meant drawing up the sail to the first row of reef points; taking a "double reef," drawing it up to the second row.

Reeve. To pass a rope or cable through an eye or other narrow opening.

Rigger. A crewman who is expert in the arts of sewing, splicing, whipping, and knot tying and who makes and maintains ropes and sail attachments.

Rudder Head. The upper part of the rudder stock, above the blade, on which the quadrant or tiller is fitted.

Rudder Stock. The part of a rudder that acts as a vertical shaft through which the turning force of the steering gear is transmitted to the rudder body.

Salvage (also Marine Salvage). The process of recovering a ship, its cargo, or other property after a shipwreck or other maritime casualty. Salvage may encompass towing, refloating, or repairing a ship.

Salvor. One who assists a vessel in distress.

Scantling. Pieces of soft wood 2 to 3 inches thick and 3 to 5–1/2 inches wide.

Schoolship. A vessel used (a) as a nautical training school in which apprentices are trained for service as sailors at the expense of the state or (b) as a reform school to which boys are committed by the courts to be disciplined and instructed as mariners.

Schooner. A vessel rigged with two to six fore-and-aft masts.

Scull. To propel a boat by working an oar from side to side, or in a figure-eight motion, over the stern.

Seizing. Line or cord used for binding one rope to another, a rope to a spar, or different parts of the same rope. Seizing stuff most commonly used is made of tarred hemp.

Settle. Ease slightly, as a rope in a tackle.

Shears (a variant of sheerlegs). A device for lifting heavy weights consisting of two or more spars lashed together at their upper ends from which a lifting tackle is suspended.

Sheave. In a block, the grooved wheel over which a rope passes.

Sheer. To deviate from a course.

Shifting-boards. One or more wooden bulkheads in a ship's hold, put up fore and aft and firmly supported to prevent a bulk cargo (e.g., grain) from shifting.

Ship. A masted vessel larger than a boat and suitable for navigation on the high seas. Also, a sailing vessel with three square-rigged masts and a full bowsprit.

Ship Chandler. A retail dealer who specializes in equipment for ships.

Shroud. One of a set of strong wires or ropes extending on each side of a masthead to a ship's sides to support a mast laterally.

Skysail. A sail set very high, above the royals.

Slack Water. The period between flood and ebb of the tidal stream.

Slip Line (also Slip Rope). A warp (rope) led through a ring or around a cleat or bollard ashore, with both ends made fast on board.

Sloop. A one-masted sailboat with a fore-and-aft mainsail and a jib.

Spanker. A gaff-rigged fore-and-aft sail set from and aft of the aftmost mast.

Speak. To hail and communicate with another vessel at sea. (Used without a preposition: "We spoke a bark.")

Spencer. A large gaff sail behind a square-rigged foremast or the mainmast of a ship or bark.

Splice. To join ropes by interweaving their strands.

Spring. A shore mooring line used for moving a vessel lying alongside a wharf ahead and at the same time thrusting her sideways from the wharf.

Square of the Hatch. The area directly below the opening in a ship's deck.

Stanchion. In wooden vessels, a rough log used as a pillar in the hold.

Stand Off and On. To approach an object (e.g., a coastline) on one tack and recede from it on the other.

Stay. Strong rope providing fore-and-aft support for the weight of a mast.

Staysail. A triangular or trapezoidal sail hoisted on a stay leading fore or aft from the head of a mast to a lower mast or to the deck.

Steerage way. The degree of forward movement that renders a ship subject to the helm.

Step. A recessed block or framing in which the heel of a mast is placed. It is fitted on the keelson or a lower deck. To place the heel in the step.

Sternpost (also Stern Frame). A heavy casting, forging, or weldment forming the afterend of the ship's structure and supporting the rudder.

Stopper. A short length of rope or chain, or a steel fitting used for checking the running of a rope or chain cable, or for holding it firmly.

Stream Anchor. An anchor stowed at the stern and used with a main anchor in narrow waterways, where there is no room for the vessel to swing with the tide.

Studdingsail (pronounced 'stun' sul). Light sail set from a portable extension of a yardarm.

Surf Boat. Open rowboat designed for beaching and launching through surf.

Surfman. Man who uses a surfboat in the lifesaving service.

Tack. The direction of a vessel's head with regard to the trim of its sails. To change the course of a sailing vessel by turning its head to the wind.

Tackle. A combination of ropes and blocks to assist in lifting a weight or applying tension.

Talk with Flags (Semaphore). To communicate between ships by using two flags (one in each hand) to indicate letters of the alphabet.

Three-Skysail-Yarder. A ship with three masts; atop of each is a yard (spar) to which the head of a skysail is attached.

Throw the Lead. To use a lead weight attached to the end of a line to ascertain the depth of water beneath a vessel.

Topgallant Sail. A quadrilateral sail extended above the topsail. In more recent vessels topgallants are divided into upper and lower topgallant sails.

Topsail. The second sail (counting from the bottom) up a mast. These may be square sails or fore-and-aft sails.

Trades (also Trade Winds). Any of the nearly constant winds that dominate most of the tropics and subtropics throughout the world, blowing mainly from the northeast in the Northern Hemisphere and from the southeast in the Southern Hemisphere.

Trestletree. One of two strong bars of timber fixed horizontally on opposite sides of a masthead to support the crosstrees and the frame of the top.

Tryworks. A brick stove built into the deck of a whaling vessel used for converting whale blubber into oil.

'Tween Decks. The decks below the upper deck and above the hold, reserved for cargo.

Union. Upper inner corner of an ensign.

Union Down. Displaying the flag with the union down is a signal of distress.

Way (also Ways and Launching Way). An incline by which a vessel slides from a building slip into the water.

Wear. To change the course of a vessel by putting its helm up and turning its head away from the wind.

Weather Quarter. The quarter of a ship on the windward side.

Western Ocean. The North Atlantic Ocean.

Windlass. A winch used to hoist anchors and house them safely.

Yard. A long, nearly cylindrical spar tapering toward its ends, used for supporting and extending sails.

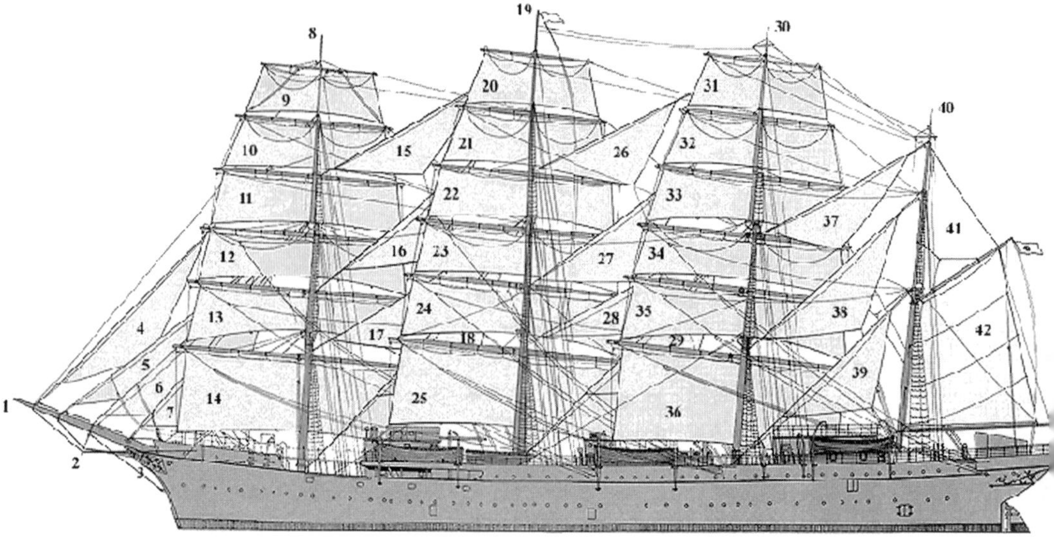

Sail rigging identification. Courtesy Tall Ships America (www.tallshipsamerica.org)

1. Bowsprit
2. Martingale
3. Figurehead
4. Flying Jib
5. Outer jib
6. Inner jib
7. Fore topmast staysail
8. Foremast
9. Fore royal
10. Fore upper topgallant sail
11. Fore lower topgallant sail
12. Fore upper topsail
13. Fore lower topsail
14. Foresail, Fore course
15. Main royal staysail
16. Main topgallant staysail
17. Main middle staysail
18. Main topmast staysail
19. Mainmast
20. Main royal
21. Main upper topgallant sail
22. Main lower topgallant sail
23. Main upper topsail
24. Main lower topsail
25. Mainsail, Main course
26. Mizzen royal staysail
27. Mizzen topgallant staysail
28. Mizzen middle staysail
29. Mizzen topmast staysail
30. Mizzen mast
31. Mizzen royal
32. Mizzen upper topgallant sail
33. Mizzen lower topgallant sail
34. Mizzen upper topsail
35. Mizzen lower topsail
36. Crossjack, Mizzen course
37. Jigger topgallant staysail
38. Jigger topmast staysail
39. Jigger staysail
40. Jigger mast
41. Gaff topsail
42. Spanker

Index

Note: Page numbers followed by "*n*" and a number indicate endnotes.